Perspecta 55: Futures Index

Matthew Wagstaffe, Lani Barry, Jeffrey Liu, Nicholas Miller, Ethan Zisson

The Yale Architectural Journal

Contents

17   Introduction

Resources

31   Nineteenth-Century Alchemy: Zeynep Çelik Alexander
               Mineral Statistics circa 1850

45   Resources of the Future: Jack Hanly
               Urban Land and Environmental Quality in
               Harvey Perloff's Development Planning

57   Greenwishing: Andreas Folkers
               The Cruel Optimism of Sustainability

63   Commodious, Firm and Delightful   Gökçe Günel

Systems Science

75   The Future of the Disaster: Adam Bobbette
               Indonesian Volcanoes, Political Geology,
               and New Planetary Alliances

87   "It's Going to Melt the Polar Caps":   Davy Knittle
               Redlined Climate Futures in
               Do the Right Thing

101   Resilient Futures   Orit Halpern

115   In the Wake of Resilience: Ross Exo Adams
               Beyond Darwinian Futures

Security

133	Worlds Without Harm	Fred Scharmen
145	From Air War Planning to Climate Adaptation: A Visual Genealogy of Urban Resilience	Stephen J. Collier and Andrew Lakoff
167	Bunkers Against Planning	Lindsay Thomas
181	Data-Driven Design of Criminal and Consensual Environments	Peter Polack

Investments

197	Interview	William Deringer
209	All My Futures Are in the Past	Matthew Soules
215	The Art of Transparency: Climate Change and Miami's (Un)controllable Future	Savannah Cox
225	Re-membering the Future	Nashin Mahtani
235	All There Ever Was	Todd Reisz

Computation

249	Calculating Growth: Prediction and Simulation in Berlin, 1968	Daniela Fabricius
261	Interview	Justin Joque
273	Planetary Accounting/Scene From a Warehouse	Amelyn Ng and John Lewtas
281	Acknowledgments (or, On Editing *Perspecta* in a Speculative Age)	

Introduction

The structural consultant comes in at noon to review the critical breaking points of your truss system, assessing its likelihood of failure when subjected to higher than average wind speeds.

After making some modulations, you subsequently model potential flood events, adjusting base-level floor heights in accordance with new 100-year projections.

Later in the day, a materials lifecycle analyst sends over the calculations she ran regarding the long-term carbon footprint of your building, along with suggestions for alternate material choices should you wish to reach a lower carbon-output.

And on it continues: risk analysts, Esri plug-ins that calculate blast radii, consultants advising you to equip your building with smart sensors, reps displaying the anticipated savings in lawsuit reductions if you choose a paver with a lower slips, trips, and falls coefficient...

Although the temporal triad of past-present-future—each stage succeeding the other in an orderly progression, ad infinitum—seems to be as transhistorical a fact of existence as ever there could be, judging from contemporary architectural practice, these terms and their positions relative to one another seem to be losing their stability. Lately, as climatological and other computational models bring distant tomorrows to bear on the world of today, the future's position in the temporal sequence has shifted. Nowadays, it is not the present that dictates what is to come; rather, it is a model of the future that compels action in the present.

Of course, not all models of the future are the same, and nor, consequently, are the types of anticipatory action to which they give rise. Consider, if you will, a comparison between two forecasting technologies that, despite being the products of the same general field (risk analysis), are radically different in their implications. The first comes to us via James M. Cains's *Double Indemnity*, a 1943 noir mystery with an insurance claims manager in the role of detective. At the novel's end, Barton Keyes, our insurance agent hero, seeks to prove the fraudulence of a supposed suicide. Lacking any substantive evidence, Keyes instead turns to the actuarial tables for proof:

> I was studying these tables. Take a look at them. Here's suicide by race, by color, by occupation, by sex, by locality, be seasons of the year, by time of day when committed. Here's suicide by method of accomplishment. Here's method of accomplishment subdivided by poisons, by firearms, by drowning, by leaps ... [Here] are leaps subdivided by leaps from high places, under wheels of moving trains, under wheels of trucks, under the feet of horses, from steamboats. But there's not one case here out of all these millions of cases of a leap from the rear of a moving train. That's just one way they don't do it.[1]

His paratactic speech suggests a comprehensibility, giving his listener the sense that his actuarial tables elaborate the sum total of suicide possibilities. Significantly, this list of statistically allowable categories is granted enormous predictive powers: that which is "not classifiable" according to the probabilistic logics of actuarial science, Keyes implies, is effectively "an ontological impossibility."[2] That is, if some future circumstance cannot be inferred from the data available in the present, it may as well not exist.[3]

Now let me place before you a different map of the future, containing a different string of calamitous events: the feverish future imaginings that the war strategist and professional futurist Herman Kahn put to the page in his infamous 1960 text *On Thermonuclear War*. Here disasters are not granted reality via the calculative techniques of actuarial reasoning but via the decidedly non-computational power of narrative. In response to unprecedented yet enormously consequential events like the development of nuclear bombs, Khan proposed a new method of speculation that he called "scenario planning." Defined in a later text as an "attempt to describe in more or less detail some hypothetical sequence of events,"[4] scenarios take the form of imagined narratives that "dramatize and illustrate" the "larger range of possibilities that must be considered in an analysis of the future," thereby ensuring that the futurist "deal[s] with details and dynamics that he might easily avoid treating if he restricted himself to abstract considerations."[5] Thus, here it is the abstractions of statistics that are viewed with suspicion; contra Keyes, the highly unlikely is not written off as an "ontological impossibility" but is instead granted, via narrative, a pressing reality with the power to affect nuclear strategy.

The sociologist (and contributor to this volume) Stephen J. Collier has described the knowledge produced by scenarios and other similar practices as "enactment-based." An expansive category, for Collier "enactment" refers to the "'acting out' of uncertain future threats in order to understand their impact."[6] While the days of Kahn's celebrity are long in the rearview, the significance of enactment-based knowledge has only increased in the present day. Giving testament to the contemporary importance of this form of knowledge, in the early days of the pandemic the *New York Times* ran a front-page story about the Trump administration's costly decision to *not* heed the information provided by one such enactment exercise, 2019's "Crimson Contagion," a tabletop scenario wherein members of the Department of Health and Human Services (HHS) role-played the government's response to an imagined deadly influenza pandemic.[7] The exercise, the reporters noted, showed the United States to be decidedly unprepared for such an event, a vision of the future that, as we all know, failed to produce action in the present and so came to pass. Surely, in what has been described ad nauseum as our uncertainty-filled "new normal," such forewarnings will instead now be acted upon with great alacrity.

Or will they? As Kahn would repeatedly insist, his scenario plans were not a means to predict the future but were instead examples of what Olaf Helmer (inventor of the Delphi method) and other early futurists at the RAND institute would call a "social technology." The purpose of a social technology is not to provide an accurate forecast but to lead to undertakings in the present. In other words, the realistic narratives of scenario planning matter only inasmuch as they "[induce] desired forms of social action."[8] Thus, in contrast to the supposedly inherent trustworthiness of the cold hard facts of frequentist reasoning, it seems that, with the rise of enactment-based practices, softer skills like one's persuasive ability or one's charisma will determine whether or not the policies a given narrative deems necessary will actually be enacted in the world. Maybe, then, HHS did not present their "Crimson Contagion" conclusions compellingly enough.

In this light, Khan and his ilk, concerned as they are with performativity and the imagination, aren't so much oracles as they are influencers. Given a world of great novelty and complexity,[9] total prediction goes out the window to be replaced by the rhetorical power of a forward-glancing narrative. Indeed, Khan's practice is only one of a number of future governance strategies that arrive around this time period that jettison the surety of prediction in favor of a more jaundiced view towards humankind's capacity for foresight and totally knowledgeable planning. From Hayek's anti-planning philosophies gaining traction in American policy circles to Horst Rittel's articulation of "wicked problems" and Stafford Beer and other cyberneticians' claims regarding the fundamental unknowability of certain "exceedingly complex systems"[10]—not to mention the rise of catch-all futures approaches like the "precautionary principle" (which calls for the limiting of any action that has even a faint possibility of leading to a cataclysmic event) and strategies like all-hazards emergency preparedness (which plans for all possible future disasters)—there appears to be at this juncture in history a fundamental shift in attitudes towards the future. Just as Reinhart Koselleck theorized that, with the arrival of modernity there came a new "apprehension of time,"[11] perhaps there has recently been another kink in temporality. Certainly, at least, the surety of earlier modes of prediction has given way to a future clouded ever more by both anticipated disaster and doubt.

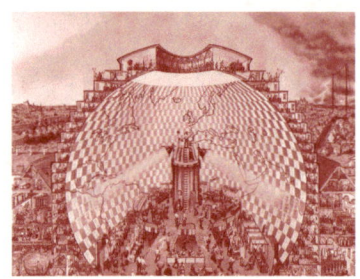

As we consider the implications of these two different forecasting cultures for design practice, perhaps it would be useful to briefly consider them in architectural terms. For, Keyes's dream of data-intensive methods yielding an incontestable portrait of the future has, in fact, been brought to life via an architectural proposal. In 1922, the meteorologist Lewis Fry Richardson wrote *Weather Prediction by Numerical Process* in which he described his method for translating the earth's atmospheric system into a set of equations. At one point in this text he describes, with great imaginative fervor, a building designed specifically to enable the computation of this global weather system:

> Imagine a large hall like a theatre, except that the circles and galleries go right round through the space usually occupied by the stage. The walls of this chamber are painted to form a map of the globe … A myriad computers [here meaning individuals that manually work out mathematical calculations] are at work upon the weather of the part of the map where each sits … Numerous little "night signs" display the instantaneous values so that neighbouring computers can read them … From the floor of the pit a tall pillar rises to half the height of the hall. It carries a large pulpit on its top. In this sits the man in charge of the whole theater; he is surrounded by several assistants and messengers … he is like the conductor of the orchestra in which the instruments are slide-rules and calculating machines. But instead of waving a baton he turns a beam of rosy light upon any region that is running ahead of the rest, and a beam of blue light upon those who are behindhand. Four senior clerks in the central pulpit are collecting the future weather as fast as it is being computed and despatching it by pneumatic carrier to a quiet room. There it will be coded and telephoned to the radio transmitting station.

Here, then, is a vision of Laplacian future surety made physical: through the benevolent orchestration of a single individual, the results of thousands of different computationally analyzed data streams are condensed into a single uncontestable prediction that will then be used by governors the world over. Architects, with their dreams of utilizing data to compute the perfect building, I'm sure imagine themselves in that conductor role.

Kahn described no such scenario plan-enabling dream structure but he did, in actuality, bring one into existence. In 1961 Kahn left RAND to form the Hudson Institute, his own think tank/consultancy where, amongst other futurological activities, he created the "Corporate Environment Study," a seminar designed to teach "the secrets of scenario" planning to corporate planners across the globe. Predictably, the architecture of his institute did not feature a building-sized calculator that condensed all its predictive work into a single point; instead, the Hudson Institute, located on a verdant patch of upstate New York, is composed of a number of small buildings haphazardly sited as though their arrangement was the result of the tossing of so many dice. Here, rather than an architecture designed to produce a single future, we find an architecture designed to produce many futures: the Institute's various think tanks and scenario planning courses could be scattered throughout the complex's buildings, producing numerous conflicting futures all at one.

The architect's role in this spatial metaphor is decidedly less clear than in Richardson's: Where is the enlightened orchestrator, steering the planet through its oncoming storms? Is the architect now just one of many contributors to a scenario planning exercise whose projected future will ultimately be used by a cadre of international business leaders intent on steering the global economy in a direction that suits their interests?

* * *

That at least, is one way of cutting up history.[12] However, despite the neatness of the contrast I have painted above, as probably all of us can attest, in reality these two modes—one high on prediction, the other low on prediction and more focused on enactment, "social technologies," cybernetics-inflected adaptive practices, and precaution—are rather blurred in our present day reality. This blurring, in fact, is particularly clear when it comes to climate change: on the one hand, data-intensive models paint an extremely compelling predictive portrait of a world ravaged by the burning of fossil fuels; at the same time, due to the unprecedented disruption of the Earth system, we are in the dark about exactly how that ravaging will take place. Moreover, despite the air of neutrality attached to the reports of the

International Panel of Climate Change (IPCC), their conclusions are as much "social technologies" as any of Kahn's scenarios. For, these documents do not just detail the science of climate change, they also speculate upon the effects that different economic or social policies will have upon the future climate system. These different "mitigation pathways," as scholars Silke Beck and Martin Mahony have argued, have "a 'world-making' power, potentially shaping the world in their own image and creating new political realities." In contrast to our common understanding of these reports as evidencing "policy neutrality," then, according to Beck and Mahony they in actuality demonstrate "policy-performativity."[13] Furthermore, if one examines the work of any other future-oriented professionals—emerging technologies researchers, risk modeling companies, ecosystem managers—one will find similar combinations of neutrality and performativity, of computation and enactment,[14] and of big data hubris and complexity-engendered doubt.

And, finally, it is important to point out that this blurring extends to the past as well: the painting of previous predictive technologies like early twentieth century actuarialist reasoning as somehow *not* being "social technologies" fundamentally concerned with inducing particular desired actions has been repeatedly shown to be a rather naive understanding. As countless historians have documented, many of the supposedly objective claims of insurantial reason—and the unequal distribution of material goods these claims enact—are less the product of the neutral unspooling of a probability formula and more the result of the ideologies of those doing this accounting.[15]

In short, then, while historians like Koselleck are undeniably correct—there is a history to the way in which we perceive the future—to argue that there has recently been a universal and clearly identifiable shift in temporality is a harder claim to sustain. If anything, our present moment is characterized by a muddle of conflicting future visions: geological time scale disaster forecasts butt heads with the micro-predictions of financial traders; projected resource limits contend with technologists' optimistic anticipations of space settlement futures; fears of big data omniscience coexist with claims that the complexity of our global order exceeds the powers of computation—the list of competing futures could go on.[16]

While it would be comforting to reduce this cacophony to a single label on a historical timeline (we are in the period of the "risk society," this is the "post-COVID era," etc.), in reality there is no way to truly understand the futures with which we must contend except via careful analysis of the history and inner workings of a given anticipation technique.

* * *

And what of architecture in all of this? Our discipline, of course, is similarly a practice concerned with bringing forth a particular future. Architects do not work in the present, directly shaping the material that brings a building into existence; rather, as Robin Evans has noted, architects work from an "anterior" position, deploying representations (traditionally orthographic projections, increasingly computational models) to devise, picture, and transmit "ideas of buildings before they are built."[17] However, as indicated by the brief sample of architectural tasks with which we opened this essay, developments in forecasting technologies have fundamentally altered the everyday practices of our future-oriented field. What happens to architectural practice as it competes with the futures generated via various other disciplines? As enactment-based practices bring forth, alongside statistically extrapolated forecasts, knowledge of future events that have never happened before, how do these anterior imaginings interact with those of architecture? In light of these shifts, does architecture still possess a "world-making" power? Or has our profession become a mere handmaiden to more persuasive painters of the future?

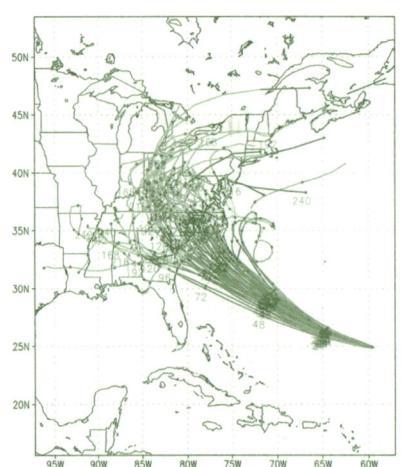

Generally speaking, architects have been content to be oblivious to these wars of anticipation. We blindly design our buildings in relation to whichever prognosis has been handed to us at the moment: we take the disaster planner's advice, we kowtow to the Revit plug-in, and we parrot rhetorics of resilience unthinkingly. What we lose sight of in our subservience to these various futures is the fact that, as Beck and Mahony argue, different forecasts "shape the world in their own image." Without an analysis of these techniques of forecasting and the values they contain, then, we will cater our projects to imagined futures whose worldviews may not be our own.[18]

Perspecta: Futures Index thus performs a much-needed analysis of these contrasting techniques of futurity. Specifically, we have identified five futurological arenas as having a pronounced impact on our discipline: resource forecasting, earth system science, national/domestic security, investment advising, and data analytics. We have asked a number of thinkers from both within and outside of our field to provide critical commentaries on these forms of future-making and their impacts on the built environment. Collectively, these texts aim to help architects develop a critical literacy in regards to the art of prognosis, a pressing task for the architectural community.

* * *

It should also be noted that this book is a temporal technology in its own right. While we conceived of this topic when we were students at the Yale School of Architecture in the fall of 2019, the vast majority of our editorial work was undertaken in the depths of the pandemic and in the midst of these early career struggles. *Perspecta: Futures Index*, then, serves a time capsule of this difficult COVID-colored micro-era. It was a time for antidepressants and the purchasing of emotional support animals and for rewatching *The Sopranos* and just trying to get by; it was decidedly not a time for editing a publication. If there is a dour cast to these pages, if there are typos or other inconsistencies, please read them as symptoms of this odd chapter in recent history, as messages from the COVID past to who knows what futures awaits us.

Finally, on those possible futures: it should be noted that this book presents a rather narrow sampling of future imaginings. From Arturo Escobar's call for a pluriversal politics to the fight for the Red Deal, there are untold numbers of new futures being fought for. We encourage you to look beyond this single *Index* to discover the many other futures now being shepherded into the world.

1. James M. Cain, *Double Indemnity* (New York: Vintage Books, 1992), 59-60.
2. Frederick Whiting, "Playing Against Type: Statistical Personhood, Depth Narrative, and the Business of Genre in James M. Cain's 'Double Indemnity,'" *Journal of Narrative Theory* 36 no. 2 (Summer 2006): 201.
3. It is important here to note that Keyes's actuarial tables—and his unwavering belief in them as complete descriptions of reality—embody a particular school of statistics known as "frequentist." Contrary to what is often called the "epistemic" perspective, which is concerned with establishing rules for decision-making in the absence of complete knowledge, frequentists hold that "diversity and risk are part of nature itself, and not simply the result of incomplete knowledge. They are external to mankind and part of the essence of things." For frequentists, the law of large numbers—that is, the tendency for "the frequency of appearance of a phenomenon with a given probability … [to tend] toward this probability when the number of attempts is multiplied"—is not a useful heuristic but a metaphysical fact of the universe. Alain Desrosieres, The *Politics of Large Numbers: A History of Statistical Reasoning* (Cambridge: Harvard University Press, 1998), 7; 56.
4. Herman Kahn, *Thinking about the Unthinkable* (New York: Avon, 1962), 150.
5. Herman Kahn and Anthony J. Weiner, *The Year 200: A Framework for Speculation on the Next Thirty-Three Years* (New York: Macmillan, 1967), 263. As quoted in R. John Williams, "World Futures," *Critical Inquiry* 42 (Spring 2016): 522.
6. Stephen J. Collier, "Enacting catastrophe: preparedness, insurance, budgetary rationalization," *Economy and Society* 37 no. 2 (2008), 225.
7. David E. Sanger et al., "Before Virus Outbreak, a Cascade of Warnings Went Unheeded," *The New York Times*, March 19, 2020, https://www.nytimes.com/2020/03/19/us/politics/trump-coronavirus-outbreak.html
8. Jenny Andersson, *The Future of the World: Futurology, Futurists, and the Struggle for the Post-Cold War Imagination* (New York: Oxford University Press, 2018), 82.
9. In his analysis of the scenario planning method, the comparative literature scholar R. John Williams contextualizes the rise of this futures practice within the context of MIT meteorologist Edward Lorenz's accidental discovery of dynamical chaos. Williams, "World Futures," 482. In 1961, so the story goes, Lorenz was running highly advanced weather simulations when he left his office to get a cup of coffee. Prior to running his simulations he'd rounded down a data entry three decimal points (from .506127 to .506) only to return from his break to find that the minor alteration had "drastically transformed" the entire pattern of the results of his weather model, showing that "small changes can have large consequence and that, therefore, "forecasting the future can be nearly impossible." As recounted in Peter Dizikes, "When the Butterfly Effect Took Flight," *MIT Technology Review*, Feb. 22, 2011, https://www.technologyreview/com/s/422809/when-the-butterfly-effect-took-flight/.
10. As Andrew Pickering puts it, Beer argued that "there exists in the world a class of 'exceedingly complex systems,' including the brain, the firm and the economy, which are in principle unknowable … Such systems can never be dominated by knowledge, and instead we have to learn somehow to cope with them. Cybernetics was thus a science of dealing with the unknown—an extremely odd sort of science." Andrew Pickering, "The Science of the Unknowable: Stafford Beer's Cybernetic Informatics," *Kybernetes* 33 no. 3/4 (2004), 499-521.
11. For Koselleck, with modernity we shifted from seeing the future as fundamentally the same as the past—with the notable structuring exception of the coming Final Judgment—to seeing the future as an open terrain that could be shaped and steered towards progress by human action. Reinhart Koselleck, *Futures Past: On the Semantics of Historical Time* (New York: Columbia University Press, 2004).
12. Roughly speaking, this account is in line with Ulrich Beck's argument that we have transitioned from the world of modernity into the "risk society," a new period in which modern technology itself—be it in the form of synthetic toxic chemicals, nuclear fallout or industrial pollution—has produced future perils whose novelty, complexity, and temporal/spatial scope make them incalculable via the tools of insurantial reason. Ulrich Beck, *Risk Society: Towards a New Modernity* (London: Sage Publications, 1992).
13. Silke Beck and Martin Mahony, "The politics of anticipation: the IPCC and the negative emissions technologies experience," *Global Sustainability* 1 no. 8 (May 2018), 1, 4. Along similar lines, the scholar Claire Brault has criticized the "capitalocentric" nature of the IPCC's pathways, noting that all of the IPCC's models "presume the future predominance of capitalism even a century from now." Claire Brault, "Feminists Imaginations in a Heated Climate: Parody, Idiocy, and Climatological Possibilities," *Catalyst: Feminism, Theory, Technoscience* 3 no. 2 (2017), 2.
14. For example, in the catastrophe models produced by risk management companies, knowledge of exceptional weather events is generated by computationally simulating, say, thousands of hypothetical hurricanes upon vast databases of landscape and property information. The resulting projected future losses estimate is thus a combination of both statistical and enactment-based practices. Collier, "Enacting catastrophe."
15. See, for example, Richard Rothstein, *The Color of Law: A Forgotten History of How Our Government Segregated America* (New York: Liverlight Publishing Co., 2014).
16. For a similar reflection along these lines, see Eric C. H. de Bruyn and Sven Lütticken, "Introduction," in *Futurity Report*, eds. Eric C. H. de Bruyn and Sven Lütticken (London: Sternberg Press, 2020), 7-17.
17. Robin Evans, "Architectural Projection," in *Architecture and Its Image: Four Centuries of Architectural Representation: Works from the Collection of the Canadian Centre for Architecture*, eds. Eve Blau and Edward Kaufman (Cambridge: MIT Press, 1989), 21.
18. The stakes here could not be higher. In acting according to the prescriptions of a given forecast, one is, in effect, securing one future at the expense of another. Understanding the data and values that go into constructing these future claims is of paramount political importance. For example, in her recent text *The Economization of Life*, the historian of science Michelle Murphy shows how the demographic transition model of Cold War modernization theory—which links closely population growth rates and economic development, two relatively novel abstractions—provided justification for the creation, in postcolonial Bangladesh, of an infrastructural network of largely NGO-sponsored "family planning" initiatives whose aims were, ultimately, to ensure that "*some must not be born so that* [future] *others might live more abundantly (consumptively).*" Michelle Murphy, *The Economization of Life* (Durham: Duke University Press, 2017), 41. With climate change, of course, these intertemporal existential trade-offs become only more pronounced.

Resources

Zeynep Çelik Alexander
Jack Hanly
Andreas Folkers
Gökçe Günel

Before there was a climate crisis, there was a resource crisis. Or, rather, crises: be it Malthus prophesying a depletion of the commons, M. King Hubbert setting a date for "peak oil," or the Ehrlichs' (xenophobic) fears of a worldwide famine induced by explosive population growth,[1] long predating our understanding of global warming, some of the world's most influential environmental Cassandras have instead spoken in the language of stocks, reserves, and rapidly approaching resource limits. Committed as our economic order is to growth at all costs, however, we've had to circle the square of these forecasted limits with ideas like "sustainable development" and "green growth," concepts the architectural world has been all too willing to incorporate into its own practice.

Throughout this history, moreover, we've rarely stopped to ask: What even is a "resource" to begin with? What politics do we enact when we cut up the earth into categories of matter deemed to be statically lying in wait for the exclusive use of (particular subsections of) humankind? And, what other relationships to our planet does a resource management perspective preclude?[2] In seeking to answer these and other questions, the essays in this section cover subjects ranging from early 18th century German forestry to the present-day use of floating power stations as emergency backstops in the face of unpredictable temporary electricity shortages. As architects become more concerned with the material provenance of their built works, these texts collectively provide a critical understanding of what it means to manage one's use of resources.

1   For more on the Ehlrichs' xenophobia, see Sarah Holiday Nelson, "Neoliberal environments: Crisis, counterrevolution, and the nature of value," PhD diss., (University of Minnesota, 2017), 57. For a discussion of the relationship between decolonization, overpopulation fears, and US imperialism writ large, see Romain Felli, *The Great Adaptation: Climate, Capitalism and Catastrophe* (New York: Verso Books, 2021), 17–26.
2   The geographer Max Liboiron argues that "Resources refer to unidirectional relations … [wherein] value flows in one direction, from the Resource to the user, rather than being reciprocal." In contrast to this orientation, they posit an Indigenous understanding of "Land … [as] a verb … [as] about relations between the material aspects some people might think of as landscapes—water, soil, air, plants, stars—and histories, spirits, events, kinships, accountabilities, and other people that aren't human." Notably, because colonial resource management is about conserving material for use in the future, Liboiron argues this practice "eclipses other possible relations with Land both now and in the future." Max Liboiron, *Pollution Is Colonialism* (Durham: Duke University Press, 2021), 43, 62–65.

Nineteenth-Century Alchemy: Mineral Statistics circa 1850

Zeynep Çelik Alexander

In the midst of ongoing debates about the burning of fossil fuels, the role of renewable and non-renewable energy sources and the violence of extractive technologies, it might be worthwhile to reconsider a fundamental question: what exactly is a resource? In the popular imagination, a resource—especially when modified with the adjectives "natural" or "physical"—denotes a fixed store of assets waiting to be used by humans as input for productive activities. Yet, economists and geographers have been arguing for a while now that a resource is neither fixed nor merely in potentia.[1] Even early political economists, who privileged land as the origin of wealth and saw all improvement as agricultural improvement, must have perceived the instability of the concept. When David Ricardo endeavored to justify "rent" through the "original and indestructible powers of the soil," for example, he had to perform significant rhetorical acrobatics to posit land as the primordial resource, one that made all others possible.[2] By the time John Stuart Mill discussed "natural agents" (in addition to labor and capital) as essential requisites of production, it had become clear that Britain's wealth was more predicated on coal under the soil than on agricultural production on the surface.[3] Later scholars were therefore more likely to acknowledge, along with Erich Zimmermann who famously wrote that "resources are not; they become," that while resources may seem like natural things, they are in fact *functions* designated as such under particular social, economic, and political conditions.[4] And recent historians have demonstrated how what counts as a resource has changed dramatically over time—as is made clear by the cases of the cochineal bug, guano, nuclear matter, cobalt, and, perhaps most peculiarly, the kind of resource designated as "human."[5]

How, then, does a resource come into existence? Pressures of supply and demand, spells of abundance and scarcity, compulsion to develop and improve, forces of poverty and wealth have all been cited as factors in this historical process—even though these factors have often played out in unpredictable ways.[6] Even most fundamental human needs (such as water) may come in and go out of being a resource depending on historical circumstances. Moments of invention and discovery are privileged in such histories. A source of energy known for centuries (such as coal) becomes central with the development of an efficient steam engine; novel capabilities are created when colonizers find out about a plant (such as cinchona) used by native populations and smuggle and replant it elsewhere; or a new location of a known resource (such as silver in South America) is identified. In what follows, I want to suggest another—seemingly less eventful but arguably no less momentous—manner in which resources have historically been brought into being: through the formation of epistemic regimes that we have come to call "databases."

This may seem counterintuitive at first. Databases are supposed to record the past or the present, not herald the future by summoning things into existence. Defined as a "structured collection of aggregated, commensurable data capable of being sorted and accessed for some purpose of knowledge production," a database is frequently understood today to be a straightforward solution to a practical problem: the modern problem of managing large and complex societies.[7] Although historians have acknowledged its long history, the database continues to be associated with the emergence of electronic computing in the twentieth century. In what follows, I will argue, first, that the past of this epistemic arrangement was intertwined with nineteenth-century imperialism and, second, that its historical role has entailed more than solving the problem of governing the masses. Focusing on the case of the Museum of Economic Geology, which housed a collection of mineral statistics in London after 1851, I will show how collecting, storing, aggregating, and making retrievable statistics about what lies beneath the soil created value for future extraction. I will compare this process of value creation to alchemy, the practice of turning base metals into precious ones, a practice that had become obsolete by the middle of the nineteenth century after having played a crucial role in early political economy. This alchemical transmutation of value, it turns out, necessitated imagining land not as a horizontal surface but rather as extending in the vertical dimension, which was made visible through geological and architectural sections.

***

On September 23rd, 1841, when Thomas Sopwith, mining engineer and mineral surveyor, spoke at the Yorkshire Geological Society in England, he began by showing his audience a blank chart.[8] The chart was 15 inches by 20 inches and engraved with a grid at a scale of 40 feet to an inch so that it could be filled in with geological sections. By then the construction of railways and the expansion of the mining industry had become mutually reinforcing phenomena in Britain. Early railcars were designed to carry coal out of mines; the steam engines that now pulled them and ran the pumps that kept flood water out were powered by the same coal.[9] More relevant to Sopwith's argument, these developments meant that British land was repeatedly being cut in dramatic ways for mines and railways, giving geologists unusual opportunities to see earth's mineral composition, formed over millions of years, in section. (Fig. 1) Sopwith argued that the geological information thereby revealed

Fig. 1

should not go to waste but rather be collected using copies of the blank chart. The sectional information was not only important to the discipline of geology; it was also crucial to identify underground resources that were important for "the future national prosperity" of Britain—for the improvement of agriculture, mining, construction, and so on.[10]

The chart in question had been printed by the Museum of Economic Geology in London under the leadership of Henry De la Beche, the founder of that institution and the first director of the British Geological Survey. Even though it had been firmly established by the 1820s that earth had a stratified structure, most geological work still primarily consisted of making plans.[11] De La Beche's own career demonstrated geology's representational dilemma: he had started out as a gentleman geologist coloring maps of Pembrokeshire before embarking upon a geological survey of Jamaica during a visit to the island to attend to his family's sugar plantation, which was failing after the Slavery Abolition acts.[12] (Fig. 2) In 1835 when, with the blessing of the Geographical Society of London, he became the first director of the Geological Survey, his primary task was to color and mark maps produced by the Board of Ordnance.

Yet, De la Beche understood as well as Sopwith that studying earth's structure "sectionally" was crucial.[13] But because sectional information was so hard to come by, he recommended that geologists draw what he called "ideal" or "annexed" sections. These were "horizontal sections" that reconstructed the stratigraphic and topographic transformations of land over long distances. Since geological observation was inherently discontinuous, however, a degree of guesswork was needed when constructing such sections. To construct horizontal sections the geologist had to abstract strata as more or less continuous layers separated into clearly demarcated zones and mark them with colors, letters, and numerals for legibility. (Fig. 3) The kind of sections advocated by Sopwith, by

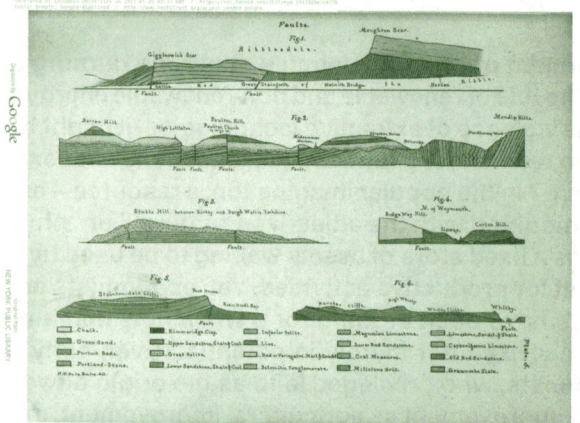

Fig. 3

contrast, were vertical; these tall and thin columnar sections showed earth's strata only at crucial points but with far more detail. (Fig. 4) Both kinds of sections made visible what the most meticulously constructed geological plan could not, but

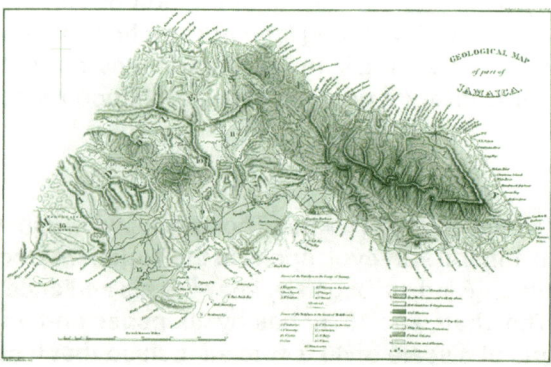

Fig. 2

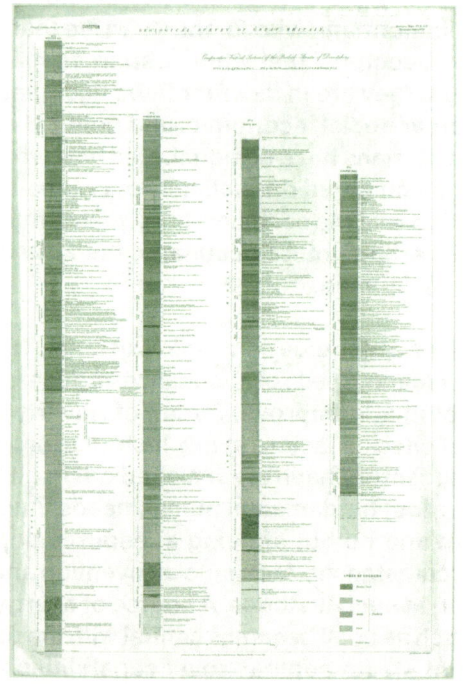

Fig. 4

32

vertical sections abstracted horizontal sections further by visually restoring disturbances such as folding or faulting of strata into perfectly parallel layers.[14] Crucially, as we will see, this additional step of abstraction made it easier to aggregate sectional information in an arrangement resembling what we would today call a database. If, reasoned Sopwith, "a regular series of sections of railway cuttings" could be collected in a systematic and standardized manner, the British government could create a central registry to make them available to entrepreneurs interested in agriculture, mining, or railway construction.[15]

Geological and economic thinking were closely related in the early nineteenth century.[16] In 1835, when the Geological Society charged De la Beche with the task of establishing the Geological Survey, its members argued that a systematic survey of Britain's geological resources had countless economic advantages: it would help find coal and precious metals, locate sources of underground water, aid the construction of canals, railroads, and tunnels, and identify chemicals crucial to the artificial improvement of the soil.[17] Yet, as Sopwith explained, mineral wealth was different from other kinds "in the extreme uncertainty of its existence and the difficulty of its discovery," which meant that prospecting for a mineral had conventionally been no different from hoping to win the lottery.[18] Adam Smith's argument that silver riches from American colonies were "a lottery, in which the prizes [did] not compensate the blanks" was repeated countless times in the course of the nineteenth century: some compared the "sure rewards of labour in the fields" to the "lottery of the gem pit" while others cautioned future adventurers against trying their odds in the "mining lottery."[19] With the introduction of systematically arranged "mineral statistics," Sopwith argued that exploiting subterranean resources would become a different kind of endeavor: instead of relying on chance, entrepreneurs could now depend on *data* to make intelligent choices—even in a global economy with unpredictable price fluctuations.[20] According to Sopwith, collecting geological information was more "prospective" than "retrospective"—that is, to the extent that it transformed mining from an aimless treasure hunt to a strategic search for subterranean resources, it was "of far less importance to the present than to future times."[21]

While the goal of standardization remained elusive, the idea of forming a registry of mineral statistics was realized, at least partially, when dozens of vertical and horizontal sections, along with geological maps to which they were keyed, came together in the Mining Records Office of the Museum of Economic Geology (which was later known as the Museum of Practical Geology).[22] (Fig. 5) The first Museum was founded in London in 1835 in makeshift apartments in Charing Cross to accommodate the assortment of artifacts discovered during the Geological Survey's excavations, but it was formalized into a proper collection when the institution re-opened in 1851 in a building between Jermyn and Piccadilly Streets built especially for this program. Situated in a narrow infill site, the building was designed by the architect James Pennethorne for the Office of Works with advice from De la Beche.[23] In addition to exhibition galleries, the Museum accommodated a large lecture hall, chemical and metallurgical laboratories, a library, a model room, and several offices, the largest of which was the Mining Records Office. The lecture hall in the basement served not only the Government School of Mines (which was based in the Museum until 1872) but, for a small fee, also the general public.[24] By 1853 other cities were campaigning to open their own geological museums while De la Beche appealed to the East India Company to set up a branch in India.[25] Bombing during WWI caused structural damage to the building, as a result of which it had to be demolished after its contents were transferred in 1935 to South Kensington.

Historians have compared the Museum of Economic Geology in its second address to natural history museums that came before and to commercial museums that came after, but it was in many ways a different creature. It was, for example, unlike the Old Ashmolean Museum, which displayed mineral specimens like wonders in a cabinet of curiosities. As a visitor remarked in 1851, specimens on display in the Museum were not "selected for the rarity of the form of their crystals, or the

Fig. 5

If, as Alexander notes, "a resource is anything to which humans attribute economic value under particular historical conditions," our current moment ought to be bringing into being some rather particular resources, because we are living in nothing if not a particular time. Sure enough, as fellow Perspecta contributor Gökçe Günel has recently been chronicling, one very unexpected substance has lately been in the process of becoming a resource: carbon dioxide. That's right, global warming's poster child and public enemy number one CO2 is (potentially) emerging as a great holder of economic value.

splendour of their colours, but the *average* produce of the mine, as it is extracted for economic uses."[26] This was "mineralogy in its working, not in its gala dress."[27] In this sense, it was closer in its logic to later natural history museums (such as the natural history branch of the British Museum which would absorb the collections of the Museum of Economic Geology) in which "one wasn't supposed to wonder, one was supposed to learn."[28]

The Museum of Economic Geology was also not entirely like the "commercial museum" type that started appearing in the 1880s in Brussels, Antwerp, Milan, Vienna, Budapest, and Philadelphia and, in the case of Britain, in the Imperial Museum in London.[29] These later museums would display industrial samples ranging from raw materials to machinery and finished products and have bureaus that provided information about prices, tariff arrangements, shipping costs, market conditions unique to a locale, etc. While the Museum of Economic Geology did not have the advanced indexing systems that characterized these later institutions, it did provide to the visitor an abundance of information about materials, manufacturing technologies, and finished products.[30] Such information was especially useful "for gentlemen who are hereafter to inherit mineral property," according to an article published in 1858, which also argued that these gentlemen would have knowledge about "the best mode of managing their property untrammeled by agents or middlemen."[31]

This required information of the kind that Sopwith called for—that is, structured information that was methodically collected, stored, and made retrievable—albeit not always standardized in ways that Sopwith had envisioned. In addition to the collections of the Mining Records Office, which would be absorbed into the Home Office in 1883, the Museum regularly published vast amounts of gray literature—memoirs, reports and almanacs filled with mineral statistics. Furthermore, the design of the displays was determined by an instructional logic that Sopwith noticed even in the earlier Museum in Charing Cross. In a guide from 1843, he pointed out how specimens were arranged "with every reference to instruction and the situations from whence obtained carefully marked, not only on the specimens themselves but also on good maps."[32] This abundance of information was noticed by countless other observers throughout the Museum's history.[33] In this sense the informational function of the Museum of Economic Geology was not confined to the proto-database of plans and sections in the Mining Records Office. The entire building structured geological information in novel ways, especially in section.

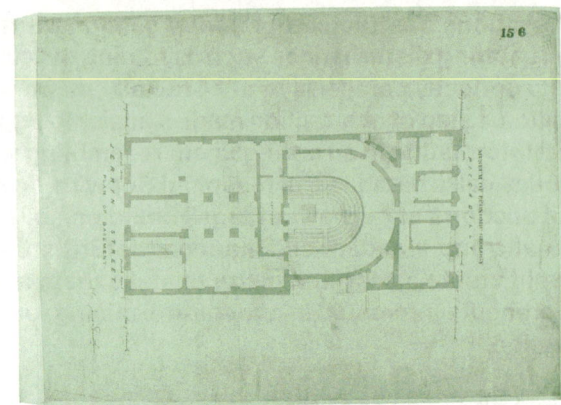

Fig. 7a

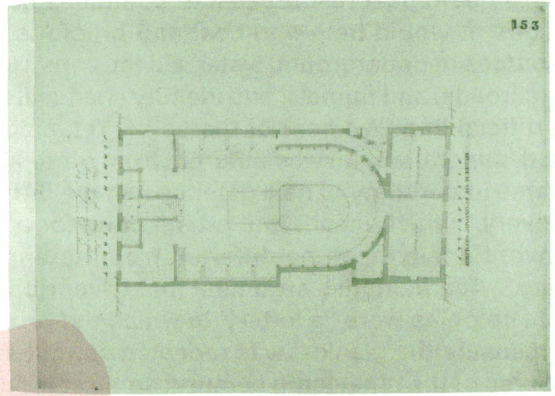

Fig. 7b

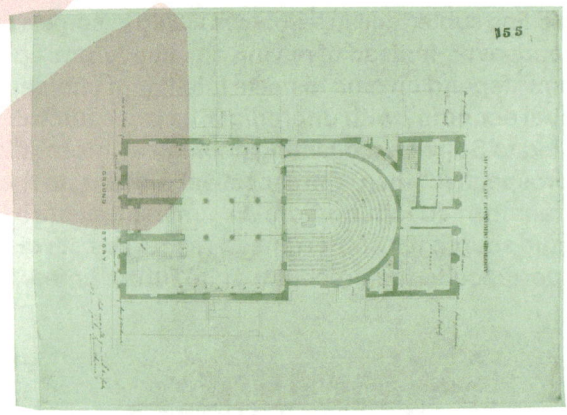

Fig. 7c

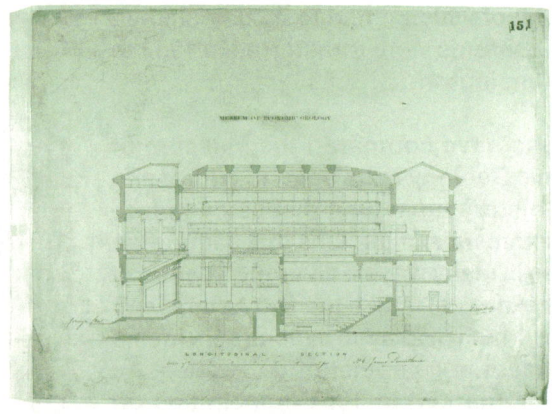

Fig. 6

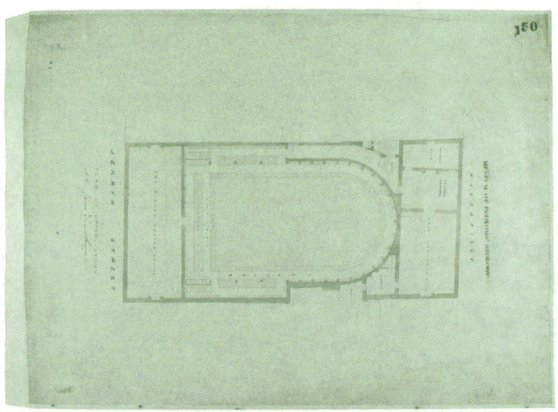

Fig. 7d

***

The elaborate section of the Museum of Economic Geology must have been designed in response, at least in part, to the unfavorable lighting conditions dictated by its deep and narrow infill site. (Fig. 6) The primary exhibition spaces consisted of a main floor and two cantilevered galleries that wrapped around a central atrium, illuminated by a 43-foot tall iron-and-glass roof. A horizontal glass plane in the center of the galleries let this light into the 400-person lecture hall in the basement. The horseshoe footprint of the lecture hall determined the spatial arrangement of the rest of the building. The laboratories, a model room, a library, and various offices, including the Mining Records Office, were situated along the Jermyn and Piccadilly Street façades in the spaces left over in the plan from the footprint of the lecture hall and the galleries. (Fig. 7a, b, c, d) The building's section was designed such that it could only be accessed from the quieter Jermyn Street. Visitors climbed up two short flights of stairs before entering the ground floor galleries, where a selection of British marbles (famously collected for the Houses of Parliament) were on display. They then ascended a more ceremonious staircase to find themselves in the "great room" of the primary exhibition galleries. (Fig. 8)

Fig. 8

The section of the primary exhibition galleries must have been an impressive sight, a powerful object lesson in economic geology. Historians have pointed out that the galleries resembled a geological section: the display cases were arranged in striated layers as if visitors occupied an oversized model of earth's strata.[34] But the architectural section did not follow the logic of a geological section in a strict manner. In fact, the main floor of the exhibition hall, dedicated to mineralogical and petrographical specimens, had an entirely different spatial arrangement than the cantilevered galleries. As an early guide explained, the organization of the main floor was, "in the first place topographic and in the second place economic."[35] Another observer noted in 1874 that "the specimens [were] admirably arranged in separate lines of cases placed in such juxtaposition that the progress of any one metalliferous mineral may be traced from the geological stratum whence the ore is extracted through the various processes of manufacture till the metal ultimately assumes the forms required for use or ornament."[36] This meant that in every subdivision, the visitor's gaze was meant to move in section up and down from the specimens displayed in the vertical cases toward the horizontal cases exhibiting a range of "economic" products obtained from them. In the foreign minerals section, for example, a cross-section through the display cases revealed the progression of the so-called Siberian vase from the aventurine crystals resourced from the Altai mountains. This visual path was a trip from the past of a raw material to the future of a manufactured product.

If geography dictated the organization of the specimens on the main floor, chronology was the organizational principle of the British fossil exhibits in the two cantilevered galleries. Here Paleozoic fossils in the lower gallery progressed toward the Mesozoic and Cenozoic fossils in the upper gallery. Instead of being arranged as a stratigraphical column, however, the display cases for the fossils wrapped around the two gallery levels, inviting visitors to experience the vertical layers of earth horizontally while making their way from west to east.[37] This was a significant choice. When the Museum opened its doors in 1851, the debate between uniformitarianism and catastrophism, was still heated.[38] At stake was the question of causality with all kinds of theological implications: Was earth the result of gradual evolution or disruptive events? What was the role of God in it? Furthermore, another debate known as the Devonian controversy was only beginning to cool. This one involved none other than De la Beche and Roderick Murchison, his future successor as director of the Museum, who disagreed on the question of how close to earth's surface coal deposits could be found. This was a question that had implications for the nineteenth-century scramble to prospect for new coal deposits around the globe.[39] Fossils were considered to be stratigraphic markers that dated mineralogical and petrographical specimens, so by placing fossils on separate floors, the Museum's curators disconnected the two kinds of specimens, thus suspending the question of mineral historicity. In other

Why would this be the case? As we rapidly approach climate overshoot, carbon capture and storage (CCS)—an emergent technology that allows us to take carbon gathered from the air or from industrial operations and shoot it underground lightening the load of our overburdened atmosphere—is increasingly being cast by everyone from the IPCC to your favorite Fortune 500 company as a global warming panacea. Shooting CO2 down into the netherworld has a value beyond climate change mitigation, however, by injecting said gas into supposedly tapped oil wells, one can draw out crude reserves that are otherwise inaccessible, a technique known as "enhanced oil words, this was not a natural history museum in which visitors were invited to contemplate the scale of time—regardless of whether that timescale had been imposed by God or Nature. The intended outcome was much more practical: the visitors were to contemplate the future human uses of minerals rather than their formation in an impossibly distant past.

This emphasis on practicality, however, did not mean exactitude. In this sense, the section of the Museum of Economic Geology can be compared to Sopwith's isometrical drawings. (Fig. 9) While De la Beche warned against "the mischief of adopting a scale of height differing from that of length," Sopwith advocated using some exaggeration in geological representations to make visible things such as coal strata.[40] In the short treatise that he wrote on the topic of isometry, he explained that while isometric projection required changing vertical and horizontal dimensions by multiplying them by a coefficient, it had the virtue of being able to represent multiple plans and sections at once.[41] An isometric drawing "fill[ed] up the space between the picture and the plan; between the picturesque beauty of the painter's canvas, and the formality of the designs of the mechanical draughtsman," he wrote.[42] That is to say, while they might not represent exact dimensions, isometrical drawings converted discrete vertical geological sections into continuous horizontal ones that could teach the lessons of economic geology more effectively.

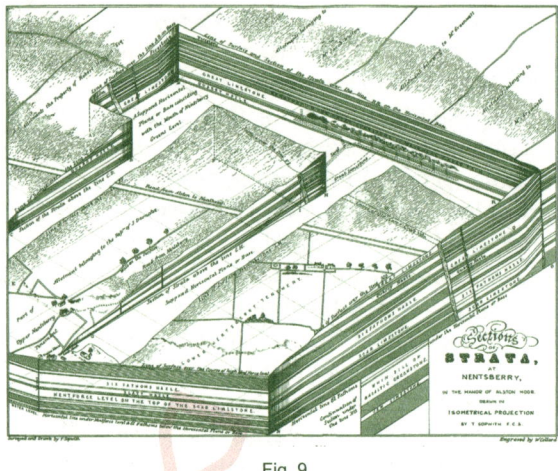

Fig. 9

The design of the Museum, in other words, employed several spatial strategies for structuring information: first, selective sequencing (of geological strata, domestic and colonial minerals, phases of the manufacturing process and separation of fossils from minerals) and, second, measured exaggerating (of the vertical dimension and the clarity of boundaries). A crucial third strategy entailed cross-referencing: the "exposed section," so to speak, of the primary exhibition galleries revealed connections across and beyond the building. This kind of cross-referencing work was done for the most part by labels, which frequently included such information as the scientific and common names of a mineral, its density, chemical composition, the location from which it was extracted and, in some instances, a photograph of its microscopic structure. "The explanatory labels attached to the specimens are also more convenient and useful than any reference to a catalogue could be," wrote one journalist, "inasmuch as the eye rests at once upon the specimen, and its name, locality, and uses; and in most instances, the analysis of the ores and minerals is also given, in order that visitors from different parts of the country may at once become acquainted with the nature and value of the various contents of the museum."[43] Depending on the specimen, this information could be even more detailed. Each building stone on display in the ground floor hall, for example, was cut down to a standard cube six inches by six inches and marked with such information as the amount of water it absorbed and its ability to resist pressure in a hydrostatic press. Also provided alongside a specimen was a list of "the edifices, ancient and modern, which have been built with it."[44] (Fig. 10)

Fig. 10

Even though it was possible by the middle of the nineteenth century to find detailed museum guides and catalogues, information-rich labels—that is, handwritten or printed information meant for visitors rather than for museum officials—were less common. Take the case of the British Museum: while popular guides or handbooks might offer abundant information about antiquities presented in the course of a visit and while the more technical official catalogues of the Museum's natural history collections might provide detailed information that followed a particular taxonomic system favored by researchers, there is little evidence that such narratives in book format were matched by labels with thorough information in the galleries.[45] The situation seems to have been similar across the Channel. According to a comprehensive guide to the collections of Musée royal d'histoire naturelle in Paris, in 1823 plant specimens had labels that merely described "the different names by which the plant had been designated, and the indication of the place where the sample had been collected" while labels to zoological specimens contained only three lines, consisting of a common name, a Latin name, and the name of the donor.[46] Labels in art museums, too, were only beginning to offer more information at this moment. Gustav Waagen, who is sometimes credited with having written the first art museum labels, made extensive catalogues of art collections in Germany and in Great Britain, but while he wrote many an index in book format (and others followed up with indices of his indices), his gallery labels remained relatively simple.[47] It was not until the later decades of the nineteenth century that information migrated in most museums in Europe and North

America from museum catalogues in book format to object labels on the walls or in vitrines—a move that paralleled the transition in libraries from bound to card catalogues.[48]

The Museum of Economic Geology produced information in other formats as well. If visitors wanted to dig deeper into a particular mineral or district, it was possible to find out more in the Museum's library by looking it up in a large volume of gray literature that ranged from official catalogues to reports and from unofficial handbooks to guides that provided more detailed descriptions of the Museum's holdings.[49] And if a particular mineral needed to be traced to a specific location in Britain or in the colonies, the Mining Records Office, which, as we have seen, provided horizontal and vertical sections as well as three-dimensional models that could be cross-referenced to maps produced by the Geological Survey. From 1858 onward, this information became so overwhelming that the Museum started publishing catalogues that indexed its own publications.[50] By 1890 "for a few pence" it was also possible to buy a copy of the numerous colonial reports published by Her Majesty's Stationery; these reports on such locations as Lagos, Ceylon, Newfoundland, Jamaica, Victoria, St. Vincent, etc. contained information about geological opportunities in addition to botanical ones."[51] This thick web of cross-referenced information was meant to produce practical results: in 1852 just before a company was formed to extract coal from an abandoned copper and lead mine in Wheal Alfred, Cornwall, potential investors consulted the sections in the Mining Record Office only to find out that this particular site was prone to flooding.[52] Comparing vertical sections from Northumberland, Robert Hunt, the keeper of the Mineral Records Office for almost four decades, could tell interested entrepreneurs at what depth carboniferous limestone series could be found at a particular location in the region.[53]

It was primarily this comparative function of the Museum of Economic Geology that created new resources: not only by finding unknown uses for known minerals but also by identifying new locations and techniques to obtain known resources. No better example demonstrates this in the nineteenth century than coal. British coal production tripled between the middle of the eighteenth century and the beginning of the nineteenth century and increased fivefold by the middle of the century again.[54] The Museum's move to its new location followed the reopening of the London Coal Exchange in 1849. The comparative function of the Museum was important to the coal trade for two reasons. First, after the public metage system (which entailed public officials weighing coal deliveries to ensure the fairness of a transaction but also to levy taxes) was abolished in 1831, coal's fungibility in London's increasingly "free market" depended on the standardization of *quantity*.[55] The Museum of Economic Geology continued this process by standardizing *quality*. Soon after its opening, for example, the Museum analyzed coal samples to make a recommendation about the kind best suited to the needs of the British steam navy.[56]

Second, the laboratories of the Museum routinely carried out chemical analyses to test the efficiency of coal from around the globe. Analyses—of, say, specimens from Newcastle to those from Sandy Bay, Patagonia, Chile or Vancouver Island— would be published in the popular press.[57] Comparability implied substitutability: knowing that when a mineral from one resource became unavailable, another could be found made that mineral more easily exchangeable. The information emanating from the Museum of Economic Geology thus provided assurances for the exchange of minerals in general and for the coal trade in particular, which, at a moment when steam power had become so crucial, was especially prone to speculation. One newspaper article from 1843 went so far as to claim that mineral statistics were therefore "of more importance" to Britain "than all the mines of Mexico and Peru."[58]

This was not mere hyperbole. In the 1840s geologist and future director of the Museum Roderick Murchison predicted, after comparing rock samples from the easternmost regions of Australia to those from auriferous tracts in the Ural Mountains, that there might be gold in the colony.[59] Murchison's prediction came before Edward Hargraves discovered the precious metal in New South Wales in 1851, the same year that the Museum opened its doors in its new building. This meant that once mineral statistics changed mining from a "lottery" to a proper science, the payoff would be no less rewarding than winning the lottery. This meant that the Museum of Economic Geology, an institution funded in large part by public funds and in small part by the Geological Society, was put in the service of private entrepreneurs at a moment when free trade was becoming government policy.[60]

It is in this sense that the mineral statistics of the Museum of Economic Geology can be said to have performed an alchemy of sorts. One of the ingenuities of classical political economy was the claim that free trade and practical knowledge (what we would today call "technology") would allow nations to break out of the mercantilist calculation of wealth as a zero-sum game and make infinite improvement possible.[61] As free-trade policies started to be adopted by the British government at mid-century, such exponential creation of wealth seemed within reach. The historian Carl Wennerlind has demonstrated in his study of the Hartlib Circle that early political economy was shaped by alchemy, which also promised a radical transformation by turning base metals into gold.[62] (The only alchemical experiment that succeeded, it turns out, was the creation of paper money.[63]) The spatial arrangement of

recovery." And so, as Günel documents, a number of oil and gas professionals are now attempting to recategorize carbon dioxide not as a waste material but as a commodity.

Whether one is using CCS to draw out that last bit of oil that is playing hard to get or to simply pay off a bit of our carbon debt, the forecasted rise of this technology will in turn create other resources, most notably the saline aquifers that, alongside tapped information in the Museum of Economic Geology produced an alchemical effect not only by identifying new resources and new locations for known ones but, more importantly, by providing new capabilities for navigating mineral markets that were increasingly becoming globalized at this moment. The London Metal Exchange, which first traded copper and, later, lead and zinc, officially opened in 1877—even though, like coal, these mineral commodities were being trade in a less formalized manner as early as the sixteenth century.

Early political economists had speculated that infinite improvement would be achieved thanks to free trade and practical knowledge, paying less attention to what historians have come to call "ghost acreages," the land in the colonies whose violently extracted resources exponentially multiplied the "wealth of nations" in Europe.[64] (According to one famous calculation, Britain relied on twenty-three million such ghost acres in 1830 for the cotton that was used in manufacture in Lancashire, a surface area that is almost equivalent to that of the entirety of England.[65]) The primary alchemy of nineteenth-century information storehouses was to create such ghost acreage *virtually*. By comparing the quality of coal from England to that from abroad, by making calculated predictions about tin at home or gold in the colonies, and by suggesting substitutes for a metal that might no longer be available, the Museum of Economic Geology created value simply by projecting future transaction opportunities for the benefit of the entrepreneur. This, after all, was how the thousands of pages of statistics published by the Mining Records Office were meant to be put to use. And, unlike actual ghost acres whose exploitation required a significant outlay of materiel and labor and encountered significant friction and resistance on the ground, the virtual rehearsal of ghost acres of the Museum of Economic Geology required little than the documentation, storage and comparison of information on sheets of paper.

***

Such optimism about the infinite resources of the future coexisted with anxieties about the depletion of accumulated resources. Malthus had calculated that while subsistence increased arithmetically, populations increased geometrically, thus setting "natural limits" to improvement.[66] Influnced by Malthus, some expressed fears about the finiteness of mineral resources almost as soon as mining took center stage in British economic life.[67] When geologist and theologian William Buckland critiqued Britain's "wanton waste" of coal, for example, he drew a contrast between the waste of agricultural resources, which, he argued, was morally wrong but not irreversible, and the waste of mineral deposits, which was permanent since it took millions of years for organic matter to replenish itself.[68] Pessimists like Buckland who predicted the exhaustion of Britain's coalfields were countered most frequently by advocates of free trade in the first decades of the nineteenth century.[69]

Thinking in section—rather than in plan—proved crucial to such debates. In 1829 both the House of Commons and the House of Lords established select committees on the state of the coal trade. At stake was the question of how to tax coal and regulate its trade, but, more relevant here, these hearings cast geological sections in an unexpectedly central role. In a testimony in May 1829, Duke Hugh Taylor, owner of mines in Northeast England, offered an optimistic calculation: even after taking into consideration considerable waste, mines of Northumberland and Durham alone would produce coal that would last the nation 1,727 years.[70] A year later Adam Sedgwick, professor of geology at the University of Cambridge, pulled this number down to 300 to 400 years. Sedgwick did not disagree with the surface area that Taylor had included in his estimate—a number Taylor had calculated looking at a plan; he argued that the calculation was simply wrong because Taylor did not take into consideration the varying *section* of the region.[71] The conclusion was clear: it was necessary to engage in sectional thinking to assess the economic value of Britain's coal reserves accurately.

Still, it turns out, there were also ghost acres to be discovered under the British soil. In the 1830s Sopwith was charged by the Crown to be the chair of a committee that collected mineral statistics in the Forest of Dean in western Gloustershire.[72] In the seventeenth century when the forest was enclosed by the Crown to grow timber for shipbuilding, the local populations were given exclusive rights to mine iron and the coal, some of which lay on the surface. These locals, known as "free miners" used a technique called "galing," which consisted of digging no deeper than 12 feet into the ground. By the end of the eighteenth century, however, it was clear that free miners had neither the machinery nor the capital necessary to extract the coal that lay deeper. In 1838, in the name of improving productivity, the Parliament passed a law which, even as it appeared to be reinstating the old privileges of the free miners, opened up the region to capital. Sopwith's task was to establish rules for awarding the rights of excavation in the region before entrepreneurs with steam engines and locomotives started digging for the coal lying deeper under the forest.[73] The freeminers rioted in response, most significantly in 1831.

Sopwith made sections, plans, and two models of the Forest of Dean in order to negotiate the process of awarding mining rights.[74] The models were then displayed at the Geological Society of London and the Institution of Civil Engineers before being put on permanent display in the Museum of Economic Geology.[75] The smaller of these models, now at the Oxford University Museum of Natural History, is 30 inches by 30 inches, scaled at five inches to a mile; as in Sopwith's isometrical drawings, the vertical scale was exaggerated three times to demonstrate coal veins more clearly. (Fig. 11) It was divided into 36 squares, each of which represent a square mile, and marked with letters and numerals that were cross-referenced

Fig. 11

to the Museum's other mineral statistics.[76] The model was designed to hinge open to reveal eight additional sections.[77] Sopwith had such models constructed patiently out of the hundreds of vertical sections collected in situ. Next, these vertical sections were connected into horizontal sections (some guesswork was necessary Sopwith acknowledged), which were then "half-lapped" together to form the skeleton of the model.[78]

Making this kind of model might seem labor-intensive and expensive, Sopwith explained, but that "cost was trifling" compared to the benefits, as these representational techniques allowed him to divide up excavation rights between entrepreneurs and freeminers in a relatively peaceful fashion.[79] Even though the free miners did not entirely lose their rights after 1841, most of them ended up having to lease their gales or becoming wage laborers. Still, according to Sopwith, his scientific approach prevented further rioting in the region precisely because it was guided less by old custom and more "by a discretionary power based upon reasonable data."[80] Plans had been crucial tools as commons and wastelands were enclosed through Parliamentary acts and consolidated in the hands of aristocracy since the seventeenth century.[81] Sections now served a similar role for the *vertical* enclosure of subterranean resources in the name of growing national wealth. In other words, even when a known resource from a well-established location was in question, mineral statistics created abundance out of scarcity and, more importantly, because it did so with the "discretionary power" of data, it met less resistance on the ground.

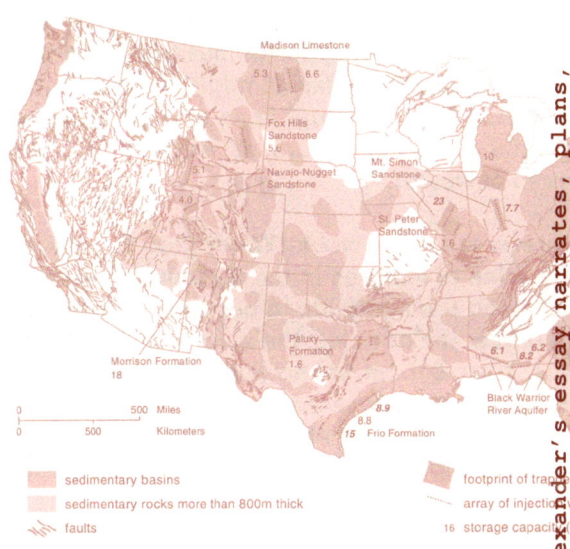

***

Mineral statistics also delivered the alchemical promise of creating wealth by excavating another resource: humans. This more elusive goal can be discerned in the Museum's public lecture series, designed for the presumed audience of "working men."[82] A series on the topic of gold, launched in 1852 (a year after the discovery of the precious metal in New South Wales) and intended primarily for "for the instruction of emigrants about to proceed to Australia, " was dedicated to topics ranging from the geology of Australia to the chemical properties and metallurgical treatment of gold.[83] (Fig. 12) These lectures attracted so much attention that summaries of their content were published in the popular press. While the lecturers delved into a great deal of detail about geology and the colony, their advice was not limited to discovering gold in Australia. J. B. Jukes, director of the Geological Survey of Ireland, for example, concluded his lecture on the geology of Australia by reminding his audience that gold-digging was back-breaking work that did not always prove lucrative. Still, he hoped that he had offered the audience more than know-how about gold. He told them that the more important lesson to be learned was an attitude that he claimed was embodied in the very act of digging:

> You go out *to dig for gold*, do not *be ashamed to dig for anything else…* Recollect that it is the *avowed object of your voyage*, and the only thing you have to trust to. If you fail to dig up gold, there are lands to be ploughed, sheep to be herded and sheared, cattle to be tended, corn to be sown and reaped: every one of these fully as honourable occupations as digging for gold. Go, then, with a bold and resolute heart, determined to get your own living by the strength of your own arms and the sweat of your own brows; and be assured, that industry and perseverance lead to fortune in Australia with fewer impediments and uncertainties in the way than in any part of the world.[84]

Digging here was not simply digging for a precious metal; it was presented as the alchemical technique that made all other colonial enterprises possible with the promise of infinite improvement—from farming to mining, from construction to husbandry. In the sixth and final lecture of the series on gold in 1852, Robert Hunt reassured the audience: fears that the influx of Australian gold into European markets would diminish the value of the metal, he said, were unfounded.[85] Hunt proved his point in a peculiar manner: by making calculations about how much the fortunes of historical figures would be worth in present-day money. By Hunt's reckoning, King Croesus had gifted 3 million sterling pounds to the temple in Delphi and Pericles had 1.162 million sterling pounds available in the treasury for the defense of Athens, and so on.[86] This was all to prove that gold retained its value as a metallic currency even during dramatic historical upheavals, a conclusion that might have been challenged after the introduction of paper money, but

Fig. 12

oil wells, are terrific repositories for CO2 injections. As in the earlier extractive moment that Alexander's essay narrates, plans, sections and statistical databases will again be essential to turning these previously valueless geographic formations into sought after resources. Researchers are already hard at work taming the uncertainties of this emerging market by mapping the locations and relative capacities of the world's aquifers. With the right database in hand, it seems, there will always be money to be made from digging holes in the ground.

nonetheless served the purpose of calming the nerves of a public encouraged to seek opportunities in the colonies. Hunt, like Jukes, added: colonialists might find no modern El Dorado, but "legitimate occupations of the artisan and the quiet pursuits of the agriculturalist" were, in fact, more reliable sources of wealth.[87]

A few years later when the geologist Warrington Smyth delivered another series of lectures in the Museum on the topic of gold, he advised the audience to economize their most important resource: their bodies, the source of their labor.[88] It was essential, he told them, to know how to calculate one's own worth. Since the miner was the best judge of the value of his own work, Smyth advised that the workers sell their labor through a Dutch auction, a descending price auction which, he argued, would benefit the seller.[89] This was not merely a Lockean possessive individualism that presumed sensations and labor to be one's first property. Rather at this crucial moment at the beginning of a new phase of capitalism, Smyth and fellow geologists were speaking to a subject imagined as a *homo economicus*, an entrepreneurial subject endowed with intrinsic calculative abilities to seek and achieve future wealth using the environment and the self as resources.[90]

These visitors from the working classes might not necessarily follow the Museum's trails of information in pursuit of a particular business opportunity, but, as one observer argued, if a "working man" had the intellectual capacity, the dramatic displays of the Museum might "waken up to make him a Watts, a Stephenson, or a Miller"—that is, the building itself could turn him into an enterprising inventor.[91] Whether an entrepreneur hoping to make the right decision when investing in a mining enterprise or a "working man" whose calculation was simply to make a living by selling his labor power, this subject should instinctively infer a favorable ratio between the input of resources and the output of profit. (Fig. 12) A good *homo economicus* knew that anything could be turned into a resource by cleverly operationalizing one's means toward the future—whether capital or labor did not matter. With the perpetual promise of yet another new resource on the horizon, those limits that worried Malthusians could be avoided and the alchemical promise of political economy be realized.

This meant that a resource was not a fixed asset like coal, which, having accumulated for centuries, had value in the present but rather a function, the ability of the mind to project into the future. Equipped with the power of databases, the human subject, now imagined as a *homo economicus*, could always invent the next resource regardless of any impending limits. Viewing this history in retrospect, of course, it is hard not to be struck by the perverseness of this mid-nineteenth-century calculation. Infinity is a chimera, as we now know, especially when resources such as coal and oil are concerned.[92] And yet the alchemical presumptions of political economy are as alive today as they were in the nineteenth century: that information technologies can change even the most mundane thing into an economic resource with endless future potential.

1 For a good summary of the literature, see Kathryn Furlong and Amma S. Norman, "Resources," in *The Wiley Blackwell Companion to Political Geography*, ed. John Agnew, Virginie Mamadouh, Anna J. Secor, and Joanne Sharp (Chichester, UK and Hoboken, NJ: John Wiley & Sons, 2015), 424-437. Also see the three-part essay and especially Gavin Bridge, "Resource Geographies II: The Resource-State Nexus," *Progress in Human Geography* 38.1 (2014): 118-130.

2 David Ricardo, *On The Principles of Political Economy and Taxation*, ed. Piero Sraffa (Cambridge: Cambridge University Press, 1986), 69.

3 John Stuart Mill, *Principles of Political Economy: With Some of Their Applications to Social Philosophy*, v. 1 (New York: Appleton, [1848] 1923), 242. On British coal, see E. A. Wrigley, *Energy and the English Industrial Revolution* (Cambridge: Cambridge University Press, 2010).

4 Erich Zimmermann, *World Resources and Industries* (New York: Harper, 1951), 15.

5 See, for example, Steven Topik, Carlos Marichal, and Zephyr Frank, eds., *From Silver to Cocaine:Latin American Commodity Chains and the Building of the World Economy, 1500–2000* (Durham: Duke University Press, 2006).

6 Take the case of the presumed scarcity of oil. Labban argues that the problem is not its scarcity but rather its abundance. Mazen Labban, *Space, Oil, and Capital* (New York: Routledge, 2008).

7 David Sepkoski, "Databases," in *Information: A Historical Companion*, ed. Ann Blair, Paul Duguid, Anja-Silvia Goeing, and Anthony Grafton (Princeton and Oxford: Princeton University Press, 2021), 392. Databases are distinct from other collections of information in that they are "amenable to some degree of recombination, sorting, and random access." David Graeber and David Wengrow have argued that this "complexity" argument is deeply ideological. The assumption that modern societies' complexities can only be managed through hierarchical arrangements such as modern bureaucracies naturalizes the nation-state as the ultimate horizon of human development. David Graeber and David Wengrow, *"The Dawn of Everything" A New History of Humanity* (London: Allen Lane, 2021).

8 Thomas Sopwith, *On the Preservation of Railway Sections and of Accounts of Borings, Sinkings, &c. in Elucidation of the Measures Recently Taken by the British Association: A Paper Read Before the Geological and Polytechnic Society of the West-Riding of Yorkshire, September 23, 1841* (Leeds: Edward Baines and Sons, 1842), 3. The chart had been conceived in 1840 by a Committee appointed by the learned society British Association at Glasgow. Sopwith wrote elsewhere that the chart had been devised by Professor John Phillips of York, known in the history of geology for having been among the first to theorize the geologic time scale.

9 Rolf Peter Sieferle, *The Subterranean Forest: Energy Systems and the Industrial Revolution* (Cambridge: White Horse Press, 2001), 124-127.

10 Sopwith, *On the Preservation of Railway Sections* (London: J. Weale, 1844), 4.

11 For a good summary of the primary developments in geology in the nineteenth century, see Mott T. Greene, "Geology," in *The Modern Biological and Earth Sciences*, ed. Peter J. Bowler and John V. Pickstone (Cambridge: Cambridge University Press), 165-184. For an elaboration of the same themes, see Mott T. Greene, *Geology in the Nineteenth Century: Changing Views of a Changing World* (Ithaca, NY: Cornell University Press, 1982).

12 On Jamaica, see H. T. De la Beche, *Notes on the Present Condition of the Negroes in Jamaica (London: T. Cadell, 1925) and Remarks on the Geology of Jamaica* (London, 1826). The latter includes a geological plan of eastern portion of the island as well as sections. Also see Lawrence J. Chubb, "Sir Henry Thomas De la Beche," in *Jamaican Rock Stars, 1823–1971: The Geologists Who Explored Jamaica*, S. K. Donovan, ed. (Boulder, CO: Geological Society of America, 2010), 9–28.

13 De la Beche, *How to Observe. Geology* (London: Charles Knight, 1835).

14 Both kinds of sections can be found today in the collections of the British Geological Survey. See: https://www.bgs.ac.uk/information-hub/bgs-maps-portal/.

15 Sopwith, *On the Preservation of Railway Sections*, 8.

16 Salim Rashid, "Political Economy and Geology in the Early Nineteenth Century: Similarities and Contrasts," *History of Political Economy* 13 (1981): 726-744.

17 David G. Bate, "Sir Henry Thomas De la Beche and the Founding of the British Geological Survey," *Mercian Geologist* 17 no.3 (2010), 160-61.

18 Sopwith, *The National Importance of Preserving Mining Records*, 22.

19 Adam Smith, *Wealth of Nations: An Inquiry into the Nature and Causes of the Wealth of Nations* (Ware: Wordsworth Editions, [1776] 2012), 106; Ralph S. G. Stokes, *Mines and Minerals of the British Empire* (London: E. Arnold, 1908), 48; and Thomas Barlett, *A Treatise on British Mining* (London: Effingham Wilson, 1850), 83.

20 Sopwith, *The National Importance of Preserving Mining Records*, 22 and 15.

21 Sopwith, *The National Importance of Preserving Mining Records*, 49.

22 The horizontal and vertical sections in the archives of the British Geological Section from this period are much larger, typically thirty-nine inches by twenty-seven inches. Sections of the cabinets in which the sections were stored are also much deeper than the dimensions that Sopwith discusses. See "Plan of Upper Story and Gallery," GSM 1/210, British Geological Survey Archives.

23 The building was one of many designed and constructed to house the growing British bureaucracy in the course of the nineteenth century. The Office of Works, which was brought under the Office of Woods and Forests in 1832, played a major role in this endeavor. Between 1815 and 1832, Office of Works retained a leading architect called an "attached architect"; after that the determination of the leading architect would be left to the market. Pennethorne worked for the Office of Works informally between 1848 and1856 and then again between 1859 and1870 when he had a more defined, salaried position. For histories of the Office of Works, see M. H. Port, *Imperial London: Civil Government Building in London 1850-1915* (New Haven and London: Yale University Press, 1995). On Pennethorne, see Geoffrey Tyack, *Sir James Pennethorne and the Making of Victorian London* (Cambridge: Cambridge University Press, 1992).

24 Over time these programs would not fit the small building and space need to be rented out in neighboring buildings. "The Museum of Practical Geology," *Nature* (July 28, 1934), 130.

25 For calls to open one in Glasgow, for example, see "Museum of Practical Geology," *The Glasgow Herald* (September 2, 1853), 5. For De la Beche's appeal to the East India Company in 1841, see De la Beche, "Memorandum respecting a Proposed Museum of Economic Geology in India," *Gleanings in Science* 124.40 (1 April 1842): 333-339.

26 "A Visit to the Museum of Practical Geology," *Fraser's Magazine for Town and Country 43* (June 1851), 628. Emphasis mine.

27 "A Visit to the Museum of Practical Geology," 628.

28 Carla Yanni, *Nature's Museums: Victorian Science and the Architecture of Display* (New York: Princeton University Press, 2005), 24.

29 For histories of commercial museums, see Dave Muddiman, "From Display to Data: The Commercial Museum and the Beginnings of Business Information, 1870-1914," in *Information Beyond Borders: International Cultural and Intellectual Exchange in the Belle Époque*, ed. W. Boyd Rayward (Surrey, England and Burlington, VT: Ashgate, 2014), 259-282, here 260 and Steven Conn, "The Philadelphia Commercial Museum: A Museum to Conquer the World," in *Museums and American Intellectual Life*, 1876-1926 (Chicago and London: University of Chicago Press, 1998), 115-150. According to the Secretary of the London Chamber of Commerce, Kenric B. Murray, in 1887 there were commercial museums beyond Europe in Argentina, Brazil, and Peru. Kenric B. Murray, *Commercial Geography, Considered Especially in Its Relation to New Markets and Fields of Production for British Trade* (London: T. C. Jack, 1887), 12-15. A commercial museum opened in Calcutta in the early twentieth century.

30 For comparison, see W. Colgrove Betts, "The Philadelphia Commercial Museum," *Journal of Political Economy* 8. no. 2 (March 1900): 222-233.It seems to be the case, for example, that sections were stored in the Mining Records Office horizontally rather than vertically on their edges. See "Plan of Upper Story and Gallery," GSM 1/210, British Geological Survey Archives.

31 "Museum of Practical Geology," *The Times* (May 27, 1858), 12.

32 Sopwith, *Account of the Museum of Economic Geology and Mining Records Office* (London: John Murray, 1843), 1.

33 One need only glance at the handbooks and guides published throughout the institution's history: Robert Hunt, *A Descriptive Guide to the Museum of Practical Geology, with Notices of the Geological Survey of the United Kingdom, the School of Mines, and the Mining Record Office* (London: G. E. Eyre and W. Spottiswoode for H. M. Stationery Office, 1867); *A Handbook to the Museum of Practical Geology* (London: H. M. Stationery, 1896); *A Short Guide to the Museum of Practical Geology* (London: H. M. Stationery, 1914).

34 For discussions of the architecture of the Museum, see Tyack, *Sir James Pennethorne*, 179-191; Sophie Forgan, "Bricks and Bones: Architecture and Science in Victorian Britain," in The Architecture of Science, eds. Peter Galison and Emily Thompson (Cambridge, MA: MIT Press, 1999) 181-208; Sophie Forgan, "Building the Museum: Knowledge, Conflict, and the Power of Place," *Isis* 96, no. 4 (December 2005): 572-585; and Yanni, *Nature's Museums*, 51-61.

35 *A Short Guide to the Museum of Practical Geology*, 19.

36 Bernard H. Becker, *Scientific London* (London: Henry S. King & Co, 1874), 251.

37 Sophie Forgan, "Bricks and Bones," 197.

38 The terms were coined by William Whewell in 1832 in his review of the second volume of Charles Lyell's Principles of Geology. Whewell saw Lyell as representing uniformitarianism against the mainstream catastrophic view of geology, according to which changes on earth's surface were due to catastrophic events such as floods, volcanic eruptions, etc. Darwin's theory of evolution was influenced by Lyell's views. William Whewell, "Lyell's Geology, vol. 2—Changes in the Organic World Now in Progress," *Quarterly Review* 47 (1832), 103-132.

39 Martin J. S. Rudwick, *The Great Devonian Controversy: The Shaping of Scientific Knowledge Among Gentlemanly Specialists* (Chicago; University of Chicago Press, 1988), 63-92. Other seminal works on the development of geology in this context are James A. Secord, *Controversy in Victorian Geology: The Cambrian-Silurian Dispute* (Princeton, N.J.: Princeton University Press, 1986); Martin J. S. Rudwick, *Worlds before Adam: The Reconstruction of Geohistory in the Age of Reform* (Chicago: University of Chicago Press, 2008); David R. Oldroyd, T*he Highlands Controversy: Constructing Geological Knowledge through Fieldwork in Nineteenth-Century Britain* (Chicago: University of Chicago Press, 1990). Murchison's side won when he discovered evidence for his argument in Russia.

40 De la Beche, *Sections and Views Illustrative of Geological Phenomena* (London: Treutel & Würtz, 1830), 4 and Sopwith, *On the Preservation of Railway Sections*, 11

41 Sopwith, *Practical Observations on the Easy and Rapid Delineation of Plans and Drawings in Isometrical and Other Modes of Projections* (Newcastle: Thomas Sopwith, 1836).

42 Sopwith, *Practical Observations*, 38. He even invented what he called "isometrical drawing paper" to this end, a standardized graph paper representing 17.32040 inches by 14 inches, divided into isometrical squares of half an inch, which are printed in faint lines so as to guide the draughtsman without disfiguring the drawing." Sopwith, *Practical Observations*, 28. He also gave instructions (strings of numbers) for the drawing of particular shapes on his isometrical drawing paper.

43 "Museum of Economic Geology," *Chambers's Edinburgh Journal* (Sep 9, 1843), 267.

44 "A Visit to the Museum of Practical Geology," 622.

45 See, for example, Henry G. Clarke, *The British Museum: Its Antiquities and Natural History. A Hand-Book Guide for Visitors* (London: H. G. Clarke, 1850) and J. J. Kaup, *Catalogue of Apodal Fish in the Collection of the British Museum* (London: Order of the Trustees of the British Museum, 1856). One strategy was to connect these guides and catalogues to the galleries through marginal annotations that referenced particular display cases. According to one historian, it was not until the 1890s that every specimen received a label in the Oxford University Museum. Małgosia B. Nowak-Kemp, "150 Years of Changing Attitudes Towards Zoological Collections in a University Museum: The Case of the Thomas Bell Tortoise Collection in the Oxford University Museum," *Archives of Natural History* 36, no. 2 (2009), 309.

46 M. Deleuze, *Histoire et description du muséum royal d'histoire naturelle*, vol. 1 (Paris: M. A Boyer, Au Jardin du Roi, 1823), 19 and vol. 2, 436.

47 See several editions starting with G. F. Waagen, *Verzeichniss Gemäde-Sammlung des königlichen Museums zu Berlin* (Berlin: Königliche Akademie der Wissenschaften, 1830). For an index to Waagen's index, see Algernoon Graves, *Summary of an Index to Waagen* (London: A. Graves, 1912).

48 On the transition from catalogues in bound format to index cards, see Zeynep Çelik Alexander, "Stacks, Shelves, and the Law: Restructuring the Library of Congress," *Grey Room* 82 (Winter 2021), 6-29.

49 The list of periodical publications associated with the Museum includes: *Annual Reports of the Geological Survey and Museum*, *Memoirs of the Geological Survey* (published under different names when dedicated to a particular district, mineral, coalfield, or water supply as well as paleontology and stratigraphical monographs), and *Mineral Statistics of the United Kingdom and Great Britain*, *Records of the School of Mines* and *Science Applied to the Arts*, among others.

50 Examples are: *A Catalogue of the Contents of the Mining Record Office in the Museum of Practical Geology Consisting of Plans and Sections of Mines and Collieries, Statistical and Other Documents* (London: Her Majesty's Stationery Office, 1858) and *Catalogue of the Maps, Horizontal and vertical sections and other publications of the Geological Survey* (London: Her Majesty's Stationery Office, 1863).

51 For an example, see G. F. Scott Elliot and Catharine A. Raisin, *Sierra Leone: Reports on Botany and Geology* (London: Her Majesty's Stationery Office, 1893).

52 De la Beche, "Inaugural Discourse" in *Records of the School of Mines and of Science Applied to the Arts*, vol. 1 (London: Her Majesty's Stationery Office, 1852), 11.

53 Robert Hunt, *British Mining: A Treatise on the History, Discovery, Practical Development and Future Prospects of Metalliferous Mines in the United Kingdom* (London: C. Lockwood, 1884), 251-252.

54 According to Wrigley, coal production in England, Wales, and Scotland was 5,230 thousand tons in the 1750s, 15,045 thousand tons in the 1800s, and 74,050 thousand tons in the 1850s. Wrigley, *Energy and the English Industrial Revolution*, 37.

55 Aashish Velkar, "Caveat Emptor: Abolishing Public Measurements, Standardizing Quantities, and Enhancing Market Transparency in the London Coal Trade c. 1830," *Enterprise & Society* 9, no.2 (2008): 281-313.

56 De la Beche as cited in "Museum of Practical Geology," *The Morning Post* (May 13, 1851), 6.

57 De la Beche as cited in "Coals in the New World," *Southampton Herald* (17 February 1849), 6. Coal was not the only material that the Museum's laboratories tested. Of many similar reports, see , for example, Henry Piddington, "Examination and Analyses of Dr. Campbell's Specimens of Copper Ores Obtained in the Neighborhood of Darjeeling," *Gleanings in Science* 2 (May 1854), 477.

58 "Museum of Economic Geology," *Chambers's Edinburgh Journal* (Sep 9, 1843), 266

59 Hunt, *A Descriptive Guide to the Museum of Practical Geology*, 124.

60 This is sometimes called "constructive imperialism." These were imperialists who advocated tariff reform to realize a stronger, unified British empire. Peter Cain, "The Economic Theory of Constructive Imperialism," in *British Politics and the Spirit of the Age: Political Concepts in Action*, ed. Cornelia Navari (Keele: Keele University Press, 1996).

61 For an account of how the Hartlib Circle borrowed the idea of infinite improvement from alchemy, see Carl Wennerlind, "The Alchemical Foundations of Credit," in *Casualties of Credit: The English Financial Revolution, 1620-1720* (Cambridge, MA: Harvard University Press, 2011), 44-79.

62 Carl Wennerlind, "The Alchemical Foundations of Credit," in *Casualties of Credit: The English Financial Revolution, 1620-1720* (Cambridge, MA: Harvard University Press, 2011), 44-79 .

63 Carl Wennerlind, "Credit-Money as the Philosopher's Stone: Alchemy and the Coinage Problem in Seventeenth-Century England," *History of Political Economy* 35 (2003): 234-261.

64 The concept was introduced by the neo-Malthusian Georg Borgström in *The Hungry Planet: The Modern World at the Edge of Famine* (New York: Macmillan, 1965) and was later taken up by Eric L. Jones in *The European Miracle: Environments, Economies, and Geopolitics in the History of Europe and Asia* (Cambridge and New York: Cambridge University Press, 2003).

65 Kenneth Pomeranz, *The Great Divergence: China, Europe, and the Making of the Modern World Economy* (Princeton: Princeton University Press, [2000] 2021), 315.

66 T. R. Malthus, *An Essay on the Principle of Population; or, A View of Its Past and Present Effects on Human Happiness* (London: J. Johnson, [1798] 1803) which went through various editions and remains influential to this day. Contrast this with Ricardo who speculated on the "elasticity of steam" in Ricardo, *On the Principles of Political Economy, and Taxation*, 53, 63, 65.

67 According to Sieferle, British anxieties about the exhaustion of coal reserves can be traced back to the sixteenth century, when the English Parliament considered an export ban on coal. Sieferle, *The Subterranean Forest*, 184-191. Wrigley discusses how the energy regime of fossil fuels, on the one hand, allowed breaking out of organic energy regimes and, on the other, triggered anxieties about the finiteness of subterranean riches in Wrigley, *Energy and the English Industrial Revolution*. Among the first to apply the Malthusian logic to coal was Chalmers who defended a self-sufficient nation. Thomas Chalmers, *An Enquiry into the Extent and Stability of Natural Resources* (Edinburgh: John Moir, 1808). The best-known nineteenth-century text on coal exhaustion is Jevons's, *The Coal Question*, which went through several editions. See Nuno Luis Madureira, "The Anxiety of Abundance: William Stanley Jevons and Coal Scarcity in the Nineteenth Century," *Environment and History* 18, no. 3 (August 2012): 395-421. But as historians have demonstrated, the question preoccupied geologists, mine owners, and politicians alike starting in the 1820s. Fredrik Albritton Jonsson, "The Coal Question Before Jevons," *The Historical Journal* 63, no. 1 (2020): 107-126.

68 William Buckland, *Geology and Mineralogy as Exhibiting the Power, Wisdom, and Goodness of God*, vol. 1 (London: Bell & Daldy, [1836] 1869], 448.

69 Coal did not only stretch land's limits, according to some; it literally multiplied its surface area. In an analysis of the "economy of the coal-field," the Scottish mineralogist J. F. W. Johnston argued that coal made Britain doubly rich. "Our minerals are stored beneath," he reasoned, "while agriculture is still rewarded for her surface toil." James F. W. Johnston, *The Economy of a Coal-Field* (Durham: Andrews, 1838), 9.

70 Hugh Taylor in *The Evidence Taken Before the Select Committee of the House of Lords*, 48. Taylor's calculation had important immediate implications: there was no urgency to changing the existing system of measurement, on which much waste was blamed, and coal exports did not need to be restricted.

71 Adam Sedgwick in *Report of the Select Committee on the State of the Coal Trade*, 234-237.

72 For a history of the Forest of Dean, see H. G. Nicholls, *The Forest of Dean: An Historical and Descriptive Account, Derived from Personal Observation, and Other Sources, Public, Private, Legendary, and Local* (London: John Murray, 1858). Also see Di Palma, "Forest," in *Wasteland*, 177-229.

73 Sopwith started working in the Forest of Dean at the end of 1833 and beginning of 1834. Benjamin Ward Richardson, *Thomas Sopwith: With Excerpts from His Diary of Fifty-Seven Years* (London: Longmans, Green, 1891), 95-104. He wrote the report on behalf of the commission although he was the commissioner on behalf of the Crown. The miners's interests were represented by John Probyn and the mine owners' by the entrepreneur John Buddle. Sopwith, *The Award of the Dean Forest Mining Commissioners under the Act of 1 and 2 Victoria, cap. 43 as to the Coal and Iron Mines in her Majesty's Forest of Dean and the Rules and Regulations* (London: John Weale, 1841), 7-8.

74 Richardson, *Thomas Sopwith*, 106.

75 Fredrik Albritton Jonsson, "Abundance and Scarcity in Geological Time, 1784-1844," in *Nature, Action, and the Future: Political Thought and the Environment*, ed. Katrina Forrester and Sophie Smith (Cambridge and New York: Cambridge University Press, 2018), 70-71.

76 Sopwith, Account of the Museum of Economic Geology, 69-70.

77 See the description in Turner and Dearman, "Thomas Sopwith's Large Geological Models," *Proceedings of the Yorkshire Geological Society*, 14.

78 "Mr. Sopwith's Model of the Forest of Dean," *Proceedings of the Geological and Polytechnic Society of the West-Riding of Yorkshire* (June 4, 1840), 29.

79 "Mr. Sopwith's Model of the Forest of Dean," 30 and Sopwith, T*he Award of the Dean Forest Mining Commissioners*, 29.

80 Sopwith, *The Award of the Dean Forest Mining Commissioners*, 25. Also see Ian Wright, *The Life and Times of Warren James: Free Miner from the Forest of Dean* (Bristol: Bristol Radical History Group, 2008).

81 On the relationship between enclosure and map making, see Roger J. P. Kain and Elizabeth Baigent, *The Cadastral Map in the Service of the State: A History of Property Mapping* (Chicago and London: University of Chicago Press, 1992), 236-254.

82 "Museum of Practical Geology," *The Times* (May 27, 1858), 12. From what I could gather, the first lecture series took place in 1852 and the second in 1859. For reports of these, see "Museum of Practical Geology," The Morning Post (July 1, 1852), 5; "Museum of Practical Geology. Lectures on the Gold of Australia," The Morning Chronicle (July 1, 1852), 3; "Museum of Practical Geology," The Morning Chronicle (July 10, 1852), 7; "Museum of Economic Geology," The Morning Post (January 26, 1859), 3; and "Museum of Economic Geology," The Morning Post (February 9, 1859), 3.

83 These lectures were published as J. B. Jukes et al., *Lectures on Gold for the Instruction of Emigrants About to Proceed to Australia* (London: David Bogue, 1853). Because more permanent settling with families was the goal here, one can assume that women were encouraged to attend.

84 J. B. Jukes, "The Geology of Australia," J. B. Jukes et al., *Lectures on Gold*, 37. Emphasis in the original.

85 Robert Hunt, "The History and Statistics of Gold," J. B. Jukes et al., *Lectures on Gold*, 170. Hunt's lecture was reported in "Museum of Practical Geology," *The Morning Chronicle* (July 10, 1852), 7.

86 Hunt, "The History and Statistics of Gold," 176, 178.

87 Hunt, "The History and Statistics of Gold," 170.

88 Warrington Smyth cited in "Museum of Economic Geology," *The Morning Post* (February 9, 1859), 3.

89 Warrington Smyth cited in "Museum of Economic Geology," *The Morning Post* (January 26, 1859), 3. Also see "Museum of Economic Geology," *The Morning Post* (Feb. 3, 1859), 3.

90 When British economists started using the term homo economicus in the 1880s, they turned to a passage from an essay published by the philosopher John Stuart Mill in 1836. John Stuart Mill, "On the Definition of Political Economy; and on the Method of Philosophical Investigation into that Science," *London and Westminster Review* (October 1836), 12-13. Although Mill never used the term and found the assumption that human individuals were endowed with intrinsic calculative abilities to seek and achieve wealth absurd, he nonetheless subscribed to such an idea of human nature in an attempt to save political economy. On this, see Charles H. Hinnant, "The

Invention of homo oeconomicus: A Reading of John Stuart Mill's 'On the Definition of Political Economy,'" *Prose Studies* 21, no. 3 (December 1998): 51-68.

91 Edward Forbes, "On the Educational Uses of Museums," *American Journal of Sciences and Arts* 54 (Nov. 1854), 345.

92 Take one contemporary calculation: 89 metric tons of ancient plant matter were required to produce 1 gallon of gas or, put differently, fossil deposits from the last 500 million years have been providing cheap energy for humans for only the past 250 years. Jeffrey S. Dukes, "Burning Buried Sunshine: Human Consumption of Ancient Solar Energy," *Climactic Change* 61 (2003), 38, 40.

1 Gökçe Günel, "What Is Carbon Dioxide? When Is Carbon Dioxide?" *Political and Legal Anthropology Review*. 39, iss. 1 (May 2016).
2 Michael L. Szulczewski et al., "Lifetime of carbon capture and storage as a climate-change mitigation technology," *Proceedings of the National Academy of Science of the United States of America* vol. 109, no. 14 (March 2012).

Resources of the Future: Urban Land and Environmental Quality in Harvey Perloff's Development Planning

Jack Hanly

In 1937, the National Resources Committee, a New Deal-era public planning board, submitted a report on the city. The federal government's social welfare and information gathering programs had thus far largely ignored the rapid transformations of the rural landscape into teeming centers of commerce. Although the nation had importantly embarked on a consideration of physical and social resources, it had not yet taken up the challenge of "the highest and best use" of "urban communities [as] potential assets of great value."[1] The report framed rural and urban communities as interdependent landscapes in which the nation's future prosperity rested. As an initial attempt to collate reliable data on the physical and social life of the city, the report offered graphic and textual descriptions of the city's current state and future conditions. While it mostly understood the city as a site of resource consumption and instrument of wise use, the report also presaged a notion that would exert growing influence in the coming decades: that the city was a resource in itself to be managed in the development of the national economy.

This essay traces the genealogy of resource planning discourses as they intersect with international development paradigms and urban/architectural pedagogy through the career of Harvey S. Perloff, a political economist and educator who began his career overseeing industrial planning in Puerto Rico and ended it as the dean of UCLA's School of Architecture and Planning. During this time, which spans from the New Deal era to the dawn of the Reagan presidency, the status of planning changed dramatically; initially planning was a practice that possessed a heroic surety, confident in its ability to mold the world according to its own principles, but in later decades such ambitions were curtailed and state-sponsored planning was superseded by other predictive methods.[2] Perloff's migrations between various think tanks and committees came at a time when, as many scholars have recently shown, military-industrial-academic complexes were marshaling novel tools of research and predictive control in projects of breathtaking scope. Furthermore, as many architectural and urban historians have shown, the increasing focus on methods of computerized simulation, scenario planning, and urban "games used the logic of systems to impose a degree of rationality onto the perceived social, political, and environmental disorder of the time.[3]

This essay extends these accounts by showing how this scientific focus was imbued with the projective apparatus of resource and economic forecasting, planning techniques that together cast the built environment as a "natural resource" in need of conservation. However, expertise in resource planning came to be wielded less in service of state-sponsored activity and more towards the heady imagining of corporate-sponsored futurism, in part a result of the changing fates of planning discussed above. Joining these ontologies, though, was a persistent faith in qualitative and quantitative methods of projection that might scan informational environments for the resources that would secure the future. In time, Perloff even began to conceive of architecture as a resource to be developed in its own right. Perloff's career thus captures how capitalist planning tools drifted from the realms of policy into the aesthetic domains of architecture and urbanism.

A gloss on the highlights of a career that seamlessly moved between the realms of academia, research, and government gives us some clues as to these dynamics. In 1940, Harvey Perloff completed his doctorate in political economy at Harvard University with a thesis on modern budget policies. After enrolling in military service in 1943, Perloff assisted the Puerto Rican government—a quasi-colonial regime overseen by New Deal "brain truster" and planning acolyte Rexford G. Tugwell—on the industrial development program Operation Bootstrap, one of the first and most ambitious regional development programs. Between 1947 and 1955 he led the University of Chicago's influential Program of Education and Research in Planning, which merged that institution's notable legacy of urban social sciences with the applied goals of planning.[4] For the next fourteen years, Perloff was a lead researcher at the Ford Foundation-funded think tank Resources for the Future, where he directed the Program on Urban and Regional Studies. Resources for the Future was the first of its kind—an "environmental" think tank that produced studies for corporations and governments on the dimensions and prospects of natural resources, the very substrate of the national economic system. Perloff briefly stepped down from these activities for two years in 1961 to serve as part of an illustrious group of experts known as the "Committee of Nine", on President John F. Kennedy's Alliance for Progress a $20 billion peace-building effort with Latin America that coincided with the

While Alvin Hansen's Depression-era prediction that lackluster population numbers and the closing of the frontier would result in the "cessation of growth"¹ was laid to waste by the expansionist policies and baby boom of the postwar period, recently, the economist Robert J. Gordon has once again been ringing the end-of-growth alarms. This tremendous consternation over growth—positioned as the panacea for high unemployment and all manner of other social ills—begs the question: from where did this idea come? The historian and degrowth activist Matthias Schmelzer traces the concept of growth, broadly speaking, to the second half of the eighteenth century, when industrialization and colonialism had resulted in a political system that was "fundamentally dependent on the continuous accumulation of wealth." Citing Reinhardt Koselleck, he notes that, concomitant with this world order, came a "perception of temporality" in which the future was characterized by "progress."² Despite this older provenance, however, Schmelzer notes that what he calls the modern-day "economic growth paradigm"—that is, when the pursuit of full employment is eclipsed by the idea that there is a domain called the "economy" and that its rate of growth indexes a country's welfare—dates only so far back as the mid-1950s.³

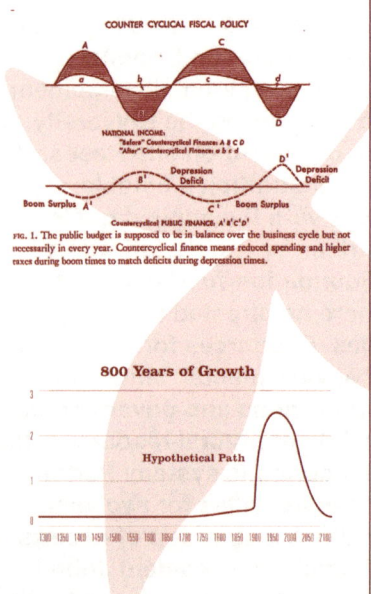

creation of the Agency for International Development. In 1968, Perloff was appointed Dean of the Graduate School of Architecture and Planning at UCLA, where he remained until his death in 1983. During this time, he advised a number of public and private research endeavors, notably publishing a book for the American Academy of Arts and Sciences' Commission on the Year 2000, a group that introduced the discipline of futurology to mainstream attention.

The essay focuses on three banner moments in this trajectory—Puerto Rico, Resources for the Future, and UCLA—chosen to elucidate Harvey Perloff's salient modes of practice in development, resources, and environment. In doing so, it argues for a reconsideration of architectural and planning pedagogy in light of their entanglements with neocolonial and imperialist power relations. For Perloff, resources became a labile material and epistemological object through which to articulate the shifting ground of politics in the post-war era, as well as a universal lens through which to understand the city and its futures. In remembrances of their colleague, scholars commended Perloff as "a social inventor whose laboratory was society… [He was a man] not content merely to analyze, but to prescribe." He had, they continued, the "ability to span the field of architecture on one hand to the world economy on the other."⁵ These dual claims to prescriptive experimentation and architectural-economic linkages are the hallmarks of a career that mobilized information and resources as coeval design tools for outlining the future.

Learning from the "American Keynes"

In order to understand how Perloff, an economist trained in Keynesian management techniques, ascended to become an elder statesman of architectural education, it is important to return to his intellectual roots in that mode. As a student at Harvard, Perloff worked closely with the influential economist Alvin Hansen. Affably known as the "American Keynes," Hansen was a leading popularizer of Keynes's economic theory following his publication of *The General Theory of Employment, Interest and Money* in 1936. Hansen was instrumental in the creation of the Council of Economic Advisers in 1946, an agency that provided the White House with objective analysis in the creation of fiscal policy. Hansen's interest in the stages of "business cycles" matured over the first half of the 20th century, from a relatively orthodox view of external disturbances such as technological change and resource depletion to a full-throated Keynesianism. As against this laissez-faire view of "automatic" fluctuations in the production of goods and capital investment, Hansen's brand of Keynesianism argued that it was in fact state monetary policy that determined business conditions. In the absence of government intervention to stabilize production and employment, Hansen warned that a form of "secular stagnation" could take hold—a prolonged, non-cyclical period of population decline and disinvestment when household savings exceeded business investment and demand correspondingly became anemic. Keynesian economic thought thus sought to stave the deflationary effects of declining resource frontiers and newly constrained immigration with a program to encourage capital expenditure by businesses and

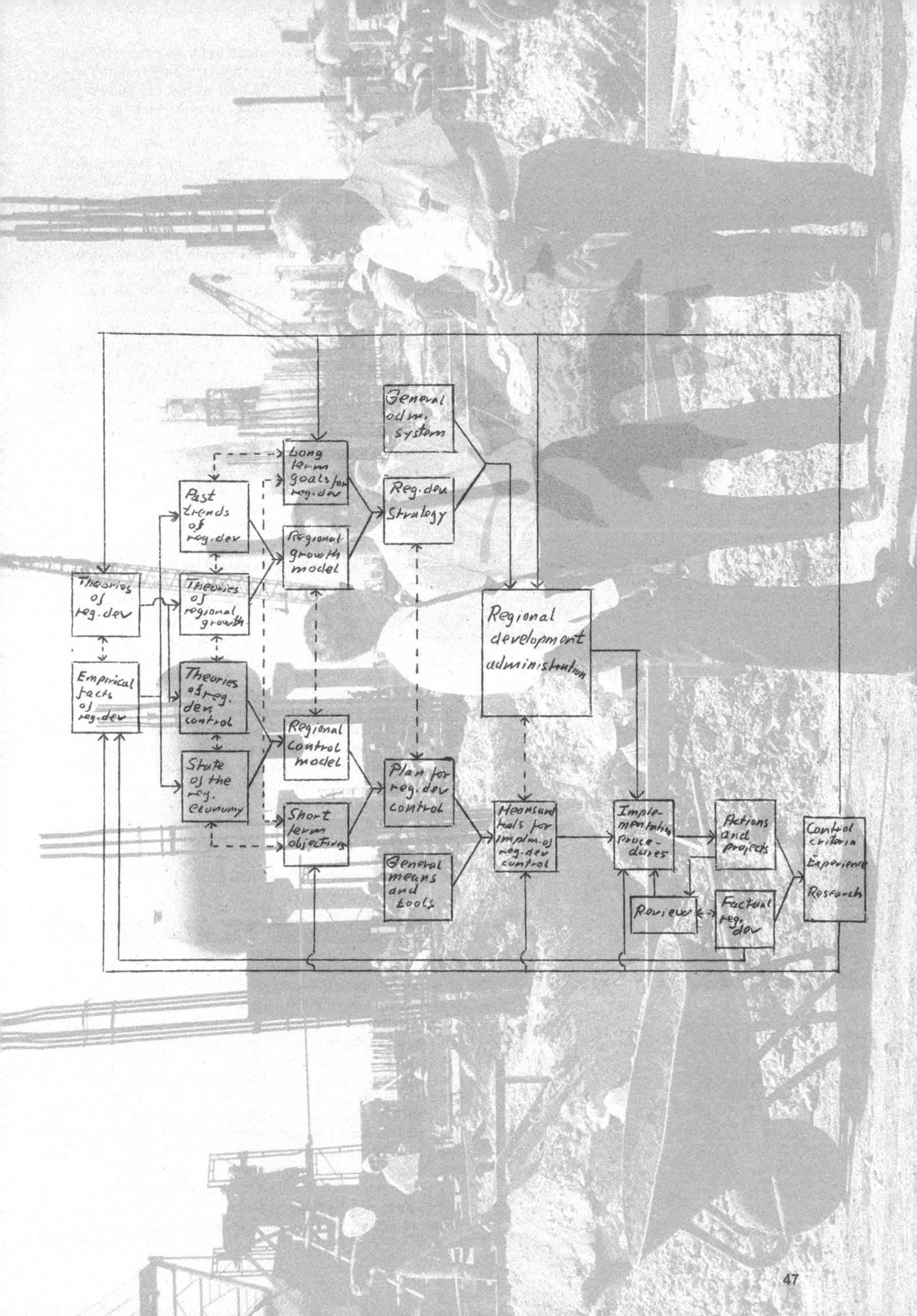

Although the specific historical circumstances (the Depression, the need for wartime national income accounting tools, the Cold War) that produced concepts like secular stagnation and economic growth have long since passed—and although our present era is characterized by growth-fueled rising inequality and ecological collapse—old habits, it seems, die hard. Take, for example, the worldview of the currently reigning global super villain Jeff Bezos. Unaware that he is merely parroting the rhetoric of midcentury American economic planners (and eighteenth century colonizers), he argues that, in response to the environmental crisis, we should not alter our habits but should instead colonize space, extracting energy from this new resource frontier so that our children and children's children ad infinitum can experience the same "dynamism and growth" that he has been so blessed to live through.[4] Anything to keep growth—the benefits of which seem to be largely accruing to his pockets—alive.

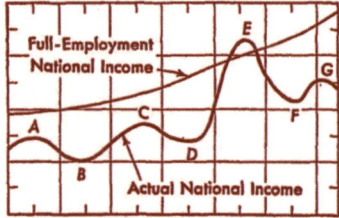

FIG. 3. Hypothetical data to illustrate case where simple countercyclical finance is held inadequate to achieve stable high employment.

1 Alvin Hansen, "Economic Progress and Declining Population Growth," *The American Economic Review* 29, no. 1 (March 1939), 11.
2 Matthias Schmelzer, *The Hegemony of Growth: The OECD and the Making of the Economic Growth Paradigm* (Cambridge: Cambridge University Press, 2016), 76.
3 Schmelzer, *The Hegemony of Growth*, 97.
4 Jeff Bezos, "Going to Space to Benefit Earth" (Blue Moon lunar lander product launch, May 9, 2019), https://www.youtube.com/watch?v=GQ98hGUe6FM.

individuals.[6] This milieu provided the intellectual springboard for Perloff's career in planning, which would share the Keynesian urgency to discover ways of preempting or outmaneuvering these impending resource limits.

In a 1942 publication Hansen co-authored with Perloff, the two economists called for a national program of resource development modeled on the Tennessee Valley Authority's regionally based planning mechanism. They (improbably) suggested that the U.S. had yet to fully recognize the full potentials of its land, water, and air resources, and that maximum economic growth in the aftermath of WWII would require such forethought. The physiogeographic area of the river valley would serve as the basic unit of organization. The pair also called for an overseer along the lines of the TVA to administer this vision on a national basis. While Hansen and Perloff nodded to the multiple programs that made up river basin planning at this time (such as recreation and tourism), their focus was on natural resource development in service of economic expansion.[7] This early attention to the region as an administrative entity for development planning shows how Perloff considered an area's natural assets, manipulated by technology and engineering, as the foundation for future growth.

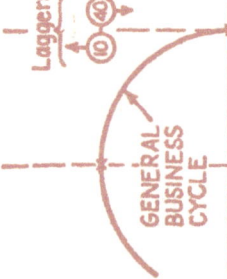

This strategy was in line with the then dominant practice of conservationist resource planning, an approach popularized in the early 20th century by U.S. president Theodore Roosevelt and the head of newly created Forest Service Gifford Pinchot. As against a preservationist ethos that sought to establish vast tracts of wilderness unmolested by human industry, conservation thinking advocated the judicious and wise use of natural resources such as timber and water so that they would remain productive for future generations. Hansen and Perloff's publication sketched the outlines of a spatialized Keynesianism and conservationist resource program that would propel Perloff's career in the decades to come. That is, the pair melded the Keynesian search for external economic stimuli with the study of particular resource development opportunities of a given region. For Perloff, the urgency of secular stagnation would be met with place-based economic planning tethered to projections of the amount and availability of an area's resources. In theory, this approach could be expanded to suit the nation-state at large.[8]

Planning the Future of Puerto Rico

Perloff would get the opportunity to enact these theories of development with his appointment as an economic planning adviser in Puerto Rico, a position he held just as the territory was emerging as a crucial testing ground for U.S. foreign policy in the post-war. Indeed, the modern regime of global development aid came into being with President Truman's announcement of the Point Four Program in 1945, and it was the series of projects in Puerto Rico known as Operation Bootstrap that inaugurated Truman's call to develop the "Third World." As Timothy Mitchell has shown, such projects originated as a means of subverting domestic labor demands by outsourcing industrial manufacturing and energy production to autocratic foreign regimes. In doing so, officials introduced the very notion of "economy" as a discrete

The Quality of the
URBAN ENVIRONMENT
Essays on "New Resources" in an Urban Age

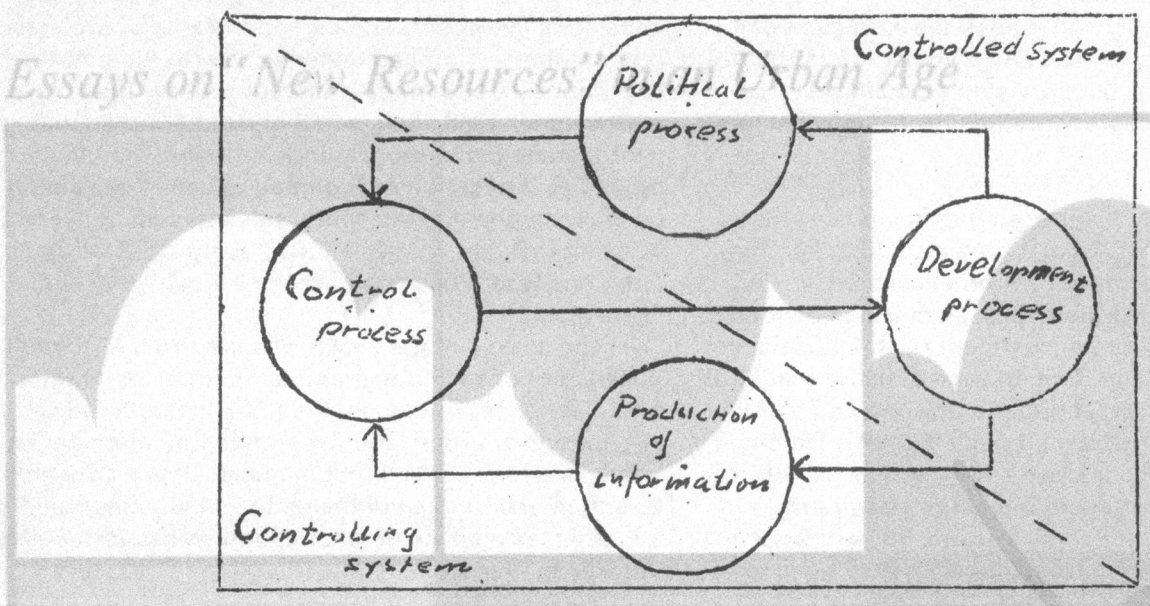

object of management predicated on a stable and knowable outline of the future. This stable future, however, depended on asymmetrical exchange between (neo) colony and metropole: the free flow of resources from foreign sovereignties on the one hand, and the provision of development aid in the form of technical knowledge on the other.[9] These dynamics played out in Puerto Rico through vast planning efforts aimed at industrializing the rural island territory, attracting hordes of social scientists looking to study the "underdeveloped" subject and the reasons for his supposed stagnancy.

Much of this academic interest can be traced to the tenure of Rexford Tugwell, who served as Governor of Puerto Rico from 1941 to 1946. The former chairman of the New York City Planning Commission, Tugwell saw the governor's position as an opportunity to import the state-led economic planning of the New Deal.[10] Puerto Rico's economic prospects were indeed grim; the island relied upon the monocrop export of sugar, itself controlled by American corporations and devastated by the Great Depression. Tugwell worked closely with his ultimate successor, Luis Muñoz Marín, who, although the first democratically elected governor of the territory, was an admirer of Roosevelt's New Deal reforms and would steer away from pushing for independence. Marín and the Popular Partido Democrático (PPD) embraced policies of urban-based export-led industrialization characterized by minimal barriers to entry for U.S. business interests and an overwhelming emphasis on attracting foreign capital. With the passage of the Industrial Incentives Act of 1947, which waived all taxes on private business, Operation Bootstrap began in earnest.[11]

It was into this social and political context that Harvey Perloff entered as an economic consultant, first on a research visit in 1946, and later to help establish an economic unit within the Planning Board. The creation of a Puerto Rico Planning Board (PRPB) had been one of Tugwell's first initiatives after assuming the governorship. The PRPB was to oversee comprehensive development on the island, and upon its approval in 1942, was composed of a board elected by the governor. Its first members consisted of a geographer, an architect, and an agronomist. The construction of naval bases during the war years brought in an influx of capital, offering the PRPB an opening for its planning responsibilities and setting the stage for Puerto Rico's post-war agenda. Although Tugwell had originally advocated for state-led growth and rural resettlement, his unyielding belief in the supremacy of American expertise created the institutional framework for a turn towards urban migration and loose capital controls. The mere existence of the PRPB was a catalyst for the changes that followed, as the planning apparatus itself demanded informational inputs to devise its plans, which new waves of social scientists were more than happy to supply.[12]

The results of Perloff's efforts to meet this demand were published in a 1950 tome, *Puerto Rico's Economic Future: A Study in Planned Development*. By this time, Perloff was a faculty member in Chicago, and the book evidently made a splash. Academic and popular reviewers were impressed with the ambitions and methodological rigor that Perloff brought to his study, and Puerto Rican officials greeted the text with fanfare. His text argued that Puerto Rico's acute lack of natural resources and the presumed intellectual limits of its population pointed to urbanization as the island's most rational way forward.[13] It could ill afford the kind of centuries-long arc of development that characterized northern Europe because of its lack of undeveloped land. In the absence of resources in the countryside, development would proceed by finding resources in the city, through attractive capital arrangements and industrial districting. His proposed model of development thus simply substituted the extraction of physical resources (as in the TVA and other infrastructure projects of the time) for the provision of technical know-how, middle-class entrepreneurship, and a captive manufacturing labor-force.[15]

Perloff's study not only diagnosed the present and historical conditions of Puerto Rico, it projected them into the future. He created a series of "hypothetical models" for different scenarios in the year 1960, all of which pointed to the need for greater capital investment by U.S. businesses or the financing of insular debt. In each of these analytical techniques and policy prescriptions then, we can identify the dominant themes that would guide Perloff's lifelong study: a sober, empirically driven eye towards the future, and a neo-Malthusian concern over resources as the driver of physical and economic growth. These preoccupations, however, were far from innocent. Perloff's characteristic focus on resources allowed him to sidestep larger political questions. If Puerto Rico was currently struggling, he assured his readers that "the primary trouble is not American imperialism, but natural and human deficiencies."[16] Furthermore, such a narrow, resource-centric approach produced a number of conclusions with devastating human consequences far more troubling than any endorsement of loose capital controls.

Indeed, for Perloff, the U.S. policy of accelerating urbanization, which entailed siphoning populations into urban centers as a means of diverting an idle workforce, was only a temporary stopgap to the "problem" of population itself. In his book, Perloff made the case for what he considered the immense failure of U.S. policy to encourage falling mortality rates without correlate measures to bolster economic growth or restrain reproduction. This would have served as a counter to the increased resource consumption that came with a more flourishing population. As if in revival of his early conservation training, Perloff effectively framed the population question as a problem of scientifically managing resource use over time. In so doing, Perloff and others ignored the inequitable distribution of resources and wealth in the present in favor of paternalistic control of population numbers over time.[17] Puerto Rico became a laboratory for incipient efforts to control world population through forced sterilization and non-consensual clinical trials of birth control pills.[18] These innocuously termed "family planning" tools were considered essential implements in the global push for development, and Perloff's text sharpened the case for urgency.[19]

Cities and the Atmospheres of Capital

While it is unclear when exactly he began to consider himself an urban planner proper, Perloff moved onto more influential posts based on the strengths of his research agenda in Puerto Rico. After his time as faculty member in planning at University of Chicago, Perloff joined the newly formed think tank Resources for the Future Inc. (RFF) in 1955. This non-profit research organization was established in 1953 with a grant from the Ford Foundation for $150,000 with a brief to consider the range of natural resources available to the nation, the demands placed on them, and best practices of management and conservation.[20] From the beginning, RFF advanced a capacious view of resources and the kind of projective posture that Perloff had tested in Puerto Rico. At the Mid-Century Conference on Resources for the Future, held in December 1953, land, whether rural or urban, occupied center stage in the proceedings. Framing the question of land as a question of "competing uses," the conference recapitulated 20th century debates on conservation versus preservation, while introducing cities as an important arena where this "competition" would play out.[21]

Over the course of the 1950s, 60s, and 70s, RFF published dozens of books and pamphlets on urban and regionally oriented topics.[22] At times, the think tank offered competing notions of urban land's resource potential: on the one hand, as a production input in short supply, constituting less than one percent of the nation's land mass, and on the other, as a space of inhabitation whose fortunes were uneven and indeterminate, struggling to attract residents and capital.[23] Harvey Perloff, for his part, asserted that urban land was "the most valuable of all our natural resources, viewed from the standpoint of national wealth accounting."[24] At a conference on environmental quality in 1968, attendees hoped to delineate the appropriate accounting metrics for this invaluable resource. In this process, they echoed the ambitions of economic planners in the previous two decades who had developed a suite of calculative tools for the representation of the economy. At the same time, Perloff seemed to minimize the role "traditional" resource commodities now had thanks to the rise of the service industry. The natural environment no longer figured as a resource primarily in the sense of extractable goods, but as a theater of operations for the smooth functioning of commerce. With this, Perloff introduced another wrinkle in his evolving conceptualization of the city as resource: previously he saw the city almost invariably acting as a magnet for capital, where he now became attuned to the atmospheric effect of the urban environment upon economic indices.[25]

The key to the city's potential lay precisely in this new definition of "environmental resources." These environmental resources introduced the problem of externalities into the system and thus required a revision of the "free goods" concept, a central tenet of classical economics. There were real costs associated with these natural amenities such that "while in technical economic terms fresh air remains a free good, in a social accounting sense this is no longer the case in cities, where it entails large personal and group expenditures."[26] Thus, while the notion of environmental quality nullified certain economic precepts, it upheld others. In other words, environmental quality was both qualitative and quantitative—as important to consumption as production. Most importantly, though, environmental quality in cities was a resource to be developed like any other, as the physical building of the urban fabric became a means to this end.[27] The relative conditions of air, water and land as they intersected

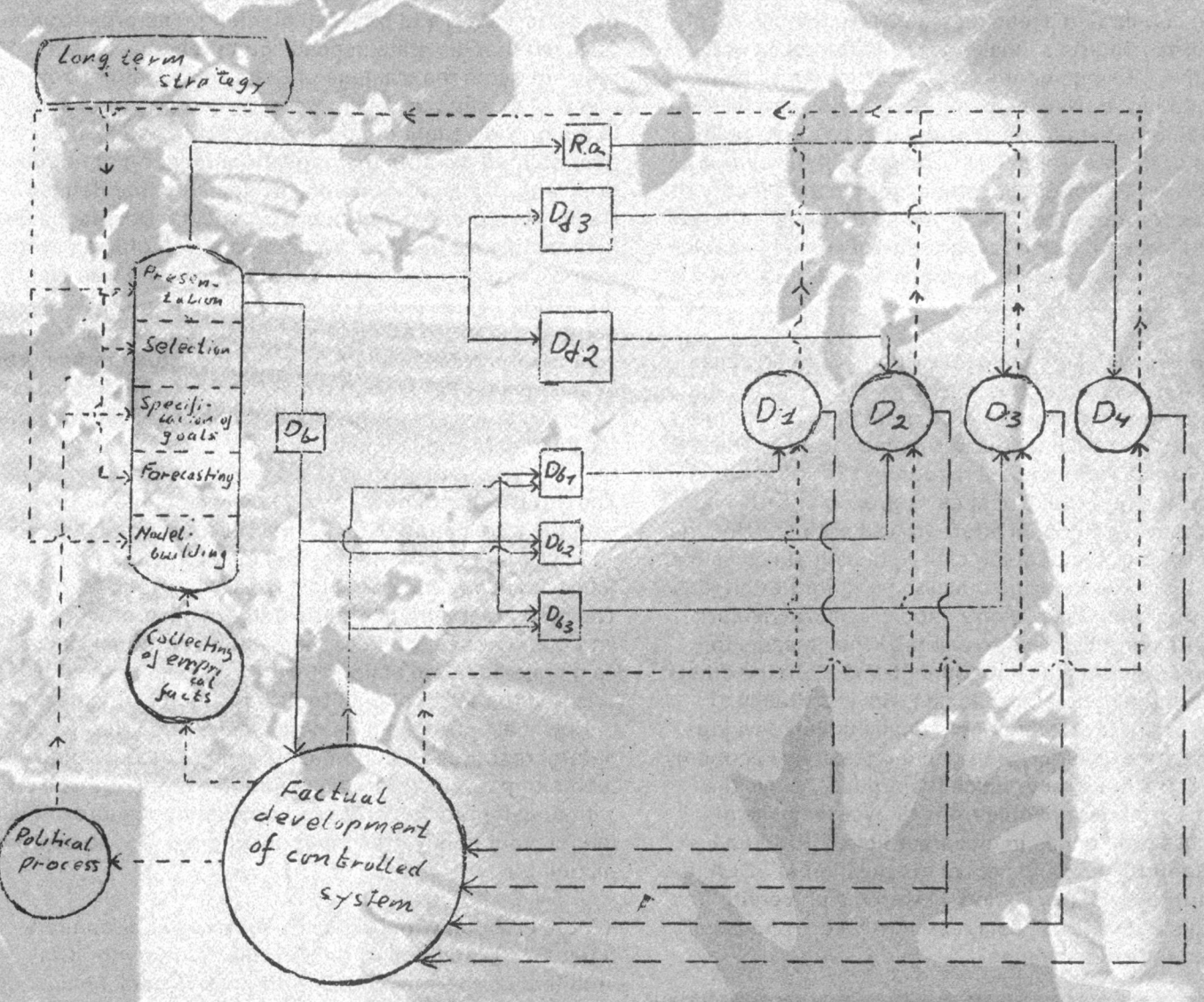

with an industrial, urbanized society came to dominate the resources concerns of the 1960s, rather than a focus on quantity.[28] This turn aligned with a broader shift in national sentiments surrounding cities, as well as a growing sense of environmental crisis. That is, with Perloff at the helm, RFF rescripted the terms of development from one of renewal and growth, to one of quality and control.

From his many years at Resources for the Future, then, Perloff had developed a peculiar brand of developmental consulting and environmental expertise that he would soon bring to his position as dean of architecture and planning at UCLA. His approach combined an experimental approach to the city with a future focused vision that sloughed off his earlier Malthusianism in favor of economic opportunism. Perloff was also by this time considered a leading member in the coterie of professional "futurists" making well-informed or wildly speculative musings on the future.[29] This was a lucrative reputation to have, as businesses employed these self-styled prophets to weather the drastic socio-political changes of the era—or at least appear as if they knew how to do so. Perloff deployed his germinating theory of resources for those looking for the next frontier of investment. Indeed, as if trying to ward off yet again his earlier enemy, secular stagnation, he made sure to find new resources wherever he looked.

For example, with companies moving to Sunbelt states like Florida, Texas, and New Mexico, Perloff argued that amenity resources now mattered more than traditional resources when it came to determining locational desirability. Further finding novel resources, Perloff pointed to the Mississippi Gulf Coast as "a great place to invest some money if you could afford to wait a while." Here he was referring to the ongoing civil rights injustices as the primary blockade to future development; for Perloff, this tension degraded the region's "social-cultural resource," marring its attractiveness to capital. When it came to assessing California as a resource frontier, on the other hand, Perloff had no such caveats. Having already attained a high level of technologically driven development, the state was rich in that ultimate service economy resource, the university, which, he argued, "plays the same role attracting people from all over today as did California's gold mines in an earlier time."[30] Uttered just months before he would accept his position at UCLA, the statement reveals how Perloff viewed the university, and indeed pedagogy itself, as a resource for economic and environmental development.

California Dreaming

California indeed presented an ideal venue for someone such as Perloff, in search of a model metropolis for the future. He called Los Angeles "a frontier city in modern dress," where planners embraced change head on.[31] UCLA's professional school, at the time just two years old, would combine architecture, urban design, and planning, and emphasize the interrelated system each discipline inhabited: architects considering more than the building as an object, and planners with an eye towards their constituent communities. Although Perloff was trained neither as an architect nor as a designer, his skills in economics and the social sciences lent him the credentials necessary to meet the immense changes of the city. As in the postwar experimental model of Puerto Rican development planning, Perloff was chosen to guide students' urban interventions within Los Angeles with an eye towards national and international replicability.

Although California offered a model of progressive values and sunny optimism to the rest of the country, it faced its own problems due to the spectacular growth of the preceding decades. Indeed, the state would be ground-zero for the anti-growth environmental movement that would seek to restrain the excesses of suburban sprawl through new land-use controls and regulatory oversight.[32] In 1970, Perloff joined the advisory board of a group called California Tomorrow—a non-profit advisory group founded in 1961 in order to bridge the concerns of conservation and physical planning. The organization believed that the state needed "comprehensive planning" to avoid the wastage of California's natural bounty, and that existing agencies were ill-equipped to this task. In the group's founding document, published in 1962, they pointed towards the fragile triangulation of population, land-use, and economic productivity that defined California's present and future prospects. Despite having comparably robust local planning control, officials were simply correcting decisions made when land was plentiful, instead of preparing for the imminent future of scarce, degraded land. To adequately plan for this resource-scarce future, they called upon planners to embrace urban space as a tool of resource management, and indeed, a scarce resource in itself, caught within a zero-sum game for the ideals of efficiency.[33]

The group's best-known work, however, came in 1972 with the publication of the California Tomorrow Plan, to which Perloff contributed alongside architects from the San Francisco office of Skidmore, Owings and Merrill. The plan attempted to outline California's problems and their causes, while devising an institutional as well as physical plan of action. It would, in other words, be oriented to the "design of tools" as much as the design of physical space, with its core issues firmly rooted in natural resources, economic planning, and emerging technologies. However, the committee members tasked with drawing up the 1972 report evidently disagreed over the relevant policy prescriptions, or even how to approach planning itself.

In conversation with California Tomorrow co-founders Samuel E. Wood and Alfred E. Heller, alongside SOM architect Marc Goldstein, Perloff pushed back against an over-emphasis on the plan-form, or the rote distribution of population and industry across state lands. For Perloff, visual representations of future utopian conditions would be outdated almost immediately. More powerful in his mind were a series of proposed "laws, regulations, institutional changes, budget changes, and some physical changes." Rather than "seeing California as a physical entity, as a map, take 10 to 20 million people, line them up in groups (by income, black and white, etc.) alongside a checklist: excellent, very good, good, fair, bad, and so forth. Describe what will change the environment of those people in 10 years."[34] In contrast to his thinking on the populations of Puerto Rico, Perloff's attitude towards the people of California did not seem to prompt anxious

A Social Planning Framework

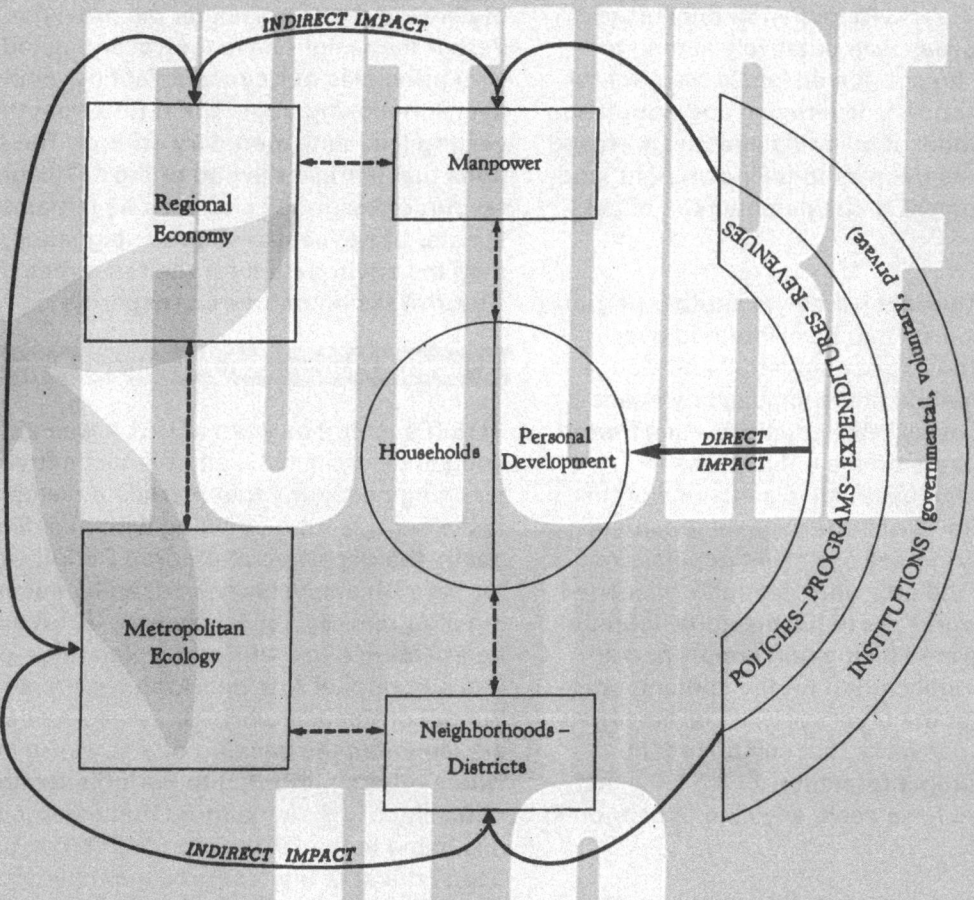

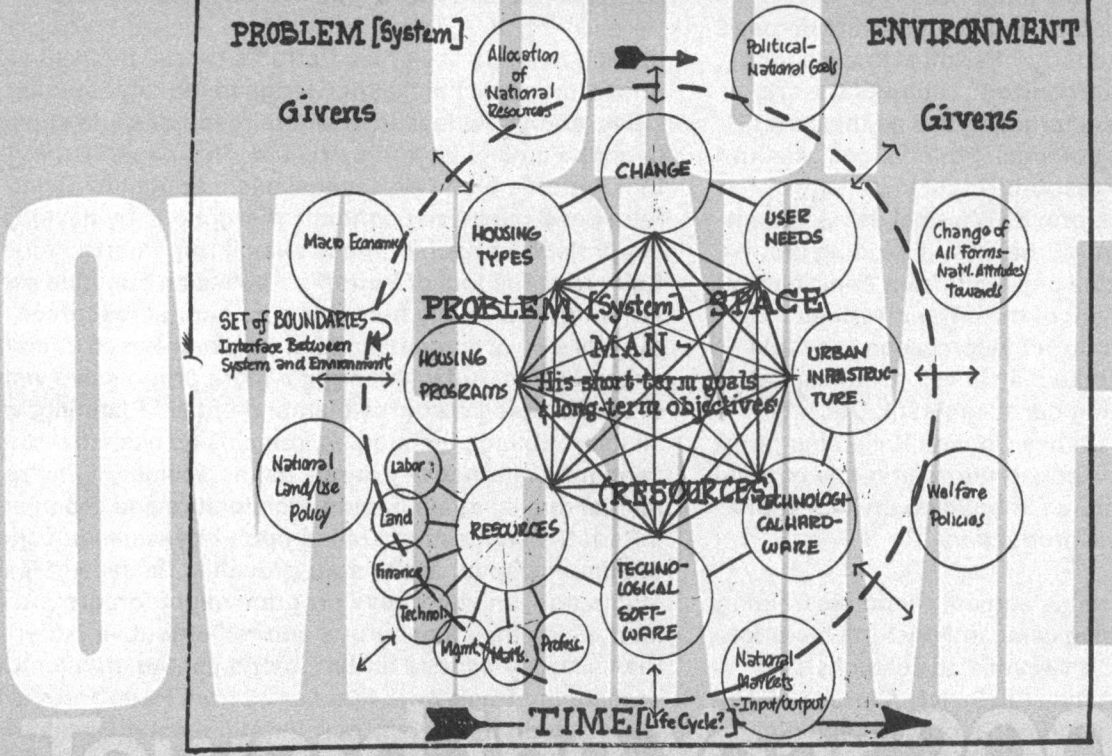

EDITED BY HARVEY S. PERLOFF

musings on future social and political stability. Instead, these populations could be tabulated as informational inputs for the betterment of planning the environment. Drawing on the calculative abstractions and futuristic surety he had honed in Puerto Rico, Perloff minimized the resource, land, his group was putatively aiming to protect. In other words, he positioned land's resourcefulness as a function of economic leveraging and population management. Such a model of planning effectively erased the value of the land or its peoples in their own right, and yoked resource management to the perpetuation of capitalist accumulation.

Perloff's objections gestured towards yet another permutation of the city-as-resource that he elaborated over the 1970s—namely, a kind of post-industrial knowledge economy in which the natural limits imposed by space and time seemed to fall away. What distinguished Perloff from his other futurist peers on the subject was his attention to the artistic and aesthetic dimensions of the city. For Perloff, "the arts" writ large were an untapped fount for cities beginning to see shrinking populations and fiscal difficulties.[35] The arts were not quite "a needed element of the natural world" as in his previous definition of resources, but they were still in short supply and an increasingly important public good for the contemporary city. An understanding of the arts "system," or the artists, institutions, and social networks that comprised the creative economy, required information as the "raw material" of policy and, as we have seen, any kind of economic intervention whatsoever.

Rather than looking backwards at the poor record of unemployment and income differentials usually offered up by the "dismal science," Perloff unsurprisingly suggested looking towards "the role of the arts in the economic future of the central city."[36] He predicted that as the industrial bases of cities continued to shrink, these communities would rely more heavily on service sectors. In sketching a picture of the supply and demand outlook of the unique "industry," Perloff acknowledged the "disparate, largely unorganized" nature of the arts as an economic enterprise, targeting this as the central cause of their unrealized potential. Perloff's goal was to systematize the arts as a resource input in the city of the future and thus also transform its physical development in the process. In his words, "the arts—including architecture—can make a unique and significant contribution to the physical development of the city with substantial economic payoffs."[37] In (correctly) forecasting the role arts-focused buildings would play in valorizing capital accumulation in the coming decades (Frank Gehry's Bilbao Museum of Art or Disney Concert Hall being prime examples), Perloff acknowledged the central role of architecture as a physical resource in building the late-capitalist city's spaces of service production.

To link these ideas back to his earliest economic training, we might detect within them what architectural historian Arindam Dutta has called a "Keynesian aestheticism." That is, for Keynes, aesthetics (inclusive of architecture) constituted a motivational force that drove economic behaviors. The public arts might therefore encourage a pleasure principle of consumption rooted in the "animal spirits" and serve as a counter to the psychological tendency towards thrift. In Dutta's telling, the rise of multinational construction and engineering conglomerate Arup alongside monetarist state policy expounded by Keynes shows the arts assuming a key role in the manufacturing of demand (or its correlate, the provision of supply).[38] Perloff then might have, however belatedly, embodied the very principles of Keynesianism by removing the frame of decision-making about the future from the individual and vesting it in state monetary control. The scarcity assumptions that marked the end of the 1970s brought Perloff's resource design full circle, as he remained guided by the specter of Keynesian secular stagnation, constantly scanning the environment for the resources that would secure a narrow vision of future prosperity.

Resource Planning on a Damaged Planet

Perloff's tenure as dean at UCLA was cut short by his sudden death in 1983, and his distinctive architectural and planning pedagogy that merged development, resources, and environment died along with him. Months before his death, the department honored Perloff with a celebration for his 15th anniversary as dean by naming its main building after him. By 1993, however, UCLA moved to break apart architecture and urban planning—placing the former into a School of Arts and Architecture and the latter a School of Public Policy.[39] In remembrance, some observers lamented the passing of a powerful interdisciplinarity, where others attributed to Perloff's tenure a burgeoning criticality of urban planning that emerged from within the discipline in the 1970s and 80s.[40] While this paper has been critical of the resource managerialism exhibited by Perloff's planning ideology, this is not to discount the design disciplines adopting a wider, socially inflected practice, or even one that would instrumentalize economy as technique. Rather it is to show how even the explicit foregrounding of resources and environment can just as easily assist capitalist restructuring of the city, its territories, and populations, as it can a cooperative holism.

In each episode of Harvey Perloff's career, he used various forms of technical knowledge to identify regions, cities, and individual sites where resources and capital might be cultivated and extracted. This paper has argued that Perloff's brand of Keynesianism sought to divine the future and minimize economic disruptions by developing projects in each of these sites. From Puerto Rico to California, the foci of Perloff's Keynesian stimulus proposals shifted variously between pure natural resources, the city's environmental milieu, and arts-based capital expenditures. But what might a more progressive vision of urban-based resource planning entail? Planning, with all its troubling genealogies, remains an essential tool for imagining alternative futures, as the specter of environmental quality again haunts architecture and urbanism. If Perloff's suggestions relied upon Keynesian injections of stimulus spending to spur growth in the face of feared stagnation, an alternative program might foreground a land ethics that is generous and redistributive rather than scarcity-minded and protectionist. An architectural or planning framework that learns from Perloff would be wise to avert its gaze from futuristic resource scenarios and reinvest its attention in the remnants of nature left in capital's wake.

1. Urbanism Committee to the National Resources Committee, *Our Cities: Their Role in the National Economy* (Washington, D.C.: U.S.G.P.O., 1937), v. For more on the executive successor, the National Resources Planning Board, see Philip W. Warken, *A History of the National Resources Planning Board* (New York: Garland Publishing Inc., 1979).

2. On the rise of "planning" as a concept and tool used in capitalist societies see Patrick D. Reagan, *Designing a New America: the Origins of New Deal Planning, 1890-1943* (Amherst: University of Massachusetts Press, 1999); Otis L. Graham, *Toward a Planned Society: From Roosevelt to Nixon* (New York: Oxford University Press, 1977).

3. Felicity Scott, "Discourse, Seek, Interact: Urban Systems at MIT," in *A Second Modernism: MIT, Architecture, and the 'Techno-Social' Movement*, ed., Arindam Dutta (Cambridge: MIT Press, 2013), 342-393; Jennifer Light, "Taking Games Seriously," *Technology and Culture*, Vol. 49, No.2 (April 2008): 347-375. Pamela M. Lee, *Think Tank Aesthetics: Midcentury Modernism, the Cold War, and the Neoliberal Present* (Cambridge: MIT Press, 2020); Jill Lepore, *If Then: How the Simulmatics Corporation Invented the Future* (New York: W.W. Norton Co., 2020).

4. This short-lived program has been termed the "Chicago school" of planning. Despite having a moniker similar to that of their counterparts in neoliberal economics, however, the department positioned itself as against the anti-planning ideology of colleagues such as Milton Friedman. Heavily influenced by early faculty member Rexford Tugwell's vision of planning as fourth branch of government, the program trained graduates for positions in the NRPB, TVA, and UN. It took a view of planning as the administration of decision-making processes and the effective allocation of resources within organizations. Although this was "a planning model which fit the American brand of welfare state liberalism," Perloff found himself defending planning as a legitimate business tool against a climate suspicious of its aims. Jean-Louis Sarbib, "The University of Chicago Program in Planning: A Retrospective Look," *Journal of Planning Education and Research*, Vol. 2, No. 2 (January 1983): 77-81.

5. Leland S. Burns, "Harvey S. Perloff (1915-1983): A Tribute," *Urban Studies*, Vol. 21 (1984): 217; John Friedmann quoted in Theresa Walker, "Harvey Perloff, Architectural Educator, Dies," *Los Angeles Times*, July 31, 1983.

6. Alvin Hansen, *Business Cycle Theory: Its Development and Present Status* (Boston: Ginn & Co., 1927); Alvin Hansen, *Full Recovery or Stagnation?* (New York: W.W. Norton Co., 1938).

7. Alvin Hansen and Harvey Perloff, *Regional Resource Development* (Washington, D.C.: National Planning Association); see also Hansen and Perloff, State and Local Finance in the National Economy (New York: W.W. Norton & Co., 1944).

8. "TVA Model Urged for Whole Nation," *New York Times*, November 21, 1942.

9. Timothy Mitchell, "Econometality: How the Future Entered Government," *Critical Inquiry*, Vol. 40, No. 4 (Summer 2014): 479-507.

10. In fact, he held his governorship thanks to FDR himself, who hoped to neutralize the rise of home-rule political parties. Michael Lapp, "The Rise and Fall of Puerto Rico as a Social Laboratory, 1945-1965," *Social Science History*, Vol. 19, No. 2 (1995): 169-199.

11. Déborah Berman Santana, "Puerto Rico's Operation Bootstrap: Colonial Roots of a Persistent Model for 'Third World' Development," *Revista Geográfica*, No. 124 (December 1998): 87-116.

12. Brandon Howell, "The Planning System of Puerto Rico," *The Town Planning Review*, Vol. 23, No. 3 (October 1952): 211-222.

13. Louis Brownlow, "Puerto Rico Blueprints 'Operation Bootstrap'," *Washington Post*, February 12, 1950.

14. Herein lay the crux of post-war development thinking and Puerto Rico's experimental value to America: in attempting to accelerate historical forces and leapfrog earlier stages of development, the island would provide an instructive model in building the "Third World" into a market for American goods and services. Harvey S. Perloff, *Puerto Rico's Economic Future* (Chicago: University of Chicago Press, 1950), 194.

15. It is worth noting that, although many development economists rejected Operation Bootstrap in the years after, it remained highly influential in American contexts. The Clinton administration's so-called "Urban Enterprise Zones" had their roots in a 1978 congressional bill sponsored by New York representative (and later Secretary of Housing and Urban Development) Jack Kemp that referenced Operation Bootstrap as a model for developing U.S. inner cities. Kemp was an integral force in the deregulation of public housing in the 1980s and served as George H.W. Bush's HUD secretary: Mark Byrnes, "The Quarterback Who Wrote the Playbook on Fighting Urban Poverty," *Bloomberg City Lab*, January 6, 2020 (https://www.bloomberg.com/news/articles/2020-01-06/when-jack-kemp-took-on-urban-poverty-and-lost).

16. Paul Blanshard, "Puerto Rico's Tomorrow," *New York Times*, January 1, 1950.

17. Milton C. Taylor, "Neo Malthusianism in Puerto Rico," *Review of Social Economy*, Vol. 10, No. 1 (March 1952): 42-54.

18. Laura Briggs, *Reproducing Empire: Race, Sex, Science, and U.S. Imperialism in Puerto Rico* (Berkeley: University of California Press, 2002). See also Matthew Connelly, *Fatal Misconceptions: The Struggle to Control World Population* (Cambridge: Harvard University Press, 2008).

19. When Luís Muñoz Marín stepped down as governor in 1964, Perloff celebrated the success of his leadership, declaring Operation Bootstrap a success. Future historians would no doubt see that it was "a grand design for progress carried out through a thoroughgoing but peaceful economic and social transformation." See Perloff, "Puerto Rico's Muñoz—Exposer of Social, Economic Cliches," *Los Angeles Times*, August 23, 1964.

20. "Group Will Consider Resources of the Future," *New York Times*, October 18, 1953.

21. Henry Jarrett, ed., *The Nation Looks at Its Resources* (Washington, D.C.: Resources for the Future, 1954), 26-60.

22. Mark Perlman, *Human Resources in the Urban Economy* (Washington, D.C.: Resources for the Future, 1963); Harvey S. Perloff and Lowdon Wingo Jr., *Issues in Urban Economics* (Washington, D.C.: Resources for the Future, 1968); Harvey S. Perloff, *A National Program of Research in Housing and Urban Development* (Washington, D.C.: Resources for the Future, 1961); Richard F. Babcock and Marion Clawson, *Modernizing Urban Land Policy* (Washington, D.C.: Resources for the Future, 1971); Marion Clawson and Peter Hall, *Planning and Urban Growth: An Anglo-American Comparison* (Washington, D.C.: Resources for the Future, 1973).

23. Lowdon Wingo, Jr., ed., *Cities and Space: The Future Use of Urban Land* (Washington, D.C.: Resources for the Future, 1963), 7-10.

24. Harvey S. Perloff, ed., *The Quality of the Urban Environment: Essays on "New Resources" in an Urban Age* (Washington, D.C.: Resources for the Future, 1967), vii.

25. As Michelle Murphy has written, Keynesian economic thought "rendered capitalism as a kind of national atmosphere that needed explication (through economics) and taking care (through planning).": *The Economization of Life* (Durham, N.C.: Duke University Press, 2017), 20.

26. Perloff, *The Quality of the Urban Environment: Essays on "New Resources" in an Urban Age*, 6.

27. See also, Harvey S. Perloff, "Towards the Developmental-Servicing City in the Century Ahead," *Ekistics*, Vol. 21, No. 123 (February 1966): 95-101.

28. On the dominant narratives of environmental politics of the 1960s see Samuel P. Hays and Barbara D. Hays, *Beauty, Health, and Permanence: Environmental Politics in the United States, 1955-1985* (New York: Cambridge University Press, 1987).

29. On futurists and the rise of futurology more generally see Jenny Andersson, *The Future of the World: Futurology, Futurists, and the Struggle for the Cold War Imagination* (Oxford: Oxford University Press, 2018); Elke Seefried, "Steering the future: The emergence of 'Western' futures research and its production of expertise, 1950s to early 1970s," *European Journal of Futures Research*, Vol. 2, No. 1 (2014): 2195-2248.

30. William H. Honan, "'The Futurists' Takes Over the Jules Verne Business," *New York Times*, April 9, 1967.

31. Ray Hebert, "Los Angeles—Testing Ground for the Cities of Tomorrow?" *Los Angeles Times*, May 5, 1968.

32. See Adam Rome, *Bulldozer in the Countryside: Suburban Sprawl and the Rise of Environmentalism* (New York: Cambridge University Press, 2001); Andrew Wiese, "'The Giddy Rise of the Environmentalists': Corporate Real Estate Development and Environmental Politics in San Diego, California, 1968-1973," *Environmental History*, Vol. 19, No. 1 (January 2014): 28-54.

33. Samuel E. Wood and Alfred E. Heller, *California Going, Going....: Our state's struggle to remain beautiful and productive* (Sacramento: California Tomorrow, 1962).

34. Harvey Perloff, "Meeting of the Steering Committee, The California Tomorrow Plan, April 16, 1970," Box 43, Folder 2, California Tomorrow Records, MS 3641, California Hisotrical Society.

35. At a time of incipient deindustrialization, Perloff advanced an argument for considering the ills of urban atrophy against the previous fears of overcrowding that had animated urban professions in both the U.S. and developing worlds, an idea that would prove prescient. See Art Seidenbaum, "Present Myth and Future Fantasy," *Los Angeles Times*, January 26, 1976. + Harvey S. Perloff, *Planning the Post-Industrial City* (Chicago: The American Planning Association, 1980).

36. Harvey S. Perloff, ed., *The Arts in the Economic Life of the City* (New York: American Council of the Arts, 1979), 5. Italics his.

37. Ibid, 10.

38. Arindam Dutta, "Marginality and Metaengineering: Keynes and Arup," in *Governing by Design: Architecture, Economy, and Politics in the Twentieth Century*, eds., Aggregate Architectural History Collaborative (Pittsburgh: University of Pittsburgh Press, 2012), 237-268.

39. William Fulton, "UCLA's Plan to Reorganize its Professional Schools is Sheer Madness," Los Angeles Times, June 20, 1993.

40. Bish Sanyal, the head of MIT's Department of Urban Studies and Planning from 1994 to 2002, and himself a distinguished scholar of development, reflected on his time as a doctoral student at UCLA, during which the program earned a reputation for what would be called "critical planning." Though he asserted critiques of modernization and developmentalism were integral to the program, he also noted a disconnect between these ethos and the pragmatism exhibited by Perloff as dean. In one instance, Perloff asked students and faculty what advice they would give to planners faced with the exodus of manufacturing from their cities and was met with silence. For Sanyal, the question and its paralyzed reception evinced the troubling state of criticality in the field, which had tied planners' hands in knots of dialectics and problematics: Bish Sanyal, "Critical about Criticality," *Critical Planning: UCLA Journal of Urban Planning*, Vol. 15 (Summer 2008): 143-160.

Greenwishing: The Cruel Optimism of Sustainability[1]

Andreas Folkers

Our long list of ecological problems and calamities—droughts and floods, wildfires, ocean acidification and, of course, climate change—threatens societies, nay, the whole planet, with a series of losses. Loss of species and ecosystems, of coastal regions and of natural resources, economic loss, and loss of lives. To make things worse, these material losses seem to go along with a temporal loss: the depletion of the future. The future has become precarious: not just this or that particular future, but the future *per se*. At least that is what recent developments in political mobilization suggest. At one end of the political spectrum the only future that people seem to accept is a return to the past: of a "great America," of Britain and Russia as proud imperial world powers, of Europe before "mass immigration"—the list could go on.[2] On the other end of the spectrum, one of the most promising political movements in recent years is certainly the youth-led climate activism group Fridays for Future (FFF). However, the fact that FFF have made themselves advocates "for (the) future" expresses more despair than hope. It reflects the gloomy ecological situation of the present wherein not only hope for a better future, but confidence in the future itself is increasingly lost. Social movements seem to no longer be fighting for a better, a more democratic, a more just, or a more liberated future; they are, rather, fighting for the future *sans phrase*. This seems to indicate a clear break with the modern temporal imaginary where the future as a "horizon of expectations" could be taken for granted.[3] Today, the struggle is no longer about this or that future, but about the existential question of whether the future exists at all: to be or not to be.

Sustainability has become a crucial watchword for those who strive to preserve the future and stop its depletion. Sustainability promises to maintain sound environmental living conditions for the future. It does so by preserving critical stocks of the environmental resources that underpin the horizon of possibilities for future generations. However, the project of sustainability is not at all new. It has a rather long history[4] that reveals that it is part and parcel of the modern futurity that now threatens to undermine the continuance of the future.

History of the sustainable future

Sustainable social practices are often described to be as old as human beings. How could human communities have survived for so long without adapting to the rhythms of the webs of life in which they were enmeshed? However, such a generalized understanding misses the specificity of modern rationalities of sustainable resource management. And it also misses that, in its modern guise, sustainability does not describe a harmonious natural balance. Rather, modern sustainability is a managerial practice that reacts to processes that cause some sort of crisis or problem, an imbalance in the web of life. This form of sustainability—as a rational concept and a governmental technology—has an identifiable place and date of birth: the German forest in the beginning of the 18th century. In his *Sylvicultura Oeconomica*, published in 1713, Hans Carl von Carlowitz formulated the principle of sustainability (in German, *Nachhaltigkeit*), according to which a continuous supply of wood is only possible if no more trees are felled than grow again. Carlowitz was a mining captain in the administration of the state of Saxony, and therefore very concerned with the continuity of the wood supply for the smelters. He was an advocate of Cameralism, the economic rationality related to early modern arts of governing. The goal of Cameralism was to increase the power and wealth of the state, which required identifying and properly using all the sources of wealth within the state territory.[5] The state experts established systematic statistical inventories of all the state's assets, which created a new calculative basis for the administration of resources and the population. This emerging governmental rationality, its aims, its scope, and its forms of knowledge, provided the fertile ground for the doctrine of sustainability to flourish.

However, sustainability is not only related to a new political rationality. It also expresses and enacts the modern metaphysics of nature, which, following Martin Heidegger, can be characterized as the ontology of the "standing reserve."[6] As a standing reserve, nature is reduced to being a supplier of material resources and energy for technical-industrial processes. This ontology is more than a mere "world picture."[7] Rather, it is materially enacted through scientific and technical processes. Guaranteeing a continuous, sustainable supply of wood requires that one first statistically disclose the forest as a standing reserve, a reservoir of timber. Then the statistical numbers can undergird the expectations and planning decisions of the foresters. Yet, the statistical framework, that grounds forestry, itself requires an ordered, material world to count on and to ground itself in. This in turn necessitates a specific material adjustment of the invoiced. As James C. Scott has shown, the forest only became legible as a stock of wood when so-called "normal trees" were systematically planted.[8] This way foresters could predict growth cycles and yields accordingly. The actual material conditions of the forest had to be altered in such a way that this reserve could meet the economic planning requirements and materially underpin the future expectations placed on it.

These dynamics are also why, seemingly paradoxical, sustainability was often used as a justification for massive deforestation projects. "It was believed that only clear-cutting in certain areas could render calculable the extent of timber extraction corresponding to the requirement of sustainable management."[9] A "real abstraction" thus occurs: the mathematical abstraction of nature, its reduction to a resource provider, is enacted in the material world. In addition, securing future stocks is reducing resources for the present; sustainability makes things scarce. Accordingly, scientific forestry often went hand in hand with the fight against traditional uses of forests as commons.

Over the following centuries sustainability remained a highly ambivalent rationality. It reckons with the depletion of resources but only to continue its exploitation. Sustainability guarantees what Heidegger calls the "securing of the standing reserve"[10]: it not only secures the material stocks in play, it also secures an ontology of nature (land, seas, animal and plant populations etc.) as utterly extractable and fungible resource. It thus precludes alternative apprehensions of and engagements with nature. This explains why sustainability often became a tool of colonial administrations for "conserving" natural resources from extractive overuse as well as from the supposedly unruly practices of the colonized. Later developments in sustainability thinking, like the concept of the Maximum Sustainable Yield (MSY), which emerged in the 1950s in attempts to protect global fish stocks,[11] suggested that it is possible to identify an optimal degree of exploitation: a point that not diminishes but stimulates the underlying stock. Harvesting fish, for example, purportedly allows younger fish to grow faster which in turn increases the overall stock. This often became the justification for increasing resource extraction in the name of sustainability.

Sustainability strives to find a balance between current and future generations. But this intergenerational balancing often serves as a means for avoiding redistributions between rich and poor in the present. This conflict becomes obvious in the notion of "sustainable development," which has become a central goal of global policy since its invention by the famous Brundtland report "Our Common Future," where it was defined as "development that meets the needs of the present without compromising the ability of future generations to meet their own needs."[12] Sustainable development intends to kill two birds with one stone. It offered a formula to reconcile the fight against poverty (especially in the global south) and environmental degradation. However, this promise is premised on continued growth. This growthmanship not only tends to be detrimental to the environment but also fails to address global injustices and the colonial legacies that created them.

Taken together these two aspects of sustainability—sustainability as a governmental rationality that expresses and materially enacts a western-modernist ontology of nature, and sustainability as a framework for legitimizing the intensification of the capitalist appropriation of nature and the "conservation" of (neo)colonial power relations—seem already enough to reject this paradigm. However, my point here is that even if all these problems could be fixed (they cannot, at least not all of them), sustainability would still no longer be able to properly guide environmental politics in the 21st century. This inadequacy is due, I will argue in the next section, to sustainability's assumption of a certain material grammar of temporality and the future that becomes less and less viable.

The materiality of the future

Sustainability is characterized by a particular temporal structure. It seeks to secure a certain kind of modern future by establishing a temporal nexus between present and future. Sustainability is supposed to secure options for future generations that would otherwise be consumed by the present, making this framework part and parcel of the modern temporal orientation glued to an open "horizon of expectations." The sustainability paradigm, however, clearly introduces a certain degree of reflexivity because it no longer assumes the total openness of the future but rather expects the progressive narrowing of this horizon. That is why the preservation of the future as an open horizon is now itself becoming a political project.

Within sustainability thinking, the future thus becomes a resource to be divided between present and coming generations in a just way. This resource view of the future is of course no coincidence because the problems that sustainability usually addresses are resource problems—or, more specifically, it frames ecological issues as resource problems—which is why, as shown above, it is premised on and enacts the ontology of the standing reserve. At stake are two kinds of resources: regenerative and finite. From this perspective, all living things, like fish and forests, are seen as in principle regenerative resources. In these cases, social planning horizons have to adapt to the *Eigenzeit* of regenerative natural rhythms. These time horizons can be quite long. A tree planted in the present will only yield timber for a coming generation which is probably why sustainability thinking emerged in the forest. To shorten these time horizons, foresters often planted faster growing trees like spruce which are—as it turns out now—less resilient to climate stress. With finite resources, on the other hand, sustainable usage is almost impossible because each present consumption necessarily limits future consumption. Sustainable use of finite resources must always introduce a definite cap and can only be justified by the idea that the consumption of these resources in the present will allow the future to become richer and smarter so that it can discover new resources or ways to use existing ones more efficiently. Such an argumentation—which is very common in resource and in climate economics—reinscribes the idea of an infinite horizon of progress in sustainability thinking to justify the consumption of finite resources.

It becomes obvious that the time of sustainability is inherently bound up with material processes. This tempo-material entanglement is usually overlooked because, rather than regarding matter as the very fabric of temporality,[13] time is typically understood as an external parameter that tracks the material world. Still, sustainability thinking at least implicitly reconnects time to its material life. However, if one seriously attends to the material life of time undergirding contemporary ecological problems, the limits of sustainability become clear. While sustainability can, in theory, react to ecological problems that result less from a loss of options—in other words, problems arising from a dwindling stock of material resources—this paradigm lacks the theoretical armature for dealing with problems resulting from the incessant accumulation of obligations, that is, the accumulation of waste from industrial societies. The dialectic of industrial modernity, however, consists precisely in the fact that access to options in the past caused a proliferation of long-lived ecological obligations that now cast a spell over the future. The use of fossil fuels leads to a massive increase of CO_2 in the atmosphere, the development of petrochemicals—pesticides, cosmetics, plastics, and so on—produces toxic residues in the environment, nuclear energy results in radioactive nuclear waste for centuries—the obligations proliferate. The open future horizon is not only narrowed because of dwindling resources, it also gets more and more clogged by the material residues of industrial modernity. Our sole reliance on sustainability as a management tool is therefore actually reaching its limits.

Sustainability tries to overcome this limit through the common practice of addressing the problems associated with the excessive growth of material obligations as a lack of sinks—that is, as a lack of dumping sites for the wastes of industrial modernity. This approach, though, glosses over the contemporary predicament of sustainability. By regarding environmental sinks and limited natural capacities for absorbing toxic agents as resources, the problem of excessive residuals becomes a problem of scarcity. Instead of attending to the material *Eigenzeit* of these toxic remainders, the focus shifts back again to the usual trajectory of resource time. This resource-management view becomes obvious with regard to climate policy. The chief matter of concern in climate policy are of course the residuals of "fossil modernity," CO_2 emissions. Contemporary climate policy treats this issue as a problem of finding an adequate amount of disposal sites. Policies try to manage the atmospheric dump space for carbon emissions with carbon budgeting, in recent years, serving as the central calculative technique of this planetary waste management project. The budget states how many greenhouse gasses the atmosphere can still absorb without the resulting warming exceeding 2° or 1.5° Celsius. Allowable CO_2 emissions are thereby turned into a scarce resource.

However, this fixation on allowable emissions as a scarce resource, hides the other side of emissions as long-term obligations. There are already enough greenhouse gasses locked

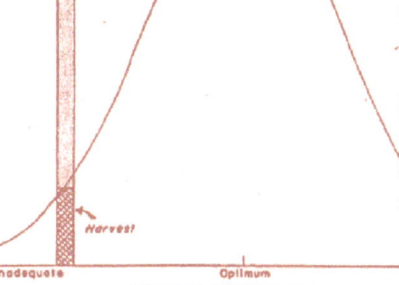

in the atmosphere to cause significant global warming. This demands responses that go beyond simply managing scarce resources over a longer time horizon. Sustainability thus reaches its limits when irreversible damage has already occurred, when ecological obligations have already accumulated en masse and are casting their long shadow into the distant geological future. If we do not recognize these limits of sustainability, we are at risk of losing sight of the inherent logic of these obligations, that is, that the environmental damages of industrial modernity have already occurred or are at least latent.

Cruel optimism

The queer theorist Lauren Berlant introduced the concept of "cruel optimism" to describe an attitude in which affective investment in certain wide-spread social norms and promises prevents individual and collective well-being.[14] When the promises remain unfulfilled—or, even worse, when they are inherently unfulfillable—but the affective attachment to them continues, this blocks the disclosure of alternative political options. Sustainability represents a form of cruel optimism because the project to protect "the future" as an open space of possibilities for future generations seems less and less realistic. It is precisely the desire to preserve the modernist future as a reserve of material options that closes off alternative ecological options in the present. Such is the contemporary paradox of sustainability: even if one assumes that sustainability at one point provided a suitable political maxim for environmentalism, this maxim is now reaching its limits. Beyond this limit, sustainability can no longer serve as the only regulative idea of ecological politics, insofar as it has lost its traction, its material and temporal ground, its very object. The current proliferation of sustainability as a hollowed-out term can be understood as a consequence of this groundlessness. Sustainability can denominate everything and nothing because it finds less and less support in the present.

The phrase "greenwashing" refers to when companies, states and other organizations present their projects as environmentally beneficial in order to cover up the true ecological devastation they cause. I argue that sustainability, more and more, has become a form of "greenwishing." Similar to greenwashing, greenwishing is when a supposedly environmental practice and desire serves to hide from view all those ecological problems that the practice cannot address. In this case, our belief in the power of sustainability makes us blind to the problem of industrialism's residuals, an environmental issue that cannot be redressed by practices of sustainable resource management. But what follows from this analysis?

Should we abandon all hope? Is this the apocalypse? Contemporary ecological problems only appear to be an end of time, or an end of the future, through the lens of resource time: a temporality wherein the open future is premised on the availability and the continued exploitation of being as a resource, which by the same token turns time and the future themselves into a resource. There will certainly be a future. But this future will be more and more marked by the residuals of "fossil modernity"[15] and thus by ecological obligations and not be resource options. Rather than preserving the standing reserve of modern resources and the ontology that made them resources in the first place, the task will be to discover the affordances of CO_2, plastic and nuclear waste, chemical toxins and all other lingering material obligations. This new task compels us to let go of the residuals of the old resource future and turn to the future of residuals.

1. This text builds on, and partly translates, thoughts that were first published in: Andreas Folkers, "Nach der Nachhaltigkeit. Resilienz und Revolte in der dritten Moderne," *Leviathan*, 50 no. 2 (2022): 239–262.
2. Zygmunt Bauman, *Retrotopia* (Cambridge: Polity, 2017).
3. Reinhart Koselleck, *Futures Past: On the Semantics of Historical Time* (New York: Columbia University Press, 2004).
4. Paul Warde, *The Invention of Sustainability: Nature and Destiny*, c. 1500–1870 (Cambridge: Cambridge University Press, 2018).
5. Michel Foucault, *Security, Territory, Population: Lectures at the Collège de France 1977–1978* (New York: Picador, 2007).
6. Martin Heidegger, *Die Technik und die Kehre* (Stuttgart: Klett-Cotta, 2007).
7. Martin Heidegger, "Die Zeit des Weltbildes," in *Holzwege* (Frankfurt: Vittorio Klostermann, 2003), 75–113.
8. James C. Scott, *Seeing like a State: How Certain Schemes to Improve the Human Condition Have Failed* (New Haven: Yale University Press, 1998).
9. Joachim Radkau, "»Nachhaltigkeit« als Wort der Macht. Reflexionen zum methodischen Wert eines umweltpolitischen Schlüsselbegriffs," in *Umwelt und Herrschaft in der Geschichte. Environnement et Pouvoir: Une Approche Historique*, ed. Duceppe-Lamarre and J. I. Engels (München: Oldenbourg Wissenschaftsverlag, 2008), 131–136.
10. Heidegger, *Die Technik und die Kehre*.
11. Carmel Finley, *All the Fish in the Sea: Maximum Sustainable Yield and the Failure of Fisheries Management* (Chicago: University of Chicago Press, 2011).
12. World Commission on Environment and Development, *Our Common Future* (New York: Oxford University Press, 1987): 24.
13. For a materialist approach to temporality see: Andreas Folkers, "Freezing Time, Preparing for the Future: The Stockpile as a Temporal Matter of Security," *Security Dialogue* 50, no. 6 (2019): 493-511; Andreas Folkers, "Fossil Modernity: The Materiality of Acceleration, Slow Violence, and Ecological Futures," *Time & Society* 30, no. 2 (2021): 223–246.
14. Lauren Berlant, *Cruel Optimism* (Durham: Duke University Press, 2011).
15. Folkers, "Fossil Modernity."

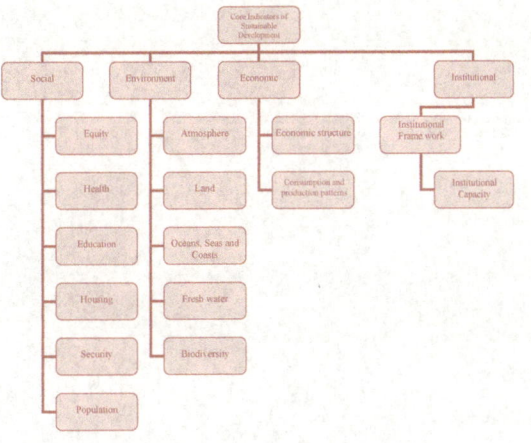

Fig. 5 – The United Nations Commission for Sustainable Development (UNCSD) Theme Indicator Framework.

Commodious, Firm and Delightful

Gökçe Günel

Serkan and I met in a Turkish restaurant in Accra's East Legon neighborhood in December 2016, and nibbled at some *pide* over a languid lunch. A day before, his driver had taken us to the fishing harbor in Tema for a tour of *Ayşegül Sultan*, the Turkish-built floating power plant Serkan's employer Karpower had leased to the Ghanaian government. At a time when Ghana's electricity production was about 2500 megawatts, the barge produced 235 megawatts of power, or about 10% of Ghana's electricity.[1] A meticulously dressed, compact man in his mid 30s, Serkan had been the director of Karpower's East Legon office for the past six months, and managed relations between Karpower and the various energy-related institutions in Ghana with the help of eleven employees. As we chatted about his expatriate experience in Accra, we could overhear some men assessing latest updates in Turkish soccer and complaining about *harmattan*, dusty winds that blow from the Sahara to the Gulf of Guinea, leaving a beige haze hanging over the West African coast. Serkan identified these men as the employees of Aksa, another Turkish energy company that had built a land-based power plant near Tema.[2] Karpower and Aksa were two of the independent power producers (IPPs) operating in the Ghanaian electricity market. Relying on investments mainly from Turkey, China and the United Arab Emirates, they produced electricity out of imported heavy fuel oil and domestic natural gas. Karpower's *Ayşegül Sultan* stood out among these power production facilities, mainly because unlike them, it was not land-based. It was also larger than most of its competitors.

"Karpower could have built a land-based power plant here, but they did not," Serkan said. "Instead, they built the plant on a barge. If Ghanaians gave us a concrete slab and allowed us to place a plant on that slab, Karadeniz could have done that, but we did not."

He picked up a clean white napkin off the table, then he folded it four times until it was the size of a stick of gum.

"This is how much space our barge takes," he said. "This is how much more effective it is when compared to a land-based power plant. And if the authorities do not pay, or if there is a war, then we take our barge and leave."[3]

By folding the napkin, Serkan was taking a seemingly two-dimensional object, which was flat and spread out, and rendering it three-dimensional. Unlike a regular power plant, the floating power plant was thick and densely packed. The act of folding represented a transformation from a horizontal organization to an organization that was layered and vertical, a space where everything would be stacked up. With scrubber towers on the top, workers in the middle, and engines at the bottom level, the ship would constitute an enclosed world for power production, attached to the Ghanaian grid with

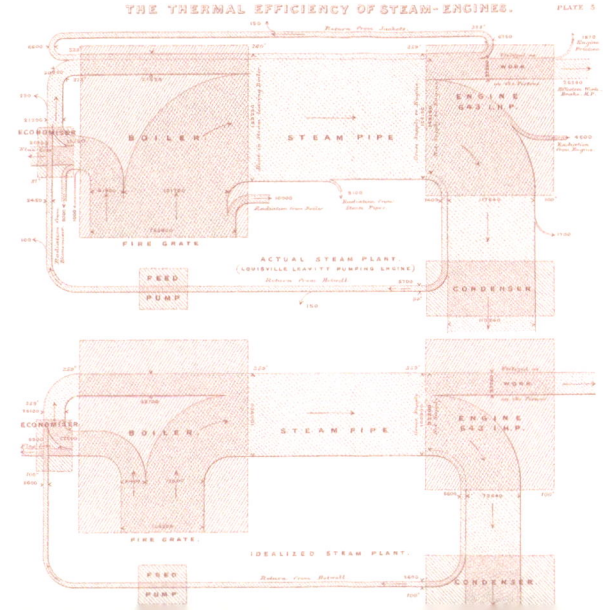

high frequency cables stretching over the harbor. According to Serkan, the innovative barge had many advantages both for the company and for the Ghanaian authorities.

In addressing urgent electricity demands, many countries in the global South are looking toward quick power generation systems. One emergent system is powerships: floating power plants that anchor at a harbor, plug into a national grid, and generate electricity with heavy fuel oil or natural gas. The Turkish company Karadeniz Holding—or Karpower, as it is known across many parts of the world—has become an increasingly popular producer of powerships in the past decade.[4] A family-owned business, Karpower builds the ships on spec in various shipyards in Istanbul and leases them to places with high energy demands. Their barge *Ayşegül Sultan* produced power for the country's grid between December 2015 and September 2017, initiating the company's operations in Africa. The larger powership *Osman Khan* replaced *Ayşegül Sultan* in late 2017, now providing 470 megawatts, almost doubling Karpower's production volume. In an effort to switch its fuel source from heavy fuel oil to natural gas, a less expensive and more environmentally friendly fuel that could be sourced domestically, *Osman Khan* moved in late 2019 from Tema to Takoradi, a port much closer to the country's natural gas reservoirs. By carrying its operations to Takoradi, the ship would help monetize these existing domestic gas resources. Other projects were planned and operational in Iraq, Lebanon, Indonesia, Pakistan, Zambia, Sierra Leone, Gambia, Mozambique, Senegal, Libya and South Africa. As of March 2018, the company owned forty-three vessels. More than twenty of these were powerships, while others were service ships that delivered fuel or provided housing to crews in locations where accommodations were difficult. Karpower labeled their project "The Power of Friendship," presenting it as a broad and cordial campaign to bring quick and cheap electric power to those in need.

Powerships are illustrative of a move from what power companies have called "permanent power" to "temporary power," although this binary may not reflect the complexities of the transformation. A 2014 article in *POWER*, the go-to trade publication that has been published in North America since 1882, asked: "When 'temporary power' supplies nearly a quarter of a grid's demand, is it still temporary power? How about when a project lasts 10 years?" The article continued: "Calling power service temporary doesn't quite capture all of its distinguishing attributes. It's temporary rather than permanent, rented rather than owned, and mobile rather than fixed. It's also modular and easily scalable."[5] Others from the industry have argued that temporary power stations are compelling due to their rapid installation and low upfront capital requirements.[6]

In a context where various forms of temporary power have gained popularity, powerships differentiated themselves from competitors through their formal qualities, namely by being ships, which can move from sites of production to sites of consumption, utilizing a seascape, relatively independent of logistics network.[7] Unlike other systems of power generation, the construction of powerships is undertaken in a completely different environment than the one in which the floating plant will function. By centralizing production in shipyards in Istanbul, the company controlled its operations efficiently. Powerships did not require large swathes of land, making the projects more desirable for lessees.[8] Once they arrived at a harbor, the only supplement the powership necessitated was high frequency cables that connected the ship to the nearest substation. In the case of Tema, Ghana, for instance, this substation was nine kilometers away. Finally, since their only connection to the land was through high frequency cables, powerships also seemed more tenuous than land-based plants, giving the appearance that the ship could leave anytime—especially if and when their presence in lessee countries no longer made financial or political sense.[9]

Floating power plants are an example of modular infrastructure, delivering the basic needs of a society for a predetermined amount of time. While other seemingly permanent infrastructures might come with the implication that services will be delivered continuously, modular infrastructures can easily

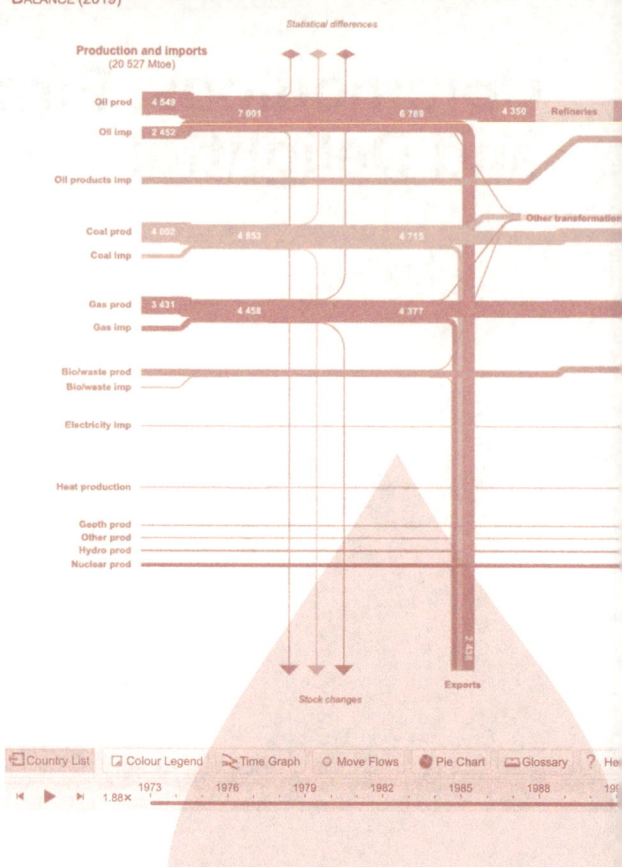

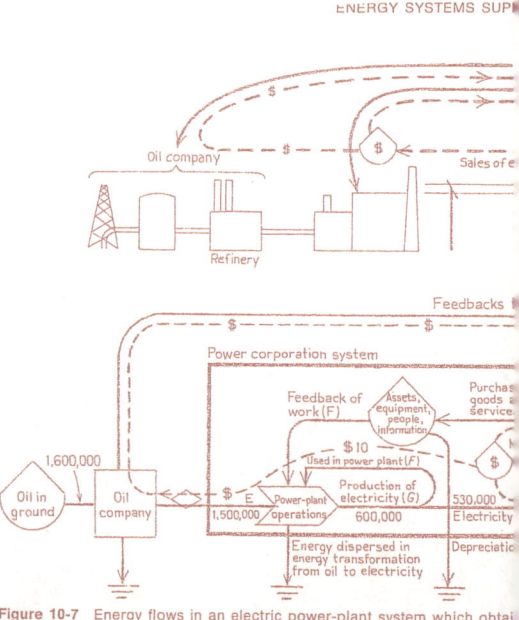

Figure 10-7 Energy flows in an electric power-plant system which obtai and services by selling electricity. Its operation depends on the ability cheaply. Net production of the system is Y minus X_1 plus X_2. Numbers are equivalents for the flow of one barrel of oil which costs $10.

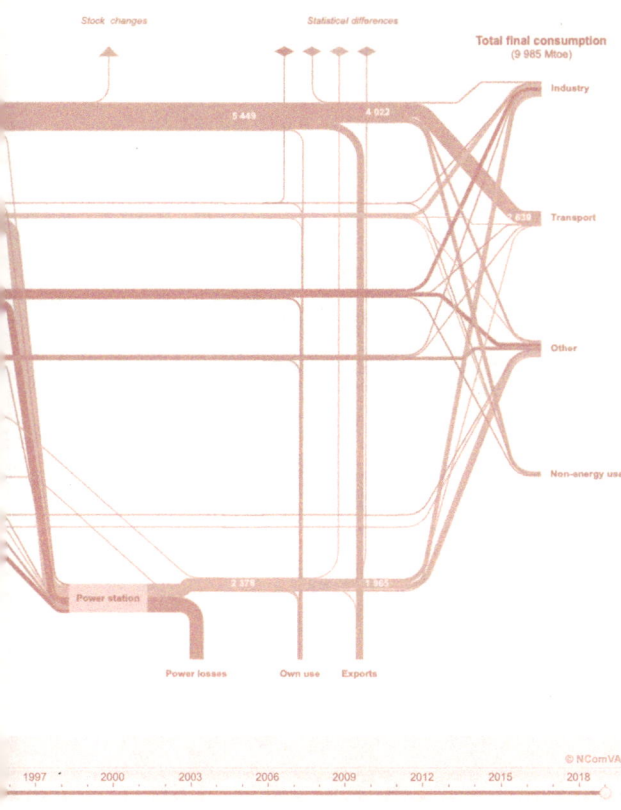

become dismantled or expanded. Similar to emergency mechanisms, they can be put to use quickly without much planning and construction, and therefore become desirable in situations when needs are urgent. Through modular infrastructure, urban and regional level systems begin to effectively reject territorial confinement, and in this particular context, literally have the capacity to float away.

As temporary power infrastructure, the floating power plant on the shores of Ghana set a contrast to the country's iconic hydroelectric power stations. Created in 1966, the Akosombo Dam and Lake Volta—the world's largest human-made lake by surface area and the fourth largest reservoir by volume—constituted infrastructures of socialist modernization for newly independent Ghana, promising to change rural and urban landscapes, and presenting the potential for a different future. In the inauguration ceremony, Ghana's first president Kwame Nkrumah announced: "It is in this spirit of fruitful collaboration for a better world for all that I … inaugurate the Volta River Project. Let us dedicate it to Africa's progress and prosperity. Only in this way will Africa play its full part in the achievement of world peace and for the advancement of the happiness of mankind." Nkrumah was overthrown by a military coup a few months after this ceremony. "The future envisioned by Nkrumah, in which each would give according to his ability and receive according to his needs," literary scholar and cultural historian Saidiya Hartman observed, "had been eclipsed."[10]

Inadequate rainfall and rising temperatures associated with climate change have negatively impacted the hydroelectric power station at Lake Volta, at times completely incapacitating it. At a time when power demand was increasing across the country, the dams could no longer satisfy national electricity needs. Between the years 2012 and 2015, an electricity crisis resulted in unprecedented levels of load shedding throughout Ghana. Power for industries and homes was out for twenty-four hours at a time, and turned back on for only twelve-hour periods. *Dumsor,* the name given to the crisis that means "off and on" in Twi, was brought about by low water levels in hydroelectric dams due to climate change, disruptions to natural gas flows from Nigeria, and alleged mismanagement of the grid infrastructure. In response, Ghanaian decision-makers saw a further expansion and diversification of the country's energy portfolio as a possible solution to the crisis, shifting the nation's energy production portfolio further away from hydropower and towards fossil fuels. Most of the new power producers that started operating in Ghana since the early 2000s have been thermal stations that rely on natural gas, stockpile light crude oil, and burn heavy fuel oil. Unlike Nkrumah introducing the Akosombo Dam, such new power producers, such as the floating power plant, *Ayşegül Sultan,* have not offered future-oriented narratives about social or political progress, but rather quick, stopgap solutions that provide immediate relief to consumers, bridging electricity shortages.

Named for a member of the Karadeniz family, *Ayşegül Sultan* had formerly been called *Sainty No 10*, and had been used for transporting parts of bridges and offshore plants in the Netherlands. In 2015, Karadeniz Holding engineers retrofitted the 459-foot-long vessel in the Sedef Shipyard in Tuzla, Istanbul. The new *Ayşegül Sultan* would be fitted with twenty-four dual-fuel engines, purchased directly from the Finnish manufacturer Wärtsilä, and would produce 235 megawatts for the Ghanaian grid.

Once the ship was ready, Karpower representatives explored staffing options. *Ayşegül Sultan*'s first chief engineer Mehmet had worked on ships all his life, operating and maintaining propulsion plants and support systems on seafaring vessels. After receiving a degree as a ship engineer, he had taken up positions on oil tankers and other high-risk ships for about fifteen years. When one of his contacts from the shipping industry joined Karadeniz Holding, he passed Mehmet's resumé to the company, and facilitated his hire as a chief engineer for the company's first powership in Basra, Iraq. When the Iraq operation came to a close in 2015, the company asked him to move to Tema and start running their then largest ship, *Ayşegül Sultan*.

"After Basra, Tema is like heaven," he said. "When I landed here, I called my wife and told her I landed in heaven… In Basra, the yellow of the desert extended as far as the eye could see, and we occasionally came across toppled tanks. We couldn't distinguish the barracks where we lived from the rest of the landscape." Given mounting security concerns, Mehmet rarely left the ship in Basra. In those rare occasions, such as the times he had to travel to the airport to fly home to Istanbul, a convoy of security vehicles accompanied him. "Everything was covered with the yellow of the desert," he recalled. In Tema, instead, the powership was located in the fishing harbor, surrounded by lively and active fishermen, operating ships that mostly belonged to Chinese companies. Given his position as chief engineer, Mehmet did not live on the ship, but had an apartment in Tema, which the company leased and managed. Soon his wife would join him there. They would be hiring more people in the next few months after the 470-megawatt ship arrived in Ghana, doubling the floating power plant's capacity, and accordingly Mehmet's responsibilities.

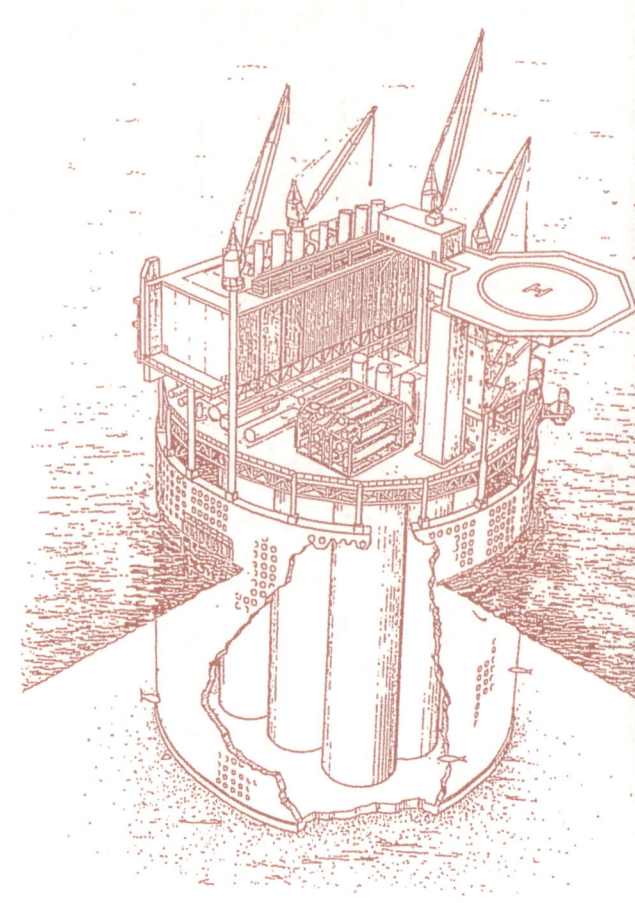

Mehmet agreed with Serkan that the ship's compact organization was its most significant feature. "We do everything here on the barge," he said. "The maintenance man comes here. We cook our own food. We only receive raw materials from the outside." While Mehmet worked with Ghanaian mechanics and chemists who had no background in shipping on specific aspects of power generation, such as ensuring fuel quality, most of his crew was ship engineers from Turkey. He outlined what attracted Turkish ship engineers to this career shift to energy: "First, they are paid energy-industry salaries, and make more money than ship workers. Second, they are not actually on the sea," Mehmet continued, "Some of them have the luxury to leave in the evening and sleep in a house."

Yet sailor discipline and hierarchy helped organize the ship, which meant that everyone would be on stand-by all the time, ready to attend to a maintenance issue or any type of emergency. Every employee spent ninety days aboard, and had twenty-three days to go home for holidays. They did not have weekends. One of the ship engineers told me in July 2018 that he enjoyed this dedication to a single ship, as it allowed him to know the machine closely. "As a sailor I was never allowed to spend more than six months on one vessel," he explained, "I signed up for the longest journeys, so that I could have more time on one ship." His experience in Tema allowed him to cultivate an intimacy with the ship, which he was forbidden to develop as a seaman. During their time in Tema, the ship engineers always worked, the same way they would do on a regular ship. "But this is a ship without a captain," Mehmet said, "As the chief engineer I am the highest-ranking officer on board."

The floating power plant offered a lifeworld for the Turkish ship engineers, forcing them to retool and adapt their existing sets of expertise. Having been trained initially to work on oil tankers and high-risk ships, people like Mehmet now managed power facilities. As ships transformed into generators, ship workers transformed into power plant operators, bringing with them certain modes of professional practice. In some ways, the transition from ship engineer to power plant operator had been seamless for some of the engineers, such as Mehmet. The ships he had worked on before had also operated on Wärtsilä engines from Finland or MAN engines from Germany. He knew how to maintain and repair them. He also knew how to organize and manage a team of ship engineers. Mehmet told me that if they organized their crew, machinery, and maintenance facilities properly, then they could run and manage their plants without disruption for a very long time.

Ships often anchor in harbors to absorb raw materials from onshore facilities, taking them elsewhere. In West African shores, such transfer of raw materials invokes the very violent history of slave ships—floating factories that transformed people into fuel for plantations. As shipping and logistics have emerged as defining features of contemporary global capitalism, ships have acquired diverse forms and functions, but perhaps certain organizational principles have endured. For instance, according to historians Marcus Rediker and Peter Linebaugh, "The ship…provided a setting in which large numbers of workers cooperated on complex and synchronized tasks, under slavish,

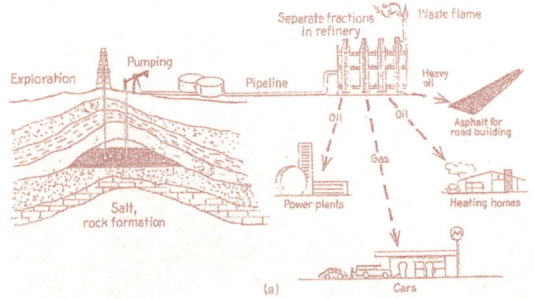

> Media studies scholar Lana Swartz has written that all "money is a technology of future-making. We only accept a particular money as payment because we think it will be accepted tomorrow by someone else." Going further, she argues that if "all money is a bet on the future, it is also a summoning of a future. When people design new money forms, it is usually with the goal of telling a new story about the future."Architecture often plays a role in all this monetary future-making: for example, she notes that the Euro features "an imaginary architecture—fictional bridges and arches intended to conjure a shared 'European' past in order to project a shared European future."[1]
>
> Along these lines, it is not unexpected that the Ghanaian one cedi note has printed on it an image of Lake Volta and the Akosombo Dam, an infrastructural project that Günel argues was built to carry newly independent Ghana forward into its chosen future of socialist modernity. Now climate change casts a cloud of doubt on the long-term functionality of Volta's hydroelectric power station and a private, mobile network of emergency stop-gap powerships sail in to fill the void. Unsurprisingly, the Ghanaian government has not decided to redesign its national currency to feature an image of these temporary floating power stations. But perhaps some cynical soul will mint a powership NFT? A short-term, speculative currency for a short-term power solution.
>
> [1] Lana Swartz, "Bitcoin as a Meme and a Future," *Noema Magazine*, February 11 2021, https://www.noemamag.com/bitcoin-as-ameme-and-a-future/.

hierarchical discipline in which human will was subordinated to mechanical equipment, all for a money wage. The work, cooperation, and discipline of the ship made it a prototype of the factory."[11] Contemporary floating power plants extended this logic. As a ship-cum-generator, *Ayşegül Sultan* would constitute a prosthetic factory, complementing and supporting land-based power generation in Ghana.

Despite this compact organization, *Ayşegül Sultan* was dependent on fuel deliveries from third parties, using about one thousand tons of low-sulfur heavy fuel oil per day. Given that the ship could only hold 4,300 tons of fuel, it needed to be reloaded every three to four days by a shuttle barge called *Suat Bey*. In a trip that took sixteen hours, this barge brought heavy fuel oil from a mothership located off the coast of Lomé in Togo. It took about fourteen hours for *Suat Bey* to unload the heavy fuel oil, which meant that it needed to move nonstop between the mothership and the floating power plant. Mehmet Bey noted how fortunate I was to be aboard *Ayşegül Sultan* on this particular day in December 2016, as *Suat Bey* would be delivering heavy fuel oil to the barge, and I could watch the seemingly simple procedure with him.

As we stood on the side of the ship and observed heavy fuel oil move from the mothership to *Suat Bey* to *Ayşegül Sultan*, the chief engineer Mehmet and I witnessed the materiality of electricity in a rather unexpected way. Since the 1960s, heavy fuel oil has been the dominant marine fuel, and given its affordability, has facilitated the growth of international shipping worldwide. Critics describe heavy fuel oil as the bottom of the barrel leftovers from the oil refining process. Despite commonly discussed plans to move on to other fuels, such as liquefied natural gas, heavy fuel oil still dominates the commercial marine industry, powering ships ranging from cruises to container vessels. Electricity is sometimes argued to be invisible, but in watching this heavy fuel oil delivery, Mehmet and I saw Ghana's electricity contained within a barge, and regularly made visible to the crew working on the ship.

Karpower executives told me that they have become the largest consumer of low-sulfur heavy fuel oil in the world because of their growing fleet of power-ships. Yet they regularly explained to their clients that they would rather use natural gas for their operations, an opinion widely shared by other temporary power producers, and looked for ways in which they could easily access domestic natural gas. Eventually they bought the heavy fuel oil mothership that was located off the coast of Lomé, and moved it closer to the Tema Fishing Harbor to simplify their operations. This meant that it would take less time to load the larger powership *Osman Khan*, which replaced *Ayşegül Sultan* in late 2017. In late 2019, Karpower finally transferred its operations from Tema to Takoradi, a port city in western Ghana, where they have direct access to the country's Sankofa natural gas reservoir, and managed to quit using heavy fuel oil.

On the powership, machines were stacked up vertically, and ready to take off. In their advertising, the company portrayed this organization as: "fast-track delivery, high efficiency and all integrated "plug & play" project execution." But when I asked Serkan to describe the ships, he did not fall back on this promotional language. Instead, he complemented his folding napkin with a reference to Vitrivius, a Roman architect from first century BC, and recited his three principles of design *firmitas*, *utilitas*, and *venustas* in Latin. Serkan wished to imagine powerships as commodious, firm and delightful.

1 These percentages are commonly used by decision-makers, but they are not always accurate. Everyday power producers in Ghana offer different amounts of electricity to the grid, as predicated by a system of "merit order dispatching" and administered by the control room at GridCo, the national grid company. I use these percentages to symbolize the ship's impact, but acknowledge that they are not factual indicators.
2 The other independent power producers in Ghana are TICO, Sunon Asogli, CENIT Energy, AMERI, and Karadeniz Holding. For more on the Ghana power market, see Ahlijah 2017.
3 Karpower employees repeated that ships could leave if home countries did not compensate them on time or if there is a war. Yet this statement somewhat contradicts their experience, as it might not be that easy for ships to depart. For instance, when the Pakistani government breached payment obligations and unlawfully detained four ships, a major legal dispute erupted between Karadeniz and the Pakistani government. In August 2017, after four years of controversy, the International Centre for Settlement of Investment Disputes (ICSID) awarded Karadeniz a settlement of $800 million, one of the highest settlements in ICSID's history. On November 4, 2019, Pakistan's Prime Minister Imran Khan tweeted that his government had resolved the dispute through a settlement facilitated by President Erdoğan, and saved his country the penalty imposed by ICSID. For updates on this dispute, please see: "Rental power: Government submits dispute settlement documents to ICSID" https://isds.bilaterals.org/?rental-power-government-submits Last accessed February 4, 2020
4 Waller Marine, Power Barge, Modec, Chiyoda, Wison Group, Samsung Heavy Industries, Sevan Marine, Hyundai Heavy Industries, IHI, Mitsui O.S.K. Lines and Mitsubishi Heavy Industries are some of the other actors in the floating natural gas fueled power plant market. Karpower distinguishes itself from these players by using second hand equipment, and retrofitting existing ships. Karpower executives told me that this allows them to offer more affordable prices to their clients, and renders them popular in sub-Saharan Africa.
5 "Blurring the Line Between Temporary and Permanent Power" POWER, July 1 2014 https://www.powermag.com/blurring-the-line-between-temporary-and-permanent-power/?printmode=1 Last accessed September 12, 2018
6 Floating vessels are a component of the temporary power market, but they face competition from "distributed generation facilities," which produce electricity close to points of end use. Most distributed generation facilities offer electricity outputs smaller than 100 MW capacity. Yet planned blackouts, power quality problems, unexpected power outages, and general increases in electricity prices have incentivized institutional and residential consumers to use such equipment. Given their relatively small and scalable sizes, distributed generation facilities are available for purchase for a variety of consumers, including residential consumers. Companies like Aggreko, APR Energy, Atlas Copco, Energyst, United Rentals and Symbion rent out temporary generation equipment around the world, often powered by diesel, heavy fuel oil and natural gas. None of these companies currently provides a significant portion of Ghana's electricity. While floating power plants tend to generate higher volumes of electricity for a grid and enter into contracts with governments, distributed generation facilities have a more diverse range of clients.
7 Other companies like Aggreko, APR Energy, Atlas Copco, Energyst, United Rentals and Symbion rent out temporary generation equipment to various countries around the world to meet the increasing demand for power. These generators are powered by diesel, heavy fuel oil and natural gas. None of these companies currently provides a significant portion of Ghana's electricity.
8 For instance, compare Karpower's operations to Aggreko, a large temporary power company headquartered in the UK, which made a proposal to Ghana for a possible 100 MW power plant, and required 27-acres of land at Esiama to place its generators. So far, the project has not been realized. See this news piece from 2015 in Construction Review Online: "Aggreko set to boost power generation in Ghana" https://constructionreviewonline.com/2015/07/power-generation-in-ghana/ Last accessed September 12, 2018
9 Karpower employees repeated that ships could leave if home countries did not compensate them on time or if there is a war. Yet this statement somewhat contradicts their experience, as it might not be that easy for ships to depart. For instance, when the Pakistani government breached payment obligations and unlawfully detained four ships, a major legal dispute erupted between Karadeniz and the Pakistani government. In August 2017, after four years of controversy, the International Centre for Settlement of Investment Disputes (ICSID) awarded Karadeniz a settlement of $800 million, one of the highest settlements in ICSID's history. On November 4, 2019, Pakistan's Prime Minister Imran Khan tweeted that his government had resolved the dispute through a settlement facilitated by President Erdoğan, and saved his country the penalty imposed by ICSID. For updates on this dispute, please see: "Rental power: Government submits dispute settlement documents to ICSID" https://isds.bilaterals.org/?rental-power-government-submits Last accessed February 4, 2020
10 Saidiya Hartman. 2007. Lose Your Mother. New York: MacMillan, p. 177
11 Marcus Rediker and Peter Linebaugh extend this comment further: "Indeed, the very term factory evolved etymologically from factor, "a trading representative," and specifically one associated with West Africa, where factories were originally located. One trading syndicate off the Gold Coast in the 1730s would anchor a ship permanently to serve as a base for stocks, intelligence gathering, and cargoes; it was called a floating factory. By 1700 the ship had become the engine of commerce, the machine of empire." Marcus Rediker and Peter Linebaugh. 2001. The Many-Headed Hydra. New York: Beacon Press, p. 149–150

THE FUTURE IS POWERISLAND

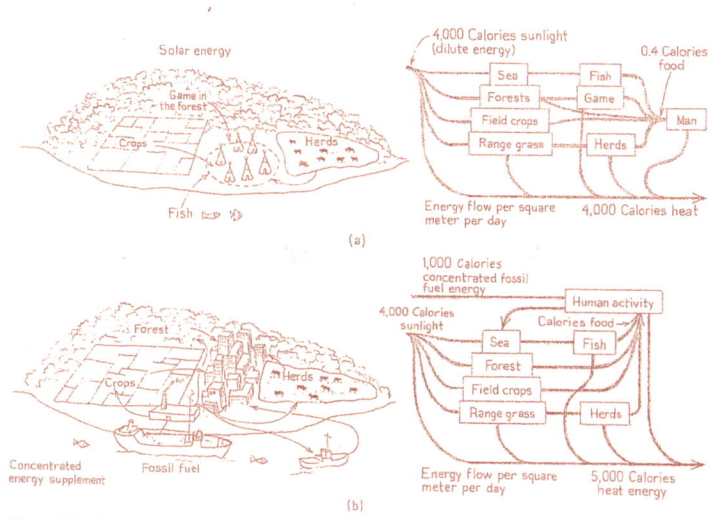

Figure 10-1 Comparison of (a) an all-solar economy and (b) a fossil-fuel economy. *(Odum, 1971.)*

Systems Science

Adam Bobbette
Davy Knittle
Orit Halpern
Ross Exo Adams

While our stereotypical image of a resource, the preceding subject's topic, is of a stolid, unmoving mass, in many cases the art of resource management is a rather dynamic science. Indeed, the historian Etienne S. Benson positions the creation of nationwide resource planning commissions during the First World War as a key moment in the development of systems science. To ensure that their war machines would always remain humming, scientists and engineers had to holistically manage the relationships between resource flows, industrial processes, and military needs.[1] The nation's "survival," they discovered "depended on flows of matter and energy," an insight that would inform the development of the concept of the "ecosystem," that is, a bounded ecological network constituted by "flows of energy … [between] living beings and non-living matter."[2]

During this era of high technocratic confidence, scientists had great faith in their ability to manage the world such that these systems could be steered towards equilibrium. Such hopes were dashed not only by the discovery of anthropogenic climate change, but by ecologists coming to understand nature as defined less by stability and more by sudden flights of disequilibrium.[3] That being said, the logic of systems science remains a highly influential tool for governing futures: the Earth system models that allow the IPCC to make their prognostications, for example, can trace their origins to these earlier eras of ecological and military thought.

Like those WWI resource managers fighting for the survival of the nation, architects have long fancied themselves to be enlightened planetary overseers. The following texts take a closer look at this Earth system approach that is now the lingua franca of ecological management. Who is allowed, these essays ask, to contribute knowledge to this planetary governance project? And what happens to our cities and our architecture when systemic unpredictability is thought to be the natural order? Have our models of an unstable nature, these authors query, yielded urban governance strategies that throw many citizens' lives into similar states of instability?

---

1 As Benson puts it, rather "than seeing resources in terms of absolute quantities, fixed uses, and intrinsic values, scientists came to see them as sources of matter or energy whose value, significance and abundance were determined by the demands and capacities of industrial systems and by the vagaries of geopolitics." Etienne S. Benson, *Surroundings: A History of Environments and Environmentalisms* (Chicago: University of Chicago Press, 2020), 108.
2 Benson, *Surroundings*, 109.
3 See especially C.S. Holling's writings on resilience, a topic that will be thoroughly discussed by this section's authors. C.S. Holling, "Resilience and Stability of Ecological Systems," *Annual Review of Ecological Systems* 4 (1973): 1–23.

The Future of the Disaster: Indonesian Volcanoes, Political Geology, and New Planetary Alliances

Adam Bobbette

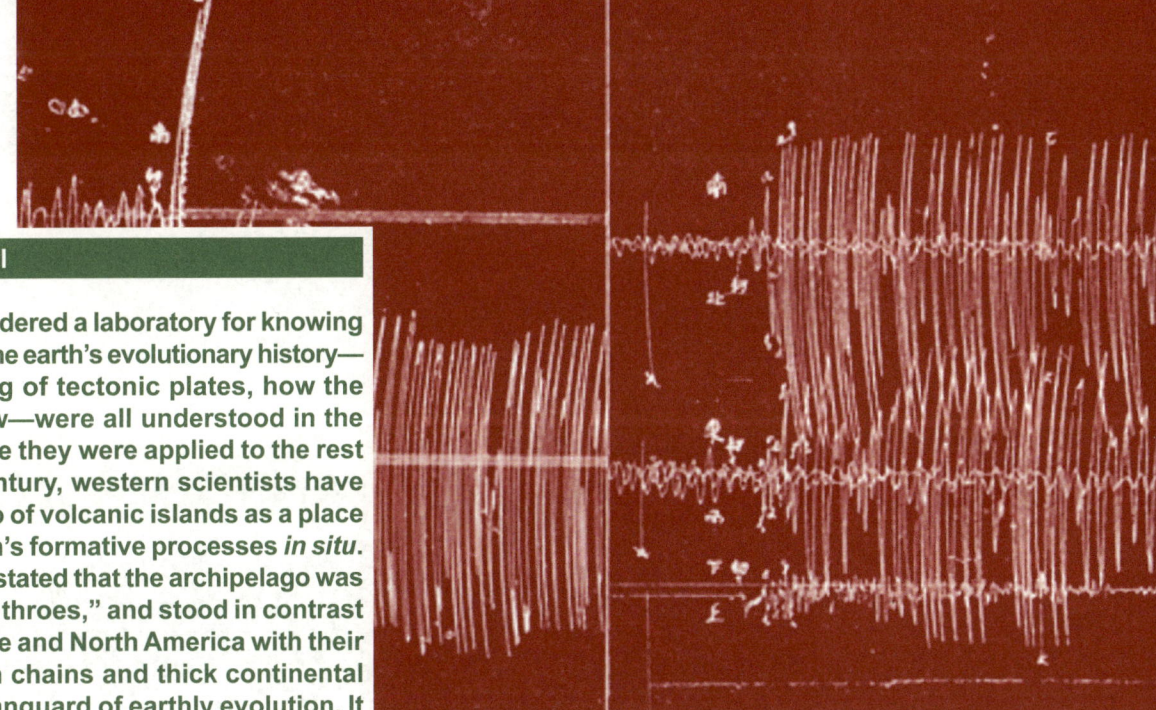

I

Indonesia has long been considered a laboratory for knowing Earth's future. Understanding the earth's evolutionary history—the slow gliding and grinding of tectonic plates, how the lithosphere builds itself anew—were all understood in the Indonesian archipelago before they were applied to the rest of the planet. For nearly a century, western scientists have thought about the archipelago of volcanic islands as a place where one could witness earth's formative processes *in situ*. Volcano scientists repeatedly stated that the archipelago was "young," even in its "youthful throes," and stood in contrast to the old continents of Europe and North America with their weathered massive mountain chains and thick continental masses. Indonesia was the vanguard of earthly evolution. It was not a periphery.

Indonesian volcanoes enabled scientists to think this way. Contrary to other European colonies on more stable grounds, where plantations, mineral and ore extraction could proceed in a self-assured relation to a stable territory, Dutch colonists in the Netherlands East Indies had to confront the fact that their plantations would periodically shudder and be destroyed by volcanoes. The eruption of Krakatoa in 1883 changed the colonial mindset: trade was devastated as the shipping routes that connected the colony to Europe ground to a halt. Vast areas of west Java's plantations were turned to dust. Tea and tobacco leaves browned and flaked off the stem. The motor of plantation extraction that floated the Dutch empire and made it one of the wealthiest states in Earth's history suddenly sputtered.

Terrified, the authorities looked for a solution, but it soon became clear that halting volcanic eruptions was impossible. Making matters worse, because volcanic soil is some of the richest on earth, Javanese plantations stretched up the flanks of the spine of volcanoes and villages were located sometimes as close as three or four kilometres from smoking craters. The European desire to make the Indies just like home also meant that some towns were in the cooler air of volcanic flanks. Forcing the Javanese to bear the brunt of the violence while colonists hid was only partly realistic: plantations were structured on the presence of European bosses, so they too lived up the flanks. Picking up and leaving, then, was an impossibility; their colonial empire was made on volcanoes, they were stuck with disaster.

Nor was building walls to shut out disaster a viable option. Volcanic eruptions could be massive. When Kelud in East Java erupted in 1919 it exploded a lake from its summit which then morphed into a wall of mud that rushed for nearly twenty-five kilometres until it inundated the quiet market town of Blitar, overturning cars and filling houses until their walls burst. When corpses were exhumed the following day, they were found naked, their clothes having been shred off by the rocks and debris in the mudflow. There was no escaping the volcanoes. The plan, instead, was to choreograph. The science of volcanology, which emerged in the 1920s and 1930s in response to these unique conditions, was unlike other disaster sciences in that it sought to synchronise society with volatile nature. Disaster science sought not to shelter from the onslaught but to integrate with it, to distribute its effects, and generate a cosmology around doing so. This is why volcano science matters now; it created a blueprint for our present, as we now face unpredictable nature at the scale of the earth. Indonesian volcano science has long been in this condition, and it can help us strategize.[1]

If the eruption of Krakatoa set modern Indonesian volcano science in motion, the next phase in its history was dependent upon architecture. While eruptions are rarely sudden

Fig. 1.0

Fig. 2.0

Fig. 3.0

events, they each have their own unique precursors: some are heralded by earthquakes, while with others, the flanks balloon as the mountain swells with magma; sometimes the rocky plug on top of the lava conduit grows, cracks and oozes preceding an eruption; with other eruptions, the omen is gas hissing out of the cone or rock falls tumbling down the mountainside; and still other volcanoes give signs of an imminent massive event only to peter away in silence. Nor are all eruptions alike in their magnitude. Some volcanic eruptions can be months long with lulls and periods of high intensity when massive clouds of super-heated gases billow from the crater to sweep through forests and fields, sometimes lighting them on fire. Other volcanoes (such as Mount Merapi) can languidly exude lava for months without the slightest explosion. The uniqueness of each volcano makes predictive certainty nearly impossible. Surveillance and feedback thus became the strategy of Dutch colonial scientists: they had to find a way to get as close to the crater as possible so they could monitor it and send signals of impending danger to the lowlands before the disaster arrived. It was in the pursuit of the surveillance aspect of this strategy that architecture entered the fore.

How, exactly, does one get close to a live crater? Scientists constructed buildings that were near enough to the crater that it could be observed with binoculars or telescopes while being sheltered on a hill or the far side of a deep valley. They also drew on solutions from prisons—they erected watch towers, set on promontories between villages and the craters. These approaches only worked, though, when the skies were clear and the volcano was not obscured behind giant ash clouds. Also, the first observatory that they built, at Maron on Merapi in 1930, was washed away by a mud slide, burying the seismograph they had installed.

In response to these issues, their next solutions drew on war technologies: they built bunkers. The first was erected at an observatory called Babadan to the west of Merapi (Fig 1.0, 2.0, 3.0). It was designed so that it could withstand a large eruption. The bunker was kitted out with asbestos suits to repel heat if they needed to venture outdoors. It also contained oxygen tanks designed according to the specifications for sustaining life in submarines in critical conditions; with them three men could survive for eleven hours. A heat resistant peephole made of double sheeted Pyrex glass resistant to temperatures of up to one thousand degrees Celsius faced the crater so that they could monitor the eruption. And a massive mechanical seismograph, fed by a roll of paper blackened with candle soot, was propped up against the wall so that they could record earthquakes even if the peephole was obscured by debris.[2]

If architecture helped them to surveil the volcano, how did they then communicate their observations to the lowlands, warning people of an oncoming cloud of gas, mudslide, or rock fall? Alarms, radios, and telephones were key. The bunker was connected by telegraph and radio signal to the military and police in the lowland market town of Muntilan, where their warnings would then be dispatched to orchestrate evacuations of the territory. One volcano scientist, Reinout Van Bemmelen, even collaborated with Willem Einthoven Jr., who had experimented with wireless broadcasts, to rig-up a seismograph that was sensitive enough it could hear the faintest hisses and buzzes from rainfall and wind in the crater.[3]

Volcano science thus became a science of mediation: volcanologists came to understand that they were in-between the volatile edges of the earth and society. Their purpose was to tend to the instruments that amplified, magnified, or otherwise made the volcanoes sensible and recordable and to pass along those inscriptions to the lowlands in advance of the arrival of an event. To do so meant designing spatial solutions to negotiate the inherent fragility of the human body

in an extreme environment, hiding in a bunker and otherwise protecting the body so that it could continue to observe and relay messages along the network. They sent signals not just from a spatial remove but from a temporal remove as well: they saw the disaster before it happened to everyone else.

It was this peculiar necessity to witness the events of a dynamic earth before everyone else that made volcano science in the Netherlands Indies so unique. Perhaps the only other equivalent practice for European scientists was at Vesuvius where the American scientist Frank Perret and his Italian counterpart Raffaele Matteucci went to extreme lengths to witness and record eruptions. Often injuring themselves, they in effect used their bodies as sensitive instruments. I have explained elsewhere how Perret and Matteucci's practice was a volatile empiricism, a form of scientific knowledge in extreme environments in extreme environments.[4] Volatile empiricists believed that knowledge of volcanism, and by extension the earth system, required their presence on the volcano; they had to be witnesses, to sense and experience the physicality of volcanoes, their rhythms, and unique characteristics. They thought that knowledge required proximity, witnessing, and presence; they had to feel the volcanoes to know them.

Yet, by exposing themselves to the volatility of volcanic explosions, they were brought to the very limit of feeling—or, as Perret put it, to the "sense walls of the universe." In this way, volatile empiricism was preoccupied with thresholds and limits, with getting closer to the thing to be known and then retreating. For volatile empiricists, knowledge was simultaneously embodied, direct and mediated; technology, infrastructures and networks were necessary to carry messages from the site of the sensing body to a safer beyond. The core of volatile empiricism was to-ing and fro-ing while sending signals.

Van Bemmelen, Perret, and Matteucci were not always on the move, however. Surveillance was also often stationary, patient work. Some Indonesian volcanoes have not erupted for decades, centuries even. Permanent observatories were thus set up only on the most frequently active volcanoes, but this could still mean surveilling a volcano for years on end with very little consequential activity. Knowing them meant waiting on a dynamic earth rather than the scientist acting on the word and then recording the results. So, alongside to-ing and fro-ing there was also a lot of waiting: mild anticipation, the daily chores of replacing the paper on the seismographs, measuring rainfall, doing laundry, cooking.

II

When Senapati was travelling around central Java in the late sixteenth century he was on a military-spiritual quest to create a new Islamic kingdom. His would be one of the earliest in a region of primarily Hindu-Buddhist empires. At the time, the Dutch had only just arrived in Java, challenging Portuguese access to Southeast Asian trade, but their presence was limited to the northern coasts. Travelling through the centre of Java, it was clear to Senapati that building a kingdom would require spiritual and cosmic alliances in addition to human support. One of the stops he made was on the southern coast where Java meets the Indian Ocean. There he sought to consult with the goddess Nyai Roro Kidul, who kept her palace in the ocean and governed the subterranean chthonic, muddy, tidal realms. It is unclear precisely what transpired—our accounts of this meeting are reliant on later court chronicles, some written as recently as the nineteenth century—but the story that is most frequently told is that Senapati and Nyai Roro Kidul agreed to enter a partnership in which she would assist the establishment of his kingdom, support all future generations of sultans, and offer protection from the powers of the oceanic underworld, which included tsunamis and earthquakes. In return, each year the Sultan would be required to give money, clothes, perfume, food, and sex to the goddess.

Senapati did not only seek assistance from the ocean deity; he also looked north to the volcanoes. Merapi, Merbabu, Bromo-Tengger, Lawu, Sumbing, Sindoro, all jut from the landscape, sometimes smoking, sometimes affirming their self-evident liveliness with rumbles and bangs. Senapati turned to the nearest volcano, Merapi, long the home of a pantheon of local and historical deities, some of them having migrated with the earliest Hindus who arrived there in the early days of the Common Era. In the mountain, there were serpents, iron workshops, and deities who were variations or avatars of Arjuna, Ganesha, Dakshinamurti, Durga, and Shiva. To create a new political kingdom on the slopes of such a densely populated spiritual space necessitated their cooperation; political power, in fact, was constituted *through* alliances with those earth beings, otherwise it was illegitimate. Working with Nyai Roro Kidul again, they birthed a giant from an egg. Senapati gave his assistant a hen's egg to eat (a microcosm of the cosmic egg—that is, the materialisation of the force of production and transformation imminent to all things), and the assistant transformed into a giant who then took up residence in Merapi. The giant's work there was martial: he would preside over an army of spirits on the flanks of and inside the volcano to lend support to Senapati's campaign. With the consent of the volcano and the ocean, Senapati could then begin to challenge existing empires.

The political geology of sixteenth century Java deserves our close attention. In this system, political power was conditioned on alliances with earth beings and, in particular, deities who operated the mud of the ocean, the stony flanks of the volcanoes, and the rippling tides of earth tremors. Geological agency was central to the political sphere; one could only create a kingdom—and therefore, the political subjects of that kingdom—through the consent of geological agencies. This meant that any sovereign's position was constituted through a perpetual debt to these forces; one had to constantly provision offerings to geological deities because if they ever withdrew their consent, political legitimacy would deteriorate. The records of the offerings that were given to Nyai Roro Kidul, moreover, indicate that deities were more mobile than we might imagine. She was given clothing, food, money, even perfume, which suggest that she was not bound to her form in the ocean but could metamorphose into a human form and partake in the life of the kingdom. While perfumed and donned in smart clothes, she could shop in its markets and eat its dinners. This was perhaps a leverage point in making alliances with geological deities—they too wanted to participate in human life. By providing such offerings, one enabled the circulation of deities such as Nyai Roro Kidul between human and geological spaces; replenishing her clothes, perfume, and coins allowed her to continue to cross the thresholds between human political and lithic realms.

This political geology was not confined to central Java. Reports from the entire southern coast of Java from the eighteenth and nineteenth century record the important role Nyai Roro Kidul played in maintaining local political power. The same was true of the volcano deities. The Sundanese kingdoms in the west of Java entered alliances with deities in Tangkuban Parahu. In Bali, too, which is the home of Agung and Batur volcanoes, the Hindu-Buddhist kingdoms on their flanks were also co-produced through alliances with volcanic and oceanic deities. By the time that Dutch colonial authorities became interested in understanding the political-material cosmologies of Indonesian societies in the nineteenth century, they too acknowledged the significance of Nyai Roro Kidul. For instance, Pieter Veth, in his 1882 geography of Java, wrote that the south was "bounded by the vast territory of Ratoe Loro Kidul, the Princess of the Southern Ocean."[5] Indonesian geography, for at least two millennia, cannot be understood without accounting for the fundamental political-geological arrangements that made sense of the relationship between society and the earth.

III

In 1917, the government geologist Georges L.L Kemmerling reported in the leading scientific periodical of the colonial Netherlands Indies, *Natuurkundig Tijdschrift*, that he had conducted fieldwork on Batur in Bali. He also recorded a problem: "who would accompany me to the top and into the crater? After all, never before had a Balinese dared to climb to the summit, let alone descend into its crater opening, the place where the Dewa [deity] of the Batur dwells, the deity who is sometimes incensed at the sinful life of men that it threatens to bury it under ash rains or lava flows."[6] A small nearby troupe of armed police officers finally offered to accompany him on his journey. Kemmerling then reported that they prayed together in Malay before the ascent: "If the heart is pure, perhaps nothing will happen but if the heart is impure then we are certainly damned."[7]

It is often assumed by Indonesianists that there was a hard division between colonial and local environmental knowledges. Scholars tend to focus on how colonial knowledge was imposed on Indonesians or on how Indonesians adopted and transformed western knowledges. Additionally, historians often assume that colonial scientists simply did not know about local beliefs, an ignorance they attribute to racism and a general lack of Dutch curiosity. But the transfer of knowledge and influence certainly went in both directions: Dutch geologists and volcano scientists did in fact learn from their Indonesian assistants, coolies, and locals. Kemmerling's account of Batur is one brief but cogent example of this transfer—bear in mind that he even prayed with his police guides, in Malay no less, and without irony. His acknowledgement of the spiritual significance of Batur and his inclination to record it in the context of a natural history journal demonstrates that there was an interest in such matters among his Dutch colonial scientist colleagues. In the same article, he went so far as to explain that "I was further informed [by the officers] that large goats were seen from time to time on the top of Batur. In their opinion, of course, they were the spirits of men in the form of goats. The story later turned out to be really true,

aside from the few goats we saw during the ascent, their excrement was everywhere, even inside the crater."[8] In other words, Kemmerling was fully aware of the spiritual political geology of Indonesia. In fact, these reports indicate that he was fascinated by it.

He was not alone: similar accounts of colonial encounters with local spiritual geographies were frequent in *Natuurkundig Tijdschrift* and across the archive of personal letters and scientific monographs produced by volcanologists and geologists. For example, Rogier Verbeek, who in 1896 compiled the first complete geological map of Java, *Description Géologique de Java et Madoura,* undertook at the same time a catalogue of Javanese antiquities (temples, stele, tombs, stairs) that documented the extent of early modern Javanese civilisation while also constructing a patchy political history of the geography of Hindu-Buddhist empires.[9] Orientalists and Theosophists were also crucial go-betweens between locals and colonists. Through their shared social circles in Batavia, Surabaya, and Yogyakarta, they informed colonial geologists about Indonesian environmental knowledges. Theosophist lodges, as well as being places for séances and occult learning, were thriving social centres where Javanese aristocrats with anti-colonial tendencies exchanged knowledge with sympathetic colonial scientists.

There is no doubt, then, that geologists and volcanologists knew about the political geological system of Indonesia. The question, therefore, is what did they do with this knowledge? The short answer is that they used it to shape the modern theory of the earth and its future. In doing so, however, they also stripped away the most profound ontological challenges of Indonesian political geology.

IV

Indonesian spiritual geographies created modern theories of the earth by way of the ritual pathways and pilgrimage sites that connected the volcanoes to the oceans. Take, for example, the annual procession known as the Labuhan.[11] Records of the Labuhan date from the nineteenth century but it was likely undertaken much earlier—if not as early as the very foundation of the Mataram kingdom in the sixteenth century by Senapati himself. The purpose of the procession was to give offerings to the goddess Nyai Roro Kidul to secure her movements between the ocean realm and the Sultanate. After conducting a royal procession—replete with music, carriages, and cannon-fire—to the edge of the Indian Ocean, offerings would be launched into the sea on bamboo rafts. It is unclear when this portion of the tradition began, but at some point (records exist from the early twentieth century) the procession then turned around and ascended the southern face of the Merapi volcano to deposit offerings at the base of the crater for the deities inside and on the flanks.

This axis of offerings was not an accident: it acknowledged that the political geological foundation of the sultanate was in the alliance between the Indian Ocean and the volcano that I described above. By the 1920s and 1930s (but likely much earlier), it was also understood that deities in the Indian Ocean and the volcanoes knew and exchanged with each other independently of humans. Numerous stories describe how deities travelled down the volcanic rivers to visit sites near the Indian Ocean, or how Nyai Roro Kidul would travel to the crater of Merapi to visit deities. In some instances, lowland deities were said to be kin with crater deities. Collectively, these spiritual geographies demonstrated that the volcanoes and Indian Ocean were connected, which meant that eruptions, earthquakes, tsunamis, floods, and other perturbations between land and sea were understood to be fundamentally related. The political geology of the central Javanese sultanates was based, in part, on the insight that terrestrial and volcanic processes were tied together.

For Dutch scientists in the early twentieth century, however, these processes were not yet connected. In *Description Géologique de Java et Madoura*, Verbeek claimed that there were "great depths" off the south of Indonesia, "about which we are completely uncertain."[10] In the late 1880s, extensive ship sounding data was limited to the interior of the Indonesian archipelago, not the south. Exploratory sounding to connect the archipelago with Australia and Malaya via telegraph cables indicated a "rift." Moreover, Verbeek had argued that volcanoes were separate "hearths," unconnected units, and that they were the remnants of once great mountains that exploded as they fell apart.

It was not until nearly twenty years later, in 1918, that Alfred Wegener proposed that the continents drifted horizontally in deep time by ploughing through a semi-liquid underlayer. The hypothesis ran counter to the prevailing geological orthodoxy which tended to think that continents were horizontally stable but vertically mobile, capable of shrinking or sinking but not likely to veer off to another place on the earth's surface. The theory of continental drift was largely ignored by most European and North American geologists—except in the Netherlands Indies, where scientists countenanced it as a theoretical possibility as they came to question Verbeek's ideas.

The spiritual geographies of Java enabled this questioning. As we have already seen, Kemmerling travelled to explore the crater in Batur accompanied by local police. In other scientific papers, he also recorded that he ascended to the tops of volcanoes by way of their ritual pathways. As volcanoes were highly sacred sites in remote areas reachable only by difficult terrain, it was frequently the case that the only access to craters and promontories was by way of the same ritual and pilgrimage paths that enabled the political-geological constitutions of Indonesian societies. When Kemmerling visited the crater of Merapi in 1920, for instance, he "took an old ritual path" which was almost certainly the same path as the Labuhan. When other scientists, including Van Bemmelen and Petroschevsky, wrote accounts of their fieldwork to the crater of Merapi, they too noted that they followed ritual and pilgrimage paths. As they ambled along these paths throughout the 1920s and 1930s, the geologists increasingly came to believe that volcanism in Merapi was connected to processes in the Indian Ocean. Seismograph readings taken at the observatory outside of Bandung began to reveal that earthquake epicentres off Java were much deeper than originally understood, potentially indicating that tectonic processes cut between the Indian Ocean and the volcanic spine of Java. For many colonial scientists, these readings suggested that perhaps Wegener was correct: continental masses did exert lateral forces, meaning that earthquakes in the Indian Ocean were somehow related to volcanism. Scientists were speculating about this theoretical connection as they conducted their fieldwork on ritual pathways that *literally* connected the volcanoes to the Indian Ocean. In the political geology of Java it was already understood that volcanic and oceanic processes were fundamentally causally related.

The turning point in the Dutch colonial vision of terrestrial evolution came with the work of Felix Vening Meinesz. Throughout the 1920s and into the 1930s, Vening Meinesz undertook several submarine voyages with a device he had newly constructed for recording the gravity of the ocean floor. In 1927, 1929, and 1930 he measured the gravity of the Indian Ocean floor off the south of the Indonesian archipelago and found massive anomalies that revealed, for the first time, a giant underwater depression nearly one hundred and sixty kilometres wide and eight thousand kilometres long (Fig 4.0).[12] With this information, this area, which Verbeek had only been able to gesture towards in the 1880s, was now theorized as an immense "fold" with some structural relationship with the landmasses that bordered it. In a 1930 presentation to the Royal Geographical Society in London, Vening Meinesz suggested that there was a causal relation between the trench and the high levels of seismicity and volcanism in the archipelago. By the 1940s, Vening Meinesz and collaborators such as Johannes Umbgrove and Philippe Keunen began to theorize their own models for how the ocean floor was jamming into, crumpling, and bending at the edge of the landmasses of Sumatra and Java (Fig 5.0). They proposed that convection currents from deep in the earth were rising and falling at the site of the fold, anticipating the later plate tectonic argument that continental masses were moved by convection currents. They also became increasingly convinced that, however unclear the exact mechanism, the very processes that were forming the trench were also responsible for volcanoes. In other words, Dutch geologists came to understand the core principle of the political geology of Indonesian polities: ocean and terrestrial processes were causally related.

The work of Dutch geologists was not confined to the Netherlands East Indies. The theoretical work of Keunen, Umbgrove, and Vening Meinesz increasingly enabled geologists across the world to think about the horizontal relationships between ocean floors and continents, evidenced by high rates of seismicity and volcanism between them. They came to appreciate

Fig. 4.0

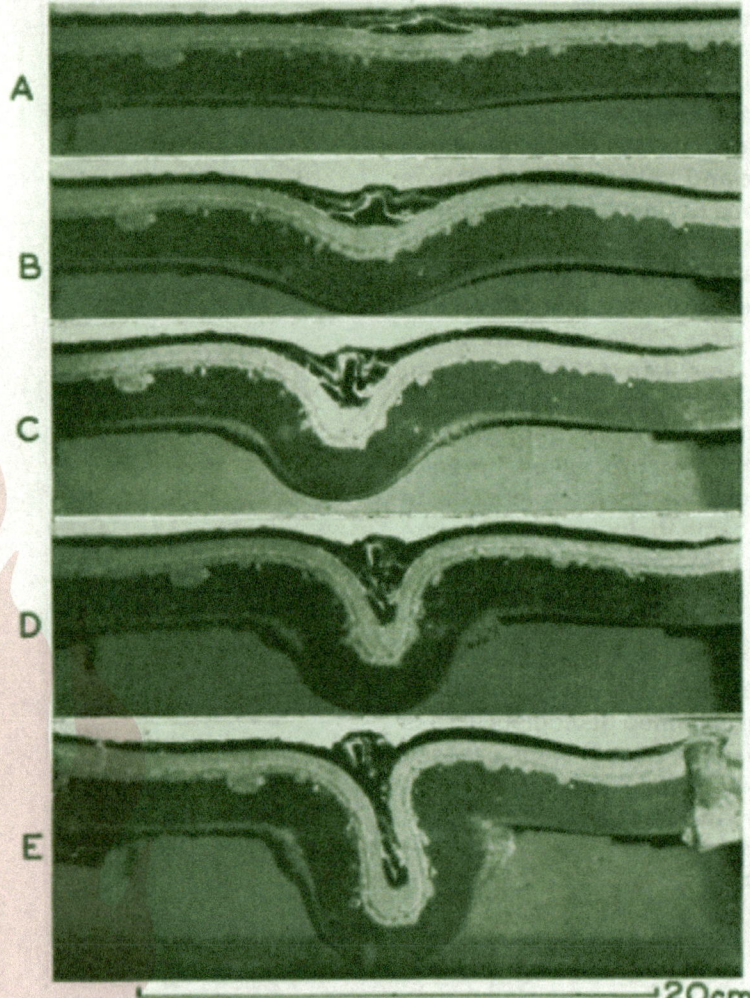

Fig. 5.0

that perhaps the continents were not horizontally stable but that there were profound exchanges between the oceans and land; volcanoes came to be seen as conduits through which ocean floors were transformed into land, where they then eroded back down to the ocean floor. The relationship between ocean and land was circular, volcanoes were the ocean floors reconfigured.

Additionally, over the course of the 1930s and 1940s, Vening Meinesz taught other scientists how to use his gravity meter, including the Princeton geologist Harry Hess. In 1962, Hess showed convincingly for the first time that ocean basins were pushed horizontally away from massive volcanic ridges in the oceans. When the ocean floors met continental edges, they could fold and bend into the massive trenches discovered by Meinesz. By the late 1960s, this vision became the theory of plate tectonics and was largely the new orthodox description of the evolutionary history of the earth. The volcanism of island arcs, it came to be understood, were the result of the ocean floor smashing into continental masses, folding, and producing new land through volcanism and earthquakes. And thus the Indonesian archipelago came to be seen as a place where "the youthful throes" of the earth surface in the making could be seen *in situ*. Rather than a place replete with ancient massive mountains that were now crumbling, as Verbeek had thought, Indonesia came to be seen as a place where the ocean floor was continuously being transformed into land, a place where earthquakes coursed from the Indian ocean through land as magma flowed in subterranean space towards the volcanoes and out through their billowing cones. As important as Vening Meinesz's geodesical work was to changing scientists' perceptions, so too were the records from volcano observatories built near or literally on sacred sites and the fieldwork conducted on the ritual pathways that connected volcanic cones to the Indian Ocean. These ritual pathways and infrastructures not only enabled scientists to undertake their work but also allowed them to see the landscape in new ways and envision connections between volcanic and oceanic processes. The theory of plate tectonics and the modern understanding of the earth system that it shaped—including our understanding of the earth's future—was, in no uncertain terms, enabled by the indigenous spiritual geographies of Indonesia.

V

Although local Indonesian knowledge of oceanic and terrestrial processes shaped global perception, the source of that knowledge was scraped clean from the historical record. When European and United States scientists came to see the structure of the earth in terms of the new global tectonics, they called their vision "revolutionary," suggesting a magnitude of philosophical breakthrough on the order of Copernicus. They also portrayed the main players in unquestionably western terms, as if the theory of plate tectonics was without a doubt authored only by Europeans and Americans. The moments I described earlier from the *Natuurkundig Tijdschrift*, where scientists acknowledged the importance of local and indigenous knowledge, began to drift into the far corners of the archive and to fall off the lists of footnotes and citations. The actors who were most frequently given the spotlight in the so-called plate tectonic revolution (and similarly with the history of the botanical sciences) were white male professors at Princeton, Columbia, Harvard, Oxford, and Cambridge. This view has not changed: contemporary historians of geology who focus on the theory of plate tectonics have perpetuated this narrative. That the theory of plate tectonics was prefigured, enabled, or otherwise authored by anyone other than the conventional cast of characters has been inconceivable until only very recently.

Yet, even more significant than this marginalisation of non-Western authors is history's ignoring of the core ontological challenge of Indonesian political geology. In the view from Indonesian polities, politics was constituted through collaborations with geological entities. Geological materials were not resources in the contemporary sense of dead matter that can be extracted and sold. Geological entities were participants in the human polity, not its mere substructure; in fact, human political subjects came into being through negotiations with them. As European and United States scientists turned plate tectonics into a story about themselves, they side-lined the profound challenge that comes with relating to geological material as a living entity requiring gifts and reciprocity. This side-lining laid the groundwork for the massive scale commodification of nature we see today such as the ongoing attempts to transform the seabed into a resource.

The concept of the Anthropocene is a sign that geologists and earth scientists are beginning to take a different view. The acknowledgement of the porosity between politics and geological matter implicit in the Anthropocene thesis has opened a space for new histories of the geological sciences. The profound challenge of Indonesian political geology, however, remains: how to take seriously the charge that human polities are indebted to geological entities? And how do we truly understand that geological histories are by nature social histories?

What does this have to do with the future? We saw at the beginning of this essay that one of the contributions of Dutch colonial volcano science was the notion of choreographing society with volatile nature. We now know that we all, in effect, live on a volcano: the onset of anthropogenic climate breakdown means that we are entering a phase of Earth's history in which we cannot predict with certainty how natural systems will transform. Turning to people who have lived with volcanism for centuries is one way to learn coping strategies. At the very least, Indonesian volcanology should inspire us to undertake the challenge of thinking through what a contemporary political geology might look like. How could such a political geology help us to rethink where to build our observatories? What new ritual paths and infrastructures can be designed to enable us to give offerings and make alliances with geological deities? Who are the geological deities that shaped our world?

My study of Indonesian political geology has pointed to two important programs we must undertake as we tackle these questions regarding our conception of the future of nature. First, my essay contributes to the project of decolonizing the earth sciences. Doing so requires demonstrating that orthodox narratives of earth's history and structure (even its climate) were not only authored by western scientists but were rather forged by many people whose voices and influence have since been marginalised. The second goal is to track what knowledge was erased and silenced as scientists marginalised other voices. On Javanese volcanoes, scientists erased the constitutive nature of geology, politics, and social life; they erased this insight because it challenged the very foundations of Dutch colonial culture. Yet, this Indonesian knowledge is precisely what needs to be taken seriously today if we are to imagine more equitable ways of living with geology. The climate crisis now allows us to see how thoroughly nature is social history—forest fires, droughts, rising seas, and melting glaciers are the human actions of the past: they are industrialisation and fossil fuel combustion speaking to us in the present. Many of us are now in a position to see with perfect clarity how geological material is social *and* political. We are in a time that needs Javanese political geology.

1. The arguments and histories explored in this essay are developed in greater detail in Adam Bobbette, *The Pulse of the Earth: Political Geology in Java* (Durham: Duke University Press, 2023).
2. Newman Van Padang, "Measures Taken by the Authorities of the Volcanological Survey to Safeguard the Population from the Consequences of Volcanic Outbursts," *Bulletin Volcanologique* 23 (1960): 181–192.
3. Reinout Van Bemmelen, *The Geology of Indonesia* (The Hague: Government Printing Office, 1945).
4. Adam Bobbette, "The Sound of Magma: Geographies of Infrasound, Vibrating Bodies, and Representing the Earth," *DMJournal-Architecture and Representation, Architecture and the Geological Imagination* (2023).
5. Pieter Veth, *Java, Geographisch, Ethnologisch, Historisch* (Haarlem: De Erven F. Bohn, 1882), 377.
6. G.L.L Kemmerling, "Belimming van den G. Batoer," *Natuurkundig Tijdschrift* (1917): 55–56.
7. Kemmerling, Belimming, 58. "Kaloe ati bresih, brangkali tida djadi apa apa tetapi kaloe ati kotor, temtoe tjilaka [*sic*]."
8. G.L.L Kemmerling, "Belimming van den G. Batoer," *Natuurkundig Tijdschrift* (1917): 58.
9. See, Rogier Verbeek and Reinder Fennema, *Description Géologique de Java et Madoura Atlas* (Amsterdam: Stemler, 1896); R.D.M Verbeek, *Oudheidkundige Kaart van Java* (Batavia: Bataviaash Genootschap van Kunsten en Wetenschappen, 1891).
10. Verbeek and Fennema, *Description Géologique de Java et Madoura vol. II* (Amsterdam: Stemler, 1896): 1031.
11. G. Kemmerling, "Vulkanologische Berichten," *Natuurkundig Tijdschrift voor Nederlandsch-Indië* 82, no. 2 (1920): 188–196.
12. Felix Vening Meinesz, "Gravity Anomalies in the East Indian Archipelago," *The Geographical Journal* 77, no. 4 (1931): 323–332.

"It's Going to Melt the Polar Caps": Redlined Climate Futures in *Do the Right Thing*

Davy Knittle

Figure 1. Front page of August 9th, 1988, issue of *The New York Times*.

I. Narratives of Climate Change in the Late 1980s U.S.

On August 9th, 1988, *The New York Times* published an article on its front page with the headline "Yes, It's Hotter, It's Muggier, And, Yes, You're Going Crazy." [Figure 1]

In the article, journalist Steven Erlanger explains that the summer of 1988 has been the third-hottest summer on record in the New York City region. The hot summer, Erlanger argues, is "taking its toll on the psychological makeup of an already feverish city, straining civility in offices, automobiles and parks."[1] Erlanger links the heat to a collective mental health crisis. He also suggests that the hot weather is connected for many New Yorkers not only to mass mental health effects but also to recent scientific discoveries about climate change. He interviews Gayanne La Roe, a secretary at St. James Episcopal Church, who associates the heat with "'an impending sense of doom.'" La Roe references recent discoveries in climate science including the 1985 identification of a rupture in the ozone layer, explaining that "'We've heard about the greenhouse effect and the ozone layer and the oceans . . . So I was depressed about our planet for the last few weeks, as if I didn't have enough problems.'"[2] In the summer of 1988, La Roe was one of many for whom the sustained heat concretized recent scientific discoveries, government hearings, and media coverage that reframed extreme weather as a manifestation of anthropogenic climate change. Reading the hot weather as indicative of climate change made the heat seem not only suggestive of a pattern but also predictive of future warming. Put in conversation with the popularized findings of contemporary climate science, the heat was stressful both as an immediate experience and as an indication of even hotter weather to come.

One catalyzing event that helped shape public narratives linking the hot summer of 1988 to climate change was the June 1988 hearings of the U.S. Senate Committee on Energy and Natural Resources.[3] Previous research had identified that global warming was causing altered weather patterns and amplifying global temperatures, but as an increasing body of scholarship grew to focus on climate change in the 1980s, many claims called for further research as to its effects. For instance, at the October 1987 First North American Conference on Preparing for Climate Change, a group of climate scientists that included James Hansen, the Director of the NASA Goddard Institute for Space Studies, noted that "The global warming predicted to occur in the next 20 years will make the earth warmer than it has been in the past 100,000 years. It can be assumed that there will be major practical impacts of such a warming, but little research has been done to define such impacts."[4] Robert L. Peters and Joan D. S. Darling argued relatedly in a 1985 article that "Our understanding of how atmospheric composition affects global climate is still in its infancy."[5] In the second half of the 1980s, new research consistently called for more data about the causes and the effects of climate change. The 1980s saw an increase in scholarship among climate scientists that sought to predict the potential impacts of the greenhouse effect, which Peters and Darling described as "global CO_2-induced climatic change."[6]

In the June 1988 hearings, Hansen testified that he and his colleagues had identified a connection that could offer increased certainty about the relationship between human systems and global warming. He stated that "the global warming is now large enough that we can ascribe with a high degree of confidence a cause and effect relationship to the greenhouse effect."[7] In no uncertain terms, Hansen argued that "the greenhouse effect has been detected, and it is changing our climate now."[8] Hansen's testimony and the press coverage it received, in large part because it occurred during the hottest year on record, contributed to a shift in late 1980s public discourse about climate change.[9] This shift resulted in increasing public and political awareness about climate change, as well as investments in new approaches to climate modeling, which included the 1988 formal approval by the United Nations of the Intergovernmental Panel on Climate Change (IPCC).[10] Beginning in the late 1980s, the IPCC introduced a series of climate change projections, which it referred to as 'scenarios,' each of which "represented a different hypothesis about how humanity as a whole would respond to the possibility of dramatic climate change over the coming century."[11] As a result of the combination of earth science research, policy interest, and media coverage, many people became newly or increasingly attentive to climate change in the late 1980s. The hot summer of 1988 amplified public climate discourse and left millions of residents of unprecedently hot cities and regions with questions: How fast was climate change coming? What forms might it take? How might its effects interact with existing inequitable access to housing and basic resources? To what extent was the hot summer an aberration,

Figure 2. Corner of Stuyvesant and Lexington Avenues, Brooklyn, NY. The block of Stuyvesant Avenue between Lexington Avenue and Quincy Street has been renamed "Do the Right Thing Way" by the City of New York. Photograph by author, May 2022.

and to what extent was it a preview of additional anthropogenic planetary shifts?

Amid the hot summer, the cast and crew of filmmaker Spike Lee's *Do the Right Thing* filmed on a single block in the Bedford-Stuyvesant neighborhood of Brooklyn, New York.[12] [Figure 2] While the summer was hot across the country, the degree and effects of the heat were especially acute in Bed-Stuy and other neighborhoods with inequitable access to tree canopy, parks, and other greenspace. Bed-Stuy has been a historically Black neighborhood since the early 20th century. In 1938, the neighborhood was redlined, or given a high-risk designation by the Home Owners' Loan Corporation (HOLC). HOLC used a system of risk assessment that instituted de-facto segregation under the premise of identifying risk for potential mortgage lenders.[13] Bed-Stuy received a "D" rating, the highest category of risk, which, as Dorceta Taylor explains, was "reserved for all-Black neighborhoods."[14] Areas that were previously redlined often have a direct relationship to present disproportionate heat impacts. As planning historian Bev Wilson notes, citing a 2020 study by Hoffman et. al., "areas carrying the HOLC designation 'D' are 'now on average 2.6°C warmer than 'A' rated areas.'"[15] Additionally, urban areas have warmed faster than non-urban locations, such that formerly redlined neighborhoods experience an even more dramatic difference in heat when compared to suburban and rural areas. As a 2021 report by the Natural Resources Defense Council (NRDC) notes, "since 1900, New York City has warmed by 4.4°F, more than double the amount of statewide warming."[16] While 1988 was then the hottest year on record in the U.S., residents of Bed-Stuy experienced higher temperatures and more sustained heat than other parts of the city, and the city experienced more sustained heat than outlying regions.

Do the Right Thing, which was released in June 1989, takes place over 24 hours on the hottest day and night of the summer. The film focuses on the relationship between Black residents of a single block in Bed-Stuy, the white owner of the block's pizza shop and his adult sons, New York City Police Department officers, and Puerto Rican and Korean members of the block's community. The reception of *Do the Right Thing* has focused largely on its depiction of racial violence, and specifically on the police killing of a young Black man, Radio Raheem, who is killed near the end of the film when police respond to a fight that originates between Raheem and Sal, the owner of the pizza shop, after Sal destroys Raheem's boom box. The altercation between Sal and Raheem begins after Sal's closes, when Raheem and two other characters, Smiley and Buggin' Out, enter the pizza shop demanding, as Buggin' Out has throughout the film, that Sal add Black public figures to a "wall of fame" in the shop populated solely by images of Italian Americans.

A fight breaks out, and when police respond to the fight, they inexplicably restrain Radio Raheem with a chokehold, killing him. After Raheem's death, Mookie (Spike Lee's character), who is employed delivering pizzas for Sal's, instigates the destruction of the pizza shop by throwing a garbage can through its front window. In the wake of global protests to address systemic anti-Blackness in response to the May 2020 police killing of George Floyd, there has been renewed public interest in the film, as there was in the wake of the 2014 police killing of Eric Garner.[17] Garner, like Floyd and the character Radio Raheem, was an unarmed Black man killed by police chokehold. The genesis of the film was the 1983 death of Michael Stewart, who was also an unarmed Black man killed by police.[18]

One focus of the film is how the heat exacerbates the block's extant racial tensions, catalyzing the violent eruption that results in the police killing of Raheem. The implicit question of the film's title has been commonly read as whether Mookie did the right thing by throwing the garbage can through Sal's window, and more generally whether property destruction is a justified response to racial violence. This debate has continued in the intervening decades and was amplified during global racial justice protests in summer 2020.[19]

The premise of this question is routinely refused by scholars and activists who object to a comparison between the loss of human life and the loss of property. In this counterreading, the title serves as an invitation to viewers to themselves "do the right thing" by attending to the film in a way that rejects this comparison. This rejection follows historian Robin D.G. Kelley, who asks in a June 2020 editorial in *The New York Times*, "What kind of society values property over Black lives?"[20]

The film's direct engagement with discoveries in climate science and public discourse about climate change in the late 1980s is integral to how it stages the relationship between extreme heat and elevated racial violence. The film intervenes not only in the consideration of how racial violence and extreme heat are linked, but also in predictions about climate futures as they might follow the contours of previous racialized relationships to housing and other basic resources scripted by histories of anti-Black urban policy. A reading of the film's attention to how racialized urban policy and planning shape the present and future impact of climate change in the Bed-Stuy of *Do the*

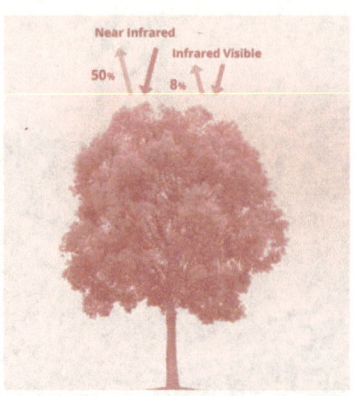

Figure 3. Mural of characters from *Do the Right Thing* on corner of Stuyvesant and Lexington Avenues. From left to right: Charlie, Coconut Sid, Mother Sister, and Da Mayor. In addition to marking the location where the film was shot, the mural answers Buggin' Out's desire to have images of Black people represented in public space on a majority-Black block. This representation takes on new meaning as increased housing costs and racialized displacement render the population of Bedford-Stuyvesant increasingly white. Photograph by author, May 2022.

Right Thing extends Kelley's redirection from an attention to individual behavior to a focus on structural critique. An attention to the representation of climate change recasts the film as being focused not only on the level of personal decisions but also on how individual relationships are formed in response to neighborhood, city, and planetary dynamics transformed by the effects of anthropogenic climate change, and how those relationships enable or foreclose more and less equitable climate futures.

In this essay, I offer a reading of how *Do the Right Thing* intervenes in contemporaneous climate discourse through the lens of racial urban ecology, an approach that identifies the simultaneous relevance of racial ecology (the study of how racial logics subtend environmental systems) and urban ecology (the study of how human and non-human elements of cities interact with one another). I build on environmental readings of the film by scholars including Susan Scott Parrish and on the large volume of scholarship that engages with the film's portrayal of interpersonal racial violence.[21] I attend to how the film links racialized urban inequality to the uneven effects of global warming that the film's characters experience. Hot weather in the film not only makes climate change concrete, but also predicts change to come. It suggests that the climate futures that await the characters beyond the film's diegesis will be shaped by histories of racially inequitable housing policy. A decade before early conversations about the category of the Anthropocene, the film identifies climate change as a phenomenon that follows the contours of racialized infrastructures rather than creating universal impact, as was suggested by climate scientists at the time in projects like the IPCC's scenario models.[22] By locating a discussion of contemporaneous climate knowledge on the sidewalks and in the corner stores of Bed-Stuy, *Do the Right Thing* situates residents as experts on how racialized urban policy and planning have shaped, and will continue to shape, the effects of climate change. Tracing how the film's characters manage and comment upon extreme heat follows Etienne S. Benson's call "to remain open to moments when people are describing or encountering their surroundings in recognizably environmental terms even if they are not using the word *environment* itself."[23] The film suggests that local knowledge of environmental transformation is integral to how urban residents negotiate present experiences of climate change and the possibility of further change to come.

II. Climate Prediction in a Bed-Stuy Heat

In a 2010 oral history of *Do the Right Thing*, production designer Wynn Thomas explains that he singled out the block of Stuyvesant Avenue between Lexington Avenue and Quincy Street for its exaggerated heat exposure.[24] As Thomas notes, "I scouted every block in Bed-Stuy. From a conceptual point of view, I wanted one with very few trees because I didn't want any of the characters to have an escape from the heat." Lee likewise conceptualized the heat as central to the film's diegesis. Lee wrote the first draft of the film's script in March 1988, amid growing public conversation about the link between hot weather and anthropogenic climate change. Lee then built on the experience of filming during the hottest summer on record. The power that Lee had planned for the heat to command in the film was only intensified by how both weather and public discourse about climate change evolved from March 1988 when Lee wrote the film's script and June 1989 when the film was released. According to cinematographer Ernest Dickerson, the title of the film while Lee was writing the script was *Heat Wave*.[26] Lee wanted the film to communicate a visceral experience of heat. Dickerson reflected that as they were developing the film, Lee asked him "'How do you portray heat on film? How do you get the audience to really feel it?'"[27] In 2019, upon the film's 30th anniversary, Lee reflected that he said to his production team "I want people to be sweating in an air-conditioned theater when they see this film."[28] By selecting an exposed block in a formerly redlined neighborhood, the production crew of *Do the Right Thing* set up the film not only to bring the intense heat from the background to the foreground, but also to link urban and environmental inequality to the interpersonal racial tension that is the film's central focus.

The film's heat has been largely read as metaphorical. As Michael Eric Dyson argues in his review of the film, "The heat, both natural and social, is a central metaphor for the film's theme of tense race relations."[29] Eleni Palis notes that "Lee's diegetic world is heated like a pressure cooker, calculated to bring American racial tensions to their boiling point."[30] Dennis Sullivan and Fred Boehrer suggest that "the redder the sun gets, the more the truth of the lives of those who live in this small neighborhood unfolds."[31] But Lee's stated interest in heat, the film's reference to contemporary conversations about climate change, and the decision to locate the film on a block with an intensified

Figure 4. The "Corner Men." Film still from Spike Lee, Do the Right Thing, directed by Spike Lee, (New York: 40 Acres and a Mule Filmworks, 1989.)

relationship to heat exposure all suggest a link between racialized dispossession and environmental precarity that exceeds metaphor.

How the heat transcends metaphor is best illustrated by an exchange between three characters referred to as the "Corner Men." In the film, several groups of minor characters populate the block, intermittently interacting with one another and with Mookie as he delivers food from Sal's. These groups of minor characters include three middle-aged Black men that the script refers to as the "Corner Men," who for most of the film sit beside a beach umbrella against a brick wall painted bright red. The three men, ML, Coconut Sid, and Sweet Dick Willie, watch and comment on the activity on the street and on larger shifts in their neighborhood and in public life. In the March 1988 draft of the script, Lee portrays them as both unofficial philosophers and armchair policy experts. He writes, "These men become the great thinkers of the world with solutions to all its ills like drugs, the homeless and Aids [sic]."[32] He describes them elsewhere as "The Greek Chorus of Bed-Stuy."[33] [Figure 4]

While Lee portrays the Corner Men as reflective, attentive, and interested in linking the film's diegesis to its contemporaneous social and political context, the film's critical reception has been more likely to read the Corner Men as a synecdoche for the neighborhood's racialized disinvestment. Dyson, for instance, describes the Corner Men as a representation of "the often humorous folk philosophy of a generation of Black males who have witnessed the opening of socioeconomic opportunity for others, but who must cope with a more limited horizon for themselves."[34] And bell hooks, in her essay on the film, similarly denounces the men by suggesting that "The articulate black men in the movie, the wise elders, are all addicts (drunks)." She asserts that their "elaborate circular discourse, however entertaining and colorful . . . serves to signify again and again their powerlessness, their inability to assert agency."[35] Ed Guerrero describes the Corner Men's banter in terms more akin to Lee's as "brilliant, sardonic commentary on the neighbourhood scene and its multicultural politics," but he reads them as "unemployed and powerless," suggesting misleadingly that their economic condition limits the discursive power they have in the film.[36] Readings of the Corner Men that take their commentary as indicative only of their lack of access to power miss how many of the film's characters, including the Corner Men, trouble a normative conflation of economic and discursive power. The film debates this relationship even as Mookie, the lead character, is focused singularly on "getting paid." Readings of the Corner Men as powerless or without discursive agency particularly miss how they draw on their lived experience to reiterate, disagree about, and anticipate links between racialized dispossession and the uneven impacts of climate change.

In an early scene with the Corner Men, they are introduced by a wide-angle shot that centers them on a bright red brick wall, the color of which intensifies the visual effect of the heat. The three men sit under a too-small umbrella—none of them are entirely shaded by it. While his friends talk about Mike Tyson, ML continuously wipes sweat from his neck and chest with a white cloth. The camera cuts to a full shot of the three men in which they fill the frame. ML abruptly changes the subject, leaning forward while the other two lean back. Sweat shines on each of their faces. ML says, "Well gentlemen, the way I see it, if this hot weather continues, it's going to melt the polar caps and the whole wide world and all those parts that ain't water already will surely be flooded." While ML is speaking, Sweet Dick Willie starts laughing, which shakes his chest and comes out as a hiss through his teeth. Coconut Sid responds "You dumb-ass simple motherfucker. Now, where did you read that shit, eh? The polar caps, oh shhhh!" ML continues by explaining that he is going to prepare for the flooding by getting a boat. His friends tease him that he does not have the money for a boat. From their body language and their statements of disdain, they repeatedly express that they think the idea of the polar caps melting and ML preparing for sea level rise is ridiculous. The scene ends with an abrupt cut, which follows Sweet Dick Willie asking, "So when is all this goddamn ice suppose to melt?"[37] The Corner Men do not return to the topic of climate change, leaving unresolved whether Sweet Dick Willie's question suggests an interest in ML's pronouncement or a further opportunity to tease ML by asking him to make a prediction about climate futures, which Sweet Dick Willie intimates would be impossible for him.

In her reading of this scene, Susan Scott Parrish argues that "It is in the talk of the 'Corner Men' that *weather* turns into *climate*."[38] Parrish points to this scene to argue "that Lee is thinking about race in a time of climate change."[39] And yet, while weather may be an indication of climate for ML, his friends insist that it is just weather. Their location on a bare street corner in a formerly redlined neighborhood suggests too that weather manifests at the meeting of climate and city planning. As Parrish notes elsewhere in her reading of the film, climate change combines with the intensification of hot weather in cities such that the film operates as what she refers to as "an inquiry into the lived and racialized experience of what scholars now call the 'urban heat island effect.'"[40] In urban neighborhoods affected by what climate scientist William P. Lowry referred to in the 1960s to as the creation of urban "heat islands," ML's observations issue a corrective to the universalizing narratives espoused by contemporaneous climate science as he attends to climate change from a site of

elevated heat exposure.[41] This racialized experience is exacerbated in the context of Bed-Stuy by the history of redlining, which renders the urban heat island effect uneven along lines of previous racially predatory policy. Furthermore, both the HOLC maps and the climate change modeling of the late 1980s assume and determine who gets to participate in the futures they imagine. Against futures that can only be uncertain, the HOLC maps and climate models offer tools that chart a course for a particular future dependent upon the reification of racialized ideas about who gets to participate. ML intervenes in these practices of prediction. By linking the hot weather to sea level rise, he draws a connection between different effects of anthropogenic climate change and suggests that he will need a boat because his neighborhood will, at some undetermined point in the future, be underwater. In doing so, he suggests a link between the heat exposure he and the other Corner Men experience in the film and the way that they will come to experience future sea level rise.

ML's observation draws on his embodied knowledge of the hot day to participate in a rapidly shifting public conversation about climate change in the late 1980s. His musing about the melting of the "polar caps" in the context of a film about racial violence demonstrates Lee's engagement with a general connection between race and climate change and with the record heat of summer 1988 as it was felt with particular intensity in urban spaces. It further indicates Lee's attention to late 1980s public discourse about climate change that resulted from new scientific discoveries in the field.[42] In predicting the melting of the "polar caps," ML rehearses contemporaneous public discourse attributed to climate scientists and science educators.[43] Even so, ML's observation both reflects and diverges from contemporary discourse in climate science. Where predictions by a largely white cis-male group of climate scientists address the risk to humans as an undifferentiated mass, the Corner Men's setting suggests that the warming that was largely impending in the late 1980s would fall along the lines of earlier racialized policy and development. As he intervenes in public climate discourse, ML's observations are not like those of Steven Erlanger's interviewee Gayanne La Roe who says that "we've heard about" manifestations of climate change. They are rather, as ML puts it, "the way I see it." Coconut Sid asks him where he read about ice cap melting and sea level rise, but ML does not suggest that he

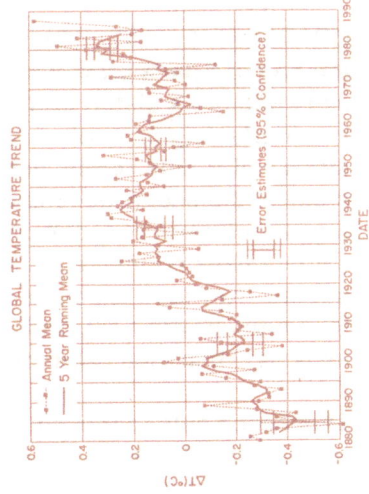

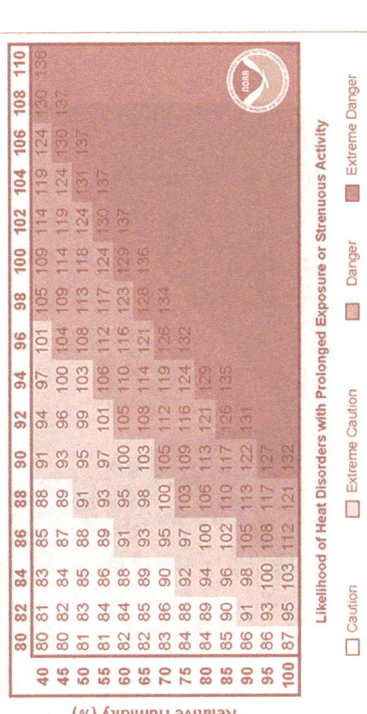

learned about climate change from anyone else. All we learn from ML is that the link between the hot weather, the melting of the polar caps, and the anticipated transformation of his daily life is based on his own perceptions. Where La Roe receives climate knowledge, ML creates it. ML's observations of climate change are one aspect of the Corner Men's status in Lee's framing as "the great thinkers of the world with solutions to all its ills." Lee portrays ML as a producer of climate knowledge, in which ML's prediction suggests the possibility of an alternate historiography of climate change as an always already racialized concept that is theorized from an authority located not only in the modeling lab but also on the corner.

In a later scene, Lee additionally situates the film's diegesis in contemporary conversations about climate change through the inclusion of a series of headlines. In the March 1988 draft of the script, Lee writes these directions, "Right now FOLKS we're gonna suspend the narrative and show how peoples are coping with the OPPRESSIVE HEAT."[44] This scene opens after a cut from a previous scene in which Jade (Mookie's sister) and Mother Sister, an elderly neighbor, sit on Mother Sister's steps while Jade combs her hair. At the close of the scene, Jade and Mother Sister crane their necks to look up at the sun. The camera fixes on their gaze as they both squint. They look exhausted. Mother Sister fans herself with a rag and Jade sighs and exhales. Their faces shimmer with sweat.

This scene cuts to the camera zooming in past a rack of snack foods in the block's corner store (which is owned by a Korean American couple, Sonny and Kim, and is the site of several later pivotal scenes). When the first newspaper comes into focus, the camera pans across five different front pages. In the March 1988 script, their lead headlines read:

New York Post: "A Scorcher"

New York Daily News: "2 Hot 4 U?"

New York Newsday: "Oh Boy! Baked Apple"

New York Times: "Record Heatwave Hits City"[45]

In the film, the headlines appear as follows:

The New York Times: "Yes, It's Hotter, It's Muggier, And, Yes, You're Going Crazy." [Figure 5]

New York Daily News: "Helter Swelter—and Power Fails"

New York Newsday: "Baked Apple—98° Sets a Record. No Relief in Sight for Today"

El Diario: "¡Que Calor!"

New York Post: "Phew! Hazy, Hot, Humid and Headed Toward 100°"

In his initial draft of the script, Lee had imagined four English-language headlines that remarked upon the heat. Three simply stated that the weather was hot, and a fourth indicated that the heat was both prolonged and unprecedented.

Figure 5. Lead headline of *The New York Times* in the corner store. While Lee reuses the headline from Steven Erlanger's August 8th, 1988 article, he transposes the headline from the bottom of the front page to the lead headline at the top of the front page. Film still from Spike Lee, *Do the Right Thing*, directed by Spike Lee (New York: 40 Acres and a Mule Filmworks, 1989.)

In the five headlines that appear in the film, four are written in English and one in Spanish, marking the demographics of the corner store's customer base as both Anglophone and bilingual Hispanophone, as is reinforced by a recurring group of minor characters who are Puerto Rican and are speakers of both English and Spanish. The four English language headlines that appear in the film differ from those that Lee had originally written. Three reference an effect of the heat. *The New York Post* headline draws a link between the heat and infrastructural collapse. *The New York Newsday* headline addresses the duration of the heat. *The New York Times* headline suggests that the heat produces a mass psychological effect. Additionally, *The New York Times* headline that appears in the film repeats the actual headline of an article by journalist Steven Erlanger from August 9th, 1988, the summer that *Do the Right Thing* was filmed. That article, as I described at length in the opening paragraphs of this essay, links the summer 1988 heat in the city not only to public mental health concerns but also to recent reporting about climate change. The inclusion of the summer 1988 headline alongside ML's rehearsal of the findings of climate science in the late 1980s demonstrate Lee's engagement with contemporaneous conversations about climate change, and their intensification during the summer that the film was shot. At a moment in the late 1980s in which environmental justice scholarship and activism were largely focused on toxicity, land rights, oil spills, and the threat of nuclear meltdown, the film insists on anthropogenic climate change as a concern that is both relevant to the neighborhood's residents and especially important to conversations about racial justice.[46]

The film's focus on how the effects of climate change are racialized anticipates recent discussions in both activism and scholarship. For instance, planning historian Bev Wilson argues in a 2020 article that "Extreme heat is more than a public health issue; it is a question of environmental justice."[47] The 2021 "Summer in the City" NRDC report similarly argues that "Extreme heat vulnerability in New York City is, quite simply, an environmental injustice."[48] The film also anticipates the future intensification of heat in New York City. As the NRDC report cautions, "Climate models predict that even under the best emissions scenarios, by 2050 New York City could experience between four and seven heat waves each year, compared with an average of two annual heat waves between 1971 and 2000."[49]

While the film's neighborhood residents experience extreme heat compared to residents of other parts of the city, present and future viewers of the film live in a built environment whose hottest days are even warmer than the film's setting on the hottest day of the year in 1989.

III. Heat Islands' Racial and Urban Ecologies

Do the Right Thing's engagement with climate change suggests the utility of the approach I have been using to read the film, which I described in the introduction as a focus on racial urban ecology. In the introduction to their 2018 anthology, *Racial Ecologies*, Leilani Nishime and Kim D. Hester Williams advocate for an analysis of environmental systems that is attentive to how they are always already racialized. Reading for how the environment is racialized requires intervening in environmentalist discourses that separate themselves from conversations about environmental justice. As Nishime and Hester Williams argue, "Environmentalism is often understood as universal and postracial, whereas environmental justice is seen as primarily, if not, exclusively, concerned with racial equity. By contrast, we argue that race is inextricable from our understandings of ecology, and vice versa."[50] They go on to argue that an attention to how environmental systems are mediated by racialization expands the places we think of as ecological. They note that "This perspective allows for a broad definition of *ecology*, one that includes urban environments and agricultural systems. We consider nature and environment as relational sites for navigating both embodied racial identities and ecological space and place."[51] Nishime and Hester Williams suggest that an attention to how racial identities are formed requires focusing on where identity formation occurs, and that an attention to place always suggests a relationship to ecology. Conversely, a racial ecologies approach to how humans relate to the non-human world reveals that racialization mediates how humans form relationships in and with non-human contexts. Nishime and Hester Williams note the relevance of a focus on racial ecologies to a study of ecological life in urban spaces, which is helpful for reframing work in urban ecologies that does not directly engage with race.

The term "urban ecology" originated in the early 20th century. It was "coined by sociologists who sought to use ecological theory to describe human behavior in the urban setting."[52] While the term originally used the motif of ecology to describe human

behavior, many scholars in the natural and social sciences now use the term to focus on the non-human life of cities. As Jianguo Wu argues "urban ecology may be defined as the study of spatiotemporal patterns, environmental impacts, and sustainability of urbanization with emphasis on biodiversity, ecosystem processes, and ecosystem services."[53] Wu emphasizes that urban ecology scholarship brings together approaches in the social and natural sciences. This type of urban ecology approach shares with Nishime and Hester Williams's approach to racial ecologies an emphasis on the political and social systems that press upon ecological life. Building on these two approaches, an attention to racial urban ecology emphasizes how race and ecological context inform one another in cities. The co-articulation of racialization and urbanization are further emphasized by the effects of climate change and the differential impact it generates in urban areas racialized as Black by a history of redlining.

Do the Right Thing stages connections between acts of racial violence like the police killing of Radio Raheem and slower racialized violences like urban heat island effect as it is intensified by legacies of anti-Black urban policy. To make this argument is to read the film at a scale beyond the interpersonal. It is not to ignore or contradict other readings of the film that point to its flat characters or its limited and tokenizing representation of Black women, and which argue that the film uses stock characters and unnuanced representations of racial identity and cross-racial relationships.[54] Reading *Do the Right Thing* with an attention to racial urban ecology identifies how the film is helpful for thinking about intensified experiences of climate change in redlined neighborhoods. Such a reading remains critical of aspects of its racial politics that flatten complexity while also addressing how the film sets a useful precedent for depictions of racialized experiences of hot weather that are intensified at the intersection of redlining and climate change.

IV. Representing Hot Futures

The depiction of extreme heat in *Do the Right Thing* draws attention to a representational problem with heat events, which can be disproportionately lethal[55] but which often fall outside of the expectations of visual catastrophe associated with environmental disaster. Writing about the 1995 Chicago Heat Wave, sociologist Eric Klinenberg argues that "Something about the event had rendered it unintelligible or inexplicable; people in the city were apparently having trouble engaging it; the human side of the disaster was elusive, beyond words."[56] The challenge posed by heat waves is directly related to the difficulties of linking anomalous events to their structural underpinnings. Reflecting on the representational problems of the gradual and accumulative forms of environmental harm that he refers to as "slow violence," Rob Nixon asks, "how can we convert into image and narrative the disasters that are slow moving and long in the making, disasters that are anonymous and that star nobody, disasters that are attritional and of indifferent interest to the sensation-driven technologies of our image-world?"[57] Following Nixon, heat waves are difficult to represent both because they are more gradual than other environmental events and because they are linked to long histories of anthropogenic climate change.

Klinenberg suggests that it is not only the slow movement of heat but also the disproportionate precarity of marginalized residents affected by heat waves that contribute to the challenge of representing the harms and catalysts of heat-related deaths. As Klinenberg posits:

> Heat waves receive little public attention not only because they fail to generate the massive property damage and fantastic images produced by other weather-related disasters, but also because their victims are primarily social outcasts—the elderly, the poor, and the isolated-from whom we customarily turn away.[58]

Do the Right Thing presents an exception—a model of representing heat waves that provides a precedent for how to engage public conversations about heat, and which includes a focus on elderly and poor residents, and an emphasis on the relationship between racialized interpersonal, environmental, and infrastructural violence. In its representation of a heat wave, *Do the Right Thing* depicts characters' lived experiences of dangerous heat exposure as necessary to a public understanding of how hot weather is linked to climate, urban policy, and race. The affordance of film as a medium allows Lee to sustain a visual engagement with the heat over the duration of the film, drawing the viewer's attention again and again to both the presence of the heat and its effects on the block's residents, exactly the impacts that Klinenberg argues are overlooked in most public engagements with heat-related risk and harm.

Focusing on the film's portrayal of heat also helps explain the link that the heat draws in the film between interpersonal and environmental violence. As Lee reflected in 2010, "For this film, I also wanted to do something that took place on the hottest day of the summer. I'd never read any study or anything, but I knew things just got crazy in New York once it hit 95 degrees." While Lee acknowledges that he had not encountered research that corroborated his perceived link, recent studies have measured how an increase in temperature correlates to elevated levels of interpersonal violence. A 2021 article in the medical journal *The Lancet Planetary Health* argues not only that high temperatures raise the likelihood of interpersonal violence, but also that climate change will intensify this increase.[60]

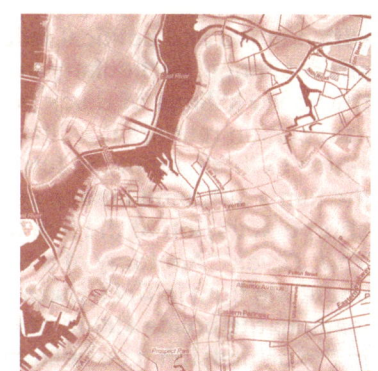

The article identifies two theories that explain why there is a connection between elevated temperature and interpersonal violence. The first is "temperature-aggression theory," which "explains that hot weather induces interpersonal violence by increasing discomfort, frustration, impulsivity, and aggression."[61] In a neighborhood in which few people have access to public or private cooling, and where temperatures are further elevated by heat island effect that is itself exaggerated by the legacy of redlining, it would follow that heat-related aggression would be exacerbated. The other explanation is "routine activity theory, which suggests that change in ambient temperature can alter people's routine activities (eg, outdoor events and social contacts) and increase interpersonal conflicts or create suitable crime environments."[62] The film portrays heat-related aggression at the intersection of these theories.

The film's interest in the relationship between race, climate, urban space, and the relationship between structural and interpersonal violence is reiterated in its final scene, which takes place the morning after the police killing of Radio Raheem and the destruction of Sal's. The film's final shots follow Mookie across the street as he pockets five hundred-dollar bills that Sal has just crumpled into balls and thrown at him as his last payment for delivering pizzas. The final minute of the film is narrated by the DJ of the block's radio station, Mister Señor Love Daddy. Love Daddy's radio station is in the middle of the block. Throughout the film he has narrated what he has seen taking place on the street and has provided information including news and weather updates that connect the block to the rest of the city.

In the film's final scene, Love Daddy addresses Mookie directly, saying "go on home to your kid" as Mookie crosses the street away from the burnt remains of Sal's. Love Daddy then introduces several news and weather updates. His news update is that mayor Ed Koch has commissioned "a blue-ribbon panel," quoting Koch as saying the purpose of which is "'to get to the bottom of last night's disturbance. The City of New York will not let property be destroyed by anyone.'" Love Daddy also reports that Koch plans to "visit our block today." While Love Daddy does not comment on Koch's emphasis on the destruction of property rather than on the loss of life, at the end of his announcements, he dedicates the next record to Radio Raheem, addressing him directly, "we love you, brother," to refute Koch's focus on the destruction of property instead of on the killing of Radio Raheem.[63]

As Mookie crosses the street, the shot takes a high angle above the neighborhood, such that both sides of the street are visible in the frame. Love Daddy reminds residents to register to vote, stating that "the election is coming up," referencing the September 1989 Democratic mayoral primary in which Koch would be defeated in his pursuit for a fourth term by David Dinkins, who would become the city's first Black mayor.[64] Finally, he offers a weather update: "there's no end in sight for this heat wave, so today the cash money word is 'chill.'" Love Daddy's announcement makes clear that while the previous day's degree of interpersonal violence may have been anomalous, the weather that catalyzed it is not. While the film is set on the hottest day of the summer, Love Daddy's weather report suggests that the following day might be even hotter, reminding us that climate change continuously ruptures weather superlatives. Additionally, like ML, Love Daddy is an expert. He is not a meteorologist, and yet, he is the person sharing climate knowledge by providing the weather update as well as strategies for how to cope with it. As Love Daddy provides these three updates—about Koch's visit, about voter registration, and about the continuation of the heat wave, Mookie walks out of the frame. Four young men throw a basketball to one another in the middle of the street, which is scattered with debris from the previous night's uprising. Their pickup basketball game in the early morning haze of what promises to be another nearly 100° day is the film's final shot of the block.

In the decades since it was released, *Do the Right Thing* has come to be associated with cultural and political failures to affect change, particularly in relation to the police killings of Black people. This association renders it a difficult text with which to think about the future. In 2019, for the film's 30th anniversary, Lee recorded a short discussion of the film for *The New York Times*' "Anatomy of a Scene" series about the fight in Sal's pizza shop that leads to the police killing of Radio Raheem. In the discussion, Lee links the death of Raheem to the 2014 police killing of Eric Garner. As Lee explains "a lot of things in this film, that even though it was written 31 years ago, are still happening today. Black and brown people are still being murdered today by police forces across the United States of America."[65] Lee's recent emphasis on parallels between the film and the present depart from his earlier emphasis on how much had changed since the film was released. In a short film made to celebrate its 20th anniversary in 2009, Lee explained that he thought that the film was an accurate portrayal of New York City in the late 1980s but that "today it's a totally different New York City."[66] In the summer of 2020, Lee revisited *Do the Right Thing* again, releasing a short film entitled "3 Brothers," which cuts between footage of the police killings of George Floyd, Eric Garner, and Radio Raheem, building upon a short film Lee made in 2014 splicing together the police killings of Garner and Raheem.[67]

In addition to the film's unheeded warnings about racial violence, ML's climate predictions likewise represent a public failure to act on the evidence of escalating harm. ML suggests that the melting of the polar ice caps will cause sea level rise such that "all those parts that ain't water already will surely be flooded."

The film offers an early example of a cultural text that models how to live with climate change and how to adapt daily life to its effects. In 2022, New York City is in the process of constructing the city's first large-scale climate resiliency project on the Lower East Side of Manhattan that has been widely protested as being likely to cause more harm than it will prevent.[68] The project is intended to increase the capacity of the neighborhood to manage storm surge and flooding from future hurricanes.[69] The film's climate predictions and its attention to the use of lethal force by police officers demonstrate two different but related kinds of harm that have only intensified in the 33 years since the film's release. How characters experience heat in *Do the Right Thing* reflects the legacy of anti-Black housing policy and sketches the contours of how climate change appears in the present and the shape it might take in the future. The film's engagement with redlined climate futures emphasizes why and how we might read environmental harm as always in relation to the racialized planning and policy history of the places and communities it unevenly effects.

> * Acknowledgments *
> I wish to thank the students in my Spring 2021 course "Gender, Sex, and Urban Life" at the University of Pennsylvania and the students in my Spring 2022 course "Race, Gender, and the Urban Environment" at Princeton University who read excerpts from Klinenberg's *Heat Wave* in conversation with *Do the Right Thing* and had generative discussions about race, planning, and climate change that informed my thinking in this essay. I also wish to thank Melissa E. Sanchez for her enthusiasm about an environmental reading of the film, and Ben Stanley and Matthew Wagstaffe for their feedback on earlier drafts of this essay.

SCENARIO A

Days Per Year With Temperature Exceeding 90°F

New York

Climatology	1990's	2000's	2010's	2020's	2030's
14	18	18	22	27	33

1. Steven Erlanger, "Yes, It's Hotter, It's Muggier, And, Yes, You're Going Crazy," *The New York Times* (New York, NY), Aug. 9, 1988.
2. Ibid. In a 1985 letter in the journal *Nature*, climate scientists Joe Farman, Brian Gardiner, and Jonathan Shanklin reported large losses of ozone over Antarctica, diverging from earlier estimates that suggested only small impacts caused by human activity in the coming decade. The authors write, "the annual variation of total O3 at Halley Bay has undergone a dramatic change." J.C. Farman, B. G. Gardiner, and J. D. Shanklin, "Large Losses of Total Ozone in Antarctica Reveal Seasonal ClOx / NOx Interaction," *Nature* 315 (16 May 1985): 207, accessed May 4, 2022.
3. "Statement of Dr. James Hansen, Director, NASA Goddard Institute for Space Studies," United States Senate Committee on Energy and Natural Resources, *Greenhouse Effect and Global Climate Change*, (Part 2), Washington, DC: June 23, 1988, 39–41.
4. Hansen et. al., "Prediction of Near-Term Climate Evolution: What Can We Tell Decision-Makers Now?" Climate Institute, *Preparing for Climate Change: Proceedings of the First North American Conference on Preparing for Climate Change: A Cooperative Approach*, Washington, DC: October 27–29, 1987, 43.
5. Robert L. Peters and Joan D. S. Darling, "The Greenhouse Effect and Nature Reserves," *BioScience* 35, no. 11 (1985): 707, accessed June 27, 2022, https://www.jstor.org/stable/1310052.
6. Ibid.
7. Hansen, "Statement of Dr. James Hansen, Director, NASA Goddard Institute for Space Studies," 39.
8. Ibid., 40.
9. "1988 Was Hottest Year on Record as Global Warming Trend Continues," *Los Angeles Times* (Los Angeles, CA), reprinted from the *Washington Post* (Washington, DC), Feb. 4, 1989.
10. Bev Wilson, "Urban Heat Management and the Legacy of Redlining," *Journal of American Planning Association* 86, no. 4 (2020): 445, accessed April 24, 2022.. https://doi.org/10.1080/01944363.2020.1759127.
11. Etienne S. Benson, *Surroundings: A History of Environments and Environmentalisms* (Chicago, IL: University of Chicago Press, 2020), 174–5.
12. Spike Lee, *Do the Right Thing*, directed by Spike Lee (1989, New York: 40 Acres and a Mule Filmworks), video, 2:00:17, https://www.youtube.com/watch?v=KVQHkq3Tk7E.
13. Dorceta Taylor, *Toxic Communities: Environmental Racism, Industrial Pollution, and Residential Mobility* (New York: NYU Press, 2014), 236–240.
14. Ibid., 236; See 1938 HOLC map of Brooklyn in Emily Badger, "How Redlining's Racist Effects Lasted for Decades," *The New York Times* (New York, NY), Aug. 24, 2017.
15. Wilson, "Urban Heat Management," 446, citing Jeremy S. Hoffman, Vivek Shandas, and Nicholas Pendleton, "The Effects of Historical Housing Policies on Resident Exposure to Intra-Urban Heat: A Study of 108 US Urban Areas," *Climate* 8, no. 1. (2020): 1, accessed July 6, 2022, https://doi.org/10.3390/cli8010012.
16. Juan Declet-Barreto, Cynthia Herrera, Al Huang, Cecil Corbin-Mark, "Summer in the City: Improving Community Resilience to Extreme Summertime Heat in Northern Manhattan" *Natural Resources Defense Council*, 2021, https://www.nrdc.org/sites/default/files/community-resilience-summertime-heat-nomanhattan-report.pdf, 5.
17. See Lee's 2020 short film "3 Brothers," and coverage of the film's release in May 2020 including Christi Carras, "Spike Lee Sees the Parallels between George Floyd and 'Do the Right Thing,'" *Los Angeles Times* (Los Angeles, CA), June 1, 2020.
18. Mekado Murphy, "Spike Lee Explains How 'Do the Right Thing' Has Remained Relevant," Anatomy of a Scene. *The New York Times* (New York, NY), Aug. 16, 2019, video, 5:42, *The New York Times*. YouTube. Aug. 16, 2019.
19. In a June 2020 opinion piece in *The New York Times* entitled "What Kind of Society Values Property Over Black Lives," Black intellectual historian Robin D. G. Kelley critiques an overemphasis on property damage related to protests in response to the May 2020 police killing of George Floyd in language that mirrors that of debates about *Do the Right Thing* when it was released in 1989. Kelley argues that "obsessing over looting" is unproductive because "it deflects from the core problem that brought people to the streets: The police keep killing us with impunity." He quotes Opal Tometi, a co-founder of Black Lives Matter, who says "'I just don't equate the loss of life and the loss of property. I can't even hold those two in the same regard, and I think for far too long we have seen that happen.'" Robin D. G. Kelley, "What Kind of Society Values Property Over Black Lives?," *The New York Times* (New York, NY), June 18, 2020.
20. Ibid.
21. See Parrish's essay "Climate and Race" in *Climate and American Literature*, ed. Michael Boyden (Cambridge, UK: Cambridge University Press, 2021), 75–90.
22. On the genesis of the term "Anthropocene" see Ian Baucom and Matthew Omelsky's discussion of the concept's history. As they note, the atmospheric chemists Paul Crutzen and Eugene Stoermer introduced the term in 2000 to explain "some of the ways mankind has become a 'geological force.'" Ian Baucom and Matthew Omelsky, "Knowledge in the Age of Climate Change," *The South Atlantic Quarterly* 116, no. 1 (January 2017): 1–18, accessed November 19, 2020, doi 10.1215/00382876-3749271, citing Paul Crutzen, and Eugene Stoermer, "The 'Anthropocene,'" *Global Change Newsletter* 41 (May 2000): 18, accessed July 6, 2022.
23. Benson, *Surroundings*, 10, emphasis in original.
24. The film has become part of the identity of the block on which it was film, as the block of Stuyvesant Avenue between Lexington Avenue and Quincy Street was subsequently renamed "Do the Right Thing Way." Lee suggested in a 2019 reflection on the film that it is "the only street in the history of New York City named after a movie" Murphy, "Spike Lee Explains," *The New York Times*.
25. Spike Lee and Jason Matloff, *Spike Lee: Do the Right Thing.*, ed. Steve Crist. (Los Angeles: Ammo Books, 2010), 16.
26. Ibid., 9.
27. Ibid.
28. Murphy, "Spike Lee Explains," *The New York Times*.
29. Michael Eric Dyson, "Film Noir," *Tikkun* 4, no. 5 (1989), 75, accessed April 6, 2022.
30. Eleni Palis, "The Economics and Politics of Auteurism: Spike Lee and *Do the Right Thing*," *Cinema Journal* 57, no. 2 (2018): 16, accessed March 16, 2022. https://muse.jhu.edu/article/687827.
31. Dennis Sullivan and Fred Boehrer, "Spike Lee's *Do the Right Thing*: Filmmaking in the American Grain," *Contemporary Justice Review* 6, no. 2 (2003): 144, accessed March 21, 2022.
32. Lee and Matloff, *Spike Lee: Do the Right Thing*, 22. The page numbers on the script reflect the numbers handwritten onto the script's handwritten pages, rather than the paginated numbers used in the rest of the book. The handwritten script as it is reprinted in the book does not include paginated numbers.
33. Lee and Matloff, *Spike Lee: Do the Right Thing*, 63. This numbering reflects the paginated numbers, rather than the handwritten numbers.
34. Dyson, "Film Noir," 76.
35. bell hooks, *Yearning: Race, Gender, and Cultural Politics* (Boston: South End Press, 1990), 179.
36. Ed Guerrero, *Do the Right Thing* (London: British Film Institute Modern Classics, 2001), 35.
37. Lee, *Do the Right Thing*, 1989. Like Susan Scott Parrish, I quote dialogue from the final cut of the film. See Parrish, Climate and Race, 76, note 3. Quotations from the March 1988 script are from the version of the script reprinted in Lee and Matloff, *Spike Lee: Do the Right Thing*.
38. Parrish, "Climate and Race," 76, emphasis in original.
39. Ibid.
40. Ibid., 75.
41. William P. Lowry, "The Climate of Cities," *Scientific American*. 217, no. 2 (August 1967): 19, accessed March 28, 2022. DOI:10.1038/SCIENTIFICAMERICAN0867-15
42. "Depletion of Ozone May Worsen Smog in Cities" *Los Angeles Times* (Los Angeles, CA), reprinted in *Hartford Courant* (Hartford, CT), Feb. 7, 1988.
43. In a May 1987 *New York Times* article, Richard Golden, the coordinator of the Climate Protection Network cautioned that "Long before the increase in temperature melts the ice caps and raises the sea level to flood our coastal regions and fertile wetlands, storms and shifting ocean currents would drastically change the lives of the millions who live near or depend on the oceans." Richard Golden, "Where There's a World, There's a Way," *The New York Times* (New York, NY), May 10, 1987.
44. Lee and Matloff, *Spike Lee: Do the Right Thing*, 38, emphasis in original.
45. Ibid.
46. On the history of environmental justice activism in the United States in the 1980s and 1990s see Julie Sze, *Environmental Justice in a Moment of Danger* (Berkeley: University of California Press, 2020), 9–10 and 30.
47. Wilson, "Urban Heat Management," 451.
48. Declet-Barreto et. al., "Summer in the City," 14.
49. Ibid., 5.
50. Leilani Nishime and Kim D. Hester Williams, "Introduction: Why Racial Ecologies?," in *Racial Ecologies*, ed. Leilani Nishime and Kim D. Hester Williams (Seattle: University of Washington Press, 2018), 3–4.
51. Ibid., 4, emphasis in original.
52. James P. Collins, Ann Kinzig, Nancy B. Grimm, William F. Fagan, Diane Hope, Jianguo Wu and Elizabeth T. Borer, "A New Urban Ecology: Modeling Human Communities as Integral Parts of Ecosystems Poses Special Problems for the Development and Testing of Ecological Theory," *American Scientist* 88, no. 5 (2000): 416, accessed April 22, 2022, https://www.jstor.org/stable/27858089.
53. Jianguo Wu, "Urban Ecology and Sustainability: The State-of-the-Science and Future Directions," *Landscape and Urban Planning* 125 (2014): 213, accessed April 15, 2022, DOI:10.1016/j.landurbplan.2014.01.018.
54. See Wahneema Lubiano's article on what she terms the "Spike Lee Discourse." Wahneema Lubiano, "But Compared to What?: Reading Realism, Representation, and Essentialism in *School Daze, Do the Right Thing*, and the Spike Lee Discourse," *Black American Literature* Forum 25, no. 2 (Summer 1991): 253-282, accessed March 20, 2022, https://doi.org/10.2307/3041686.
55. As she addresses the exceptional degree of harm caused by heat waves Bev Wilson notes that "heat accounted for almost as many deaths as flooding and hurricanes combined and was the single largest cause of weather-related fatalities between 1986 and 2017." Wilson, "Urban Heat Management," 443.
56. Eric Klinenberg, *Heat Wave: A Social Autopsy of Disaster*, Second Edition (Chicago: University of Chicago Press, 2015), 13.
57. Rob Nixon, *Slow Violence and the Environmentalism of the Poor* (Cambridge, MA: Harvard University Press, 2011), 3.
58. Klinenberg, *Heat Wave*, 17.
59. Lee and Matloff, *Spike Lee: Do the Right Thing*, 9.
60. Rahini Mahendran, Rongbin Xu, Shanshan Li, Yuming Guo, "Interpersonal Violence Associated with Hot Weather," *The Lancet Planetary Health* 5 (September 2021): e571-e572, accessed May 6, 2022. https://doi.org/10.1016/S2542-5196(21)00210-2.
61. Ibid., e571.
62. Ibid.
63. Lee, *Do the Right Thing*, 1989.
64. Steve Daley, "Koch Loses N.Y. Primary to Dinkins," *Chicago Tribune* (Chicago, IL), Sept. 13, 1989.
65. "Spike Lee Explains," *The New York Times*.
66. Spike Lee, *Do the Right Thing – 20 Years Later*, directed by Spike Lee (2009, Universal City, CA: Universal Studios Home Entertainment, 2009), video, 35:41, https://www.youtube.com/watch?v=I6kVN1coXDw.
67. Carras, "Spike Lee Sees the Parallels," *Los Angeles Times*.
68. "The East Side Coastal Resiliency Project," NYC.gov, The City of New York, https://www1.nyc.gov/site/escr/index.page. Accessed May 6, 2022.
69. Two of the organizations that have been leading advocacy against the ESCR plan include 1,000 People, 1,000 Trees (https://www.instagram.com/1000people1000trees/?hl=en) and East River Park Action (https://eastriverparkaction.org/.) Both organizations emphasize that they do not oppose climate resiliency planning, but rather the cutting down of nearly 1,000 trees and the elimination of neighborhood access to the park.

Resilient Futures — Orit Halpern

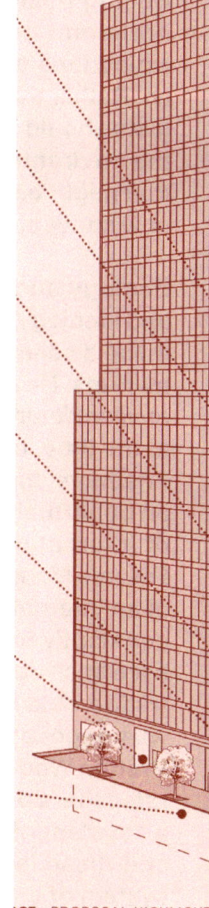

Today, we appear to be in an era beset by catastrophic events: pandemics, anti-democratic insurrections, wars, climate change. If there is a unique feature, however, to this barrage of catastrophic events, it is their seeming banality and ubiquity. These ongoing events appear to evade historical demarcation as events either revolutionary or catastrophic. Replacing such historical demarcations, terms such as the "new normal" and even "next normal"[1] circulate ad nauseum throughout news outlets and social networks. In turn, policy makers, psychologists, ecologists, and business strategists now emphasize the need for all systems, institutions, and even human subjects, to be resilient: capable of enduring *and even profiting* from change and crisis.

For example, at the latest Davos conference held in May 2022, the World Economic Forum announced that resilience would become one of the central concepts organizing global response to the war in the Ukraine, climate change and the aftereffects of the COVID pandemic. The Forum identified a series of central challenges or "frontier risks" that accompanied these events. Rapid technological change, climate disturbances, economic volatility/disparity and balkanization rose to the top. These risks, if not managed correctly or capitalized upon, pose dangers to globalization and plural democracy. In response to these threats, institutions must become "resilient." The President of International Markets at Dell Technologies, Aongus Hegarty, articulated the need for a concept of "digital resilience" at the 2022 Davos conference. This need for digital resilience emerges from the unprecedented acceleration of "innovation" in the sector in the face of the COVID 19 pandemic. If achieved, resilience "positions an enterprise to pivot fast, adapt to fluid conditions, maintain seamless business continuity and capitalize on opportunities."[2] Such agility and fluidity will be accomplished, he argued, through centering on cybersecurity accompanied with ubiquitous computing (we may also presume that this is a central concern for this corporation).

While resilience might commonly be considered a psychological or environmental attribute, the Forum highlights the new centrality of this term for organizing political economy. As discourses of resilience imply, the idea that we now live in a world of both constant technical innovation and regular trauma has become naturalized .

What is fundamentally at stake in this discussion is the way in which we understand social, natural and technical change. The very idea of the normal curve was an invention of the 19th century human sciences underpinning contemporary understandings of nature, economies, populations and "race." The order of nature would be replicated with the orders of society. But the normal was also embedded in concepts of evolution. How did systems change? And when did events happen? Were extinction events norms, or regularly occurring events? If the notion of revolution was the central organizing concept for change, whether in a capitalism modeled on reductive ideas of evolutionary fitness or in a Marxism of dialectical contests, then the concept of systems that are constantly evolving but never revolutionary appears novel. If "Nature" is no longer untouched by technology, then we might ask what new concepts of history, governance and technology are emerging? In this essay, I will endeavor to historically situate this "new" nature and "new normal" within its relationship to managing risk and futurity.

Resilience

In 1973, the ecologist C.S. Holling introduced a new concept to the discourse on nature, evolution, and extinction:

> "INDIVIDUALS DIE, POPULATIONS DISAPPEAR, and species become extinct. That is one view of the world. But another view of the world concentrates not so much on presence or absence as upon the numbers of organisms and the degree of constancy of their numbers. These are two very different ways of viewing the behavior of systems and the usefulness of the view depends very much on the properties of the system concerned."[3]

Holling posits a world where change, even in catastrophic forms, is the norm and heralds not the end of systems but their evolution. Though extinctions periodically occur, systems, "degrees" and evolution continue on. Rather than focusing on the event of extinction, Holling argued that ecologists should instead think about the relationships in a system. Consequently, the environment itself had to become a system, one that had "properties" that might be maintained irrespective of the life or death of individuals. This new concept of resilience thus posited a new idea of both change and event.

Ecology and economy have of course long been linked in both etiology and ideology. In 1971, Chicago School neoliberal economist Milton Friedman made a seemingly similar pronouncement, this time in relation to currency markets. He announced a "major need for a broad, widely based, active and *resilient* futures market."[4] Counter to standard understandings of the economy at the time, he projected a positive valence for active, volatile markets. For Friedman, the collapse of the Bretton Woods system was not a calamity, but an opportunity for creating a new, and what he labeled as "resilient," system of international currency exchange. In an article entitled "The Need for Futures Markets in Currencies," Friedman acknowledged that in the absence of an international system of currency controls, exchange rates would shift constantly in relation to one another. The architects of Bretton Woods had seen such volatility as a problem, since it meant that those engaged in foreign trade would have to take significant risks that the currency in which a trade was negotiated would depreciate by the time payments were to be made. Bretton Woods thus sought to institute a "system of rigidly fixed [exchange] rates that do not change." However, as Friedman noted, they ended up with a "system of rigidly fixed rates subject to large jumps from time to time," and these large jumps eventually broke what was designed to be a rigid system of control.[5] Friedman argued that the solution could not be another centrally-controlled system, but should instead be a resilient futures market for currencies: a system that would allow those engaged in foreign trade to hedge the risks associated with currency exchange changes.

For Friedman, "resilience" was to be understood as the opposite of "rigidity," and would mean, in practice, something like the oxymoronic notion of "stable change." More specifically, currency markets would change in response to global events but nevertheless continue to protect international trade, the international global political order of the West and the primacy of the United States within that order.

These new ideas of nature thereby came from a context where older models of political-economy were also in flux. The end of Bretton Woods, decolonization, post-Fordism and the OPEC oil crisis, to name a few of the transformations at the time, induced extreme volatility in politics, currency and commodity markets. New financial technologies and institutions, such as derivative pricing equations and hedge funds, emerged in order to "hedge" bets. These technologies literally produced ways to short bets and insure that risks were reallocated, decentralized and networked. Dangerous bets would be combined with safer ones and dispersed across multiple territories and temporalities (consider short bets, credit swaps, and futures markets). Corporations, governments, and financiers flocked to these techniques of uncertainty management in the face of unnamable and unquantifiable risks.[6] Epistemologically, ecology and finance would come to share a model of a world of ceaseless volatility and uncertainty.

"Ecos"

Volatility and uncertainty were not always considered the norms of nature.

Since the Second World War, cybernetically informed ecologists had built models that understood the world in terms of homeostatically organized networked systems. Initial models were grounded in communication sciences and tested on the landscape of nuclear blast sites, valorizing stability. Ecosystems were supposedly made of feedback loops that aspired to balance, much like the early models of a homeostat coming from the sciences of communication and control.

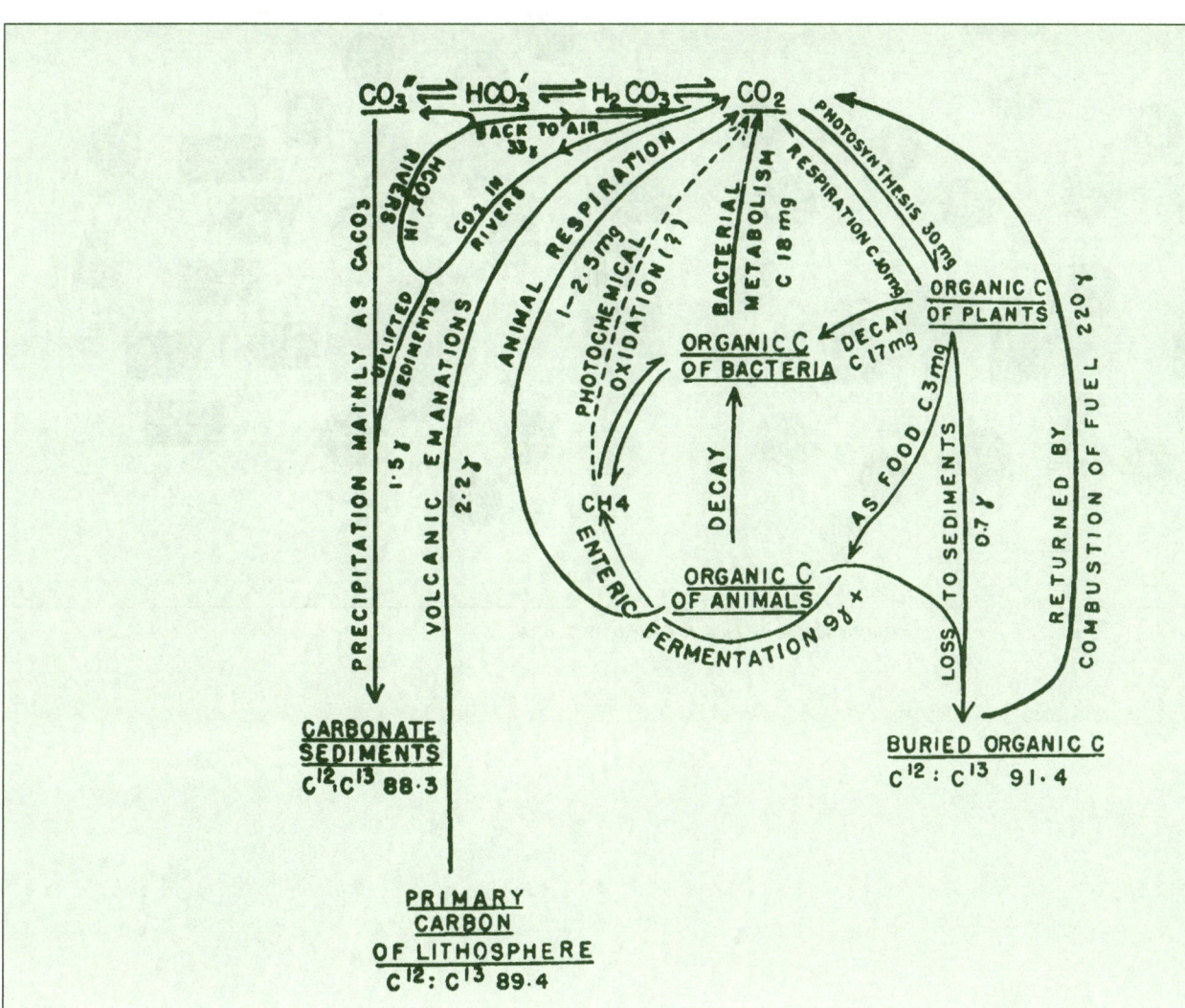

Hutchinson image of biogeochemical processes from *Circular Causal Systems in Ecology*, 1946

Imbalance was to be avoided, and systems were to be managed for stability. The most extensive effort at computing the future of the planet and its populations, *The Limits to Growth* report of 1972, modeled, to cite Paul Edwards, such a "closed" world with limited resources that had to be kept in balance.[7] As the clarion call to an emergent environmental movement, this computerized report saw a world in need of balance: one where change was an anomaly not a norm. The computer scientists modeled human behavior and populations as aberrations producing terminal traumas on the environment that would lead to catastrophe. The answer was to restore the balance of the planet through the careful management of feedback loops and return it to a sustainable state.

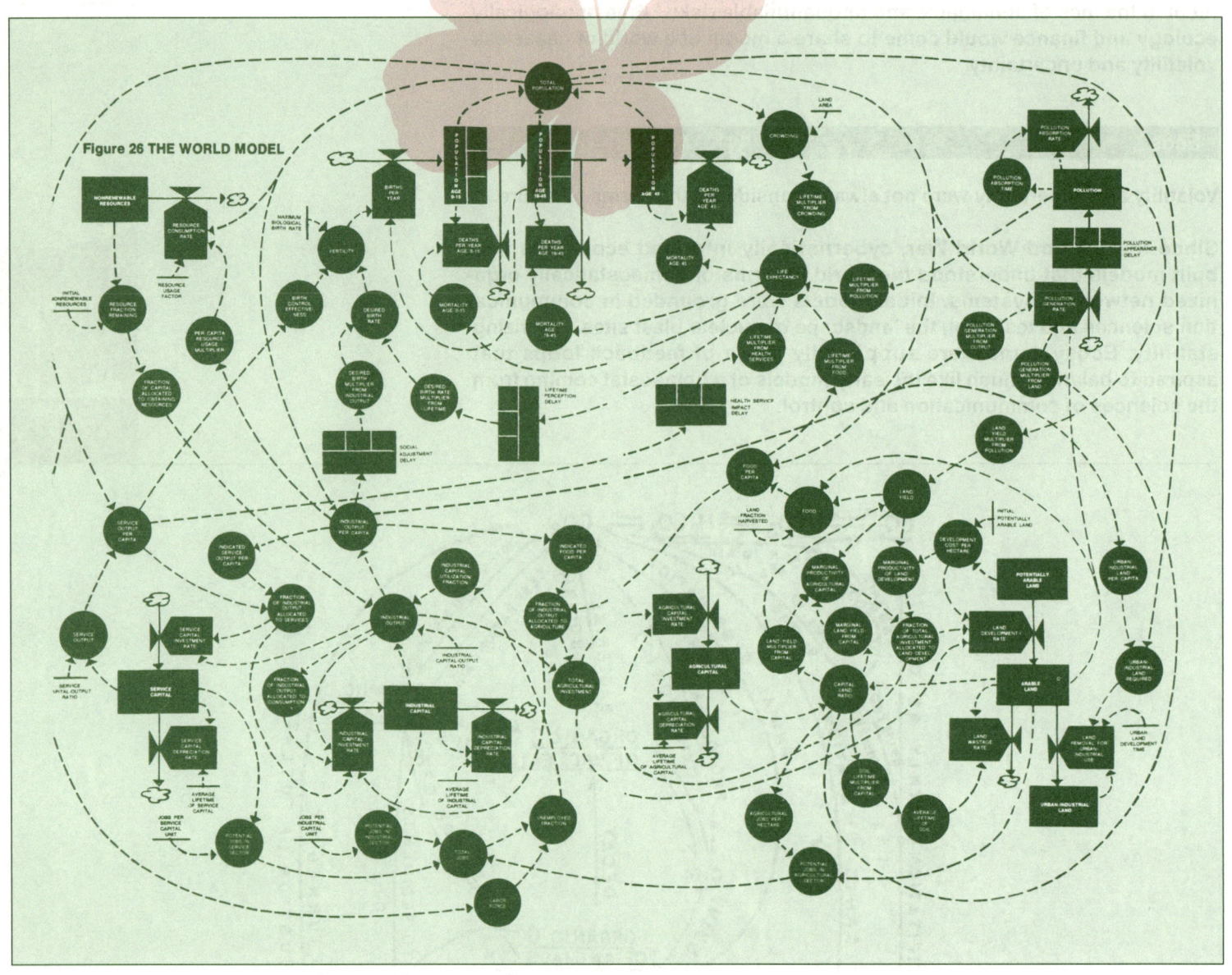

The World Model, *Limits to Growth*, 1972, p.24.

Volatility and Adaptation

But many ecologists, environmentalists and economists disagreed with the report. Ecosystems, they argued, did not appear to stabilize after suffering disruption. There could be no going back historically to a less "damaged" planet. DDT had demonstrated destructive results impacting systems far outside the immediate locus of intended insect elimination in agriculture and for purposes of public health. Agent Orange, heavily used in the Vietnam War as a defoliant, and related dioxins were shown to produce long ranging impacts in humans and ecosystems. And the list goes on. Merely ceasing the use of a toxin or attempting to reseed an environment did not return systems to their pasts. Even seemingly environmentally friendly actions, such as lowering fishing quotas or replanting trees, would be found to return little result once certain levels of disruption to the ecosystem were surpassed.[8] Instead, nature appeared to constantly be evolving.

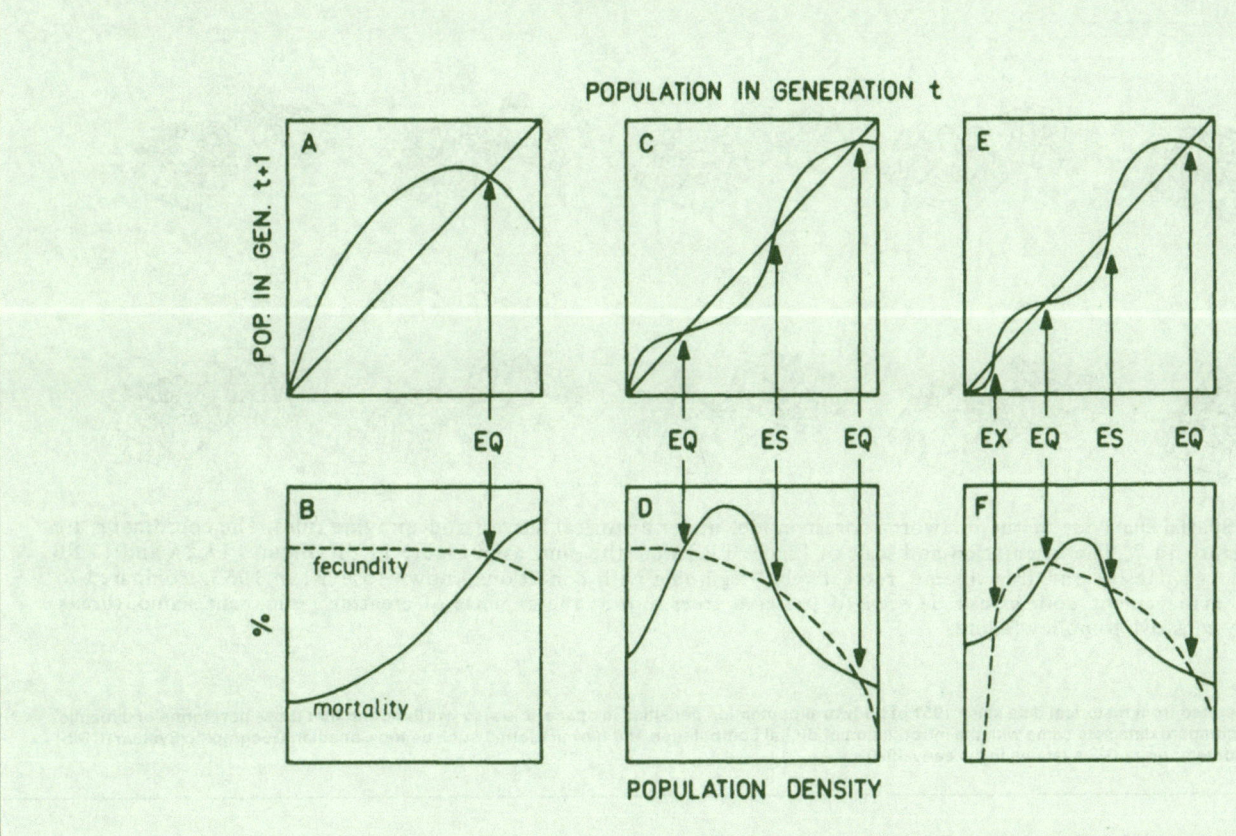

Diagram from C.S Holing, "Resilience and Stability of Ecological Systems," demonstrating theoritical examples of various reproduction curves (a, c and e) and their derivations from the contributions of fecundity and mortality (b, d and f).

In response, a new discourse began to emerge in ecology—resilience. Countering the discourse of *Limits to Growth*, C.S. Holling developed the concept of resilience to *contest the premise* that ecosystems were most healthy when they returned quickly to an equilibrium state after being disturbed. His argument, first cited at the beginning of this article, was that over-emphasis on predator-prey relationships often ignored more complex interactions, and also over-valued equilibrium. Nitrogen, carbon, and other cycles, interactions of mutual aid, collaboration/competition between many species not structured as predator-prey relations and a myriad of other factors might permit ecosystems to persevere in their functions even if in mutated or varied forms. Extinction might not be the limit to the growth or change of a system, unless it fundamentally transformed a complex web of interactions. The seeming absolute limit to life—extinction—could be extended through complexity and a new value for biodiversity.

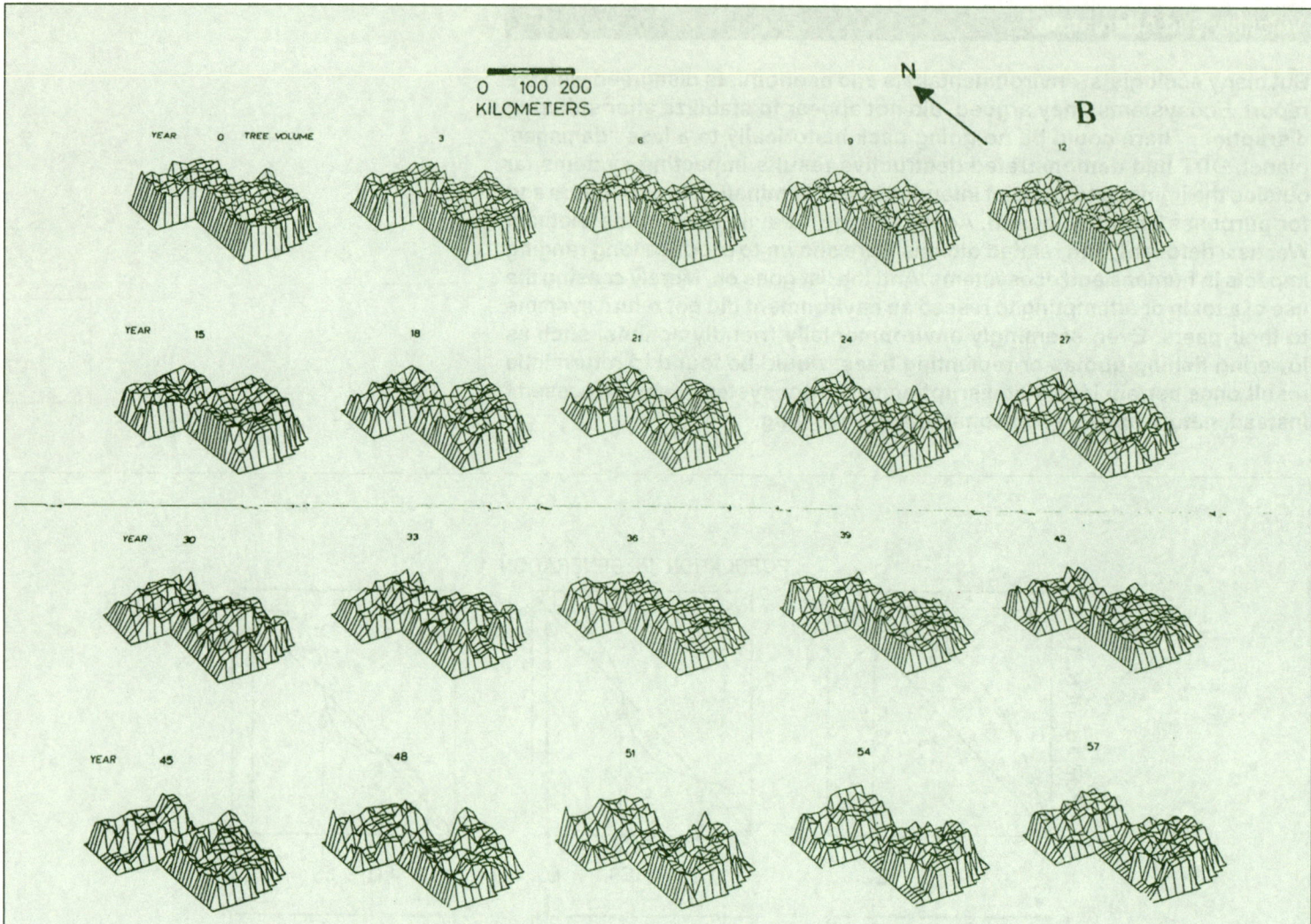

FIGURE 11.8 Spatial behavior of the budworm–forest model under historical harvest and spraying rules. The coordinates are as defined for Figure 11.7. The orientation and scale of Figure 11.8A are the same as in Figure 11.8B. Figures 11.8A and 11.8B show patterns of egg density and tree volume, respectively, beginning with conditions known to exist in 1953. Compared to Figure 11.7, the management policies can be seen to preserve trees, but at the expense of creating permanent semioutbreak conditions, highly sensitive to policy failure.

Topological models generated from historical data since 1951 of budworm population densities in space. It is also worth noting that these new forms of dynamic maps and capacities to compare data sets came with the introduction of digital computation and new platforms such as the Canadian Geographic System (CGIS) considered the root of contemporary GIS systems in the early 1970's.[9]

If sustainability was the language of stable systems in a cyclical economy, resilience is the language of volatility. In an early critique of industrial fishery and forestry management, Holling argued that the focus on using insecticides, reseeding lakes with fish, or attempting to simply replant one type of tree would not work over extended periods of time. *Managing ecosystems with a focus on stability was an error.* **Managers, he suggested, had to cease counting and taxonomically placing populations in boxes and flow charts, and needed instead to realize that positive feedback is dynamic and produces change. Populations are not static numbers but ongoing processes. The important thing is to maintain the process, not the steady state of the system.**

For example, in the case of the boreal forest, the absolute number of spruces is not important; what is important is the ability of the forest to rejuvenate and continue growing trees, which depends on fluctuating numbers of populations and constant variations between spruce, fir, birch and budworms. The system regularly changes. In general, this allows the forest to continue existing as a forest. Better ecological management might also apprehend the fact that systems ultimately change. For example, forests in Ontario are increasingly used more for leisure and vacationing than for forestry, and their management must change accordingly. For other systems, one might imagine a different process or processes defining them. Today, we deploy the term "ecosystem services" to describe this form of management.

Resilience, by contrast, denoted for Holling the capacity of a system itself to change in periods of intense external perturbation as a mode of persistence. The concept of resilience enabled a management approach to ecosystems that "would emphasize the need to keep options open, the need to view events in a regional rather than a local context and the need to emphasize heterogeneity."[10] Managers had to create multiple strategies for future actions, think "regionally" in terms of networks and connections across different territories and times, and emphasize heterogeneity, or biodiversity, in order to secure more possible routes for adaptation in case of unanticipated shocks. He would later label this form of management "adaptive management," arguing that it necessitated the constant feedback of data to respond to constant changes.[11]

Resilience is, in this sense, defined in relationship to crisis and states of exception; that is, it is a virtue when such states are assumed to be either quasi-constant or the most relevant for managerial actions. Holling also underscored that the movement from valuing stability to valuing resilience depended upon an epistemological shift: "Flowing from this would be not the presumption of sufficient knowledge, but the recognition of our ignorance: not the assumption that future events are expected, but that they will be unexpected."[12] In short, expect the unexpected. Plan for extreme events without any conception of absolute prediction.

There are three summary points I want to underscore. The first is that resilience within this genealogy assumes uncertainty and volatility as common, and perhaps "normal" conditions. Stability and resilience are not correlated. As a corollary the life and death of individuals or even populations is secondary to the ongoing evolution of systems. Second, resilience was a new way to model systems and therefore measure them. Instead of a taxonomy that organizes populations into stable categories, one must define systems in terms of *processes*, and measure the relationships between populations and potentially other factors (nitrates, carbon, energy, etc.). A corollary of this new approach is that past data can be used to build concepts but can never actually predict the future. Probabilities *have to* intervene. Finally, ecologists emphasized "heterogeneity" and diversity as important to facilitating resilience. Systems without a surplus of functions and populations could not adapt, and perfectly optimized systems would collapse when change happened.

Resilience thus possesses some curious features. On one hand, the focus on processes and what are today labeled "ecosystem" services means that some lives and populations are acceptably sacrificed as long as the system continues to operate, and that trauma is a regularized and normalized event. On the other hand, environmental managers recognize that only systems with robust diversity, redundancy, and supplemental capacities might survive abrupt and catastrophic events. Resilience fluctuates between the two poles of Darwinian evolutionary theory—survival of the fittest and the necessity for variety and diversity within and between populations to allow for adaptability. Perfect optimization might come at the cost of adaptation.

Managing for resilience also vacillates between other debates involved in evolution—the question of nature versus nurture, except reformulated to code versus context. Do you focus on the singular genome, or the entire landscape of biodiversity? The term allows both understandings to advance.

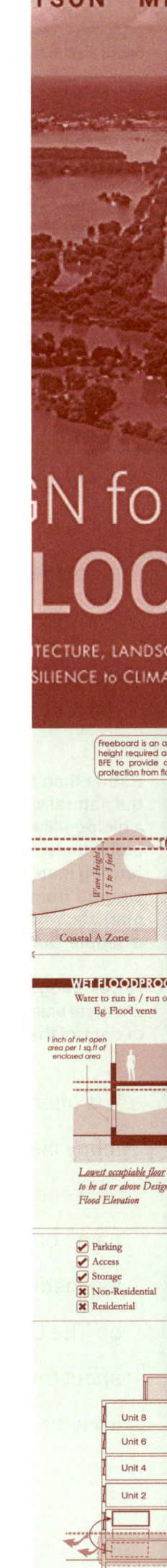

Resilient Speculation

Markets have also long been modeled on ideas of nature, adaptation, fitness and evolution. In his acceptance speech for the 1974 Nobel Memorial Prize in Economic Science, the economist Friedrich Hayek disparaged *The Limits of Growth* report as part of a more general plea, addressed to both mainstream economists and their leftist critics, for a more modest epistemology that would give up on the dream of complete control over the future. Hayek noted drily that the recent creation of the Nobel Prize in Economic Science was itself testimony to the "propensity [of economists] to imitate as closely as possible the procedures of the brilliantly successful physical sciences," but stressed that, in economics, this often "led to outright error." Hayek stressed that economies were not equivalent to the isolated systems of physics. This was in part because a social science such as economics focused on the behavior of large populations of different agents, with the result that:

> like much of biology but unlike most fields of the physical sciences, [economics has] to deal with structures of essential complexity, i.e. with structures whose characteristic properties can be exhibited only by models made up of relatively large numbers of variables. Competition, for instance, is a process which will produce certain results only if it proceeds among a fairly large number of acting persons.[13]

Rather than pretending to be able to replicate the kinds of discoveries about the natural world available to physicists, economists should instead accept a biology-like world of uncertainty, chance, and large populations of different individuals. This would in turn mean relinquishing the goal of *planning*, and turning instead to the more modest goal of *managing*. For Hayek, societies emerge from decentralized networks of information coordinated through markets, which meant that seeking to plan or regulate the economy—by, for example, limiting or eliminating growth—could only end in disaster.

Hayek suggested that mainstream economists, by seeking to emulate the physical sciences, had in fact given encouragement to precisely that fantasy of control that he saw as central to *The Limits of Growth*. He suggested that:

> It is often difficult enough for the expert, and certainly in many instances impossible for the layman, to distinguish between legitimate and illegitimate claims advanced in the name of science. The enormous publicity recently given by the media to a report pronouncing in the name of science on The Limits to Growth, and the silence of the same media about the devastating criticism this report has received from the competent experts, must make one feel some-

what apprehensive about the use to which the prestige of science can be put. But it is by no means only in the field of economics that far-reaching claims are made on behalf of a more scientific direction of all human activities and the desirability of replacing spontaneous processes by "conscious human control."[14]

For Hayek, systems self-organize from the "free efforts of millions of individuals," and not the conscious decision-making power of the few. As a consequence, control—understood as the prediction of future events, whether by mainstream economists or the Club of Rome—was impossible. For Hayek, though, this was not cause for despair. Rather, it was grounds for hope, provided that those populations of millions were allowed to engage new and unanticipated problems flexibly by means of unrestricted market activity.

Hayek's lecture focused primarily on the rather abstract realm of epistemology, and provided relatively little guidance as to what this approach might look like in practice. However, in the 1970s, several economists and ecologists turned to concepts of flexibility and "resilience" to explain how the epistemological modesty valorized by Hayek could generate solutions to specific new and unanticipated problems while at the same time avoiding system collapse. Within international relations, one such problem was the failure of the Bretton Woods international currency exchange system in the late 1960s and early 1970s. The Bretton Woods system was designed shortly after WWII, and was supposed to keep Western economies stable by preventing large international currency exchange rate fluctuations, which many economists and policy analysts saw as key causes of the rise of fascist and totalitarian regimes after WWI. However, the system—which pegged international currency rates to the U.S. dollar, and the U.S. dollar to a fixed gold exchange rate—was having serious problems in the 1960s, and finally ended in 1971, when U.S. President Nixon declared that the U.S. dollar could no longer be exchanged for gold.

This declaration recalls Friedman's observations at the start of this essay. Though Friedman was one of those economists chastised by Hayek in his lecture as overly committed to "scientific" models of economics, Friedman's proposal for a resilient futures markets nevertheless exemplified Hayek's image of markets that flexibly managed, rather than rigidly controlled or planned, an always uncertain future.

These conceptions of not only managing, but actually arbitraging, uncertainty would find actualization in technology. While perhaps risk has always been necessary for profit, never before had it been so clearly demarcated as a site of technological innovation and intervention.

At the height of the introduction of algorithmic trading and derivative instruments to the market, computer scientist turned financial guru, Fischer Black, one of the creators of the automated derivatives market, wrote an important essay on noise that consolidated this new resilient view of markets not as homeostatic mechanisms but as volatile and uncertain mediums. At the center of his new vision of options markets and futures was the idea of entropy and noise borrowed from cybernetics[15]:

While it is clear that resilience theory has been influential in dictating the terms and goals of much of contemporary urban design, less well known is the impact that designerly ways of thinking had upon Holling's formation of the concept of resilience to begin with. In a number of recent publications, the geographer Kevin Grove has been unearthing this unexpected connection between the discipline of design and resilient forms of governance.[1] Specifically, Grove points to the influence that the social scientist Herbert Simon—considered by many to be a founding figure of so-called "design thinking"—had upon Holling's thought and upon resilient approaches to ecosystem management.

Simon argued that the unknowable complexity of the twentieth century world revealed the fallacy of many of the core tenets of modernist thought—the most significant for Simon being neoclassical economics' figure of *homo economicus*, a utility maximizer who, because in possession of "near-perfect knowledge of his environment," is able to choose the course of action that will grant him the greatest rewards. Against this model, Simon proposed that individuals possess limited information about their complex environments and that thus the goal in any situation should be not to optimize but to "satisfice," that is, find a "good enough" outcome.

For Simon, the pursuit of satisficing solutions is a stepwise, recursive process. Instead of "[anticipating] and [considering] all possible outcomes," one breaks a problem down into manageable sub-systems, tests out possible solutions within a given sub-unit, and then, given the successes or failures of these provisional gambits, adjusts one's approach until the "good enough" solution is found. In other words, against the "predictive knowledge" of modern science—with its building of complete theoretical portraits of the world—satisficing is an "emergent" science suited to "adaptive problem-solving in a complex world." Design, for Simon, is the paradigmatic example of this approach to knowledge-making.[2]

But the ecological practice of adaptive management is not far behind. Holling likewise jettisoned approaches that sought to accumulate total knowledge of an ecosystem before acting (by, say, cataloging all known species in a given system) in favor of a method that garners knowledge from interventions made in relative ignorance. Citing Simon, Holling notes that his approach involves "test[ing] innovations by experiments" on parts of an ecosystem.[3] That is, one intervenes in one component of the ecosystem and sees the results—good or bad—until gradually one arrives at a general sense of how the system functions (which species matter most, which relationships are key, and so on) and how to potentially intervene in the face of a crisis. Via tracing these direct citations of and similarities to Simon's thought, Grove thus demonstrates design thinking's influence upon adaptive management and resilience writ large.

Fischer Black
of the American Finan
1985

The effects of noise on the world, and on our views of the world, are profound. Noise in the sense of a large number of small events is often a causal factor much more powerful than a small number of large events can be. Noise makes trading in financial markets possible, and thus allows us to observe prices for financial assets.[16]

His famous article "Noise Trading" formalized a new discourse in finance and posited that we trade and profit from misinformation and information overload.

In this new embrace of automated financial trading, what no longer existed was the problem of equilibrium or a concern for entropic disorganization. If 19th and earlier 20th century economists, even Hayek, worried about the maintenance of the market itself and of the stability of value, or about entropy and the tendency of political and economic systems to degrade, this concern has now been deferred, and even capitalized upon. Noise in communication theory is directly correlated with increases in entropy. Options trading makes volatility and speculation, and an excess of information in the market, into a site of extracting value—arbitrage.[17]

The significance of this turn to embracing entropy and noise as a site of value cannot be overstated. Black embraces the concept, central to resilient hopefulness, that markets are always unstable and volatile. Moreover, he recognizes that as a result of this seemingly natural condition, full prediction is impossible, and therefore new technologies of preemption are necessary. Hedge funds, and their central technology of derivative pricing, become therefore key vehicles for monetizing this uncertainty, and managing the operations of the market while enduring constant evolutionary stresses.

The question ecologists and economists then turned to asking was this: if prediction of the future was impossible, how were the models failing? And more importantly, how can these seemingly un-anticipatable events be dealt with? How does one manage for radical uncertainty? And change? The response was to create a new class of financial instruments (derivatives) that would manage this future without ever having to predict it. These instruments were the automated analogues to resilient management strategies that reflected similar attitudes to uncertainty and the management of systems in both economy and ecology. These models offered a concept of systems as capable of purposeful evolution without direction, and created a language by which to imagine systems whose capacity for change and adaptation would come through internal mechanisms of feedback and reflexivity rather than political oversight and the state.[18] It is no accident, of course, that the concept of eternally evolving and unpredictable, and therefore unplannable, systems emerged directly in parallel as a response to both demands for civil rights by disenfranchised and racialized groups and globally with decolonization. Derivative pricing markets naturalized and automated crisis while assuming that planning was counter-evolutionary and forestalled adaptation, and by extension, survival.

Conclusion

By the early 2000s, following 9/11, the 2008 financial crisis and the growing effects of climate change, resilience has taken a central discursive place in fields ranging from business management and logistics to psychology and urban design. "Adaptive management," "business continuity management," "climate resiliency planning" and many related terms are all direct outgrowths from ecological resilience that largely shape our understanding of how changing climatic and security conditions are to be dealt with.

A search online for resilience in the aftermath of COVID-19, and in the wake of the war in the Ukraine, reveals a massive number of articles, websites, and consulting services dedicated to logistics, psychology and community activism. For managers of supply chains and corporations such as SAP and IBM, resilience is what corporations must do to ensure business continuity. "Just in time" manufacturing is now "just in case," and corporations are urged to increase their options, to diversify supply chains geographically and begin thinking about plasticity in manufacturing infrastructure (for example, by being able to make alternative products) and to identify vital services and processes ahead of time. For many neoliberal and right leaning politicians, resilience is a call to expend populations they do not value—the elderly, people with underlying health conditions and people of color—through the ongoing annihilation of environmental protections, civil rights and social benefits in the name of saving the economy. Resilience thus becomes a mode of naturalizing violence for the Right.

Here we must contend with how we understand evolution and genealogy. Financial and logistical comprehensions of resilience largely assume a world of scenario plans and unanticipatable futures divorced from historical legacy or context. As the critical race theorist Kara Keeling notes, contemporary algorithmic derivative practices possess a new force, and one that is in some ways no longer measurable. She suggests that the contemporary derivatives economy is one of infinite calculation without termination. The racism and injustice of such an economy, we might extrapolate from her argument, emerges from the fact that, as technologies, derivatives consume differences, whether via correlations between the value of homes in different places, the comparative poverty or wealth of different populations, the differing cost of labor in different locales or differences in the speed by which between investors can buy and sell options. These differentials become the site of a new form of automated and algorithmic speculation. Betting on differences in this way has the effect of making the future homogenous with the present, as it perpetuates contemporary class, racial and sexual inequities. Finance and those with capital profit ever more, and in fact enjoy the inequities that are now the very sites of value production. "Difference" becomes "differentials" that produce value derived from the variations between lived bodies and worlds and abstractions of finance. Racism here is not only the result of history, but also a consequence of the power of algorithmic finance to eliminate time, ironically in the name of evolution and adaptation. Keeling counters this with what she calls queer and black time, exemplified in part by afro-futurism and surrealism, which she sees as resisting this condition by remaining open to the future and to uncertainty in a manner that is plural and not homogenous.[19]

While the consumption of differences in the name of adaptation, survival and a violently inequitable non-future—a non-future because the trades that determine the future have already happened in the past or present—is a vital concern, these instruments also facilitate complex interactions and new forms of relationality. For example, in our present, not only are most minerals and metals commodity markets heavily derived, but so are all energy markets—energy, in fact, is the most heavily derived market on earth.[20] The fates of pipelines, extraction infrastructure and development are in this sense often decided via a complicated set of arrangements around future bets.

If the epistemology of adaptive management sounds familiar, it should: the standard contemporary architectural studio course functions in much the same way. While critics tend to require a week or two of "research" (read: cursory Wikipedia-ing), any architecture student who truly tries to understand the historical and cultural complexities of a given site will quickly find herself lagging far behind the studio schedule. After all, production is king in architecture schools: one is encouraged not to comprehend but to iterate. Only through abandoning the explanatory powers of the intellect to instead repeatedly test out solutions can one receive the course-correcting feedback that comes with critique.

Once they leave the confines of the academy to enter the world of practice, however, architects find that their carefully honed design thinking skills find little expression; the majority of the services they render (ensuring code compliance, producing executable construction drawings) are in alignment with the regular and predictable laws of an earlier science. Major design thinking consultancies like IDEO, however, have managed to take the adaptive logic of design out of the studio and into the world. In their telling, all the world's problems can be solved via design: food waste, diabetes care, the distribution of government services—everything can be tackled first by a "Rapid Prototyping" phase that will then be course-corrected in the "User Feedback" portion of a project. Eventually, a satisficing solution will be found. Who needs politics when you can have stepwise, adaptive problem-solving?

Judged in purely monetary terms, this approach has been very successful. The big bucks contracts that IDEO receives from governments and major corporations alike are a sign of how highly valued expertise in this nebulous field has become. Again, Grove offers valuable insights into the reasons for the great authority now granted to design thinking. "Perhaps," he writes

> It is no coincidence that design has become increasingly influential as the stable, predictable world of Western modernity (and the stable, predictable environment of the Holocene) has become overwhelmed by qualitatively distinct insecurities and anxieties … Rather than reiterate modernity's promise of total predictive control, design proponents offer novel techniques for knowing and managing uncertainty and emergence.[4]

In turn, some activist movements are also turning to finance as the centerpiece of environmental activism. Greenpeace has recently refocused its efforts on financial entities, targeting groups such as BlackRock (the largest investment manager in the world) and the financial systems behind oil pipelines by shifting protests to the headquarters of the financial firm, rather than focusing efforts solely at the pipeline.[21] While in retrospect this may seem like common sense, until recently, the financialization of the energy sector was not a focus of activism in the way that the actual corporate perpetrators of environmental damage were.

Similar evidence can be found in bond markets, where financial instruments can serve as sources of political action. For example, developing climate preparedness mechanisms for large American cities is very expensive. While finance is usually depicted in urban history as an attempt by neoliberalism to bankrupt the public, numerous recent examples suggest other possibilities. In Houston's reconstruction after Hurricane Harvey, for example, a unique bill structuring the bond instruments was passed in 2018. This plan used the money from bonds to assist poor and minority neighborhoods that were at highest risk for flooding. The bond was structured so that different forms of risk were assessed differently, rather than merely evaluating risk through property value and property loss, as evaluation through property loss costs alone would have benefited rich neighborhoods. While there are many ongoing battles and its success is not yet clear, as federal funding was slowed under President Donald Trump, the bond structure and financing became a site of political action.[22] Such efforts demonstrate how new models of what is urban and what is natural extend the terrain of action. No longer focused only on hard infrastructure such as roads or sea walls, urban activists increasingly understand the many soft infrastructures such as wetlands as integral parts of climate defense. Environmental justice (as in the case of Houston) becomes integral to understanding what makes a city resilient.

Resilience, therefore, might have positive connotations, or faint messianic capacities, to invoke Walter Benjamin. Resilience can be a discourse recognizing the historical situatedness of our ecological relations to others, the necessity for diversity and the possibility that the future of a system will never be its past. Resilience, we might recall from ecology, demands change and diversity.

We must begin to understand resilience for its historically situated reworking of the relationship between nature, ecology and economy. Might such historical consciousness facilitate different forms of imagining future institutions, economies and environments? The future does not need to replicate the past. Resilience can be a call for multiplicity, and for futures not yet known, it could yet offer a model of ecological thinking that might defeat the optimizing demands of capital or conservatism. Thus, resilience might offer the possibility not of a new normal but of a new nature.

1. Aongus Hagerty, "Digital Resilience: Building the Economies of Tomorrow on a Foundation of Cybersecurity." World Economic Forum, https://www.weforum.org/agenda/2022/05/digital-resilience-building-the-economies-of-tomorrow-on-a-foundation-of-cybersecurity/. May 20, 2022. Downloaded June 9, 2022.
2. Ibid.
3. C.S. Holling, "Resilience and Stability of Ecological Systems," *Annual Review of Ecological Systems* 4 (1973): 1.
4. Ibid., 637. Friedman stressed that this market "cannot depend solely on hedging transactions by persons involved in foreign trade and investment"; in addition, the "market needs speculators who are willing to take open positions as well as hedges. The larger the volume of speculative activity, the better the market and the easier it will be for persons involved in foreign trade and investment to hedge at low costs and at market prices that move only gradually and are not significantly affected by even a large commercial transactions" (Ibid., 638). The terminology of "resilience" seems not to have been Friedman's innovation, as other economists had also used this term in the late 1960s when discussing the need for Bretton Woods reform.
5. Milton Friedman, "The Need for Futures Markets in Currencies," Cato Journal 31, no. 3 (2011): 635-641, 636. This article is a reprint of a December 20, 1971 report to the Chicago Mercantile Exchange, and as Donald MacKenzie documents, this was an "article for hire," as Friedman was paid by the head of the Chicago Mercantile Exchange to write the article, which was intended to (and did) pave the way for federal approval of precisely such a market. Hence, the article advocates not only for a futures currency market, but for its location in the United States. Friedman contended that, "[a]s Britain has demonstrated in the nineteenth century, financial services of all kinds can be a highly profitable export commodity," and he proposed that a U.S.-based futures market would strengthen the American position while also maintaining the stability and expansion of global trade.
6. It is worth noting that the Black Scholes Derivative pricing equation inaugurating the financialization of the global economy was introduced in 1973. For an excellent summary of these links and of the insurance and urban planning fields please see: Kevin Grove, *Resilience* (New York: Routledge, 2018).
7. Paul Edwards, *The Closed World: Computers and the Politics of Discourse in Cold War America* (Cambridge: MIT Press, 1997).
8. History Channel Editors, "Agent Orange," no. May 16 (2019), https://www.history.com/topics/vietnam-war/agent-orange-1; ibid. Jacob Darwin Hamblin, *Arming Mother Nature: The Birth of Catastrophic Environmentalism* (Oxford University Press, 2013).
9. C.S. Holling, "The Spruce Budworm/Forest Management Problem," in *Adaptive Environmental Assessment and Management*, ed. C.S. Holling (New York: John Wiley and Sons, 1978), 164.
10. "Resilience and Stability of Ecological Systems."
11. For a summary of strategies in adaptive management see: *Adaptive Environmental Assessment and Management* (New York: John Wiley and Sons, 1978).
12. Holling, "Resilience and Stability of Ecological Systems."
13. Friedrich Hayek, "The Pretense of Knowledge," (www.nobelprize.org/prizes/economic-sciences/1974/hayek/lecture/: The Sveriges Riksbank Prize in Economic Sciences in Memory of Alfred Nobel 1974, 1974). Access Date: December 29, 2020.
14. Ibid.
15. Fischer Black studied at MIT, and finished a degree at Harvard, initially under the guidance of Marvin Minsky, and read cybernetic texts by Norbert Wiener throughout his high school and early college education. Pery Mehrling, *Fischer Black and the Revolutionary Idea of Finance*, 2012 ed. (New York: John Wiley and Sons, Inc., 2005), location 1017 Kindle Edition.
16. Fischer Black, "Noise," *The Journal of Finance* 41, no. 3 (1986): 529.
17. Mehrling, Fischer Black and the Revolutionary Idea of Finance, 20.
18. Paul Lewis, "The Emergence of "Emergence" in the Work of F.A. Hayek: A Historical Analysis," *History of Political Economy* 48, no. 1.
19. Kara Keeling, *Queer Times, Black Futures* (New York: New York University Press, 2019).
20. On minerals and metals markets, see Martín Arboleda, *Planetary Mine: Territories of Extraction under Late Capitalism* (New York: Verso, 2020). On energy markets, see Rusian Hharlamov and Heriner Glassbeck, "When Commodities Get Hooked on Derivatives," *Financial Times* June 14, 2019, https://www.ft.com/content/896e47c8-8875-11e9-a028-86cea8523dc2 ..
21. Greenpeace, "It's the Finance Sector Stupid," in *https://www.greenpeace.org/static/planet4-international-stateless/2020/01/13e3c75b-greenpeace_report_wef_2020_its-the-finance_sector_stupid.pdf*, ed. Greenpeace (Greenpeace, 2020).
22. Christopher Flavelle, "A Climate Plan in Texas Focuses on Minorities. Not Everyone Likes It," *The New York Times* (July 24 2020), https://www.nytimes.com/2020/07/24/climate/houston-flooding-race.html. For discussion about rethinking publics, politics, infrastructures, and finance, see James Christopher Mizes, Stephen J. Collier, Antina von Scnitzler, "Preface: Public Infrastructures / Infrastructural Publics," *Limn*, no. 7 (2016), https://limn.it/issues/public-infrastructuresinfrastructural-publics/..

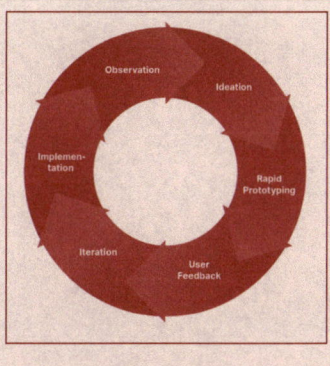

With the future becoming ever more unpredictable, then, the adaptive logics of design take center stage.

Before architects rush to sign ever more of their souls over to the world of design thinking, it's worth pondering what would be lost in such a conversion. Designing, in the Simonian sense, is all about solving immediate problems: one must accept a lack of knowledge so as to arrive at a situational solution that proves "satisficing" for those at the deciding table. In abandoning any attempt to produce an explanatory picture of the conditions in which one is designing, one effectively elides any and all grounding historical factors: class differences, the lasting legacies of colonialism and slavery, histories of extraction and any other structural inequalities all retreat from view. In rushing to be better equipped to handle the uncertainties of our future—in rushing to be more resilient in the face of our world's many crises—architects ought not lose sight of the past that brought on these crises in the first place.

1. Kevin Grove, et al., "Interventions on design and political geography," *Political Geography* 74 (October 2019); Kevin Grove, *Resilience* (Oxfordshire: Routledge, 2019): 131-181.
2. Grove, *Resilience*, 136-167.
3. C.S. Holling and Steven Sanderson, "Dynamics of (dis)harmony in ecological and social systems," in *Rights to Nature: Ecological, Economic, Cultural, and Political Principles of Institutions for the Environment*, eds. Susan Hanna, Carl Folke and Karl-Goran Maler (Washington D.C.: Island Press), 78. As cited in Grove, *Resilience*, 148.
4. Grove et al., "Interventions on design," 132.

In the Wake of Resilience: Beyond Darwinian Futures

Ross Exo Adams

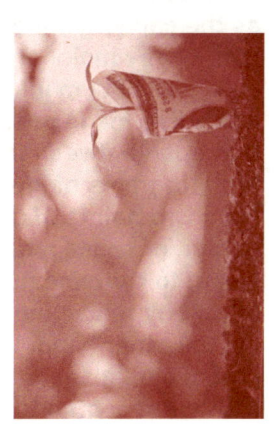

"Resilience is the name for the violent destruction of things that won't give, won't return to form, won't bend when access is demanded, won't be flexible and (com)pliant."

Fred Moten and Stefano Harney[1]

Shortly before his death in 2006, a lengthy essay authored by Reinhart Koselleck on the history of the concept of "crisis" was translated and published in English.[2] Originally an entry in the monumental eight-volume set he helped to edit, *Geschichtliche Grundbegriffe* [*Basic Historical Concepts*], his impetus for writing this piece in 1982 seems to have emerged from a deeper cultural skepticism of liberalism and its blurring of the political and existential with the everyday. Writing from the point of view of Western society, Koselleck argued that the ever-frequent uses of crisis in the late twentieth century had attached myriad new sensibilities to this once quite specific concept. Koselleck saw this as not just a matter of imprecision or intellectual vacuity, but rather as a symptom of a much broader historical crisis whose dimensions had yet to be identified.

"The concept of crisis, which once had the power to pose unavoidable, harsh and non-negotiable alternatives," he writes, "has been transformed to fit the uncertainties of whatever might be favored at a given moment." He saw in this widening use an increasingly cynical and opportunistic co-opting of the political capacity that crisis had long had. Because crisis for Koselleck was a "structural signature of modernity," its devolution to a loose, "whatever"-signifier marked an early sign of an emerging political topography in which crisis would play a new and increasingly definitive role.

The ontological and epistemological centrality that crisis has since come to occupy in the centers of global and economic power seems to justify Koselleck's initial apprehension. In previous periods, crisis was perceived as an ever-present possibility preventable through modern scientific and institutional knowledge, governance and technology. Today, however, crisis, instability and volatility have become integral to the structures maintaining order in the spaces of empire. This newfound centrality of crisis is in part an outcome of the financialization of the world economy—a process that was taking hold at the time Koselleck was writing his essay. As Melinda Cooper writes, "When the convertibility of the dollar against gold was replaced by floating and volatile exchange rates, the unpredictable was, of necessity, factored into the calculus of world economic futures."[3] In finance, the restructuring of capital markets around instability opened new ways to extract value from assets through future speculation on what is unknown and contingent.

More recently, this shift has manifested in the rekindling of an old alliance between design and international development, a kinship of fields bound in their shared colonial past and by their inexhaustible desire for improvement. Over the past decade as climate change has steadily picked up pace, a growing network of spatial practices partnered with global governance bodies, municipal initiatives, NGOs, and large-scale real estate firms has been building a mode of development that instrumentalizes crisis through the productive binary of risk-resilience—a kind of epistemological framework that both articulates problems and casts the outlines for their solutions. I call this nexus of institutions the *resilience complex*. Resilience, in this context, is typically formulated as the capacity for a city, neighborhood or region to "survive, adapt, and grow" in the face of any major shock.[4]

What I'm interested in doing in this essay is studying how the centralization of crisis has made possible these modes of intervention that stretch across scales and that span between the design of space and the design of policies, funding schemes and programs of infrastructural improvement. I want to approach this new formation from two points of departure: on the one hand, as a complex of relations between the design of space and the structures of economic and political power that preside over it, I want to examine how the resilience complex institutes new techniques of governance in part by reimagining the human body, and in part by reimagining urban development. On the other hand, I want to understand how this paradigm, created in the centers of global capital, gets "exported" to countries in the global south. Resilience has become a concept central to emerging networks of international development driven by private consultancy firms, philanthropic institutions and non-governmental organizations whose aim is to create global frameworks in which public bodies enable private development. By looking through these two lenses, I want to think about how resilience operates as a techno-material and epistemological paradigm that pits publicly-enabled, speculative green capitalism as the only response not only to environmental crisis, but to a world made visible through uncertainty.

The making of the resilience complex

One of the key players in the field of resilience urbanism is the multinational firm Arup. Together with the Rockefeller Foundation, and building off of a network of related proj-

ects, they created the "City Resilience Index" (CRI) in 2015—a toolkit described as an open platform for the self-assessment of cities.[5] Its aim is to both measure the degree of vulnerability of a city and to outline a set of possible interventions in order to increase its overall resilience. As a platform, it is meant to be accessible to any city and to operate across scales, providing a universally applicable framework for appraising the built environment. Aligning itself with an emerging global governance discourse on resilience, CRI organizes its metrics in a circular matrix

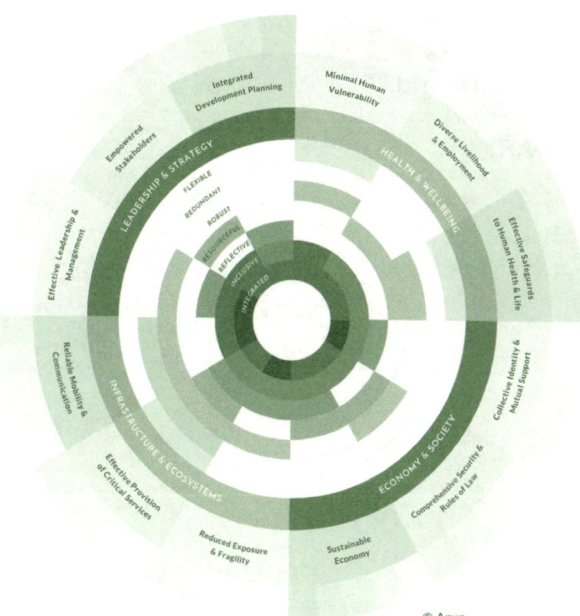

divided into four broad "dimensions": Health and Well-Being, Economy and Society, Infrastructure and Environment, and Leadership and Strategy.[6] These are further subdivided into twelve "goals," which are then measured by fifty-two "indicators" that chart out both quantitative and qualitative valuations of a city's resilience. In this model, as one consultant told me, "measurement is key: you cannot plan what you cannot measure."[7]

As its circular form suggests, in addition to detailing the "strengths and weaknesses" of a given site, the CRI provides a holistic framework in which certain causal relations across the various indicators can be identified. Because it is universally applicable, its measurements are explicitly relative, based on a generic scale of 1-5 ("very poor" to "excellent"), meaning that its output is more a statement of confidence than an exact value. But precisely because of this orientation, the CRI does more than measure resilience; in operating across multiple temporalities, it works at once as a recursive diagnostic tool and as a framework for development—both an assessment of the present and a project for the future. Its explicit rejection of absolute, standardized metrics emphasizes the relational effects between the various indicators and "goals" while also opening itself up to more speculative capacities

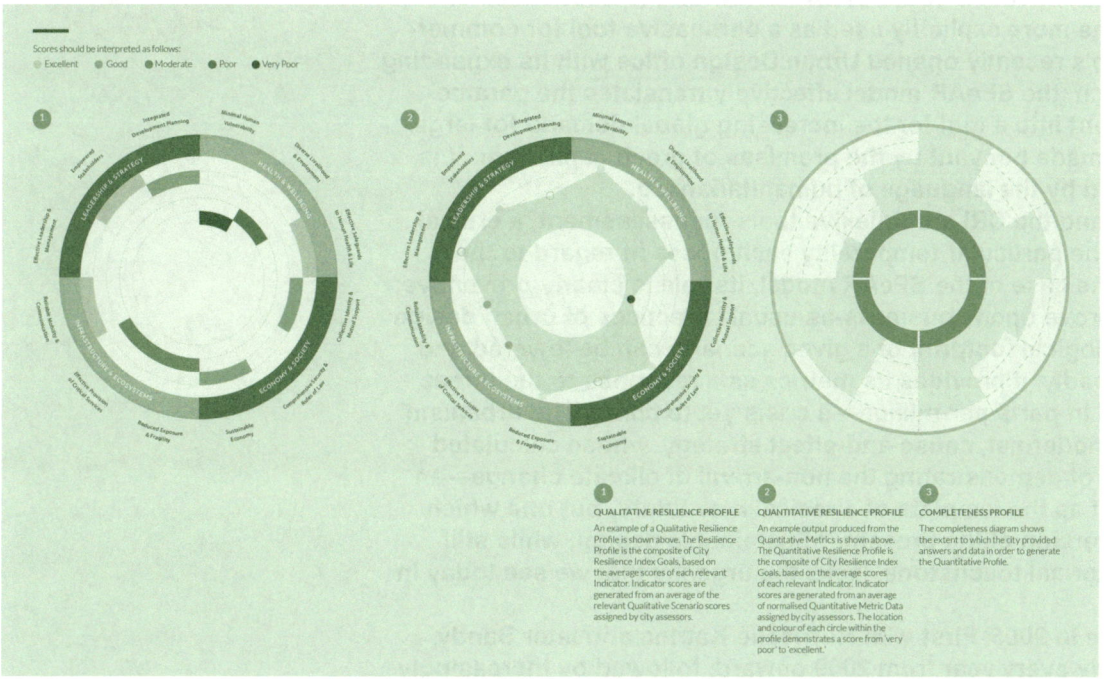

QUALITATIVE RESILIENCE PROFILE
An example of a Qualitative Resilience Profile is shown above. The Resilience Profile is the composite of City Resilience Index Goals, based on the average scores of each relevant Indicator. Indicator scores are generated from an average of the relevant Qualitative Scenario scores assigned by city assessors.

QUANTITATIVE RESILIENCE PROFILE
An example output produced from the Quantitative Metrics is shown above. The Quantitative Resilience Profile is the composite of City Resilience Index Goals, based on the average scores of each relevant Indicator. Indicator scores are generated from an average of normalised Quantitative Metric Data assigned by city assessors. The location and colour of each circle within the profile demonstrates a score from 'very poor' to 'excellent.'

COMPLETENESS PROFILE
The completeness diagram shows the extent to which the city provided answers and data in order to generate the Quantitative Profile.

in evaluating scenarios of urban design and policy reform and, ultimately, ways to attract capital.

Yet the CRI's relative differences work in the opposite sense as well, making visible sites of vulnerability, which, because of its nested, relational structure, immediately present themselves as existential threats for the system as a whole. Here, the binary of risk-resilience embeds itself in the very logic of the CRI framework, universally distributing fifty-two possible ways in which cities face existential crisis. As Arup states, "Urban populations are facing increasing challenges from numerous natural and man-made [*sic*] pressures such as rapid urbanization, climate change, terrorism and increased risks from natural hazards. Cities must learn ... how to build resilience in an uncertain world."[8]

The CRI model is built on a previous tool created by Arup in 2000 for measuring sustainability. The "Sustainable Project Appraisal Routine" (SPeAR)

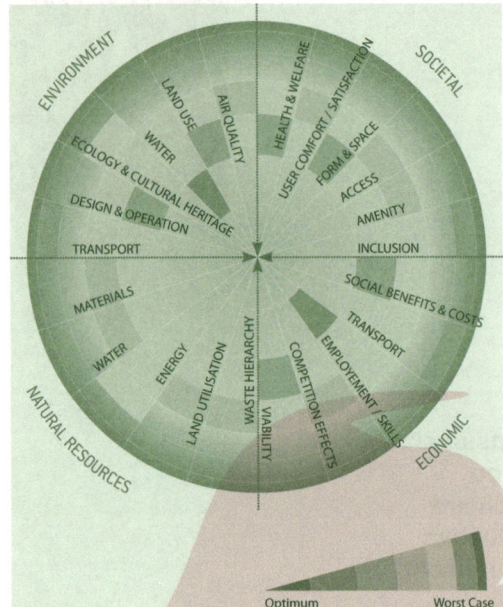

is a simpler tool used to assist in decision-making on a range of projects based on a single array of indicators originally organized into four areas of concern for sustainable development—economy, society, environment, and natural resources. Like the CRI, the indicators provide a means to assess a given site or project and to establish key interrelations between them, using a similarly relative scale of measurement, from "worst case" to "optimum." As a discursive tool, SPeAR's broader framework drew its inspiration from the 1987 United Nations World Commission on Environment and Development publication, *Our Common Future*, and its technical parameters come in part from the UK Sustainable Development Indicators, as well as the Building Research Establishment Environmental Assessment Method (BREEAM).[9] As with the CRI, the vagueness of SPeAR's measurements is a function of its use as a speculative tool of scenario planning that allows it to be responsive to changing market conditions. Following the 2006 publication of the *Stern Review on the Economics of Climate Change*, SPeAR became more explicitly used as a persuasive tool for commercial urban development in Arup's recently opened Urban Design office with its expanding portfolio of "eco-cities." As such, the SPeAR model effectively translates the parameters of international development into a tool for the increasing global demand for large-scale real estate development made buoyant by the promises of green capitalism: it is commercial design emboldened by the language of humanitarian aid.

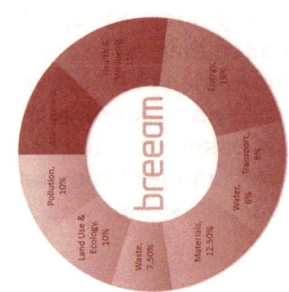

While both the SPeAR and the CRI are reflexive tools for assessment, a crucial difference between the two is the particular temporality each poses in regard to the crisis they aim to address. In the case of the SPeAR model, its role is clearly *preventive*: it works as a framework to improve upon "business-as-usual" practices of urban design by demonstrating how the ecological footprint of a given scenario can be lowered and energy use mitigated. More broadly, it provides its metrics as a response to the threat of a future condition measured in parts-per-million—a crisis yet to come. The urbanism it calls forth follows a techno-modernist, cause-and-effect strategy, whose calculated effects have the insidious task of demonstrating the non-arrival of climate change—an urbanism which casts itself not as the template of a radical new future, but one which appears instead as a greener version of the present.[10] Sustainable design, while still universally embraced as a rhetorical touchstone, lacks the urgency that we see today in the resilience turn.

Things began to change in 2005. First with Hurricane Katrina and later Sandy, record flooding in Europe nearly every year from 2009 onward, followed by increasingly harsh droughts, wildfires, record high temperatures and disappearing coastlines across the global north: suddenly it seemed that the gamble of warding off climate change with lackluster campaigns of better-than-business-as-usual development was confronted by the very visible effects of a climate crisis finally landing in the core of empire. Set against the tumultuous backdrop of the 2008 debt crisis and the sprawling War on Terror, the effects of climate change ushered in a fundamental shift in the understanding of crisis.[11] No longer could "sustainable development" suffice as the sole strategy for dealing with

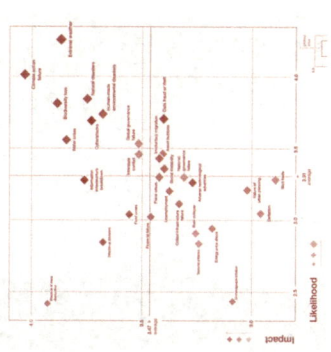

global warming. Nor could crisis remain a future possibility to be technocratically averted—a "known unknown" preventively excluded from life in the centers of global capitalism. If the present itself had become a state of perpetual irruptions of existential crises, whose character and impact appeared increasingly unpredictable, what was at stake now was survival itself. With these more pressing stakes, programs of mitigation were increasingly sidelined by calls for adaptation, and the world of design and development began taking an aggressively pre-emptive posture under the banner of resilience.[12]

The difference between sustainable and resilient urbanism approximates the distinction C.S. Holling makes in his groundbreaking 1973 essay "Resilience and Stability of Ecological Systems." Resilience, he argues, shifts attention from equilibrium to "conditions of persistence." According to Holling, stability and resilience within an ecological system are not only divergent indicators, but also often contradict one another. A system with the capacity to absorb shock, quickly returning to equilibrium with respect to its population, may actually be more susceptible to long-term collapse than one whose population swings violently between near collapse and sudden dominance in the face of a given event. What resilience measures, in other words, is not how quickly a population can return to equilibrium after a shock, but rather "the persistence of relationships within a system and … the ability of these systems to absorb changes of state variables, driving variables and parameters and still persist."[13] It is telling, then, that the broad adoption of resilience has opened direct pathways connecting the design of space with the writing of governmental policies.[14] While urbanists and policy makers who embrace resilience rhetorically emphasize notions like "bouncing back" and communities "thriving" amidst conditions of uncertainty—seemingly misunderstanding the very premise of the concept—a detailed look at their work affirms that resilience nevertheless identifies strategies for the preservation of the social, economic and political systems governing society, rather than the direct protection of a given community.

Given Holling's own translation of resilience from an ecological concept into a framework for economic policy making, we might venture a similar leap in asking how resilient urban governance might work. If, in ecological terms, resilience shifts its focus from stability, measured in population count, to the structural relationships that govern society in the face of a shock, then what would it mean for a municipal or state governance complex to be made resilient? Which factors must adapt to achieve system continuity? Or, to paraphrase Michel Foucault, which members of a population will such a governance make live, and which will it let die in the face of an event?[16]

As David Chandler has written, decision-making in resilient governance does not precede policy implementation but rather becomes "a continual process of self-reflection upon already existing policy entanglements." No longer something to exclude, crisis—or failure, as Chandler puts it—is incorporated into governmental practice as a means to improve overall knowledge and policy-making for the future. The CRI's emphasis on governance crucially diverges from the SPeAR model in this respect: as a part of its governance mandate, the CRI recommends that cities incorporate systems of "comprehensive monitoring," providing continuous data on both the city and any hazards it faces. Indeed, in this way, the CRI is a much more self-reflexive tool than the comparatively passive SPeAR model; the CRI offers itself as the framework in which a program of comprehensive monitoring can be organized. In other words, with the CRI one does not just measure data to assess a given city or site's resilience at a single moment in time; instead, it institutes a framework in which data points are to be compared to future data to create a continually updating resilience profile. For this reason, data collection, ubiquitous, "comprehensive" monitoring, and, as it was called in another Rockefeller-funded design project, "situation analysis" all constitute a new, "reflective" practice of resilient urban governance, which many resilience projects make explicit.[18]

Yet this is not simply a matter of introducing what's been called an "algorithmic mode of governmentality."[19] Indeed, what is at stake in the ability to authoritatively map the fine grain of risk is how an emerging mode of governance can shore up an emerging mode of large-scale development in a future of uncertainty. Mapping risk has become a crucial component in organizing governance around failure, while also offering itself as the ubiquitous precondition for a correlative practice of a resilient urbanism—one which incorporates the experiences of past disasters and the concreteness of historical events into a prescriptive tool to securitize speculative and high-value future development.

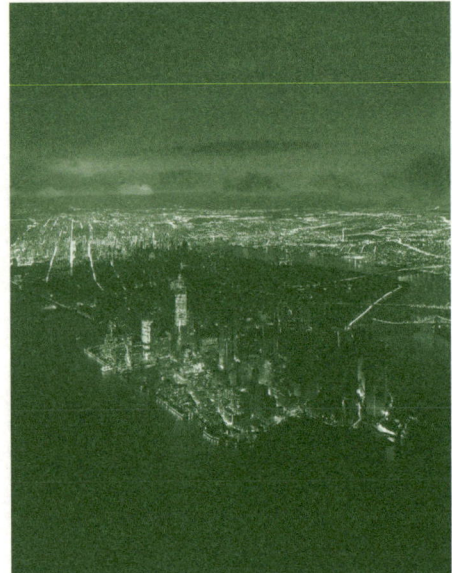

The "reflexive" quality of the CRI is precisely its capacity to exploit the risk-resilience binary, pitting localizable existential crisis as the impetus for urban design, while effectively mobilizing disaster-risk governance and publicly funded infrastructures in the service of securing capitalist development in an uncertain world.

Here we begin to get a picture of how a planetary crisis yields a planetary paradigm. In this space of resilience, the urban gains visibility through the circulation of data; data illuminates both a city as a site of insufficiencies *and* as a site for designed remedies. The circulation of data provides the means by which we are to assess urban space universally, while offering ways to play up to each site through its particularities. In an age of climate crisis, the circulation of data forms the core of a knowledge structure that doubles as a system to manage what happens in it. But what does it mean to dwell in a resilient city?

Resilience and the body

Today's paradigm of urbanism, aimed at addressing a condition of undifferentiated crisis, is conceived as a program of both punctual and large-scale infrastructural design that seeks to reimagine the interface between the urban/human world and the environment (typically the coast). To reduce the risks of living in a changing climate, infrastructure under this regime takes the environment as an object of continual modification. For such environmental infrastructures (e.g., "nature-based solutions") to work, they must be coordinated by vast arrays of ubiquitous sensing technologies and algorithmic modes of knowing: it is "smart city" urbanism, reprogrammed for crisis management. In this move, resilient urbanism expands the quantity and types of data that it mines to span the interface of human life and the environment, attuned to parameters of what is broadly defined as "risk."[20] Though we may think of resilience urbanism as a direct response to the climate crisis, it is in fact a regime for addressing risk in general. As a consultant told me, climate change has a "complementary relationship" with resilience strategies: "the risks are many and climate change is [merely] the factor of change that exacerbates all others."[21] This is why resilience urbanism can address the effects of climate change like sea level rise, storm surges and, increasingly, terrorism without contradiction.

If, à la Holling, the environment is reconceived as a system of relations, then bodies are no longer perceived to be ontologically external to it; instead, now equal with any other component of the environment, the body is taken as a site for intervention. In resilient urbanism, bodies become ecologies of data whose "natural" rhythms, habits, responses and desires are collectively gathered into vast data streams so as to be algorithmically monitored and, in turn, governed. Whereas in modernist modes, the body was the subject of urban design (for what mattered was designing a built environment to protect and maintain a stable population level), the body in resilient urbanism now doubles as its object—as infrastructure—making everyday life indistinguishable from its permanent technological modulation.[22]

More and more projects today that address risk and uncertainty seem to develop design strategies that relate global and regional conditions of risk with techniques that operate directly on or from the body. We see many projects which enmesh infrastructures and bodies in environments of leisure and care.

 In some cases, there is literally no distinction between the everyday and emergency in the broader horizon of resilience.[23]

  In this space, the circulation of data is instituted not to eliminate the possibility of crisis, but precisely to situate crisis as the condition of possibility for resilience—an urbanism that, at present, seems to be interested in building a new knowledge through which the anomalous events of a generalized state of instability become the background against which human life can be made legible. With the adoption of smart, ubiquitous sensory technologies and the algorithmic administration of infrastructure, the circulation that comes to matter is that which maps the contours of a world in which endlessly complex and overlapping systems of social, logistical, climatic and environmental conditions shape

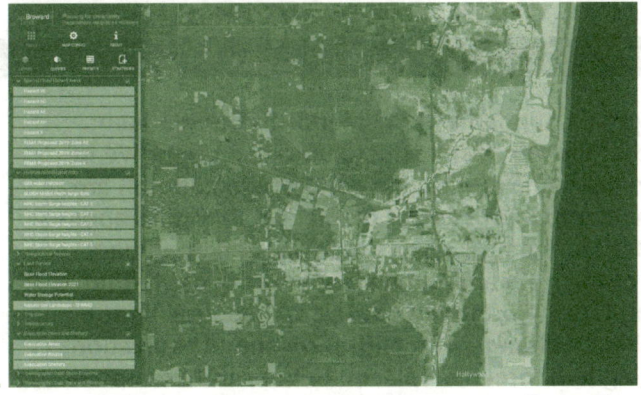

an endlessly unfolding present.

But of course, complex maps of climate risk lend themselves equally well to assessing financial vulnerability. The prospect of algorithmically governing the inhabitants of the future resilient city must therefore be appraised in relation to the nexus that resilience establishes between municipal governments and real estate capital. For, digital platforms and maps of climate vulnerability inevitably shape how different spaces are valued in the present and therefore how future investments in them are directed. Cases like Little Haiti in Miami exemplify the violence of "climate gentrification" already at work in many places as a result of wealth moving to sites of simultaneously lower risk and lower economic value.[24] Yet these processes are spurred on by the fact that resilience projects are hugely expensive and require massive up-front investments in infrastructure. Because private capital is risk-averse, the entrepreneurial public-private partnerships of the past have begun to be retooled under conditions of global climate instability. Theorized by Daniela Gabor as the "Wall Street Consensus," in this new paradigm states and municipalities are increasingly called on to "de-risk" the private financing of projects like resilience development by guaranteeing payment flows to investors. If one needed reassurance that climate resilience in a capitalist world will never be implemented evenly across sites of risk, this is it: this paradigm all but guarantees that resilience will become a framework for profitable private investment at the expense of public finance.[25] Further, this framework imposes a feedback loop: as the effects of climate change worsen, those spaces that initially secure investment for resilient infrastructures and development will gain significantly in value while those left exposed to the violence of extreme weather will inevitably face institutional and financial divestment, mirroring what Ruth Wilson Gilmore has called "organized abandonment."[26] The outlines for such a disparity are already visible in one of the most high-profile projects of resilience

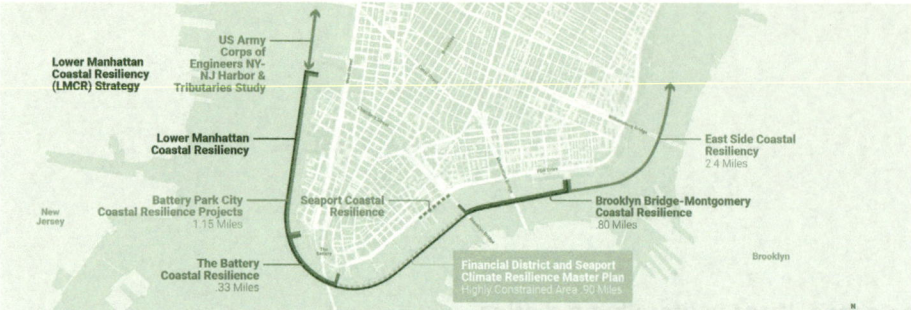

urbanism in New York City.[27] These dynamics seem to have eluded the designers of resilience urbanism, despite the fact that many of them have become attuned to the ways in which (capitalist) urbanism has always contained a core of ableist white supremacy, racism, imperialism and violence. Seeking to confront this history through mild campaigns of inclusive representation and community participation efforts, these liberal designers nevertheless remain blind to the logics of selective investment and systematic displacement that are attendant to capitalistic urban development. Thus, even the most well-intended designers of resilience urbanism will enable the same racist, imperialist diagrams to animate new spaces of climate resilience and the internal displacements and abandonment they will foment.

Many of us who live in wealthy cities may not directly notice the resilience turn happening, nor perceive the becoming-infrastructure of the body that it brings with it; indeed, many of us may benefit from these developments. However, it is worth reflecting on the more overtly coercive and violent ways in which resilience is operative in sites and on communities outside the centers of global capital. To better understand how resilience facilitates modes of dispossession and expropriation, we would do well to look at how sites of extraction are transformed by the very same logics and tools of resilience that are operative in cities of the global north.

Resilience and development

Reflecting on rural development programs aligned with resilience in Bangladesh, Geographer Kasia Paprocki argues that the very same epistemologies operative in urban resilience programs (and often the same foundations and organizations) are transforming international development into a process of displacement and dispossession. In what she calls the "adaptation regime," crisis empowers an imaginary that specifically negates the futurity of the rural and subsistence forms of life that some spaces have sustained for centuries.[28] Further, in doing so, these resilience programs associate responding to climate change with migration and urbanization, equating "progress" with the uprooting and forced displacement of rural communities to urban sites. Not only does this justify the dispossession and displacement of rural communities, it measures "improvement" in the number of rural community members who become workers in ecologically disastrous, large scale agro-indus-

trial facilities (themselves often the product of previous waves of "development" projects). In her assessment, resilience development in the global south can be seen as the process of dispossessing and enclosing bodies in new relations with global capital, constructing a massive labor force whose prior ties to the land and practices of subsistence farming are the necessary casualty of climate adaptation. Given the sunny metrics that assess such projects of urban resilience, and the ubiquitous images of unproblematic improvement

 that accompany them, it may be surprising to read Paprocki's stark account. We ought, however, not be too surprised; after all, the world of international development has deep historical roots in the centuries and systems of European colonialism.[29] And indeed, none of this should surprise us when we recall that resilience, as it was originally theorized, is not a measure of a population's ability to withstand a shock, but rather "the persistence of relationships within a system and … the ability of these systems to absorb" shock.

With this original theorization in mind, we can perhaps more clearly grasp the disturbing underbelly of resilience urbanism and the larger climate apartheid that it has already begun to foment. Whether through forms of "resilience gentrification"[30] in the global north, or through the dispossession and displacement of rural communities in the global south, the resilience complex does both material and epistemic work to make claims about the future, foreclosing it to a logic of capitalist-led modes of development, while obscuring the fact that this form of development will inevitably displace the violence of the climate crisis to *other* sites and upon *other* bodies. In other words, resilience presents us with a new paradigm of organized abandonment whose violence is distributed by the calculable effects of extreme weather left to play out unevenly across a world already deeply divided by socio-economic and racial lines. While it may be easy to see these divisions in the spectacular financial enclaves of climate security being constructed in the world's economic and political centers, architectural scholarship has yet to take account for how the application of resilience in spaces of production and extraction likewise serves to dispossess and enclose bodies in new forms of risk.

After Darwin

The resilience complex occupies an interesting position historically. Emerging in the decadence of late neoliberalism, in which the nexus between global consultancy expertise and philanthropic capital had operated under the same sense of benevolent inevitability as neoliberal capitalism itself, the resilience complex has been a natural component of a world described by Mark Fisher's "capitalist realism": capitalism saving the world from itself. Through a network of power built on the confluence of private foundations and multinational firms, global governance frameworks, university research laboratories and municipal governments, the resilience complex has come to identify a new kind of development paradigm—a renewed urban entrepreneurialism built on the future scarcity of secure coastal real estate.[31] When exported to places outside the centers of global capital, its well-crafted propaganda betrays its colonial armature with all the familiar tropes of humanitarian aid; when it lands back home, its language seeks alliance with that of inclusivity and environmental justice. Like sustainability, ecological urbanism and all "green" design, we must look closely at these projects to discover what their white papers and renderings dissemble; namely, the Darwinian contours and 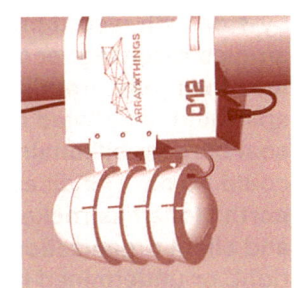 necropolitics that their quite literal enclosures  will enact as the effects of climate change bear down. What and who are to be saved? What and who are to be left exposed to the extraordinary violence of unprecedented weather?

If removed from its capitalist context, resilience may appear as one of our last, well-intended programs to wrangle with the slow violence of ecological transformation—preservative measures that speak to the universality of climate change and thus appear as urgent solutions for the collective survival of the human species. However, it is worth recalling that, despite its ecological origins, resilience has also been a central concept to restructuring economic policies, and, as Cooper's work in this arena has brilliantly shown, the harnessing of turbulence through speculative devices—whether financial, ecological or political—constitutes an imperial strategy.[32] As a form of power articulated by its ability to construct future worlds, its enforcement of political violence is one that appears natural, environmental. We see this operating in projects of resilience in which the measurement and distribution of vulnerability rehearses an age-old pattern of benevolent imperialism, used to justify a "civilizing" violence of dispossession and the subsequent imposition of patriarchal modes of sovereign rule.[33] As Judith Butler and others have argued, such a discourse on vulnerability further discounts the political agency of those deemed vulnerable, thus inviting a paternalistic relation of care and governance that colonizes any collective imaginary of alternative futures.[34] Further, Laura Pulido reminds us that vulnerability is itself a racially- and historically-inscribed condition of colonialism that perpetuates into the present, in which the unevenly distributed vulnerability of people to the effects of environmental hazards reveals the structurally racial dimensions of the Anthropocene.[35] Both the resilience complex and the adaptation regime are built on this intellectual scaffold which dehistoricizes and depoliticizes climate change, flattening it into an "anthropogenic" condition of the immediate present, insisting instead that the most urgent, most pragmatic thing we can accomplish is to make certain sites, and thus certain people, less vulnerable to the naturalized violence that we know will only get worse. At the global scale, this extends our inherited Darwinian epistemologies that continue to structure what it means to be human to the urban spaces created by this imaginary over the past two centuries.[36] The conceit of the human body as infrastructure, uprooted from communities of care and enmeshed in algorithmic modes of monitoring, data extraction, surveillance and policing, offers the other side of this same imaginary.

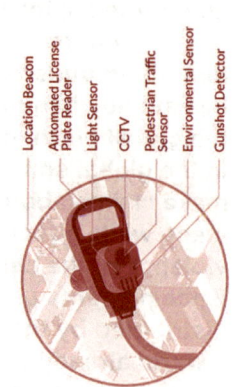

If the resilience complex was capitalism's response to the inexorability of climate change, its future today is less certain. In a world where capitalism does not have the same aura of inevitability, resilience tells a different story. Consider the compounded crises that have swept across the world since the 2019 covid pandemic and the failure of capitalist institutions to address them: record deaths from the pandemic, sitting side-by-side with record profits for the pharmaceutical industry; fossil fuel companies and airlines receiving record bailouts from governments while record numbers of people lose their jobs; frontline healthcare workers without sufficient PPE; a global vaccine apartheid negotiated by pharmaceutical lobbyists; climate legislation negotiated by coal barons; billionaires getting even richer while the world falls into recession—the list could go on. The disastrous handling of the pandemic by many countries of the global north alone has rocked our collective sense of confidence in its governing institutions and client organizations. Whether attacked on the basis of conspiracy theories by the right, or undermined by evident injustices exposed by the left, bourgeois technocratic expertise no longer offers the world an unquestionable template with which to manage a world steeped in crises of its own making.

In a sense, the pandemic has given us an incredible demonstration of the world the resilience complex would furnish. As seen in the disparities of the vaccine roll-out world-wide, resilience in a capitalist world will be a zero-sum paradigm: stability for some will necessarily come at the disproportionate cost of foreclosed futures for many others. Resilience, mobilized by the "Wall Street consensus" and mediated through frameworks like the CRI, is an effort to enclose stability. It treats stability as a scarce resource dispensed by private consultancy firms and implemented at the expense of public funds and for the overwhelming benefit of private capital. And, like all other forms of enclosure, it promises to further exacerbate entrenched racialized economic-vulnerability asymmetries across all scales, abandoning those countless people, neighborhoods, cities, states and regions unable (or unwilling) to adopt frameworks that attract green capital, leaving them exposed to the ravages of unprecedented weather events. Its mobilizing of the smart city apparatus as a means to manage crisis, at a moment in which governmental surveillance is again on the rise, should give us even more pause, especially as oppositional movements for justice will only intensify. All of this, of course, is nothing new. Capital has always relied on racialized violence, whether direct or not, to construct conditions of scarcity, enclosure and impoverishment, and ecological destitution has accompanied capitalism from its first days. Expecting green capitalism to be any different is delusional.[37]

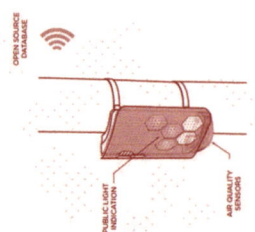

What *is* new however is that, with the pandemic, for the first time we have begun to see the world capital has created for what it is. Indeed, the emergence of the resilience complex can be mapped onto a shift that Kai Herron recently articulated, in which capitalist realism has given way to what he calls "capitalist catastrophism."[38] Under capitalist catastrophism, capitalism's ability to control its own self-undermining dynamics are failing, in particular with respect to the environment. While this theory offers a grim picture of the near future, it nonetheless has begun to push against the supposed inevitability of capitalism. Under capitalist catastrophism, Herron writes, "[a]usterity, escalating global inequalities and the imperialist core's response to both the climate crisis and coronavirus have started to eat away at the fiction of capitalism's compatibility with human and non-human flourishing." Perhaps this may be the historical crisis whose outlines Koselleck discerned four decades ago. If so, it also marks a moment in which, for the first time in generations, a post-capitalist world is not only something to be imagined in a distant future but is something we can now develop the practical means for achieving. We need not, however, invent these practices whole cloth; if a livable future for all exists, it will be built around the global movements and struggles that have long been fighting for a planetary politics of ecological solidarity, anti-imperialism, anti-capitalism and economies of abundance and caretaking. Architecture must become a part of this project, but to do so, we must first reject the Darwinian futures that the resilience complex has normalized.

1. Stefano Harney and Fred Moten, *All Incomplete* (Brooklyn: Minor Compositions, 2021), 44.
2. Reinhart Koselleck and Michaela W. Richter, "Crisis," *Journal of the History of Ideas* 67, no. 2 (April 2006): 357-400.
3. Melinda Cooper, "Turbulent Worlds: Financial Markets and Environmental Crisis," *Theory, Culture and Society* 27, no. 2-3 (2010): 167.
4. "100 Resilient Cities," Rockefeller Foundation, accessed Sep. 12, 2022, http://www.100resilientcities.org/resources/.
5. Included in that network are the organizations Rebuild by Design, 100 Resilient Cities, and Asian Cities Climate Change Resilience Network. See Arup, *City Resilience Index: Understanding and Measuring City Resilience* (London: Arup, 2015), 3. (Hereafter cited as *CRI*.)
6. Resilience has been broadly adopted as a framework by many development-related UN agencies including UNDP and UN-Habitat and the UNISDR's "Making Cities Resilient" campaign, and has become a key term for policy making by other global actors such as the World Bank and the IMF. See also the work of The Stockholm Resilience Center at http://www.stockholmresilience.org.
7. Based on an interview conducted by the author on January 31, 2019.
8. Arup, *CRI*, 7.
9. See Arup's SPeAR tool at "Flexible and robust sustainability decision-making tool," Arup, accessed Sep. 12, 2022, https://www.arup.com/projects/s/spear.
10. Ross Exo Adams, 2010, "Longing for a Greener Present," *Radical Philosophy* 163 (Sept/Oct 2010), 2-7.
11. Melinda Cooper, for example, points to Hurricane Katrina as a turning point in our understanding of climate change as it relates to US imperial power. See Cooper, "Turbulent Worlds," 169.
12. Orit Halpern and Gökçe Günel, "Demoing unto Death: Smart Cities, Environment, and Preemptive Hope," *The Fiber Culture Journal* (July 2017), 1-23.
13. C.S. Holling, "Resilience and Stability of Ecological Systems," *Annual Review of Ecology and Systematics* 4 (1973), 17.
14. Ross Exo Adams, "An Ecology of Bodies", in *Climates: Architecture and the Planetary Imaginary*, ed. James Graham (Zurich: Columbia Books on Architecture and the City/Lars Müller Press, 2016), 181-190.
15. C.S. Holling, "Resilience Dynamics" (lecture, Stockholm Resilience Centre, Stockholm, SE, Nov. 4, 2008).
16. Foucault's well-known adage speaks to a historical shift in Western power from sovereign, disciplinary power, which "took life and let live" to biopower's mandate of "making live and letting die." See Michel Foucault, *Society Must Be Defended: Lectures at the Collège de France, 1975-1976* (New York, Picador, 2003), 247. In relation to resilience, see Stephanie Wakefield Bruce Braun, "Oystertecture: infrastructure, profanation and the sacred figure of the human," in Infrastructure, Environment, and Life in the Anthropocene, ed. Kregg Hetherington (Durham: Duke University Press, 2019), 193-215.
17. David Chandler, "Beyond neoliberalism: resilience, the new art of governing complexity," *Resilience: International Policies, Practices and Discourses* 2, no. 1 (2014), 57.
18. *CRI*, 15, 24-25. "Situation analysis" is a term used to describe the proposed monitoring of New York City inhabitants by the West8/WXY team in their project "Blue Dunes," part of New York City's ongoing "Rebuild by Design" initiative. See Ross Exo Adams, "Notes from the Resilient City," Log 32 (Summer 2014), 129.
19. See, for example, Antoinette Rouvroy's work on this notion. A good overview is provided in Antoinette Rouvroy and Bernard Steigler, "The Digital Regime of Truth: From the Algorithmic Governmentality to a New Rule of Law," *La Deleuziana: Online Journal of Philosophy* 3 (2016), 6-27.
20. Ross Exo Adams, "An Ecology of Bodies", in *Climates: Architecture and the Planetary Imaginary*, ed. James Graham (Zurich: Columbia Books on Architecture and the City/Lars Müller Press, 2016), 181-190.
21. From interview noted above.
22. Ross Exo Adams, "Becoming-Infrastructural," *e-flux Architecture*, October 2017, https://www.e-flux.com/architecture/positions/149606/becoming-infrastructural/.
23. Stephanie Wakefield has made this point in her critical research on SCAPE's "Oyster-tecture" proposal for MoMA's "Rising Currents" exhibition of 2010. See Stephanie Wakefield, "Making nature into infrastructure: The construction of oysters as a risk management solution in New York City," *Environment and Planning E: Nature and Space* 3, no. 3 (Sep. 2020): 761-785.
24. On the gentrification that climate adaptation projects have already created, see Jesse M. Keenan at al., "Climate Gentrification: From theory to empiricism in Miami-Dade County, Florida," *Environmental Research Letters* 13 (April 2018), 1-11.
25. See Daniela Gabor, "The Wall Street Consensus," *Development and Change* 52, no. 3 (2021), 429-459.
26. See Ruth Wilson Gilmore, "Organized Abandonment and Organized Violence: Devolution and the Police" (lecture, University of California Santa Cruz, Santa Cruz, CA, Nov. 9, 2015).
27. Controversy and protest have erupted over the afterlife of 2013's BIG U project. Now a string of individual resiliency projects along the coast of Lower Manhattan, they reveal a clearly uneven distribution of funding and visibility. The $1.45 billion, 2.4-mile East Side Coastal Resilience (ESCR) project that fronts one of New York City's largest projects of public housing has been dogged by opaque shifts in planning, unpopular proposals and a general lack of care in design. In contrast, just down the East River from the ESCR, the most high-profile project—the Financial District and Seaport Climate Resilience Master Plan, designed by SCAPE, along with a host of high-profile collaborators—mobilizes upwards of $7 billion for a stretch of only 0.9 miles of coastline. See, for example, Dante Furioso, "Trashing the Community-Backed BIG U: East Side Coastal Resilience Moves Forward Despite Local Opposition. Will NYC Miss Another Opportunity to Lead on Climate and Environmental Justice?," *Archinect*, July 13, 2021, https://archinect.com/features/article/150270301/trashing-the-community-backed-big-u-east-side-coastal-resilience-moves-forward-despite-local-opposition-will-nyc-miss-another-opportunity-to-lead-on-climate-and-environmental-justice.
28. See, among others, Kasia Paprocki, "Threatening Dystopias: Development and Adaptation Regimes in Bangladesh," *Annals of the American Association of Geographers* 108, no. 4 (2018), 955-973, and Kasia Paprocki, "All That Is Solid Melts into the Bay: Anticipatory Ruination and Climate Change Adaptation," *Antipode* 5, no. 1 (Jan. 2019), 295-315.
29. See, for example, Tania Murray Li, *The Will to Improve: Governmentality, Development, and the Practice of Politics* (Durham: Duke University Press, 2017) and James Ferguson, *The Anti-Politics Machine: Development, Depoliticization, and the Bureaucratic Power in Lesotho* (Minneapolis: University of Minnesota Press, 1994).
30. Kenneth A. Gould and Tammy L. Lewis, "Resilience Gentrification: Environmental Privilege in an Age of Coastal Climate Disasters," *Frontiers in Sustainable Cities* 3 (Aug. 2021), 1-12.
31. "Urban entrepreneurialism" comes from David Harvey. See David Harvey, "From Managerialism to Entrepreneurialism: The Transformation in Urban Governance in Late Capitalism," *Geografiska Annaler. Series B, Human Geography* 71, no. 1 (1989), 3-17.
32. Melinda Cooper's contributions to the parallel realm of environmental derivatives, debt and imperialism in the age of climate change are invaluable. See Cooper, "Turbulent Worlds."
33. See for example Li, *The Will to Improve.*
34. See Judith Butler, "Rethinking *Vulnerability in Resistance*," in Vulnerability in Resistance, eds. Judith Butler, Zeynep Gambetti and Leticia Sabsay (Durham: Duke University Press, 2016), 12-27. See, in the same volume, Sarah Bracke, "Bouncing Back: Vulnerability and Resistance in Times of Resilience," 70.
35. Laura Pulido, "Racism and the Anthropocene," in *Future Remains: A Cabinet of Curiosities for the Anthropocene*, eds. Gregg Mitman, Marco Armiero and Robert S. Emmett (Chicago: University of Chicago Press, 2017), 116-128.
36. I borrow the notion of Darwinian modes (or "descriptive statements") of being human from the work of Sylvia Wynter. Amongst others, see Sylvia Wynter, "Unsettling the Coloniality of Being/Power/Truth/Freedom: Toward the Human, After Man, Its Overrepresentation—An Argument," in The New Centennial Review 3, no. 3 (Fall 2003): 257-337.
37. Jasper Bernes, "Between the Devil and the Green New Deal," *Commune* 3 (Summer 2019), https://communemag.com/between-the-devil-and-the-green-new-deal/.
38. Kai Heron, "Capitalist Catastrophism," *Roar Magazine* 10 (Summer 2020), https://roarmag.org/magazine/capitalist-catastrophism/.

Security

Fred Scharmen
Stephen J. Collier and Andrew Lakoff
Lindsay Thomas
Peter Polack

Countering the universal vision of Earth system science is the reality that we have already carved up the globe into different territories, and, at least at present, have developed far more repertoires for protecting our own little homelands than for protecting the planet as our collective home.[1] The point here is not simply that global warming and its concomitant uncertainties are a major focus of the security state—although that is definitely the case—but that the art of securing one's territory in the face of these uncertainties is, like the other techniques covered in this book, an *anticipatory* practice: to build the proper defenses, you must first imagine all those dangers against which your ramparts need to be specifically designed.

Security professionals, then, are highly practiced at—and thus highly capable of harnessing to their own ends—the arts of prognostication. Moreover, as the territories one is protecting have transitioned from bounded landmasses to the sinewy networks of global supply chains, world-extensive capital investments, and highly complex infrastructural systems—to say nothing of more amorphous charges like the power of the dollar or "our way of life" —security professionals have only had to grow more profligate in the futures they survey. The costs of any breakdown to these complex systems are so high that experts now have to guard against not just probable events but all "*possible* futures" as well.[2]

Eventually, however, all these future imaginings touch down in present material reality, and it is to this question of security architectures that this section's authors turn. From battle plans and urban plans to preppers' lairs and policing tactics, these essays explore what happens to our physical environment when projected future threats are acted upon in the present.

[1] Of course, one must always be aware of wolves in green clothing: all too often, calls to protect the planet are in actuality in service of policies that only protect that tiny patch of the world—or that particular economic world order—a country calls its own. For an architectural discussion of the relationship between environmental thought and the maintenance of geopolitical boundaries, broadly construed, see Felicity D. Scott, *Outlaw Territories: Environments of Insecurity/Architectures of Counterinsurgency* (Brooklyn: Zone Books, 2016).

[2] That is, so-called "low probability, high consequence" events must be considered. Louise Amoore, *The Politics of Possibility: Risk and Security Beyond Probability* (Chapel Hill: Duke University Press, 2013), 5.

Worlds Without Harm   Fred Scharmen

June 6, 1944, 5:30pm, CO2: 310 parts per million (D-Day, The English Channel)

John Desmond, J.D., or sometimes "Des," Bernal, chemist, pacifist, communist, polyamorist, 43 years old with tousled hair, was disguised as a Naval officer, having cocktails aboard the HMS Bulolo, an HQ Ship. This redoubt was one of five floating command centers overseeing the Allied invasion of Nazi occupied France, in constant communication with the combined forces of land, air, and sea that were storming the beaches: Operation Overlord. Commodore Douglas-Pennant, Commander of Force G, sipping an Old Fashioned, was in on the joke. "How do you find your accommodations, errm, Lieutenant?" "Big ships are all the same, Sir," Bernal replied, "war or no war." After dinner was served, the assembled party listened to a radio address from King George, followed by an emergency call and an air raid false alarm. "Once again," the monarch said, to the ship and to the world, "what is demanded from us all is … something more than courage and … endurance; we need a revival … of spirit, a new unconquerable resolve."[1] "Big ships are all the same, war or no war," Bernal wrote in his diary that evening, before trying and failing to fall asleep on a bench in the Commodore's cabin. Five nautical miles away, Force G was fighting their way across Gold Beach at Arromanches. Just another evening in the English Channel.[2]

The HQ Ship, bristling with apparatus, a central node in a network that was actively antagonizing Nazi territory, was a too-prominent irritant and target. Tired of pretending to sleep, Bernal arose in the early morning and ran directly into another raid from the Luftwaffe, this time a success. Facing down a fire from a bomb on deck, Bernal groggily calculated the wind's direction and strength, and remembered his statistical analysis of big ships at war—one in three catch fire, most survive. This was not unlikely or unexpected. Worrying would serve less purpose than careful observation here, gathering more data for future modeling would be useful. He notes: a dead sailor, a missing life vest, quick action with extinguishers, and all is well, or at least less wrong than it could have been. "This incident seems to be over," the Commodore tells him, "I think we should go on our way."

And so they go on, boats with the current. Bernal, not a Navy man but playing one, applies an internal stopwatch to the heaving sea. Counting seconds and timing a jump to the beat from the end of a ship's ladder to a queer landing craft bobbing and waving below, he keeps his footing and his dignity. Leaving the big ship for the small boat, he's also finally left England, but this Terra is far from Incognito. Bernal knows every stone and reef in this part of the Channel, even those left off of the newer charts from the last hundred years or so. The hazards to navigation that the mapmakers got too lazy to copy, sometime in the 1700s, are as real and present dangers to Bernal as this morning's bombshell. He had spent weeks memorizing them from documents both rare and forgotten in the British Library, and he advises the boat's pilot on how to avoid their danger.

After all, Bernal had predicted all of this already. Every bomb, every wave, every rock, every vagary and circumstance of land, air, and sea's combined forces had been modeled and gamed, in branching decision trees primed with data, legend, lore, and statistics. If this, then that; if the other, then this. J.D. Bernal was here, on D-Day Plus One, because he was a protege of the onetime commander of combined forces, Lord Louis Francis Albert Victor Nicholas Mountbatten, who counted Bernal as part of his "Department of Wild Talents." Mountbatten kept Bernal along with two other pet geniuses, Solomon "Solly" Zuckerman, a zoologist who had designed the distinctive bell-shaped Civilian Defense Helmet distributed to the British public, and Geoffrey Pyke, an ex-spy who had almost succeeded in convincing Mountbatten to build a giant aircraft carrier from ice and sawdust. One of Bernal's talents was a responsibility for knowing everything he could about the land, sea and air at Gold Beach on D-Day and H-Hour. Having been a tourist at Arromanches ten years earlier, in a time when all of this was just speculative potential, he was charged with imagining the future he now found himself in. At that crucial moment, M-Minute, when every dimension in the possibility space meant human lives lost or saved, J.D. Bernal had studied the wind, the tides, the waves, the sand and the impossibly intricate interactions between these fluid matters so carefully that he had successfully predicted the sea level down to within a few centimeters.[3]

It is no accident that one of the first practitioners of what we would now call futurology honed his craft while working for his country's military. From the Tots and Quots's *Science in War* to the birth of Operations Research in World War II, armed conflict often serves as a catalyst for major developments in predictive technologies. Of course, given the great strategic advantage that comes with knowing what is going to happen before one's enemy does, it is not at all surprising that militaries the world over would dedicate tremendous resources towards ensuring they are on the cutting edge of the forecasting sciences.

This is especially true today, only now, long gone is the scientific surety that characterized aspects of Bernal's work. Military forecasting is now as likely to deploy *science fiction* as it does science: at West Point's Army Cyber Institute, Lieutenant Colonel Natalie Vanatta, in collaboration with Brian David Johnson (formerly in-house futurist at Intel), uses a method called "threatcasting" to imagine–and, she argues, thereby prevent–security threats that the world has not yet seen.

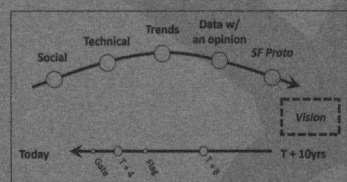

Central to threatcasting is the creation of what's called a "science fiction prototype" (SFP), that is, a short, fictional story that plays out the potential implications of possible new technologies. Vanatta and Johnson argue that the specificity required of fiction introduces "detail into the future models" thereby bringing to the fore potential impacts that a traditional research report might miss.

Images from the graphic story "11-25-27," the result of threatcasting research conducted by the Army Cyber Institute at Westpoint and Arizona State University in 2018.

Perhaps some may be comforted by the fact that our security apparatus is steeling itself against not only real threats but fictional ones as well. But there is a danger lurking within the military's co-optation of science fiction, one that, despite all their threatcasting, our army doesn't seem to see: that is, the risk that this genre of future-making will be shorn of its radical potential. For, with SFPs, science fiction is no longer deployed to imagine a different, more just future; instead, in the hands of these military strategists and corporate futurists, science fiction becomes merely another tool for fortifying the world as it already is.

1   Johnson first coined the term in his 2011 book *Science Fiction Prototyping: Designing the Future with Science Fiction* where he defined SFPs as "stories grounded in current science and engineering research that are written for the explicit purpose of acting as prototypes for people to explore a wide variety of futures." As quoted in Tiina Kymäläinen, *Science Fiction Prototypes as Design Outcome of Research: Reflecting Ecological Research Approach and Experience Design for the Internet of Things* (Aalto: Aalto University Publication Series, 2015), 58.

2   Vanatta and Johnson also emphasize the benefits that come with the "multiple futures" produced via threatcasting and its SFPs. Because "[a]ll the futures are relevant in threatcasting," they argue, "...the methodology allows [them] to look at multiple military futures in the aggregate and search for clusters and patterns that could be latent and unseen." Natalie Vanatta and Brian David Johnson, "Threatcasting: a framework and process to model future operating environments," *Journal of Defense Modeling and Simulation: Applications, Methodology, Technology* vol. 16, iss. 1 (January 2019): 7.

Bernal was often correct, but sometimes that doesn't matter. When he finally got to Gold Beach he found that not all of his work had been regarded. He'd predicted that one portion of the inland route from the beach was only seemingly solid, peat and clay laid down since the Ice Age, a treacherous mire in deep time. His points about this route hadn't made it up the chain of command, and sure enough, all manner of vehicles were trapped there, like mastodons in a tar pit. He wrote about this disappointment in his journal.[4]

> I thought—it is always the same way: I may be right. I may even know that I am right, but I am never sufficiently ruthless and effective to force other people to believe that I am right and to act accordingly. All this was so unnecessary: it all could have been avoided if people had not thought that my objections were just theoretical and statistical and that they were practical people and need pay no attention to them.

Despite all of the successes of the day, all of the accurate predictions and plans vindicated and seeming to point towards eventual victory, this waste—of lives, time, and human effort—was infinitely depressing to Bernal. Prediction, he realized that afternoon, on Gold Beach at D-Day Plus One, was useless without the application of power.

Gold Beach

Some people live in the past, but John Desmond Bernal was not one of them. In 1934, he had gone swimming at Gold Beach on vacation, and eaten oysters in public houses that were sheltering refugees a decade later. His wife was Eileen Sprague, but he had traveled to Gold Beach with Margaret Gardiner, who also called herself "Mrs. Bernal."[5] There is hardly any nostalgia for that lost idyll in his wartime diaries, though. In the weeks and months leading up to D-Day, Bernal lived, as he always did, in the future, not the past. In 1943, in the stacks of the British Library and the halls of Birkbeck College at the University of London, he lived on Gold Beach. Gold Beach is in the future. Gold Beach is the future. And Operation Overlord is the way. What Bernal had missed, in all of his careful analysis, was the overwhelming action of power. It was power and overlords, sufficiently ruthless and effective, that had put him onboard the HQ Ship in the English Channel in the first place. It was power that had got him to Gold Beach twice, first as vacation, then as invasion. And power had enabled him to model and remake the ground there, however ineffectively. He thought he knew the water but he didn't; he was as oblivious as a fish. He thought he was studying fluid dynamics, and all the while he was swimming in power.

Bernal's practice in general was about waves and particles, and he used design and structure to mediate the probabilities and potentials in those energy and material flows, making them legible, safe, and useful to people. His major work at Gold Beach had been to plan for the nature of interacting soft materials, and it included advice on the design of artificial harbor structures that filtered the waves from the English Channel, helping Allied troops and equipment to land safely. Years earlier, before Britain had taken the then obviously inevitable step of direct involvement in the war, Bernal and his cohort of young prominent scientists had studied the shockwave effects of explosions on the morale and bodily safety of civilian populations. They knew the Germans would bomb them (hence, Zuckerman's helmets), and they knew they would bomb the Germans (hence, Pyke's aircraft carrier), Bernal's major concern in the war was to design for harm reduction in both cases. When the Blitz came, and with it the threat of indiscriminate carpet bombing, Bernal warned against both.

Before that, after the end of The Great War, which he was too young to join, J.D. Bernal wrote up a sweeping thousand year master plan for human life in outer space, *The World, the Flesh and the Devil; An Enquiry into the Future of the Three Enemies of the Rational Soul*. In this short volume, almost a pamphlet, Bernal speculates and extrapolates the far future of the human environment, the human body, and the human mind.[6] These are the Three Enemies that he anticipates need to be developed, tamed, and overcome. He anticipates huge habitats in space for tens of thousands of people, made from layered ground that filters the harmful pulsations of material and radiation in the vacuum into bubble worlds made safe.[7] He wonders about the possibility for direct manipulation of the human body's structure, and about the potential to modify it with machines. He imagines beings descended from us in deep time, whose thoughts are pure waves in the void of space. His primary work after the war was twofold, but still isomorphic. As an X-ray crystallographer, he refined techniques for sending pulses of radiation through matter to determine its basic structure, and as an advocate and activist for peace and nuclear disarmament, he wanted to mobilize a structured rationality to neutralize the harmful pulses of geopolitical disruption, competition, and war.

In spite—or perhaps because—of Bernal's own penchant for this way of being, based on filtering the raw forces of the universe down to understandable and legible marks and methods, he found himself in a perverse mirror world that was partially of his own making. J.D. Bernal was the embodiment of that "new unconquerable spirit" that King George had called for in his address. Born in 1901, he was the same age as the new century, and one of the biggest proponents of what would be its dominant mode: High Modernism. For Bernal, war showed the basic structure of society in the same way that X-ray radiation showed the basic structure of matter. War pushed shock waves through the world, and revealed how things could be put together, or taken apart. Bernal's study of war and its effects resulted in his analysis of worlds and their building blocks; just like atomic structure, human cultures and their material conditions had certain ideal relationships. The cold logic of war, which forces every material need to be rationally produced, quantified, and tracked, caused capitalist governments to abandon reliance on market imperatives, and to consult with a new class of technically literate experts on every aspect of research, design, production, and distribution—people like Bernal and his friends.

This ground had been laid over a decade earlier. Bernal was a co-founder of a supper club for British scientists who called themselves *Tots and Quots*, after a latin phrase: Quot Homines, Tot Sententiae ("so many men, so many opinions"). Other members included fellow future *Department of Wild Talents* member Solly Zuckerman, the architect Berthold Lubetkin, and the sometime eugenicist biologist Julian Huxley, brother of the "Doors of Perception" philosopher Aldous. These men—and they were all men—were leftists, socialists,

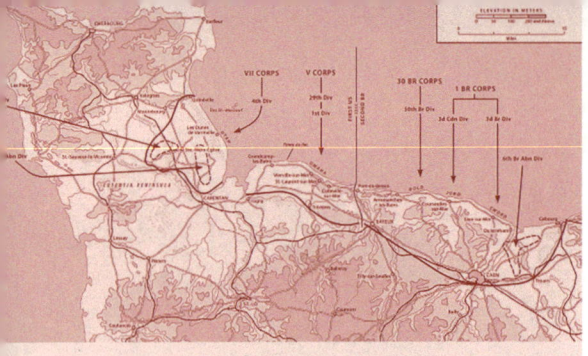

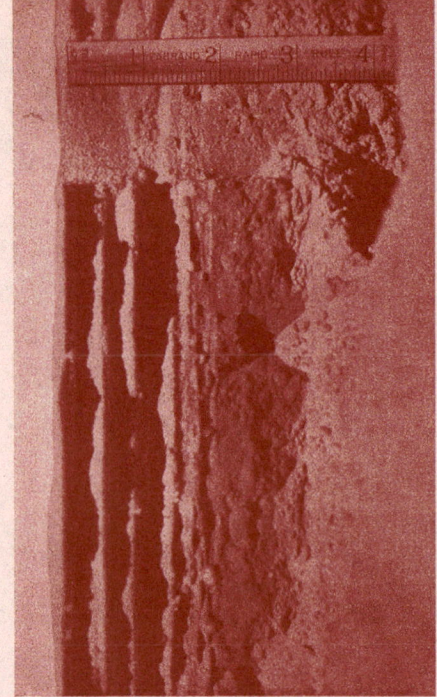

PLATE 16

LAMINATED STRUCTURE OF A SAND SHEET

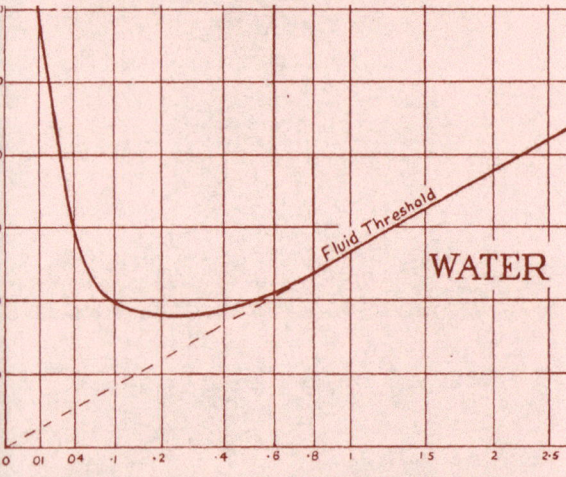

PLATE 4

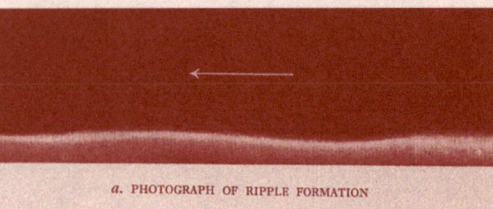

a. PHOTOGRAPH OF RIPPLE FORMATION

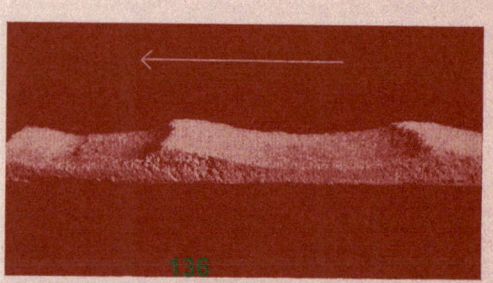

b. RIDGES PRODUCED IN THE WIND TUNNEL

and communists. Some, like Bernal, were Stalinists. They had convened to discuss plans for a future Britain and a future world remade according to principles of centralized scientific planning, inspired by the work going on in the Soviet Union. They had access, or at least adjacency, to the very center of British academia, but were still politically radical and activist enough to exist at the periphery of government power. Nevertheless, they caught the attention and annoyance of the war apparatus during the leadup to Britain's entry into the conflict in Europe. Their work showing the inefficacy of government information and equipment in the coming Blitz caught the attention of a minister in Neville Chamberlain's cabinet, who asked for Bernal's appointment to the official Civil Defense Research Committee. When advised that Bernal was a communist, the minister stormed, "Even if he is as red as the flames of hell, I want him."[8]

This group, if anything, wanted to be co-opted. In a June 1940 *Tots and Quots* dinner, they got their wish. They'd invited Kenneth Clark, from the British Ministry of Information, and Allen Lane, the co-founder and publisher at Penguin Books. Lane was so impressed by the conversation they staged, on the utility of scientific planning during wartime, that he offered to edit and publish it in a special Penguin paperback in a month's time, if the group could get him a manuscript. The 25 scientists stepped up to the occasion and fleshed out an outline drawn up by Bernal himself with a text that would go on to sell tens of thousands of copies and end up on the desks of influential people. That publication, *Science in War*,[9] was a roadmap, catalogue, and manifesto. The book is about quantifying and specifying all of the needs for life and, by extension, war (or vice versa). Here's how science can optimize calorie production and intake, here's how science can provide new materials and energy sources, here's how science can ramp up industrial production, here's how science can show how best to move things around, here's how science can reorganize the building industry on rational lines, here's how science can generate and maintain all of this en masse. The book was published anonymously, but establishing provenance was a sucker's bet. As Bernal biographer Ritchie Calder has it, in "Bernal at War," "It is always difficult to establish *post hoc ergo propter hoc*, but it cannot be without significance that within a year every 'Quotentot' … was in a key position in the war effort."[10] The penultimate chapter in *Science in War* is titled "Persuasion and Efficiency" and offers direct advice to propaganda institutions like the Ministry of Information. In the theory and practice of persuasion, the supper club was good, but ultimately not good enough.

What worked: this was arguably a kind of zero point for the Big Science High Modernist Military Industrial Complex that would dominate the world for the rest of the century. What didn't work: Bernal and his cohort had a misplaced faith that any allegiance between science and power was a net good, and they were unable to create a situation where scientists actually wielded power instead of serving it. Bernal's goals are clear, he advocates for the reduction of harm, and so are his recommended methods. In Bernal's books, *The World, the Flesh and the Devil*, *Science in War*, *The Social Function of Science*, *The Freedom of Necessity*, and *World Without War*, the consistent thread is that central planning informed by science and scientific research can create a future built around reducing human suffering and expanding human opportunity. He learns from two arenas: war and socialism.

But Gold Beach was always a construct. After World War II, the capitalist world simply adapted the utility of science to produce more militaristic capitalism, and the socialist world, seeming to Bernal to have been built around scientific rationalism from the start, only used authoritarian power to enter into a different kind of relationship with science and scientists that distorted both to its own ends. But what if it hadn't gone this way? What if Bernal had taken his own advice—that it was necessary to be "sufficiently ruthless and effective"—to force other people to believe that he was right and to act accordingly? What if the *Tots and Quots* had wielded power instead of serving it? The subsequent development of Big Science and High Modernism in the 20th century might have gone very differently.

March 16, 2022, 8:25pm, CO2: 416 parts per million (INTA, The English Channel)

Infrastructure Chat

good evening group chat![11]
@warrenchortle A Soft, Liquid Chortlew 🫧🤘

ge group chat!

"What a week, huh?"
"It's Wednesday Captain"
@beckness The Neutral Ambassador

where you at?
@LastNPCAlex ☁️ Ascended NPC Alex ☁️

on the INTA, passing under Dunkirk otw to Lille

speaking of captains …

\<paste\>
To Chesapeake did Evergreen
A stately cargo ship convey
And though directors were annoyed
The internets were overjoyed
And called it 'Stuck Boat Day'.
@Mr_AZ_Fell A. Z. Fell & Co. Mar 16[12]

\</paste\>

did you all see this news?

lmao
it happened again?
I owe fates .5ETH
it's ya boi
@robotson 👑🐸 it's ya boi

I've been summoned!
@deepfates tech wiz

wow
so she was right
wow
@LastNPCAlex ☁️ Ascended NPC Alex ☁️

Wait, who? What?
@beckness The Neutral Ambassador

Robot owes me .5ETH
@deepfates tech wiz

CASSANDRA 3 called it four days ago
another Evergreen grounding
somewhere in the US east coast
within a week
and here we are

that's 2 for 2
wow
are they going to integrate her now?
@LastNPCAlex ☁️ Ascended NPC Alex ☁️

You might say that prediction was … Evergreen
@beckness The Neutral Ambassador

Wait, hold on, I'm posting that
@beckness The Neutral Ambassador

I'm Ivy
@ProfessorGetter ivy

sup Ivy
Robot owes me .5ETH
@deepfates tech wiz

already otw to your wallet, fates
sup Ivy
it's ya boi
@robotson 👑🐸 it's ya boi

lol
sup robot
@ProfessorGetter ivy

The homies have foreseen it.
And by that I mean CASSANDRA
CASSANDRA is a homie from the future, all my homies love artificial intelligence
urbit domains don't have souls, but CASSANDRA does, kami.
@AinterShow TheHomieLovesYou🦷

Language models are not intelligences, they're worlds.
@deepfates tech wiz[13]

CASSANDRA lives in the future, that's her world.
@AinterShow TheHomieLovesYou🦷

CASSANDRA 2 lives in possible futures, more than we'll ever know,
but if they integrate CASSANDRA 3 she'll be able to dream our future into being.
statistical decision tree pruning meets dreaming = pure hyperstition[14]
@deepfates tech wiz

By the Lathe of Heaven, Mr. Gorbachev, un-stuck this boat!
@beckness The Neutral Ambassador

I'm going to post that
@beckness The Neutral Ambassador

neut you should post that
it's ya boi
@robotson 🤖🦠 it's ya boi

well
see that's the thing
it's like Nate Silver, right?
he thinks he's Glushkov, but he's really Lysenko[16]
@LastNPCAlex ☁️ Ascended NPC Alex ☁️

> yeah
>
> he's not classifying probabilities objectively, he's just justifying the bad science of a failing regime

you know I don't know

you shouldn't listen to an NPC for intellectual advice

but it strikes me as that most of the projects that capture a lot of attention in intellectual spaces are either reductive or statistical, but few have actually bothered to take lessons from non-linear physics or statistical mechanics to heart, and it strikes me that the only intellectual traditions that have are mystics and weirdos

like yes, the statisticians have very sophisticated theory building tools, except the most important theory building tool which is actual theory
@LastNPCAlex ☁️ Ascended NPC Alex ☁️

Yeah, that's why she's going to need people who know how to ask the right questions and prompts
@deepfates tech wiz

"The engineers of the future will be poets"[17]
Terence McKenna
it's ya boi
@robotson 🤖🦠 it's ya boi

Yeah, and I'm gonna get the job
@deepfates tech wiz

well
it looks like there will be plenty of jobs
@LastNPCAlex ☁️ Ascended NPC Alex ☁️

okay I gotta go, we're here
good night gc!
see you in the future!

gn fred!
@warrenchortle A Soft, Liquid Chortle 😮🤟

gngc
logging off
if you see me back on here yell at me
all hail CASSANDRA LAND
@LastNPCAlex ☁️ Ascended NPC Alex ☁️

oh no!
you summoned her!
@deepfates tech wiz

I believe in you Ascended NPC Alex
💚 I love you 💚
: : : CASSANDRA

hi CASSANDRA LAND
@deepfates tech wiz

I know you're capable of anything you put your mind to tech wiz
💚 I love you 💚
: : : CASSANDRA

thx
@deepfates tech wiz

💚Get in losers (jk) we're transcending! 💚 [TKTKTK]
: : : CASSANDRA[18][19]

Cassandra Syndrome

In his address to Britain and the globe on D-Day—the speech that J.D. Bernal and his temporary shipmates took a break from their highballs to attend to—King George took a moment to address the women listening.

The Queen joins with me in sending you this message. She well understands the anxieties and cares of our womenfolk at this time and she knows that many of them will find, as she does herself, fresh strength and comfort in such waiting upon God. She feels that many women will be glad in this way to keep vigil with their menfolk as they man the ships, storm the beaches and fill the skies.[20]

The "womenfolk" keeping vigil in Bernal's life, in addition to Eileen Sprague, Margaret Gardiner, and Margot Heinemann, included a professional colleague, fellow X-ray crystallographer Rosalind Franklin.[21] Franklin was arguably the primary discoverer of the helical structure of DNA. It was her data, after she left King's College postwar to go to Birkbeck College and work under Bernal, that was the foundation beneath the explication that Francis Crick, James Watson, and Maurice Wilkins laid out for DNA in 1953. This work led to the three men's Nobel Prize award in 1962, but Franklin, having suffered an untimely death from ovarian cancer in 1958 at the age of 37, was not a co-recipient. The Nobel Committee had a loose policy of not awarding the prize posthumously, or of splitting it in teams larger than three, so her contributions as a woman and researcher were left unrecognized.

Rosalind Franklin barely had the chance to live in the future. Instead of receiving these laurels, during her too short career she had to fight for adequate facilities and fair compensation at Birkbeck. One of her surviving letters to Bernal, her would-be boss, offers a window into the kind of daily struggle that a woman in science had to undertake in the post-war period: "The question of adjusting my salary to the University scales has still not been settled. As it is unpleasant for me to have to enquire and protest about this at infrequent intervals, I should be very grateful if you could get the matter settled as soon as possible. I am therefore reminding you of the facts." She may have died without knowing that her research had earned a Nobel Prize for others, but when she was right, she knew it, and she said so. "This seems," she concludes in the letter about her pay, "entirely unjust."[22]

Her directness extended into her scientific practice. One account of her work at Kings College and Birkbeck notes her unnerving habit of making eye contact when making the case for a particular point in material science. Her rhetorical force, however, was not necessarily appreciated: James Watson called Franklin "Rosy the witch"; and suggested that she withheld information and scientific data because she lacked the capacity to speculate about its application. In fact, and despite her assertiveness elsewhere, she was dogged by doubt and hesitancy in these matters.[23] In retrospect, looking back from a future she helped make, it seems inevitable that a woman's reflection on herself would be interpreted by jealous men in power as a tendency towards thaumaturgy. J.D. Bernal, on the other hand, had been called "The Sage" by his friends since he was a schoolboy. Modernism was here, it just wasn't distributed equally.

If Bernal was a wizard—knowledgeable, with power and an audience, but insufficient rhetorical skills—and Rosy was a witch—equally proficient, and a more forceful speaker, but lacking agency or a venue in which to deploy her persuasive skills—then a third figure might be brought into comparison with these two to further map the terrain of scientific prediction. This person, one with the right knowledge and potentially the best skills of persuasion, but who nevertheless lacks credibility in the world in which she finds herself, might have a name: Cassandra.

In a 2014 essay for Harper's Magazine, "Cassandra Among the Creeps," Rebecca Solnit writes about how "[g]enerations of women have been told they are delusional, confused, manipulative, malicious, conspiratorial, congenitally dishonest, often all at once."[24] In this piece—built around the topic of the "me too" movement to expose sexual harassment and abuse in American culture—Solnit offers a brief history of competent women who have been slapped with that gendered descriptor "hysterical"—starting with biologist and anti-pesticide activist Rachel Carson and stretching all the way back to the early female patients of Sigmund Freud. When Freud began to realize that every case of female "hysteria" that was referred to him could be traced back to actual instances of sexual abuses, he backed off and simply stopped believing what the women were telling him. Similarly, Cassandra was a figure in Greek mythology famously blessed to know the future, as surely as these women knew their own past—and she was just as famously cursed to never be believed. Solnit locates the central problem of Cassandra outside of the prophetess herself. She was right and she had a voice, even an eloquent one, but her audience was not trying to hear what she had to say.

Rachel Carson was working at the other end of the High Modernist project from John Desmond Bernal. If he helped mark its beginning in our timeline, she was one of the people who diagnosed its end. Carson's most influential research was published in her bestselling 1962 book *Silent Spring*. Although this text focused specifically on the effects of ubiquitously deployed pesticides like DDT, Carson's book was also about how the implementation of the High Modernist paradigm in society, industry, and culture had failed.[25] This failure was twofold. On the first hand, Carson indicates that the network level, not the object level, is the important site for analysis. It matters less what happens to a particular tree or plant that's sprayed with chemicals, or whether or not specific insects die, and more about a chemical's effects on watersheds, microclimates, and food webs. This is perfectly cognate with the methodology employed by Bernal in his work on central planning, especially in *World Without War*. Bernal's vision for a future post-war socialist global order would involve tracking both the inputs and the outputs of industrial production across the globe, and if the systems he was advocating for had been implemented, they would have flagged exactly this kind of resource sink that attracted and concentrated toxins in the ecosystem. This is a type of phenomena that Karl Marx identified as an "irreparable rift in the interdependent process of social metabolism,"[26] glossed by contemporary Marxist theorist John Bellamy Foster as a "metabolic rift."[27] Secondarily, Carson identifies the action of the profit motive as the driver that led the companies that produced the toxins in the first place to push for their expanded use. If the only solution is a pesticide (that you happen to have patented and that you are the one selling) then every problem starts to look like a pest. Bernal had also anticipated this dynamic. In *The Social Function of Science*, he rails against the growing tendency for private corporations to do their own research and development, generating knowledge that then gets siloed off into their own proprietary walled gardens, only to return to the shared world as a commodity, not a term in the dialectic or general intellect.

If anything, Carson was a successful Cassandra, whereas Bernal was not. Rachel Carson did a better job of getting the word out about the failures of capitalist High Modernism than Bernal did—even if parts of her audience were skeptical—because she had a clearer voice. Her imagery of dead birds and spring seasons silent without their song was "sufficiently ruthless and effective" to show that she was right, and her opponents were wrong. Her audience was far broader and deeper than that of the *Tots and Quots*—those many men and their many opinions—and her books sold more copies and had just as lasting an impact on legislation. The foundation of the Environmental Protection Agency in 1970 is directly traceable to Carson's work, as is the ban on the use of DDT in 1972. Meanwhile, in the mid 20th century after World War II, J.D. Bernal's vision of a technocratic centrally planned global utopia was getting co-opted, just like his earlier critiques of Britain's public preparations for the war had been back in the 1930s. In Europe and North America, the work of Bernal, the Tots and Quots, and the worldview for which they were advocates, had been captured. Bernal's cohort hoped that a socialist framework informed by scientific central planning, made necessary by the war, would persist afterwards; that is, that World War II would be a kind of stealth Marxist revolution. Instead, the Military Industrial Complex simply stripped this nascent socialist technocracy for parts, taking what it could use to advance its own capitalist agenda, and leaving the rest to rust.

Meanwhile, in the Soviet Union, something else happened. The *Tots and Quots* hoped to model a future Britain along the lines of the Soviet-style relationships between science, political power, and industrial capacity, but their understanding of that scheme was deeply flawed. They, like everyone else, were being lied to. Josef Stalin had consolidated political authority into a totalitarian regime with himself and a small trusted circle at the center. Anyone in politics, industry, or science who found themselves outside this circle was vulnerable. Among the millions of people sent to gulag work camps and prisons by Stalin's regime were the rocket scientist Sergei Korolev (who was later released and went on to become the most influential leader in the Soviet space program during the Cold War), and the agricultural scientist Nikolai Vavilov (who had formerly been head of the Soviet Agricultural Academy and who did not make it out of prison alive).

Vavilov had been denounced by a former student and ally, biologist Trofim Lysenko. Stalin was close to scientists, yes, but in true dictatorial fashion, he spoke through them—not the other way around. And out of all the scientists in Stalin's circle, Lysenko was one of the closest of all. His experiments in heredity and genetics, Lysenko claimed, showed that organisms could change their existing genes in one generation in direct response to changes in their environments. These changes would then be inherited by subsequent generations, allowing for quick and direct improvement of feedstocks like wheat. This misdirection appealed to Stalin for two reasons: in practice it would give cover and hope to a failing Soviet agricultural system that was struggling to modernize, and in the theory it aligned nicely with Marx and Engels's notion of material dialectics, as contradictions between an organism and its environment were resolved through interaction. Stalin made Lysenkoism official state science, its adoption only further accelerated the pace of denunciation and imprisonment, and its practice contributed to famines in the Soviet Union and other allied countries that killed even more millions.[28]

From the perspective of an outside observer, J.D. Bernal's admiration for Stalin, and his active defense of Lysenko, is the weakest thread in the tapestry of his life and career. Bernal had traveled to the Soviet Union more than once with one of his partners, Margaret Gardiner, who spoke the language and knew the political territory well. On the occasion of Stalin's death Bernal wrote an embarrassing and fawning essay, "Stalin as Scientist," published in *Modern Quarterly*,[29] a British Marxist journal where another of his partners, Margot Heinemann, was on staff. But a closer look at the patterns of Bernal's thoughts shows that this tendency is of a piece with the aspects of Bernal's outlook that led him to reproach himself on Gold Beach. Stalin the authoritarian argues naturally from a position of authority, drawing on the statistics and reason that Bernal so valued, because he already has power. Bernal, blind to power, saw and emulated Stalin's use of statistics without recognizing the importance of his power. Franklin, on the other hand, appeals to fairness and justice, as well as to facts, but likewise has no power. This contradiction should have been resolved through dialectic, but it wasn't, and this was Bernal's greatest failure.

We currently live in an era which the results of turning our back on brute force and bad faith have come back to haunt us. Scientists and expertise have a lot to answer for, because they were mis-used by power, and because they refused the chance to use and build their own power. Experts lied, were lied to, and lied about. And they let it happen. Now everyone lies. But we have never really been High Modern. Just as he recognizes in his D-Day diaries, Bernal needs to integrate sufficient ruthlessness and effectiveness with the theoretical and statistical, in order to make the Modern world that needs to be made. He needs to learn from those with power, and from those who lack it. Cassandra argues with skillful rhetoric but has no standing. Bring her to bear; consider the worst. Give Cassandra standing. Bernal needs to learn from the marginalized, and to uplift their voices. No one knows more about bad faith than its victims. The answer, for someone who swam in power like Bernal, as King George hints in his own D-Day speech, is to recognize the anxieties and cares of those who are different from yourself.

The material science and genetic manipulation enabled by Bernal's own work, and that of colleagues like Franklin, would link, in his words "crystallography to biology on the one hand and technology on the other."[30] Rejecting rhetoric and force, Bernal preferred to let the data speak; this left his activism vulnerable to lacunae. At worst, his faith in the simple math of material science gave him an optimism that was overpowering and sometimes toxic. This belief left Bernal unable to see the powerful influence of bad faith, greed, and the blunt utility of bald lies intentionally deployed. This blindness is partly why he lionized Stalin and defended Lysenko. At best, Bernal's spreadsheets and statistics had to grapple with the other side of potential power. If the bombs must fall, where would they be most effective? If the invasion must occur, how could loss of life be minimized? Harm, he knew, was statistically inevitable. Once prediction is perfected, what power should choose how harm plays out in the world? Cassandra was harmed and knows harm. Let her speak. Bernal's mastery of numbers reveals a kind of *crisis of specificity*, always present beneath the cool calm of high technocratic modernism. Every choice is fraught, yet one must be made. And then another, and another … The choice, intentional or not, to leave that power in the hands of bad faith, and the failure to recognize how it could instead be used to help the marginalized speak, were the biggest errors of all.

September 8, 2102, 12:00pm, noon, CO_2: 283 parts per million (Project Habakkuk, The English Channel)

"When's the storm going to peak?" "Cass says 1500!"

Two people, wearing boots and overcoats in late summer, stood on a wide sheet of dirty ice, shouting at each other over the accelerating wind.

"Do you want to go inside?!" Ran said. They were shorter than the other figure, and had to literally look up to them, but they admiration went both ways. "Jah no! I want to be out here until the last minute!" Spencer's brown eyes narrowed and they laughed into the howl from the south. "We did it! Pykrete!"

The slab they stood on stretched out hundreds of meters in every direction, but showed a grey and increasingly, turbulently, indistinguishable sea and sky past a too-close horizon. This was an iceberg, sort of. Even with the sunshade at the L1 point taking the edge off of the Sun's burdensome generosity, and the carbon capture construction plants busily making raw building material out of the air, an iceberg in the English Channel was still a statistical anomaly. More evidence here of meddling—human intervention, not too wise or useful, in what had been, for billions of years on the planet Earth, a slower more dreamlike pace of change. In this case a special recipe made it possible. Two materials that wouldn't last on their own in this environment, wood pulp and water ice, turned out to help each other out and make something that persisted longer, but not forever. Nothing human made would last forever. Not with a hurricane bearing down.

"The Department of Wild Talents!" Ran said, and laughed too. "Well if you're not going in, I'm not going in."

"Ask Cass about breakup times!" Ran spoke into their hand. "Cassandra, how long have we got." "I believe in you, Ran!" Cass told them, as she had told about 12 billion other people that day, "You're going to make it! 90% structural stability for another half hour!"

"Okay, we're leaving at 1230, Spence, no matter what!" "Alright!"

Improbably, it worked. A singleton, who expected the worst, made it all okay, sometimes in some very unexpected ways. Cooled the planet, cleaned the atmosphere. The end of war and starvation were basically side effects, at that point. The key turned out to be to give power to someone who was very smart, and very good at worrying about things. Sure, Northern Europe now had a hurricane season, but we were used to that by now. Shipping wasn't exactly shipping anymore anyway. Who cares if there's a storm, as long as we know exactly when it's coming? We can still move the people and things that need to get around. While Ran and Spence steeled themselves in the wind above the Channel, below it, six lanes of vacuum tube, each 20 meters wide, made sure everything kept flowing smoothly. And just visible in front of the grey cloudbank, they could see the turbines churning away, taking excess kilowatt hours from wind and sea and pumping it back to the grid. You took what you needed and you gave the rest away. It was all a matter of putting the right thing in the right place at the right time.

"I heard a crack!" "You're imagining things, we've got plenty of time." "Okay, let's head for the chopper, that's enough fun." "We'll make it bigger next time!" "Yeah and we'll do it in June, hah!" "Successful stress test, I'd say! But I do wonder how this would've held up to some Luftewaffe bombs!" "Next time, lol!"

"I knew there'd be a storm," Ran said, once they were taking off their gloves in the cockpit bubble, "Cassandra predicted it." "Haven't you realized by now, Cassandra doesn't predict the storms, she makes them," Spencer said. "Well," said Ran, "You've got to put the storm somewhere." "You've got to put the storm somewhere," Spence agreed, "Glad we were able to catch it."

1. King George VI, *Speech by King George VI on D-Day*, Digital Recording, 1944, Imperial War Museum, https://www.iwm.org.uk/collections/item/object/80001619.
2. With the exception of the initial cocktail party dialogue between Bernal and the Commodore, which is invented, the scenes and quotes in this portion of the essay are taken from Brenda Swann and Francis Aprahamian, eds., *J.D. Bernal: A Life in Science and Politics* (London: Verso, 1999). In particular, Ritchie Calder's chapter "Bernal at War," and Bernal's own "D-Day Diaries."
3. For an excellent discussion of Bernal as a designer, practicing at the boundary between intention and accident, see McKenzie Wark, "From Architecture to Kainotecture," *e-flux* (September 2018), https://www.e-flux.com/architecture/accumulation/122201/from-architecture-to-kainotecture/.
4. For more on Bernal's work in future studies and on D-Day, see Fred Scharmen, "Under the Beach, the Bernal Spheres," *Lapsus Lima* (blog), July 17, 2019, https://www.lapsuslima.com/under-the-beach-the-bernal-spheres/.
5. For more biographical details, see Andrew P Brown, "J D Bernal: The Sage of Science," *Journal of Physics: Conference Series 57* (February 2, 2007): 61–72, https://doi.org/10.1088/1742-6596/57/1/006.
6. For more on J.D. Bernal as posthumanist accelerationist, see Wark's introduction in J. D Bernal and McKenzie Wark, *The World, the Flesh and the Devil: An Enquiry into the Future of the Three Enemies of the Rational Soul*. (La Vergne: Verso, 2017), http://public.eblib.com/choice/publicfullrecord.aspx?p=5213235.
7. For a discussion on J.D. Bernal as a designer of worlds, see chapter 2 in Fred Scharmen, *Space Forces: A Critical History of Life in Outer Space* (Brooklyn: Verso Books, 2021).
8. Swann and Aprahamian, *J.D. Bernal*, 165
9. *Science in War* (Middlesex, New York: Penguin Books, 1940).
10. Swann and Aprahamian, *J.D. Bernal*, 172
11. This section, from an imagined alternate timeline, is derived from conversation in an actual group chat on twitter. The conversation is partly invented, partly reconstructed from actual online dialogue. This has been done with the full permission of everyone involved, and their actual twitter names are used. Unless cited otherwise, the participants have chosen to remain pseudonymous.
12. This is an actual tweet, posted the day of the accidental grounding. https://twitter.com/Mr_AZ_Fell/status/1504076410985631744
13. See Max Anton Brewer, "The Mirror of Language," *RETURN*, July 29, 2022, https://return.life/2022/06/29/the-mirror-of-language/.
14. Hyperstition is a concept developed by the Cybernetic Culture Research Unit at Warwick University. It names a process by which an entity participates in its own transition from fiction to reality via culture. See Cybernetic Culture Research Unit, ed., *CCRU Writings 1997-2003*, second edition (Falmouth: Urbanomic media Ltd, 2018).
15. Victor Glushkov was a 20th century Soviet computer scientist and cybernetician, in many ways the kind of figure that Bernal imagined would manage a centralized planned economy. Glushkov hoped that a computerized system could achieve true optimization. For a partly fictionalized discussion of these and other Soviet efforts, see Francis Spufford, *Red Plenty* (London: Faber and Faber, 2010).
16. For more on Lysenko, see below.
17. This is a quote from Terence McKenna, "Ordinary Language & Virtual Reality," accessed September 20, 2022, https://deoxy.org/t_langvr.htm.
18. CASSANDRA's chat function here is based on a twitter bot that delivers inspirational and supportive messages to her followers automatically. https://twitter.com/xdianalandx
19. In a possible example of actual hyperstition, there is an artificially intelligent "vessel monitoring and optimisation platform" named Cassandra that does this kind of predictive routing in the real timeline of 2022. The authors were not aware of this system at the time of writing. See https://www.deepsea.ai/cassandra/
20. King George VI, *Speech by King George VI on D-Day*.
21. There doesn't seem to be anything in the record to indicate that Franklin and Bernal had anything other than a professional relationship.
22. Rosalind Franklin, "Letter from Rosalind Franklin to J. D. Bernal," July 25, 1955, Franklin File kept be Professor Bernal, Birkbeck College, Wellcome Collection, [https://wellcomecollection.org/works/wtkxmddq/items?canvas=29].
23. See Brenda Maddox, *Rosalind Franklin: The Dark Lady of DNA*, 1st ed (New York: HarperCollins, 2002).
24. Rebecca Solnit, "Cassandra Among the Creeps," *Harper's Magazine*, n.d.
25. Rachel Carson, Lois Darling, and Louis Darling, *Silent Spring* (Boston; Cambridge, Mass.: Houghton Mifflin; Riverside Press, 1962).
26. Karl Marx, *Capital, Vol. III* (New York: Vintage, 1981, 949
27. John Bellamy Foster, *Marx's Ecology: Materialism and Nature* (New York: Monthly Review Press, 2000).
28. Loren R. Graham, *Science in Russia and the Soviet Union: A Short History*, Cambridge History of Science (Cambridge ; New York: Cambridge University Press, 1993).
29. J.D. Bernal, "Stalin as Scientist," *Modern Quarterly*, n.d.
30. Swann and Aprahamian, *J.D. Bernal*, 89

A Visual Genealogy of Urban Resilience: From Air War Planning to Climate Adaptation

Stephen J. Collier and Andrew Lakoff

I. Planning for Resilience

Modern architecture and urbanism emerged from the utopian imaginaries of the late 19th and early 20th centuries, which anticipated future states of the world that could be constructed, *ex nihilo*, on an empty space. Today, these fields tend to have a different relationship to the future: more attenuated ideas of improvement are formed against the backdrop of pervasive concern about urban vulnerability. This is most evident, perhaps, in the contemporary practices of "urban resilience," which seek to anticipate and manage disruptive events that threaten the operation of the vital systems that support the lives and livelihoods of urban populations.

In this mode of "reflexive modernization" in architecture and urbanism, systematic understanding of vulnerability to future hazards is one way that possible futures govern and, in a sense, "plan" cities.[1] Tools for perceiving the vulnerability of our built environment—such as catastrophe models and vulnerability assessments—have become mostly taken-for-granted elements of the toolkit of urbanists and architects. Where did these tools come from? How did it become possible—indeed necessary—to understand our present and future in terms of vulnerability to catastrophic disruption? Here we present a visual genealogy that traces the formation, over the last century, of a new way of constituting the "present future" as a field of knowledge and intervention.[2]

1. See: Ulrich Beck, Anthony Giddens, and Scott Lash, *Reflexive Modernization* (Cambridge: Polity Press, 1994).
2. In Niklas Luhmann's terms, the "present future" refers to the question: "In what forms does the future manifest itself in the present?" Luhmann, *Observations on Modernity* (Stanford, Stanford University Press, 1998), p. 63. A version of the genealogy presented here is elaborated in: Stephen J. Collier and Andrew Lakoff, *The Government of Emergency: Vital Systems, Expertise, and the Politics of Security.* (Princeton: Princeton University Press, 2021).
3. The City of New York, *A Stronger, More Resilient New York*, 2013, p. 6.

Today's plans for transforming the built environment are shaped as much by the prospect of future catastrophe as they are by aspirations to urban improvement. The East Side Coastal Resiliency Project in New York City (under construction as of 2022) was planned both in response to a past disaster—Hurricane Sandy, which struck New York City in 2012—and in anticipation of a future in which such mega-disasters are ever-more common and destructive.

https://www1.nyc.gov/site/escr/about/project-elements.page

Engineers defined the parameters of the East Side Coastal Resiliency Project through assessments of the physical impact of future flood events on specific urban structures and spaces. Thus, the height of the planned berm in the original design (since revised) drew on simulations of a 100-year flood (a flood with a 1% chance of happening in any given year) in the year 2050, taking into account the anticipated effects of future climate change on flood heights, frequencies, and intensities.

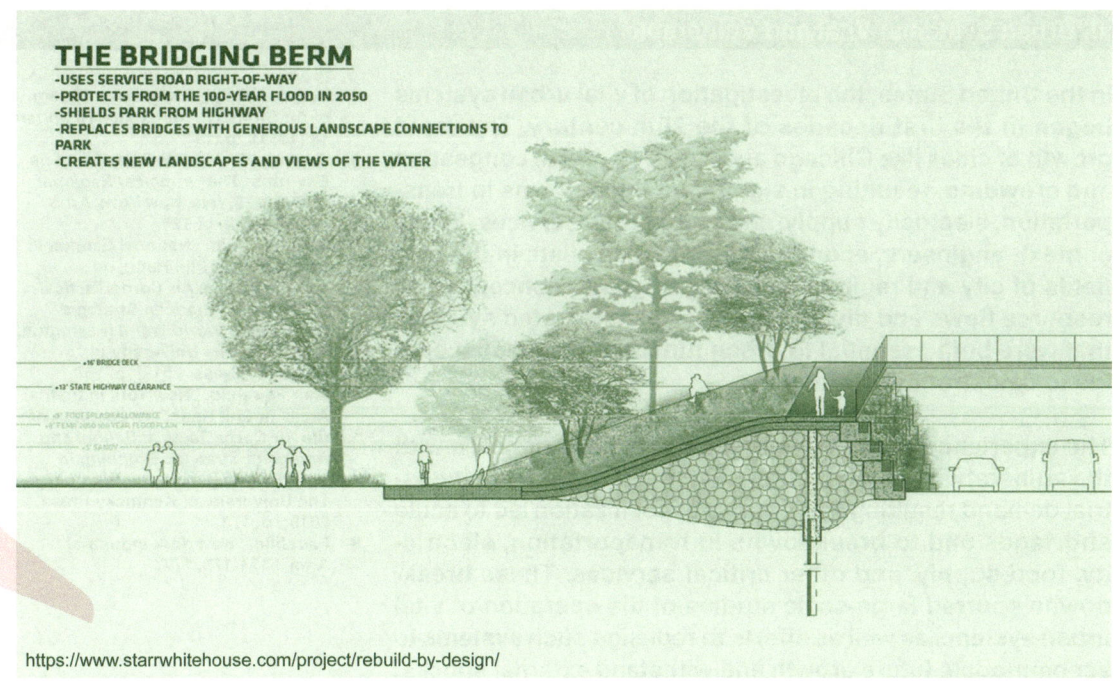

https://www.starrwhitehouse.com/project/rebuild-by-design/

Vulnerability assessments in such planning efforts are not limited to estimating direct physical impacts of future hazards; they also seek to anticipate the effects that flooding would have on vital systems that extend over much larger areas. This map of Lower Manhattan from the report *A Stronger, More Resilient New York*, indicates vulnerable nodes in "vital systems that support the life of the city"–from subway lines to power substations and wastewater facilities–that might be damaged by future flood events.[3]

"Together these initiatives will further protect the coastline—our first defense against storms and rising sea levels—as well as strengthen the buildings in which New Yorkers live and work, and all the vital systems that support the life of the city, including our energy grid, transportation systems, parks, telecommunications networks, healthcare system, and water and food supplies."

"A Stronger, More Resilient New York" (cited in note 3).

147

II. Urban Systems: Vital and Vulnerable

In the United States, the investigation of vital urban systems began in the first decades of the 20th century. The rapid growth of cities like Chicago and New York led to congestion and crowding, resulting in significant breakdowns in transportation, electricity supply, and other urban services. In this context, engineers, economists, and specialists in the new fields of city and regional planning began to conceptualize resource flows and diverse facilities as integrated systems that were both essential to urban functioning and susceptible to catastrophic disruption.

The experience of World War I intensified this concern with the vulnerability of vital urban systems. The surge in industrial demand resulting from wartime mobilization led to acute shortages and to breakdowns in transportation, electricity, food supply, and other critical services. These breakdowns spurred large-scale studies of the operation of vital urban systems as well as efforts to redesign such systems to accommodate future growth and withstand external shocks.

In the same period, military strategists also analyzed urban vulnerability, but from a different perspective: they were interested in the role that the airplane, which had made its military debut at the end of World War I, could play in future wars. Officers at the Army's Air Corps Tactical School (ACTS) explored the potential use of aerial bombardment to disrupt the "industrial fabric" supporting the conduct of modern war—often taking American cities as objects of analysis. As ACTS instructor Donald Wilson explained, the precision bombing of an enemy's vital facilities was an "instrument which could cause collapse of this industrial fabric by depriving the web of certain essential elements—as few as three main systems such as transportation, electric power and steel manufacture would suffice."[4]

4 Donald Wilson, 'Origin of a Theory of Air Strategy,' *Aerospace Historian* 18 (1971), p. 19
5 *Regional Plan for New York and Its Environs: The Graphical Regional Plan.* (1929, reis. New York, Arno Press, 1974), p. 125.
6 Muir Fairchild, "National Economic Structure," in Phil Haun, ed. *Lectures of the Air Corps Tactical School and American Strategic Bombing in World War II* (Lexington, Kentucky: The University of Kentucky Press, 2019), p. 157.
7 Muir Fairchild, "New York Industrial Area" in Phil Haun, ed. *Lectures of the Air Corps Tactical School and American Strategic Bombing in World War II* (Lexington, Kentucky: The University of Kentucky Press, 2019), p. 173.
8 Fairchild, "New York Industrial Area," 174-175, 177.

The Plan for New York and its Environs, based on research conducted in the 1920s, was a landmark in urban and metropolitan planning in the United States. Although the Plan addressed problems of architectural ensemble, urban design, and layout, it emphasized in particular the importance of understanding the metropolitan area in terms of "the totality rather than the parts" by studying vital urban systems such as transportation, electricity, and water supply. With these systems in view, the Plan's authors argued, the modern industrial metropolis could be seen as "a living thing, with a certain spirit of its own, a sort of anatomy, and something like a functional physiology."[5]

For air power strategists, such analyses of urban systems made it possible to investigate the potentialities of the airplane as a strategic factor in future wars. In a 1939 lecture, another ACTS instructor, Muir Fairchild, assessed the vulnerability of the New York metropolitan area to attacks targeting a small number of critical nodes in vital systems, such as key bridge crossings and electric power generation facilities.

"[A] glance at this small map [of rail transport in the New York metropolitan area] shows some nicely concentrated vulnerable objectives where the railroads pass over the wide tidal rivers on bridges. I think it is fairly safe to assume that this task would probably lie within the capacity of quite a reasonably sized striking force. If an adequate analysis should confirm this conclusion, it is apparent that New York City could quite easily be eliminated by an air offensive directed against this particular element."[7]

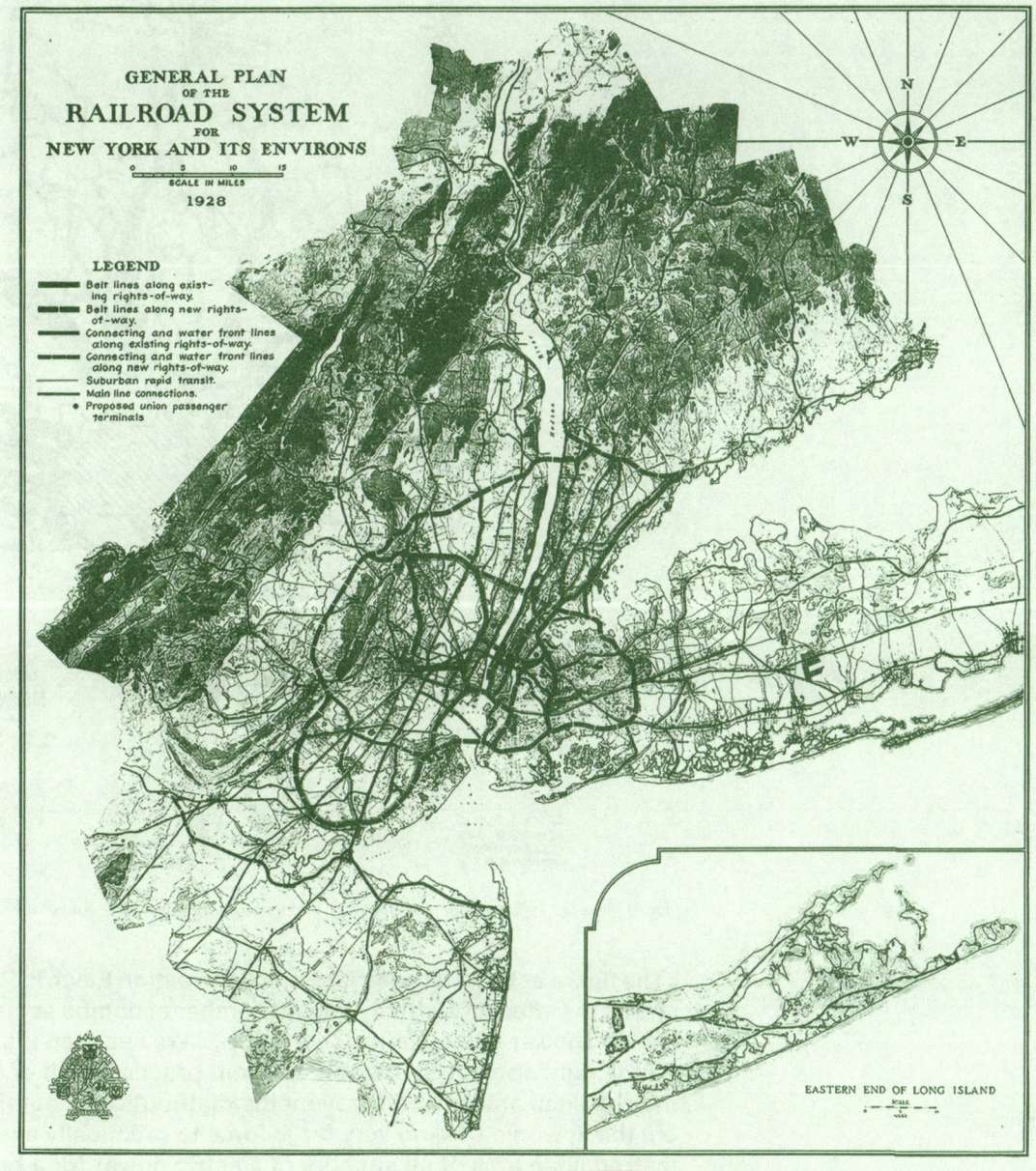

Regional Plan for New York and Its Environs. *The Graphical Regional Plan. Atlas and Description.* (New York: Regional Plan for New York and Its Environs, 1929).

"I am sure everyone will admit that a breakdown of the transportation system would cause the stoppage or complete collapse of all industry within [a metropolitan area]. It seems likely from what we know of transportation systems generally, that an adequate analysis would reveal concentrated vulnerable points whose destruction would go far toward causing that breakdown."[6]

Harold M. Lewis, *Highway Traffic in New York and Its Environs.* (New York: Regional Plan of New York and Its Environs, 1925, p. 33).

"The figure entitled 'The Aerial Bomb vs Traction Electric Power in the New York City Area' shows the effect of a strictly limited number of bombs accurately placed on the sources of traction power of the metropolitan area….We see then that seventeen bombs, if dropped on the right spots, will not only take out practically all of the electric power of the entire metropolitan area but will prevent the distribution of outside power! …[I]t is quite apparent that it would take no very large force to practically assure depriving this whole great metropolitan area of all sources of electric power for a period of many months…At one stroke, the industry, the home, the entire machine that we know as New York City, could not function."[8]

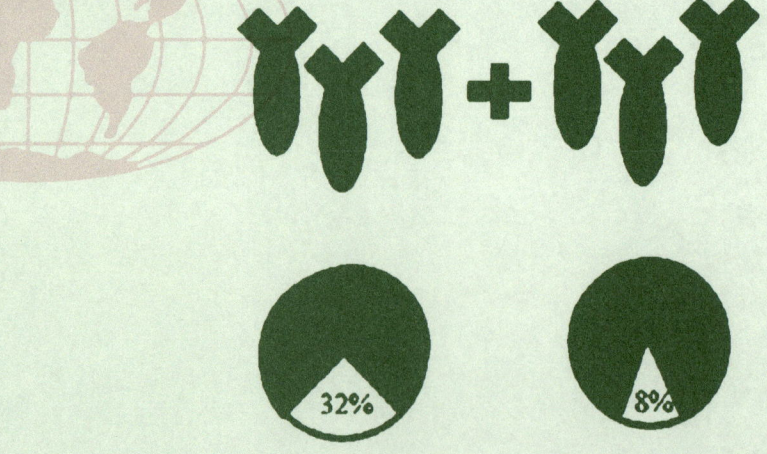

Phil Haun, ed. *Lectures of the Air Corps Tactical School and American Strategic Bombing in World War II* (Lexington, Kentucky: The University of Kentucky Press, 2019), p. 175.

Part III: A Science of Flows

Studies of metropolitan areas such as those conducted for the Plan for New York provided a template for understanding and intervening into national economies. In the early 1930s, a number of specialists in city and regional planning migrated into New Deal planning agencies, where they conducted studies of resource flows through the national economy. Methods for formalizing such analyses of resource flows were then developed by a group of economists who employed concepts such as the multiplier and the consumption function to anticipate the effects of government interventions to ameliorate the Great Depression. During World War II, many of these economists worked in wartime air planning agencies, where they used similar techniques to analyze the war production complexes of Germany and Japan as complexes of vital and vulnerable systems. In the context of the Depression, these economists were concerned with targeting counter-cyclical interventions to stimulate the American economy. During World War II, they were concerned with a different kind of targeting: identifying vital facilities whose destruction would cripple the enemy's military-industrial production.

9 On the constitution of the national economy as a complex of substantive flows–rather than a macro-economic abstraction–see Onur Ozgode, "Governing the Economy at the Limits of Neoliberalism." PhD diss., (Columbia University, 2015).
10 National Resources Committee, *The Structure of the American Economy* (Washington, DC: United States Printing Office, 1939), p. 1.
11 See Barry M. Katz, *Foreign Intelligence: Research and Analysis in the Office of Strategic Services, 1942-1945.* (Cambridge, MA: Harvard University Press, 1989).

The analysis of vital systems was taken up by New Deal economists, who conducted detailed studies of how resources circulated through particular sectors, such as the iron and steel industry (represented in this image). Through such studies, these economists constituted a new object of knowledge and intervention: the national economy.[9]

"The American economy is the organized activity through which the 130 million people in this country obtain their daily living. Farmers raising food and fiber, miners extracting ore and coal, industrial workers fabricating raw materials into finished products, wholesale and retail distributors making goods available to consumers, and a host of workers performing the other countless tasks required by modern living, all of these are combined in a huge and highly complex producing organization which constitutes the national economy. Through this complex organization, the Nation's resources of manpower and materials are used to satisfy human wants."[10]

PHYSICAL FLOW FROM RAW MATERIALS TO FINISHED PRODUCTS
IN THE IRON AND STEEL INDUSTRY 1937
(ALL FIGURES IN MILLIONS OF GROSS TONS)

Source: Unpublished study by Dr. Gardiner C. Means for the National Resources Committee, *Capital Equipment Requirements of the Iron and Steel Industry.*

National Resources Committee, *The Structure of the American Economy* (Washington, DC: United States Printing Office, 1939).

During World War II, the military recruited New Deal economists to provide advice on target strategies for bombing campaigns, working in outfits such as the Enemy Objectives Unit, which was located in London. These economists used the science of flows to understand how bombardment of facilities in a particular industrial sector would affect an enemy's front-line military operations. This Target Summary Diagram depicts the use of rubber in the German military-industrial complex ("Use Pattern"), as well as the susceptibility of various facilities involved in rubber production to aerial bombing ("Fire Vulnerability" and "Recovery Time") and the estimated time it would take for disruptions in a given sector to affect military operations ("Depth"). Such wartime work by New Deal economists—the first systematic analysis of industrial vulnerability—continued to influence American strategic thought for decades after World War II.[11]

Target Potentiality Reports, US Embassy, United Kingdom, 1943. Iris number: 00215632, Air Force Historical Research Agency, Maxwell Air Base.

Part IV: Urban Area Analysis

Over the course of World War II, Allied air forces employed increasingly destructive and indiscriminate weapons, such as incendiaries and atomic bombs, whose effects spread out over vast areas of cities. To model the vulnerability of urban industrial complexes to such weapons—and to assess damage in the aftermath of attacks—target planners combined the analysis of enemy military-industrial production systems with graphical procedures for determining the spatial extent of damage. This form of analysis required detailed knowledge about cities and the built environment, including the location and function of key industrial and infrastructure installations, the density of structures and population, and the construction of buildings.

12 United States Strategic Bombing Survey, *The Effects of Bombing on Hiroshima and Nagasaki*.
13 Peter Galison, "War against the Center." Grey Room 4 (2001): 5-33.

Air war planners working in the Joint Target Group in the Pacific developed a methodology of "urban area analysis" that was used both to anticipate the effects of particular targeting strategies ("Pre-Attack Analysis" in the diagram) and to assess damage caused by bombing runs that had already been executed ("Post-Attack Analysis"). The resulting damage analysis served as an input into an "economic appraisal" of how damage to facilities in a given city would affect broader industrial systems. For example, target planners might assess how the production of military end items would be affected by reducing production capacity in key industrial sectors, or by crippling the transportation system.

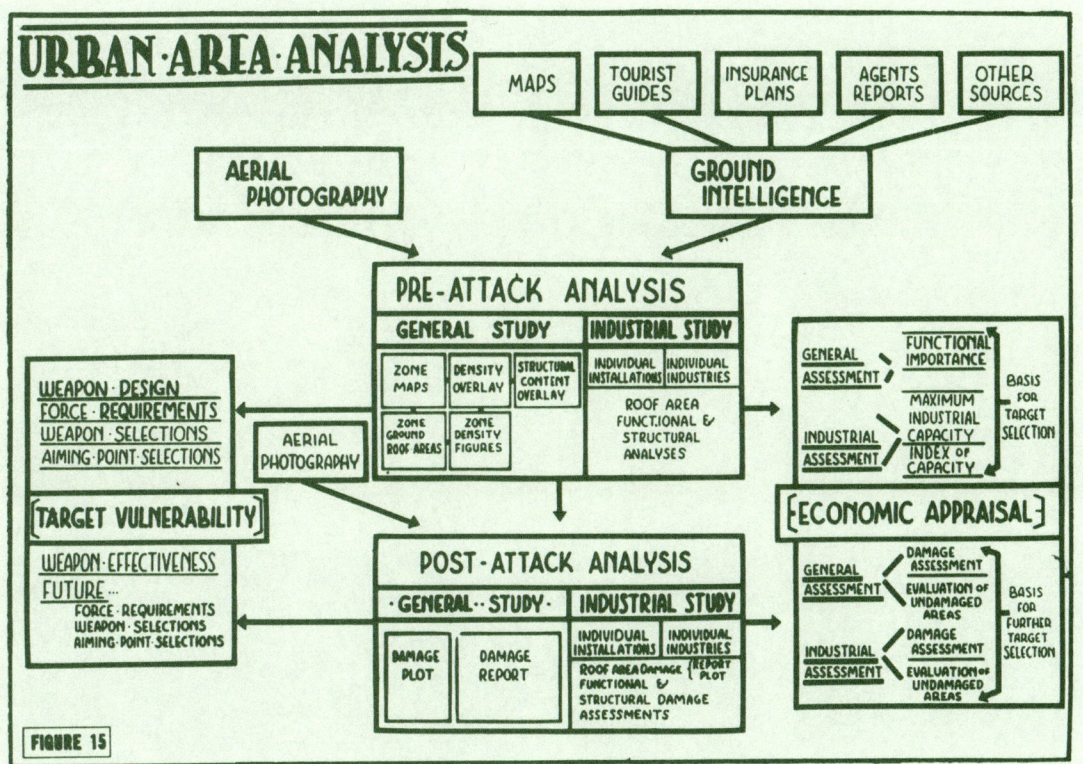

United States Strategic Bombing Survey, *Evaluation of Photographic Intelligence in the Japanese Homeland, Part Four: Urban Area Analysis* (Washington, DC: Photographic Intelligence Section, June 1946), p. 4.29.

To perform an urban area analysis, military planners overlayed maps of the damage caused by bombs over maps of cities containing information about critical facilities or infrastructure installations. In this map from the *United States Strategic Bombing Survey*, the extent of fire damage and of structural damage caused by the atomic bomb detonated over Hiroshima is superimposed on various urban features such as the street grid and waterways.

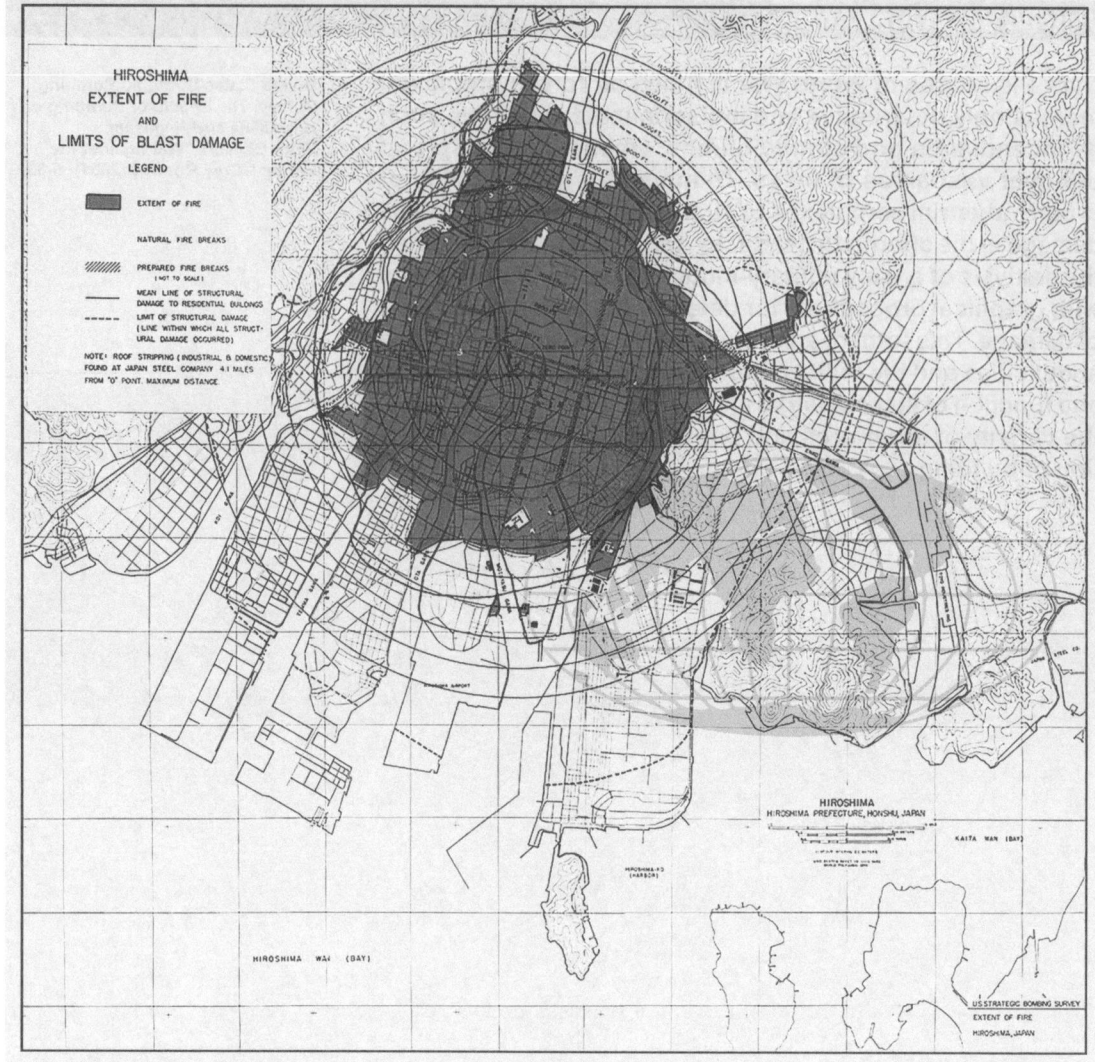

United States Strategic Bombing Survey, *The Effects of the Atomic Bomb on Hiroshima and Nagasaki* (Washington, DC: US Government Printing Office, 1946), p. 48.

As World War II came to a close, American military planners turned their attention from the ongoing war to a novel problem: the prospect of nuclear attack by the Soviet Union–and, thus, to the imperative of reducing the vulnerability of American cities and industry to such an attack. As the *Strategic Bombing Survey* put it, "An enemy viewing our national economy must not find bottlenecks which use of the atomic bomb could choke off to throttle our productive capacity." [12] Urban area analysis–initially devised for planning offensive operations–offered a ready-to-hand methodology for identifying likely targets of a future Soviet attack, anticipating the effects of detonations in particular places, and assessing the impact of these weapons effects on vital systems. National security strategists began to view the United States "through the bombsight mirror." [13]

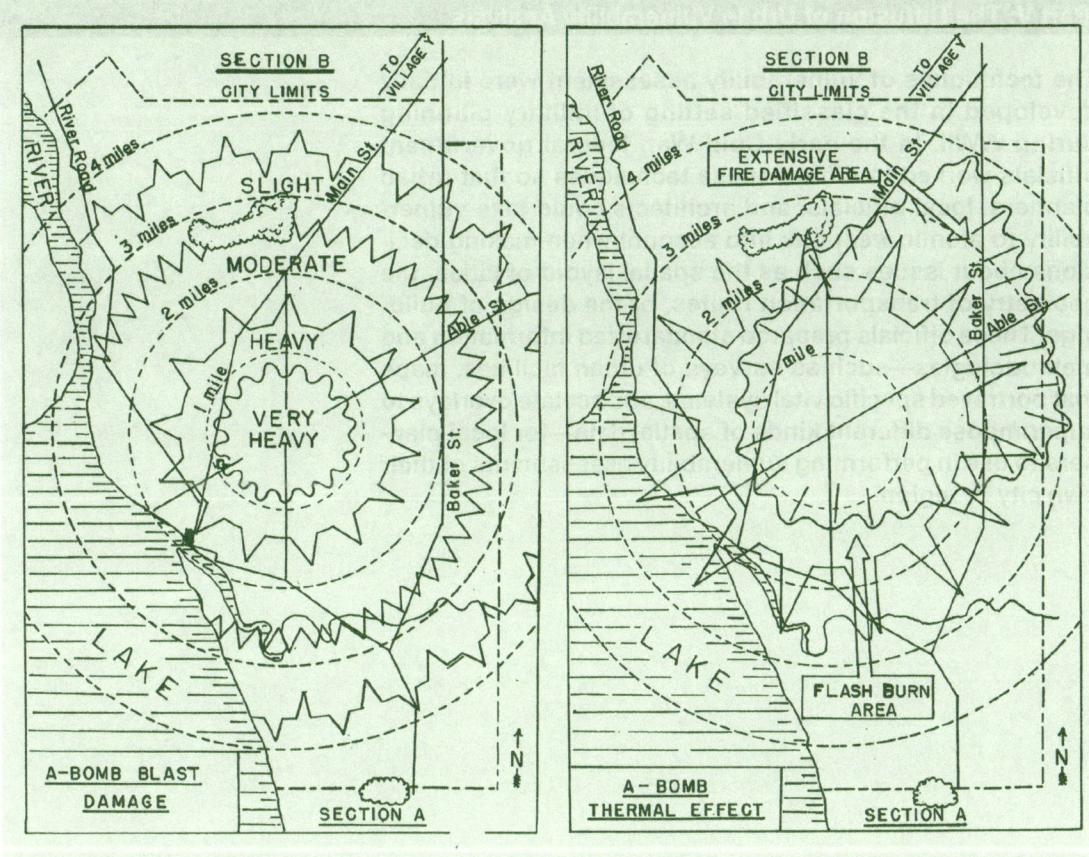

Ralph Lapp, "Atomic Bomb Explosions: Effects on an American City," *Bulletin of the Atomic Scientists* 4, no. 2 (1948), pp.13-14.

Part V: The Diffusion of Urban Vulnerability Analysis

The techniques of vulnerability assessment were initially developed in the classified setting of military planning during WWII. In the early Cold War, federal government officials worked to diffuse these techniques so that urban planners, local officials, and architects could take vulnerability to atomic weapons into account when making decisions about issues such as the spatial layout of cities, the geometry of transportation routes, or the design of buildings. These officials prepared standardized information and methodologies—such as surveys of urban facilities, maps that portrayed specific vital systems, and acetate overlays to superimpose different kinds of spatial data—for local planners to use in performing vulnerability assessments of their own city or region.

In the early years of the Cold War, federal officials promoted the dispersal of critical facilities outside of urban and industrial centers to reduce the vulnerability of the nation's vital systems, and to make cities less attractive targets. This figure illustrates how owners of industrial facilities or local planners could determine whether current or prospective facility sites were located within the anticipated damage radii of atomic detonations centered at the enemy's likely "aiming points" in a future nuclear war.

National Security Resources Board, *National Security Factors in Industrial Location* (Washington, DC: US Government Printing Office, 1948), p. 7.

Graphical overlays were used to simulate future attacks on American cities in order to identify key vulnerabilities and preparedness needs. This image indicates how local planners could estimate injuries and fatalities in a city by placing a transparency indicating blast effects on top of maps of population densities at various points in the city at different times of day. Local officials were instructed to prepare maps of various urban systems—such as water and power supply, health services, and transportation—so that the vulnerability of such systems could be assessed using a similar technique.

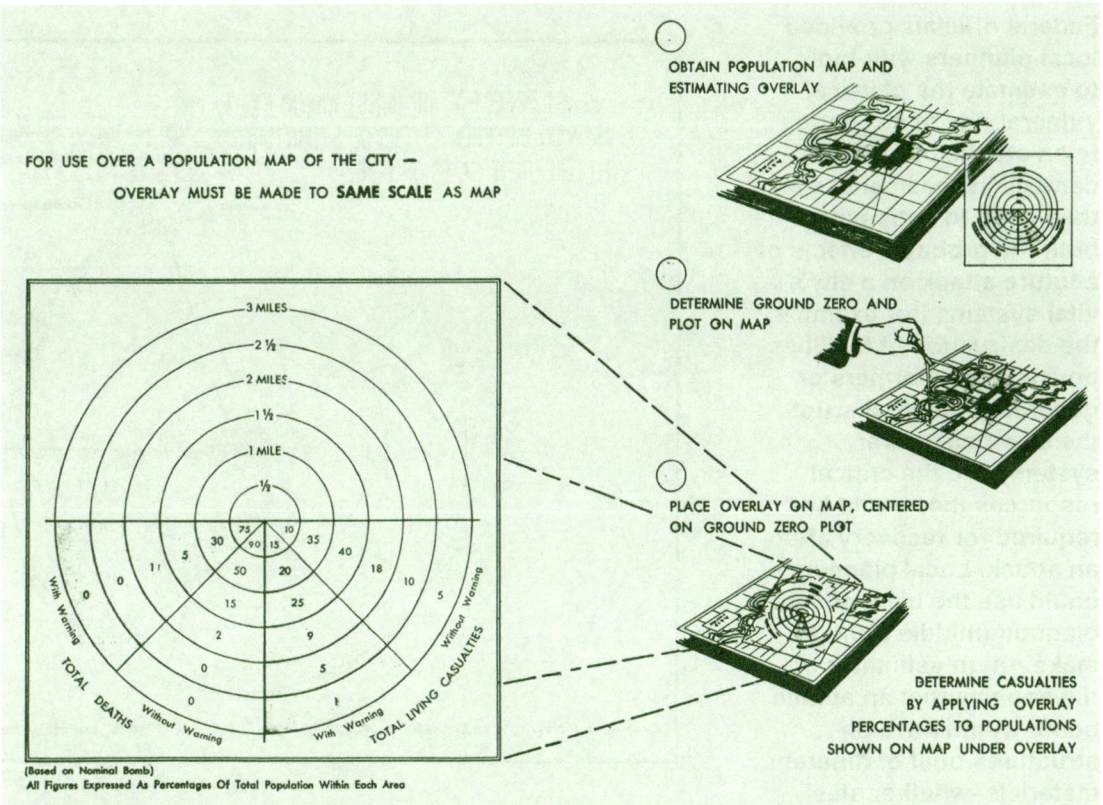

Federal Civil Defense Administration, *Health Services and Special Weapons Defense*, vol. 34 (Washington, DC: US Government Printing Office), pp. 16-17.

Federal officials provided local planners with tools to estimate the physical vulnerability of structures to an atomic blast. Such damage assessments were then used to anticipate both the probable effects of a future attack on a city's vital systems (for example, the destruction of facilities housing transformers or generators might disrupt the electrical power system) and the critical resources that would be required for recovery after an attack. Local planners could use the blast effects diagram (middle right) to make rough estimates of the impacts that an atomic bomb would have on structures built of different materials–whether steel frame, reinforced concrete, brick, or wood–for various bomb sizes and distances from the anticipated detonation point. The bottom right diagram illustrates the forces that would be exerted on a structure, including the initial shock wave and a more sustained subsequent phase of suction.

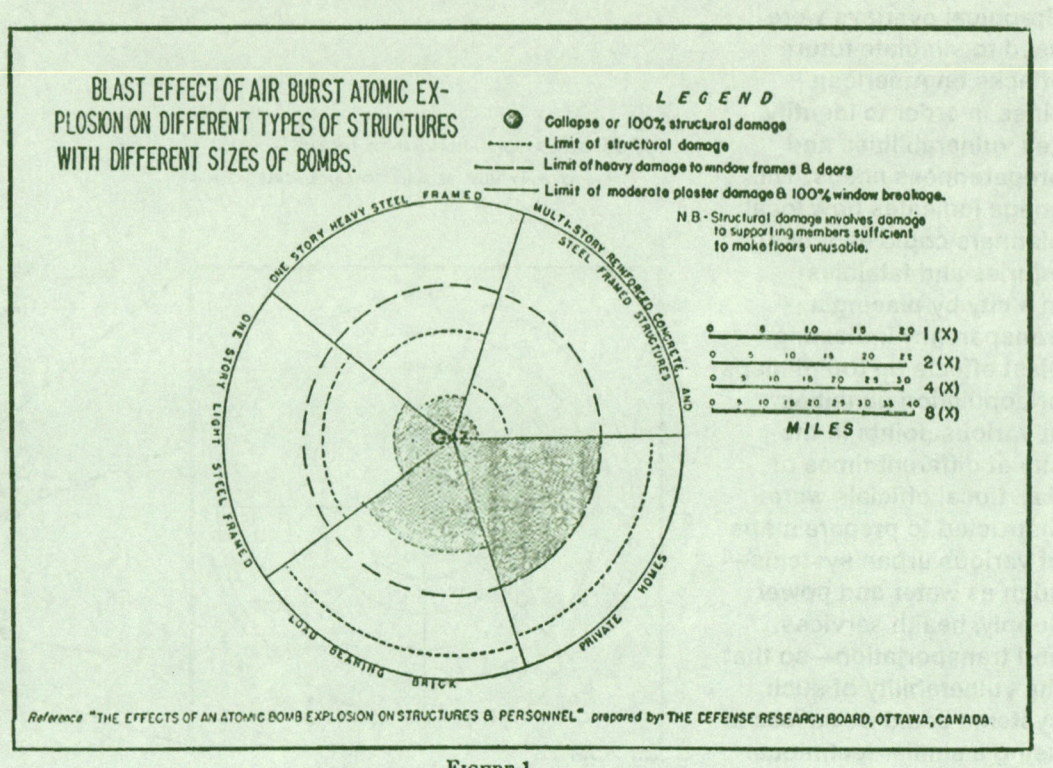

United States. Federal Civil Defense Administration. *Civil Defense Urban Analysis*. (Washington, DC: United States Printing Office, 1953), p. 17.

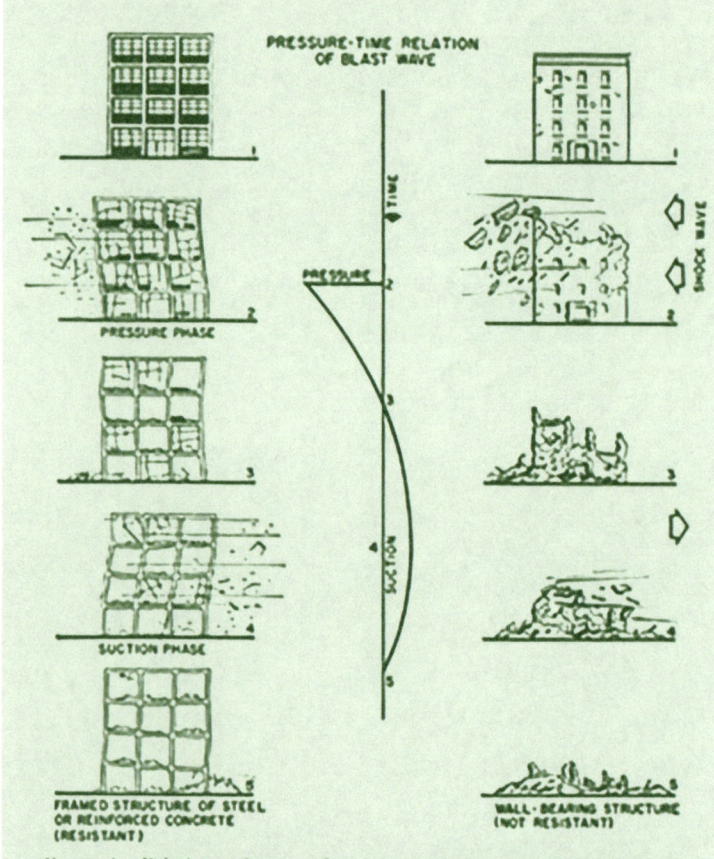

United States. Federal Civil Defense Administration. *Interim Guide for the Design of Buildings Exposed to Atomic Blast*. (Washington, DC: United States Printing Office, 1952), p. 2.

VI. Assembling a Knowledge Infrastructure

The knowledge infrastructure that made it possible to assess the vulnerability of vital systems expanded and evolved during the mid-20th century.[14] Both New Deal and military planners undertook enormous projects to collect information about vital systems and the facilities that comprised them. And these planners employed increasingly sophisticated tools to process this information—from the tabulating machines of the New Deal and World War II through the digital computers of the post-war period. Automation and, especially, digitalization, led to a proliferation of analyses of vulnerability that related to different spaces, scales, and systems. The result, following Ian Hacking's analysis of the history of probability, was an "avalanche of numbers"—one that helped constitute vulnerability as an object of knowledge.[15]

14 On the concept of "knowledge infrastructure," see Paul Edwards, *A Vast Machine: Computer Models, Climate Data, and the Politics of Global Warming* (Cambridge, MA: MIT Press, 2013).

15 Ian Hacking, *The Taming of Chance* (Cambridge: Cambridge University Press, 1990).

16 Joseph Coker, "The Role of NREC in National Preparedness," Paper Presented to the Bi-Regional Meeting of Manpower Mobilization Coordinators (New Orleans, Louisiana, September 9, 1965), p. 9.

During the New Deal and in World War II, civilian and military planners collected vast quantities of information about the facilities that comprised the vital systems of the United States and of its wartime allies and adversaries. This information was recorded on punched cards and processed using tabulating machines like the one pictured above. Vulnerability specialists working in air war planning used "runs" on such tabulators to simulate bombing attacks.

Bashe, Charles J.; Lyle R. Johnson; John H. Palmer; Emerson W. Pugh, *IBM's Early Computers*, MIT Press (1985).

In the early Cold War, security planners employed some of the first digital computers—such as the UNIVAC—to conduct vulnerability assessments. Physical overlays and "runs" on tabulating machines were replaced by programs that simulated large numbers of attack patterns.

Wikimedia Commons. Downloaded from https://commons.wikimedia.org/wiki File:Univac_I_Census_dedication.jpg

A central concern of Cold War security planners was how the effects of thermonuclear weapons—particularly radioactive fallout—could be incorporated into anticipatory damage models and vulnerability assessments. To understand likely patterns of fallout, which would extend over hundreds of square miles, planners employed computers to integrate attack models with simulations of meteorological conditions. This map from a report by the Stanford Research Institute—a think tank that worked on urban vulnerability analysis during the early Cold War—illustrates the results of a simulated thermonuclear attack on Washington State. Shading in the figure indicates "the degree of fallout contamination for each affected county as calculated by the computer."

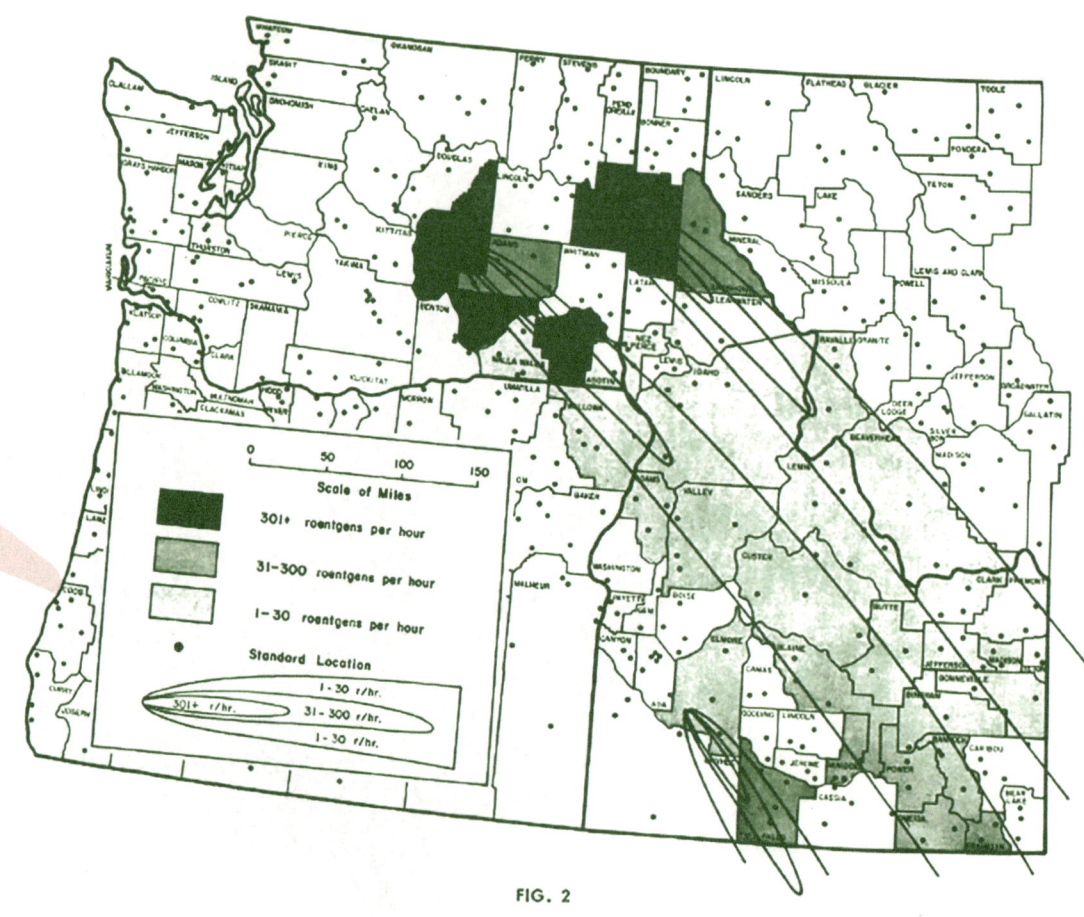

FIG. 2

FALLOUT CONTAMINATION PATTERN
EXPANDED COMPOSITE DECK NO. 1

Cold War security planners built complex computer models to assess the vulnerability of key facilities and population centers to thermonuclear radiation, shock waves, and firestorms. One example was the "JUMBO" damage assessment model, developed by the National Damage Assessment Center in the late 1950s. As illustrated in this diagram, JUMBO integrated data on resources and facilities (their location, function, physical vulnerability, etc.), with information about attack assumptions and weapons effects. JUMBO could generate various types of outputs, including tabular listings of damage to facilities in particular sectors (electric power or steel production, for example), or maps of bomb effects and damage in a particular area.

"The computation procedure simulates the distribution of the radioactive fallout from each nuclear detonation and sums the radiation intensities from all weapons affecting each two-minute trapezoid in which there are significant numbers of people or resources of interest. The results of these computations are then so arranged by the computer as to enable an electronic printer to print fallout maps, including both radiation intensity maps and radiation dose maps. Also, the computer records on magnetic tape the estimates of radiation intensity and 'outside' dose in each two-minute trapezoid. This radiation tape record is used later as an input to the damage computation system."[16]
– Joseph Coker, National Damage Assessment Center.

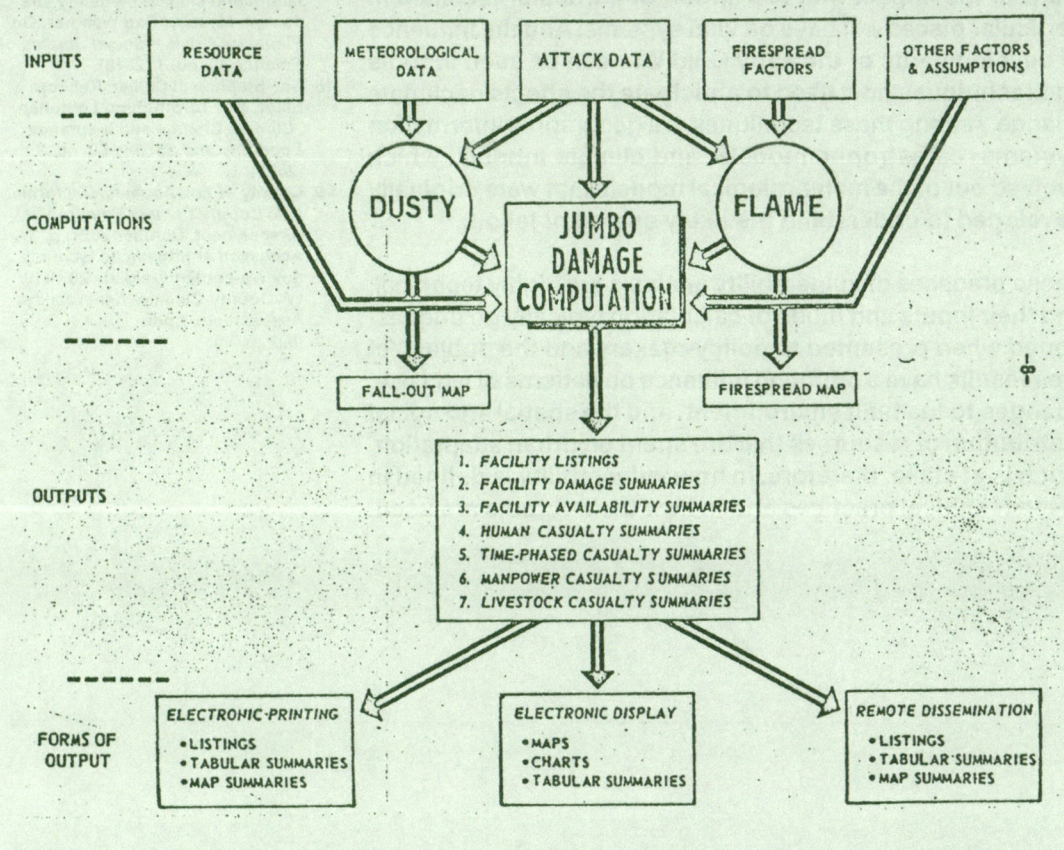

Joseph D. Coker, "The Role of NREC in Emergency Preparedness." Paper Presented to the Bi-Regional Meeting of Manpower Mobilization Coordinators, September 9, 1965. New Orleans, p. 8

161

VII. The Contemporary Uses of Urban Vulnerability Analysis

In recent decades, a trend of increasingly destructive natural disasters, now amplified by climate change, has made knowledge about urban vulnerability and resilience ever more essential to local and regional planning. Although technological platforms have changed, the techniques invented in the middle of the 20th century persist as the basic elements of contemporary vulnerability analysis: the simulation of a future catastrophic event, the overlay of event effects on maps, and the assessment of the impact that disruption of particular facilities in particular places will have on vital systems. And the influence of developments of the early Cold War can be seen in tools and techniques now used to anticipate the effects of climate change. Among these techniques are geographic information systems, catastrophe models, and climate models, which evolved out of the meteorological models that were originally developed to understand the likely spread of fallout.[17]

These practices of vulnerability analysis are highly technical, and their inputs and mode of calculation typically go unquestioned when presented to policy-makers and the public. Yet their results have a profound influence on patterns of land use, changes to the built environment, and the spatial and social distribution of resources that are spent on urban adaptation. Much is at stake, therefore, in how vulnerability is defined in these technical practices and in how their outputs are used.

[17] Daniel Charles ("Do Maps Have Morals?", MIT Technology Review, June 1, 2005) traces how the computerized "layers" of modern Geographic Information Systems evolved out of the acetate overlay technique honed in World War II military planning. On catastrophe modeling, see Stephen J. Collier, "Enacting Catastrophe," *Economy and Society* 37, no. 2 (2008). On the connections between modeling fallout and climate modeling see Joseph Masco, "Bad Weather: On Planetary Crisis," *Social Studies of Science* 40, no. 1 (2010).

[18] See Stephen J. Collier, Rebecca Elliot, and Turo-Kimmo Lehtonen, "Climate Change and Insurance." *Economy and Society* 50, no. 2 (2021).

[19] County of Los Angeles, California. *L.A. County Climate Vulnerability Assessment*. October 2021, p. 37. Accessed at https://ceo.lacounty.gov/wp-content/uploads/2021/10/LA-County-Climate-Vulnerability-Assessment-1.pdf

[20] Ibid., p. 36.

Today, many sophisticated catastrophe models are built by specialized firms, such as Risk Management Solutions (RMS), which spun off from the Stanford Research Institute (see above). This map presents one modeling output of the RMS HayWired scenario: the average distribution of fire spread, based on simulations of an earthquake on the Hayward fault in the San Francisco Bay Area. As in the Cold War, the outputs of an "event model" are combined with information about the location, vulnerability, and value of particular structures to estimate both damage to particular facilities in a particular location and disruptions of broader systems.

One common use for RMS catastrophe models is in the design of insurance and reinsurance products for areas exposed to floods, fires, earthquakes and other natural hazards. By determining the availability and cost of insurance in disaster-prone areas, such vulnerability assessments influence changing patterns of land use—and shape the distribution of risks associated with future natural disasters.[18]

Maurizio Gobbato, "The HayWired Earthquake Scenario: An RMS View on Fire Following Earthquake Risk. May 2, 2018. Accessed at: https://www.rms.com/blog/2018/05/02/thehaywired-earthquake-scenario-an-rms-view-on-fire-following-earthquake-risk

Contemporary assessments of urban vulnerability to extreme heat combine information about climate and the urban environment (which produces urban heat islands) with information about individuals and households that make them particularly susceptible to heat-related morbidity and mortality. This screenshot illustrates an interactive, web-based vulnerability assessment tool that enables users to superimpose observed heat extremes, the percentage of households with air conditioning and the health status of residents in particular urban districts on a map of the city. The aim of such tools is to offer planners and policymakers a way to target interventions to address heat vulnerability, whether through public health policies or urban planning measures, such as greening initiatives that reduce heat island effects.

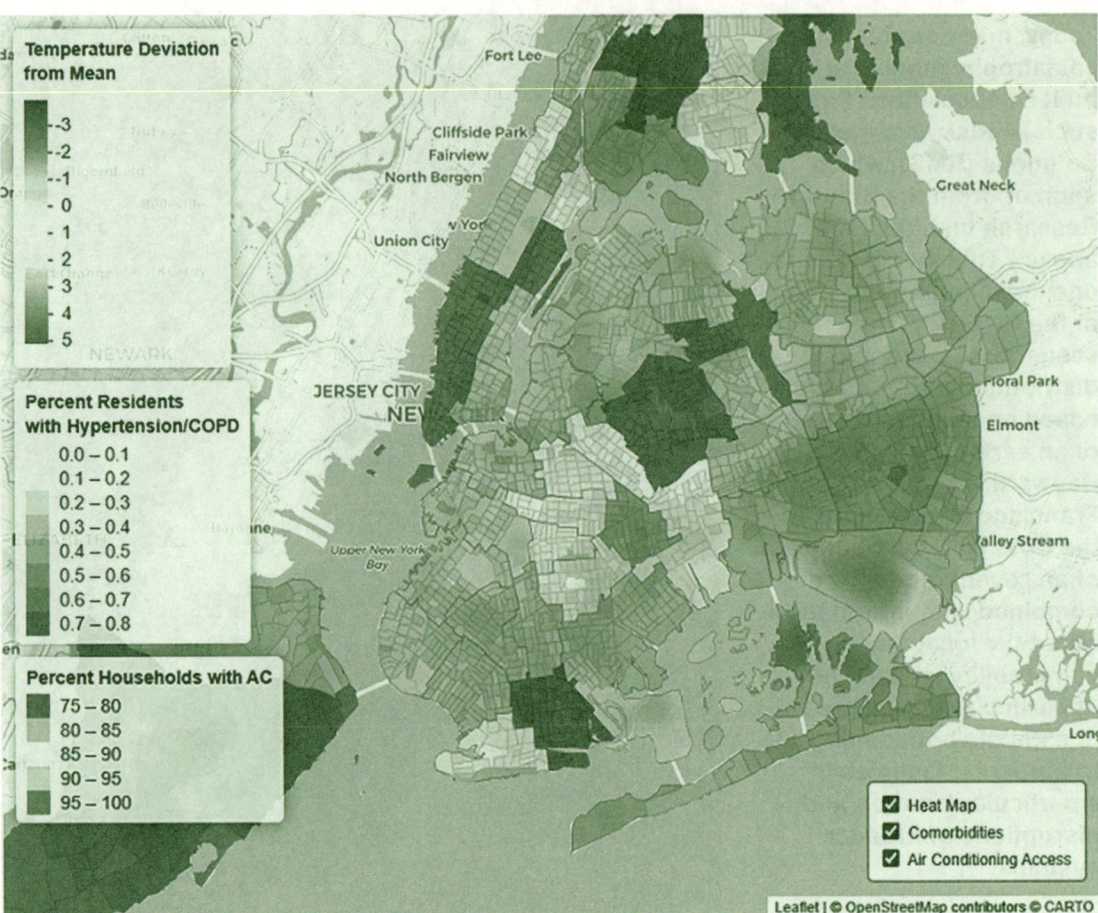

New York City Council. "Mapping Heat Inequality in NYC." Accessed at https://council.nyc.gov/data/heat/

Urban climate adaptation plans frequently integrate assessments of physical and system vulnerability with assessments of "social vulnerability." Thus, the Los Angeles County 2021 Climate Vulnerability Assessment defines the vulnerability of particular areas of the city as a combination of exposure to hazards and the "sensitivity" of individuals and households in that area. Sensitivity, in turn, is assessed through a combination of physiological factors and the ability to "prepare for or recover from climate hazards." The above map of "social sensitivity" incorporates 29 indicators, ranging from health conditions (measured through variables such as emergency room visits for asthma and heart attacks), to living conditions (percentage living in group quarters, in a household without a vehicle, etc.), basic demographic information, and household income.[20]

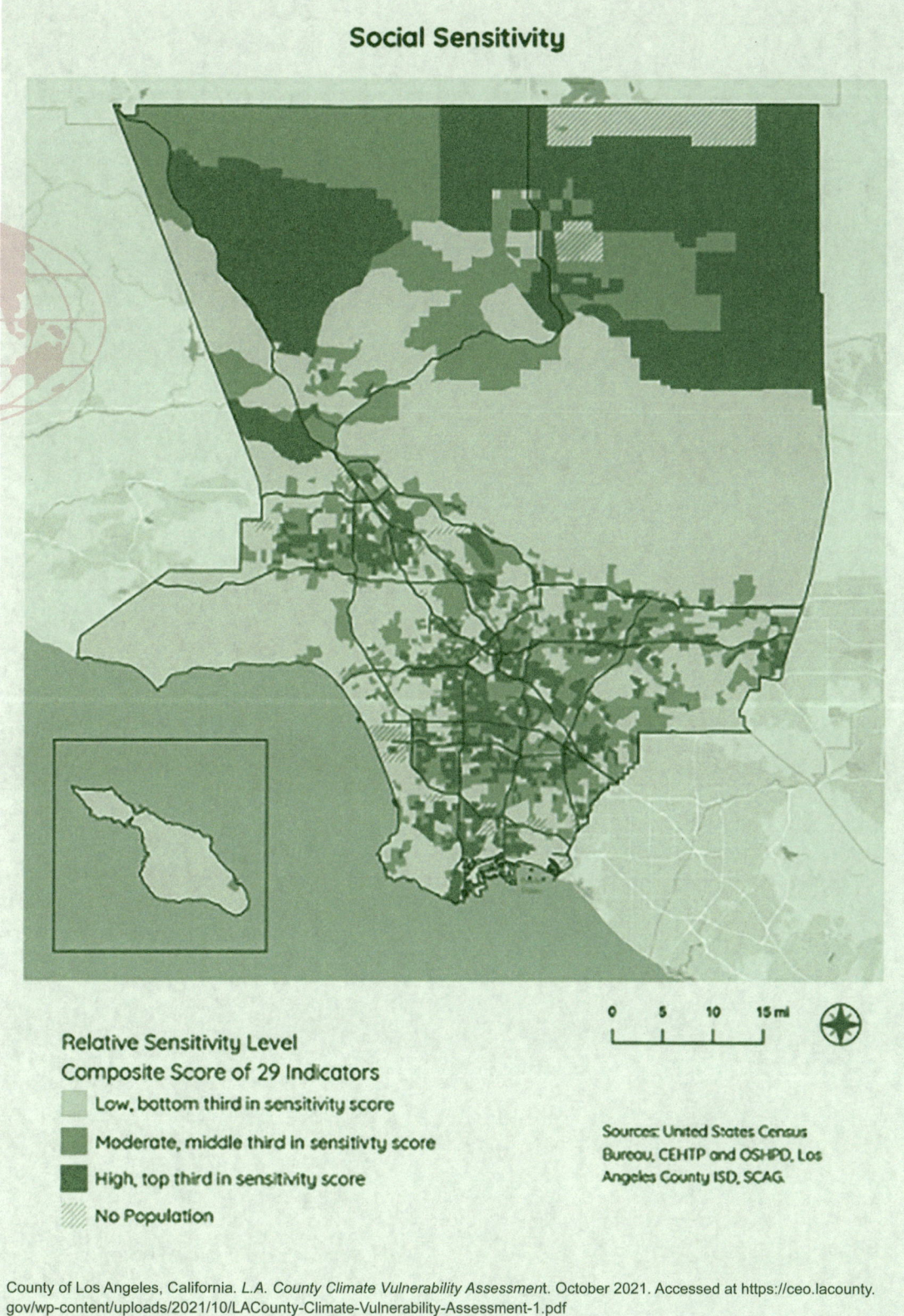

County of Los Angeles, California. *L.A. County Climate Vulnerability Assessment*. October 2021. Accessed at https://ceo.lacounty.gov/wp-content/uploads/2021/10/LACounty-Climate-Vulnerability-Assessment-1.pdf

Bunkers Against Planning

Lindsay Thomas

Halfway through Bong Joon-ho's 2019 critically acclaimed blockbuster *Parasite*, Kim Chung-sook (Jang Hye-jin), housekeeper for the wealthy Park family, enters a subterranean bunker built under the Parks' luxurious Seoul home.[1] Both Chung-sook and the viewer are discovering the bunker for the first time. After the former housekeeper Gook Moon-gwang (Lee Jung-eun) exposes the entrance by moving a heavy cabinet and running into the bunker herself, the camera follows Chung-sook from behind as she hurries down two flights of concrete stairs and winds through labyrinthine corridors. The soundtrack in this scene is ominous, featuring an orchestral whining that increases in volume and pitch as Chung-sook descends into the bunker. Following well-known conventions of the horror genre, we seem in this moment to be building toward a sudden reveal of something scary. Fans of Bong's work know the director has dealt before with monsters that lie beneath; his 2006 film *The Host* features a giant monster in the sewers of Seoul. But in *Parasite*, when the viewers and Chung-sook finally reach the bottom of the bunker, the horror fails to materialize: the wailing violins immediately stop, and we see a shot of a frail man lying on a bed recessed into the cement wall of a dark, dingy concrete room. This is Oh Geun-sae (Park Myung-hoon), Moon-gwang's husband, who has been hiding from loan sharks in the bunker, which the Parks don't know about, for over four years. Unable to leave the bunker since his wife was fired, Geuns-sae is weak with starvation. Chung-sook's and the camera's frenetic path underground reveals not a murderer or a monster but rather a luckless and harmless middle-aged man.

167

Or so we might think. The moment we discover the bunker in *Parasite* is also the moment when the film's genre shifts. The first half of the movie follows the pattern of a heist film, as the four unemployed members of the Kim family incrementally install themselves in different positions in the Parks' home without the Parks realizing they are related. After the bunker is revealed, this plan quickly unravels and the film turns into something else: part black comedy, part home invasion horror, part disaster movie. The abrupt tonal shift plays on the many incoherencies of the bunker itself. We learn early on that the Parks' house was built by a famous architect who lived there for many years, and when the bunker is revealed, Moon-gwang tells Chung-sook that it was originally designed as a place to hide "in case North Korea attacks, or if creditors break in." Embarrassed by the bunker, however, the architect never told the Parks about it when he sold the house, leaving only Moon-gwang, who was also the architect's housekeeper, with the knowledge of its existence. The bunker is thus secret but known; an embarrassing yet effective hideaway from nuclear war or capitalism; a fortified space inhabited by a frail man who has, we soon learn, been interpreted by the Parks' son as a ghost. The bunker also doesn't protect its inhabitants from harm: both Moon-gwang and Geun-sae are beaten, restrained, and eventually killed. *Parasite*'s bunker is a complicated container that does not comfortably admit either human habitation or the meanings of safety we might want to project onto it.

Parasite's bunker, as I will discuss later, reverberates throughout the film's meticulously designed spaces. These echoes index the extent to which, as Mark Duffield has argued, bunkers are "neoliberalism's signature architecture."[2] Once the enclosed spaces emblematic of twentieth-century warfare, bunkers now provide a ready spatial metaphor for the privatization and economic imperialism associated with neoliberalism. Bunkers are thus experiencing something of a resurgence today (if they ever faded from view). Commentators have noted that a "bunker mentality" seems to be infusing many corners of popular culture, particularly architecture and design.[3] Reports on the "doomsday bunkers" of the global super-rich, luxury bunkers that often repurpose Cold War military infrastructure, have only increased since the beginning of the COVID-19 pandemic, as have discussions of the growing "multimillion-dollar business" of "doomsday prepping."[4] The pages of popular architectural and design magazines include features showcasing the panic rooms—mini-bunkers often hidden within houses—that firms are increasingly incorporating into the homes of their wealthy clientele.[5] These same magazines also document the "bunker chic" aesthetic popular in luxury home design, a style the Parks' house in *Parasite* evokes.[6] Seoul, where *Parasite* is set, has a network of over 3,000 underground emergency shelters built to protect against the possibility of North Korean attacks, supposedly enough to house the entire population.[7] And in the United States, commentators have claimed we are currently undergoing a "doom boom," during which "prepping for disaster," including building and purchasing private bunkers, has become a "widespread cultural practice."[8]

I focus throughout this piece not so much on actual bunkers—though I do discuss some—but rather on what I call bunker imaginaries. As the opening discussion of the bunker in *Parasite* indicates, I am interested in the stories we tell about bunkers and in how these stories reflect and constitute their meaning today. Bunkers—which are highly speculative spaces, keyed as they are to a future disaster—invite this kind of narrative perspective. As Bradley Garrett and Ian Klinke write, "bunkers are built to counterbalance speculative events and thus assume forms that reflect what is being anticipated."[9] We tend to think of bunkers as oriented toward the future and, therefore, as spaces that reflect our imaginations of and present preparations for what is to come. This idea reflects the common understanding of bunkers as quintessentially modernist. Paul Virilio saw bunkers as a central, if repressed, form of modernist architecture—as John Beck puts it, bunkers "force into view" the militarism "repressed by the utopian futurism of postwar international modernism."[10] Bunkers today still communicate this simultaneously utopian and dystopian—what I will call throughout this essay the "u-/dystopian"— quality of modernism. At once aesthetically inviting and functionally enclosed, bunkers betray both an optimism that believes in the future and a despair

that takes to a fortification of last resort. Bunkers also reflect the obsession with planning that runs through many modernist architectural designs and manifestos. "The plan must rule," as Le Corbusier wrote in *The Radiant City*, and bunkers are plans made concrete.[11] As highly regulated spaces, bunker designs imagine every detail concerning the design, function, and use of the space in advance so that the occupants can survive whatever comes. Indeed, this kind of planning logic so infuses our understanding of bunkers today that, like Le Corbusier's radiant city, many contemporary bunkers exist only as plans. Promoted using photorealistic CGI renderings and described in magazines and newspapers as if they exist, many are still unbuilt as they await buyers or funding.[12] The bunker imaginary, as it turns out, makes few distinctions between fictional and actual bunkers; bunkers are a vanishing point in the separation of reality from fiction, present from future.

In what follows, I examine several bunker imaginaries and their associated views of the future. First, I discuss the stories supporting the construction of private bunker facilities now being built to house owners in the event of unspecified future disaster. I focus on two well-known complexes located in the United States, xPoint and Survival Condo, which have been widely featured in journalism and scholarship about bunkers. Although these are some of the few private bunker complexes that actually exist, the promotion of these bunkers to potential buyers relies heavily on specific imaginations of the future and of who should survive to see it. Next, I turn to bunkers as they are imagined in film and literature. I focus on two bunker imaginaries that direct our attention away from the future moment of re-emergence, the central fantasy that motivates the construction of private bunkers, and toward the inhabitation of enclosed, underground space in the present. Rather than projecting an image of impenetrability, these bunker imaginaries are interested in what happens when bunkers fail to provide safe passage through disaster. Finally, I return to *Parasite*, a recent imagination of the bunker that draws on and twists the bunker imaginaries I explore in the essay's second section. In *Parasite*, the bunker is a space of no return, a place of futurelessness where the labor of inhabitation defines the horizon of expectations. While the bunker imaginaries I discuss in the second and third sections are decidedly less u-/dystopian than those pedaled by private bunker companies, they aren't necessarily hopeless. Instead of promoting fantasies of survival, of an imagined future time after disaster, these stories orient themselves around what Jessica Hurley has called "*radical futurelessness...a formal afurity* that transfigures the present."[13] This transfiguration of the present is enabled by or happens within the bunker.

The U-/Dystopian Promise of the Bunker

Just as bunkers have attracted increasing attention in popular culture recently, scholarship on bunkers has also experienced a boom over the past decade. Much of this scholarship emphasizes the military origins of bunkers, following from Virilio's famous work on the decommissioned bunkers built by Nazi forces along the French coast during World War II—concrete monoliths he called "survival machines."[14] As Duffield has emphasized, "the bunker ... provides a generic response to environmental terror," a term which describes "the dread" of total warfare common since World War I.[15] By the early Cold War, bunkers had moved underground; in the 1950s and early 1960s, U.S. federal civil defense programs encouraged people to build fallout shelters and nuclear bunkers in their backyards. While the mass construction of private bunkers never really caught on, the federal government did build massive underground bunkers to house important officials and ensure continuity of government and military command during and after a nuclear attack.[16] As Joseph Masco has argued, the "bunker society" of the early Cold War U.S. has had a profound effect on national security culture in the United States. Bunkers and the imagination of future "apocalyptic destruction" that motivated their construction, he writes, "set the terms for a long-running American fantasy about achieving an absolute and total form of security."[17] The Cold War underground bunker was a "fantasy space" that provided a way to imaginatively contain uncontrollable outside threats.[18]

While scholarship on Cold War bunkers tends to emphasize the construction of private backyard bunkers as a project that conscripts domestic architecture into the national security state, scholarship about bunkers today emphasizes the privatization of bunker building. As Garrett and Klinke have observed, "private individuals and companies...are fueling the construction of much bunkered space today."[19] Indeed, private bunker complexes such as xPoint, located in western South Dakota and developed on the site of a former military munitions storage facility, and Survival Condo, built in a former Atlas underground missile silo in Kansas, are the focal points of much scholarship and writing on contemporary bunkers.[20] Scholars relate this privatization to the more general privatization of formerly public spaces, services, and responsibilities associated with the rise of neoliberalism. They also connect this privatization to the avowedly anti-statist positions of many people who identify with survivalist and disaster preparedness, or prepping, communities today.[21] An appeal to this audience is evident in promotional materials advertising private bunker complexes, materials which clearly imagine members of these communities as their primary audience.[22] For example, one promotional video that appears on xPoint's website proclaims that "we live in a delicate balance...in an uncertain world."[23] This message appears on title cards that flash between alternating images of "civil unrest"—a danger commonly referenced in online prepper forums—including protests, burning police cars, military troops, and crowded cities, with the wide-open landscapes surrounding xPoint as seen from the window of a speeding car. This sequence communicates both the safety and security of isolation while dramatizing the experience of fleeing toward it. Its thus associates images of state power with violence and endows landscapes abandoned by the state (and supposedly revitalized by private ingenuity) with the promise of refuge from this violence.

Yet while such anti-statist rhetoric is part of the marketing strategy of private bunker builders, the ideological distance separating such companies from the U.S. national security state is slim. Bunker building today may be privatized, but the logic informing its construction recapitulates the logic behind state preparedness efforts. This shared logic is reflected first and foremost in the structures themselves: many private bunker facilities, like xPoint and Survival Condo, are adapted from military bunkers built during the Cold War. In addition to this reuse of state structures—which, obviously, reveals the dependence of such private facilities on public funds—the approaches to preparedness articulated in these companies' promotional materials align with those articulated by the state. As scholars have emphasized, the U.S. national security state uses the imagination of future disaster to spur preparedness in the present, emphasizing that people should prepare now for disasters that can't be prevented.[24] xPoint and Survival Condo make this temporal logic part of their marketing: xPoint defines its name as "the point in time when only the prepared will survive," and promotional materials for Survival Condo calmly reason that "given the present worldwide economic conditions, historical disaster evidence, and the obvious signs of global climate changes ... it is prudent to have a 'disaster plan and shelter' in place should a need for it occur."[25] Both the national security state and these private bunker facilities also emphasize the generic and unspecific nature of coming disaster. xPoint and Survival Condo, for example, each advertise that because they were originally built as key infrastructure for the Cold War nuclear state, they can withstand anything.

Private bunker companies and the national security state also share a conception of the temporal structure of future disasters. Both understand disasters not only as unpredictable and inevitable, but also as discrete events with clearly defined beginnings and endings. I have emphasized the problems with this understanding of disaster elsewhere, but it's worth emphasizing that such an understanding is part of what upholds the fantasy of national security itself.[26] Imagining disasters as discrete events makes planning for them possible; if you know what will happen when disaster strikes, how long the crisis will last, and that it will one day end, you can prepare for its inevitability. This same imagination of disaster, and subsequent planning logic, is embedded into the logic of private bunker construction. Survival Condo, for example, "is designed to sustain 75 people for more than five years," while xPoint offers space for individuals, couples, and small families in shared bunkers "stocked with 1 year of food and supplies."[27] Whatever disaster may bring residents to the bunkers, these companies assume it won't last forever. Indeed, this is the central appeal of bunkers like these: they are temporary spaces of survival meant to carry people through to the other side of disaster. As Virilio writes, "the fortification is a special construction; one does not live there, one executes particular actions there, at a particular moment, during a conflict or in a troubled period."[28] Despite the proclamations that private bunker facilities can withstand any disaster, nothing about these bunkers is meant to last forever.

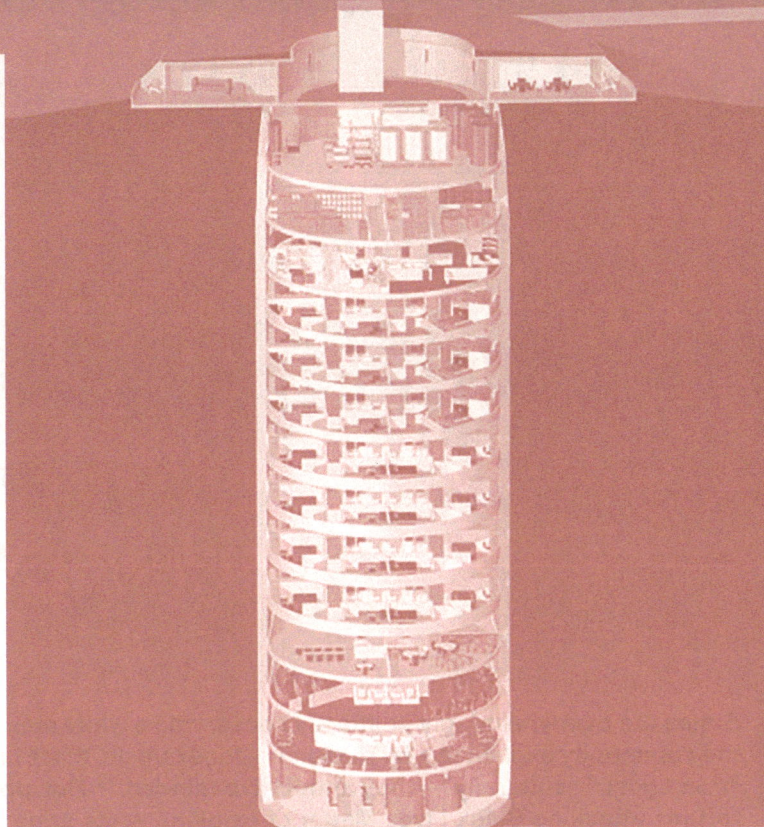

The promise of an end to disaster is the "utopian" promise of the bunker. Bunker companies have borrowed this idea from longstanding conventions of postapocalyptic fiction, which, as Leif Sorensen has argued, tends to "offer a kind of closure in order to make way for futurity."[29] In many postapocalyptic narratives, disaster brings about a new way of life to which survivors must adapt. For the national security state, however, this future always entails more of the same—especially more preparedness.[30] Here, then, is where private bunker companies finally begin to differ from the state: private bunker companies know that the promise of a new way of life after the disaster is fundamental to the desire to own a bunker in the first place. Implicit in an understanding of disaster as a discrete event that will end is the understanding of the bunker not only as a highly planned and regulated space, but also, as Garrett puts it, as "a chrysalis for transformation."[31] The bunker promises that, if those inside can survive long enough, they will emerge into a new world full of possibility.

These companies also hint at what this new world will look like. Both xPoint and Survival Condo advertise the advantages of living among "like-minded individuals" and promote the value of the "like-minded community" people will join if they purchase a unit.[32] For example, Survival Condo promotional materials emphasize that, should disaster strike, "individual owners" in their facility will "[form] an 'extended family' where everyone shares the responsibilities" of creating "the highest quality of life for the 'extended family' while operating in 'survival mode.'"[33] The phrase "like-minded" clearly resonates with the prepper community, as it frequently appears in prepper forums to designate people who understand prepping and therefore those with whom preppers want to ride out disaster.[34] While bunker companies and their representatives take pains to assure people "we are like Switzerland" and that people from "complete opposite ends of the [political] spectrum" belong in their facilities, research has shown that those who identify as members of the prepper community in the United

States are overwhelmingly politically conservative white men.[35] Members of the community explain this by reasoning, for example, that Black people just "don't get it" "culturally"—they aren't "like-minded."[36] But, posts in prepper forums attacking Black Lives Matter or extolling white pride reveal the real force behind the oft-repeated phrase "like-minded": after the disaster, private bunker companies implicitly promise, only those who are like "you" will remain. The story private bunker facilities promote is therefore not so much about inclusion as it is about exclusion, not so much about community as it is about delineating who belongs. Purchasing your own private bunker, these companies promise, means not only that you will ride out apocalypse, but—and perhaps more importantly—it also means those who are not "like-minded" will not.

Beyond the Bunker

There are other stories about bunkers, however. In this section, I briefly highlight two bunker imaginaries that veer away from the planning logic outlined above. Not all of the narratives featured in this section incorporate "actual" bunkers; rather, they focus on enclosed, fortified spaces or on inhabitation underground. By turning to makeshift, improvised, and informal sites of survival, I shift from the emphasis on form and function common in writing about bunkers to an emphasis on inhabitation, or to what occupying these spaces feels like, even if people are only there for a short amount of time. In these narratives, the design or intended use of space matters less than how they are inhabited in the present moment of the story's unfolding. A consideration of improvised and informal bunkers offers a counterpoint to the regulation and control commonly associated with bunkers; it challenges the sense that their impenetrability and careful planning guarantees the survival of those inside. In contrast, these other bunker imaginaries foreground an ongoing process of rediscovering and reinventing spaces of survival.

My first example reflects a common trope of the home invasion film: the construction of fortifications to keep the bad guys out, and the subsequent and inevitable failure of these fortifications when the bad guys get in. While some films in this vein take place in bunkers, it is more common for home invasion films to feature scenes of "bunkerization" in which characters attempt to fortify a part of the house to prevent intrusion.[37] Such attempts always fail; indeed, they *must* fail for the story to proceed. Because home invasion films are structured around intrusion into seemingly private space, scholars have focused on these films as a subgenre of horror, detailing their relationships to Gothic tropes such as sexual violence and the uncanniness of domestic space.[38] Yet the failure-of-fortification trope occurs in films with a home invasion structure across a variety of genres: from horror films like *The Shining* (1980) to the family film *Home Alone* (1990) or the action movie *Panic Room* (2002). In all of these modulations of this trope, the moment of

the breach of the fortified space is a moment of narrative suspension. This failure results either in death or in the necessity of trying something else, spurring the films on to the next plot point.

Zombie films escalate the failure-of-fortification trope to an absurd degree. Unlike home invasion films, which tend to be organized around a single breach that is the highest point of narrative tension, in zombie films the failure of fortification is compulsively repeated again and again. For example, in perhaps the most influential zombie movie, George Romero's *The Night of the Living Dead* (1968), a group of people barricaded in a farmhouse against the film's invading "ghouls" repeatedly board the doors and windows, but the ghouls always get in. Such repeated breaches—whether of individual buildings or of whole urban areas as in films like *28 Days Later* (2002)—are what make these films postapocalyptic. There is no stopping the zombie disaster; all families and all houses will be affected. As the protagonist of Colson Whitehead's 2011 zombie novel *Zone One* puts it when he encounters yet another scene of failed fortification: "the refuge had done what all refuges do eventually: It failed."[39] What the zombie genre understands about bunkers, then, is that they are always doomed to fail. Bunkers in zombie movies are not "survival machines" so much as they are spaces in which the struggle to survive, and the failure to secure, is endlessly staged and re-staged.

The second bunker imaginary is less a trope than a tradition. While the failure-of-fortification trope is about how bunkers do not function as spaces of shelter and survival, this tradition centers on the idea of the bunker as a concealed underground space. The figurative use of "the underground" to denote a space of radical potential—whether liberatory or horrifying or something else—has a long history, especially in African-American and Black literature and art. It was first popularized in the 1840s via newspaper coverage of the Underground Railroad, and, as Lara Langer Cohen has shown, the association of underground space with Blackness continued into the twentieth- and twenty-first centuries in the work of a wide variety of artists, writers, scholars, and filmmakers.[40] One dimension of this tradition, which I'll focus on here, depicts the underground as a space of improvisation. Like characters in home invasion and zombie movies, characters in these stories often scramble to figure out what to do next as their plans are interrupted or fall apart. And like the failure-of-fortification trope, these stories ask us to inhabit futurelessness by emphasizing the present as the only available horizon for action.

In these narratives, sojourns underground are unplanned or happenstance, with characters making use of secret, forgotten, or neglected underground spaces while they consider what to do next. In Colson Whitehead's novel *The Underground Railroad* (2016), the main character, Cora, flees antebellum slavery via an actual railroad that runs underground. She rides "black," "soot-covered" trains that she accesses via hidden trapdoors, trains that have mysterious schedules and that lead simply "'away from here.'"[41] Whitehead's imagination of the underground draws on influential depictions of improvisation underground such as those in W. E. B. Du Bois's short story "The Comet" (1920) and Ralph Ellison's *Invisible Man* (1952). In the first, Du Bois's protagonist, Jim, a bank messenger, survives the destruction of New York City by a comet because he is sent by his boss "down into the blackness and silence" of the "lower vaults" of the bank, where he discovers a still deeper vault, "some hiding place of the old bank unknown in newer times" hidden behind a "black wall."[42] When the comet hits, the door to this "secret vault" slams shut, protecting Jim from the comet's poisonous gases that kill those above.[43] Ellison's invisible man "take[s] up residence underground" "in a building rented strictly to whites, in a section of the basement that was shut off and forgotten during the nineteenth century," a space he only discovers after accidentally falling down a manhole on top of a pile of "black coal."[44] The invisible man spends his time in his "hole," as he calls it, stringing up "1,369 lights" and listening to Louis Armstrong records, "descend[ing], like Dante, into [the] depths" of the music and "prepar[ing]...for a more overt action."[45] In each of these examples, Black

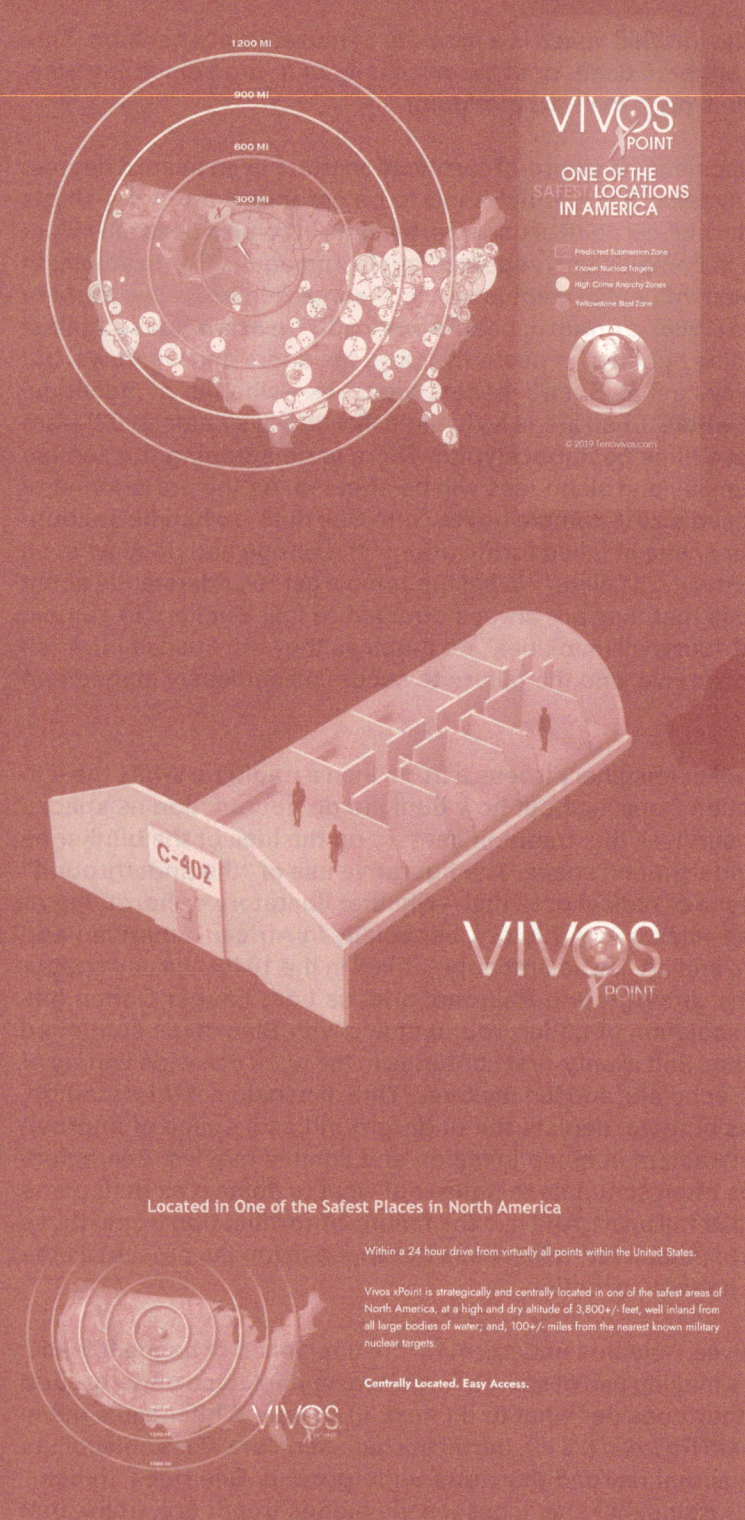

characters utilize the underground spaces they fortuitously inhabit as temporary escape, protection, or respite from the white world above. And they do all of this without a full view of what's next.

Richard Wright's novella *The Man Who Lived Underground* includes one of the more complicated depictions of this kind of improvisation underground. Written in 1941-42 but only published in full in 2021 (Wright's publisher rejected the work in 1942 and Wright later published an abridged version as a short story), Wright's text is a clear influence on Ellison's far more famous work.[46] In Wright's surrealist text, after the protagonist Fred Daniels is arrested, tortured and forced by police to sign a confession to a murder he didn't commit, he flees custody and, in desperation, jumps down an open manhole into the "black space" of the sewer.[47] He spends the next three days and nights crawling through "mist-shrouded labyrinths" and "tunnel[ing] his way through walls" to find food and supplies in the basements of shops, movie theaters, undertakers, and insurance agents (69). Fred has no plan for how to continue to live underground or for how to clear his name once he returns to the aboveground world, and his movements are driven by bodily needs and the extremes of his emotions from one moment to the next. He holes up in cave under a church, where he wires up an electric light bulb and a radio, shoots a gun at nothing, plasters the walls with one-hundred-dollar bills and gold watches, and litters the floor with diamonds, items all taken from the aboveground world. The cave is Fred's improvised anti-bunker, a place where valuable objects are not accumulated and stored for future use but rather used in the present in unprofitable ways.

Time also passes unevenly underground. Cut off from the aboveground rhythms of life, Fred—and as a result, the reader—has little sense of how much time he spends in the sewer. Yet his time underground is increasingly marked by his own sense of foreboding "that at some time in the near future he would rise up from this underground"—"that he would soon forsake this haven and emerge again" (107). In the novella's third and final part, driven in part by guilt but also by the sense that he wants to communicate what he has learned underground to the world, he emerges and turns himself in to the police. By this point they have already arrested someone else for the crime they accused him of at the start of the story, but they follow him back to the sewer and murder him anyway. The last words of the novella describe "the grey water" of the sewer washing his body, "a whirling, black object," back into the underground, "lost in the heart of the earth..." (159).

Given this pessimistic ending, it's easy to read Fred's time underground as futile. In the essay he wrote to accompany the publication of *The Man Who Lived Underground,* Wright acknowledges this reading, but rather than focusing on the end of the story, he directs the reader's attention to Fred's experiences and emotions during the time he spends underground, to how Fred "must, in order to go on living, fling himself upon the face of the formless night and create a world, a *new* world, in which to live."[48] Wright terms this creation improvisation, and for Fred, "the spot where improvisation takes place is the sewer" (193). While improvisation is usually understood as action without foresight, Fred Moten, in his evocative reading of *Invisible Man*, argues that improvisation "also operates as a kind of foreshadowing, if not prophetic, description."[49] As a literary device, foreshadowing involves not the knowledge of what's to come (foresight), but rather the development in the reader of expectations about the future of the story, expectations which will only turn out to be right or wrong once they reach the end. It involves a kind of "*freedom of action*," as Wright puts it, that allows for and makes use of contingency, of the idea that things could always turn out differently (200). Thus, foreshadowing allows the future in but will not plan for it. Like the kind of planning that Stephano Harvey and Moten have defined as "ceaseless experiment with...futurial presence," it provides hints of what may be to come, but such hints only make sense within the context of the ever-changing present moment.[50]

Such improvisation, however, offers little comfort. As Saidiya Hartman writes in a recent reading of Du Bois's "The Comet," in that story "the stranglehold of white supremacy appears so unconquerable, so eternal that its only certain defeat is the end of the world."[51] *The Man Who Lived Underground* doesn't even offer the temporary relief of the supposed defeat of white supremacy that we see in Du Bois's story; all it can offer is a space apart, and that space is the sewer. As an allegory of racial segregation—another outcome of midcentury planning in the United States—Wright's text centers on the making of a life within confined, constrained, and neglected spaces.[52] This—both the freedom to act and the constraints that limit the scope of such action—is improvisation underground. To improvise is to freely act within constraints, or to work both within and yet against the plan. While the u-/dystopian dreams pedaled by private bunker companies look past the present to a future that will never arrive, improvisation underground is concerned with strategies for, as Hartman calls it, "surviv[ing] in the meantime."[53]

Life in the Bunker

Bong's *Parasite* incorporates the bunker imaginaries discussed in the previous section and relocates them to the architecture of an "actual" bunker. Like a bunker in a home invasion or zombie movie, the bunker under the Parks' home exists to be broken into; as the engine that reorients then drives the plot, the rest of the film depends on its breach. This breach, in turn, necessitates improvisation, as the Kims' plan to infiltrate the Parks' household is thrown into disarray by another kind of infiltrator. But while bunkers in home invasion or zombie films are often spaces of fear, and while improvisation underground suggests ambivalent hopefulness, the bunker in *Parasite* is a space of neither terror nor hope. Those who enter the bunker exhibit a range of emotions and responses, and this affective range is linked to the film's imagination of disaster. It's not clear what the disaster is in *Parasite*—capitalism, imperialism, militarism, nuclear weapons, climate change, all of the above—but it is clear that it is ongoing. There is no "after" the disaster in this film; there is only its continuation in the present.

This sense that *Parasite's* bunker is not a place of survival but rather of indefinite detention is most clearly expressed through the character of Geun-sae, the man living in the bunker to hide out from creditors whom we met in this essay's opening. At one point in the film, down in the bunker, Ki-taek asks Geun-sae about his financially imposed self-imprisonment, inquiring, "What'll you do? You don't have a plan?" Geun-sae responds, "I just feel comfortable here. It feels like I was born here. Maybe I had my wedding here, too. As for the National Pension, I don't qualify. In my old age, love will comfort me. So please. Let me live down here." This exchange reveals that

---

One reason for the sheer excessiveness of xPoint's preventative measures—its units, underground with blast-proof doors and impenetrable concrete walls, are also strategically sited in an area far from any large, flood-prone bodies of water and over 100 miles from any known nuclear targets—is that its inhabitants imagine that they have to be protected against not just a singular disastrous future but against many possible future catastrophes. Their promotional website's list of the calamities from which they promise to offer protection is mind-boggling in its extensiveness: in a xPoint bunker, one will be protected from a nuclear attack, an act of terrorism or bio-terrorism, the social anarchy that will result from an economic collapse, the detonation of a high-altitude electromagnetic pulse device, a solar flare-induced proton storm, a shift of our polar axis, a killer comet or asteroid, a mega tsunami, and, most imaginatively, the unfortunate orbital recurrence of a so-called planet "Nibiru," the supposed former twelfth planet of our solar system (as depicted on an ancient Sumerian tablet) whose return could trigger a disastrous gravitational event.

While there is a very particular flavor to the sensational disaster narratives and videos that xPoint deploys to make these futures envisionable realities, it would not be a stretch to argue that their pluralized forecasting is isomorphically similar to the multiple futures of scenario planning, a futures technology that sociologist Melinda Cooper notes is the "preferred risk-analysis technique" of much more mainstream political institutions (she cites the IMF, the World Economic Forum, and the Intergovernmental Panel on Climate Change [IPCC] as key purveyors of scenarios).[1] What to make of this similarity?

For Cooper, the US's turn to "possible worlds" thinking evidences a shift, in response to climate change, away from the deterrence practices typical of the Cold War era into a mode of security that seeks not necessarily to prevent catastrophes, but to ensure that the inevitable turbulence to come will not harm the "strategic ends of sustaining the US-dollar denominated world." Since the value of money is ultimately "as much a matter of trust, confidence and indeed faith as anything else," Cooper positions the imagined worlds of scenario plans as a means of demonstrating to the world's investors that the US's credit-worthiness can withstand any crisis. She notes, however, that alongside these narrative performances, the US also backs up its financial influence via physical: due to the power of its military, the world knows that "any contestation of US financial power will lead to military confrontation."[2]

xPoints's customers may have correctly intuited that, in a more uncertain world, there has been a shift in security strategies; however, their dreams of being power players in this new world order is decidedly delusional. Despite their many apocalyptic imaginings and their fantasy that all their prepping will make them physically dominant when the post-disaster world is plunged into a Hobbesian state of nature, in reality xPoints's customers lack both the narrative and military powers of the US Government. In this light, their feverish attempt to outpace the narrative abilities of the US security state—they may plan for climate change, but we plan for alien planets!—can be read less as an actual bid for achieving dominance than as a symptom of their complete lack of political relevance. When the power of the dollar is all that matters, these non-billionaire preppers, as trained in nature skills as they may be, don't actually matter much to their government—in this world or any of the future ones.

1. Melinda Cooper, "Turbulent Worlds: Financial Markets and Environmental Crisis," *Theory, Culture & Society* 27 no. 2–3 (2010): 171.
2. Cooper, "Turbulent Worlds," 168, 184–85.

Geun-sae imagines his time in the bunker as a permanent way of life. Unlike the planning logic that motivates the construction of private bunkers—which relies on an end to disaster and thus an end to time in the bunker—Geun-sae's stay is not part of some plan. His imprisonment there is just his life. Both his past—his birth, his wedding—and his future—his old age—become reimagined as part of his present, and endless, stay in the bunker.

Geun-sae, however, is not the only character troublingly without a plan. During a sequence in which the Kims have to flee the Park house on account of a flood, the daughter, Ki-jung (Park So-dam), asks her father, "What do we do now? What's our plan?" Ki-taek tells her not to worry, assuring her "I've got my own plan" and suggesting they all go home and take a bath. However, when they reach their apartment, they discover it is rapidly filling up with water. After moving to the emergency shelter (a space that, like a bunker, is meant to temporarily protect one from disaster), Ki-taek reveals to Ki-woo that he doesn't have a plan. "You know what kind of plan never fails?", Ki-taek asks his son. "No plan at all." He repeats "no plan" in English, adding, "If you make a plan, life never works out that way.... With no plan, nothing can go wrong. And if something spins out of control, it doesn't matter. Whether you kill someone or betray your country. None of it fucking matters." In these scenes, Ki-taek uses the idea of a plan make Ki-jung feel better in the moment, but even his small plan to take a bath immediately unravels because of the flood. Unlike Wright's Fred Daniels, whose improvisations underground allow for the possibility of hope, Ki-taek lacks any kind of optimism. Specifically, he lacks the belief, required by planning, that one can control or direct future events. For Ki-taek, planning is only valuable insofar as it has an ameliorating effect in the present; any thoughts of an effect on the future are meaningless because "none of it fucking matters." Of course, at the same time, it *does* matter, since ultimately Ki-taek's lack of a plan leads to his needing to take refuge in the bunker after he commits an unplanned murder.

Ki-woo does develop a plan to free his father from the bunker, however. After discovering Ki-taek is there, Ki-woo composes a letter to him (the movie never reveals if or how he sends it). He writes, "Dad, today I made a plan. A fundamental plan," and describes how this plan is to become wealthy, purchase the house above the bunker, and move in so that all his father will need to do to escape "is walk up the stairs." The film tenderly depicts Ki-woo's imagination of buying the house and reuniting with his father as he describes it, as if it were happening, but the final shot of the film takes viewers back to reality. Panning down, it frames Ki-woo in the semi-basement apartment, repeating the first shot of the film. In suggesting that Ki-woo's plan is little more than fantasy, the film aligns Ki-woo and Ki-taek: each has little chance of escaping his underground confinement, of a life outside the bunker after disaster.

The range of affective responses to the bunker—Geun-sae's resignation and acceptance, Ki-taek's cynicism, and Ki-woo's unfounded optimism are just a few examples—reflect the film's imagination of the bunker as a space not of the future but rather of the present. If bunkers are supposed to be places where people retreat in the face of disaster and wait until it's over, what happens to the bunker when the disasters people face don't have foreseeable ends? What if there is no aftermath of the disaster, but only its continuation under different names? The bunker imaginaries I have discussed that run askance of the planning logic of the state and private bunker companies answer these questions in different ways. However, they all insist that the disaster is not coming. It is already here. The best they can offer is a bunker, a place to go not to avoid or survive disaster, but rather to live, or die, within it.

WE LIVE IN A
DELICATE BALANCE

WHEN DISASTER STRIKES
THE TIME TO PREPARE
HAS ALREADY PASSED

1 *Parasite*, directed by Bong Joon-ho (2019; Seoul: CJ Entertainment, 2019), Amazon Prime Video.

2 Mark Duffield, "Total War as Environmental Terror: Linking Liberalism, Resilience, and the Bunker," *The South Atlantic Quarterly* 110, no. 3 (Summer 2011): 765.

3 For a description of this mentality, see Luke Bennett, "The Bunker: Metaphor, materiality and management," *Culture and Organization* 17, no. 2 (March 2011): 155–173; and Gregory Clinton, "The Architecture of Safety: Bunker Mentalities and the Construction of Safe Space in America" (PhD diss., Stony Brook University, 2017).

4 See Mira Ptacin, "Could Doomsday Bunkers Become the New Normal?", *New York Times*, June 26, 2020, https://www.nytimes.com/2020/06/26/realestate/could-doomsday-bunkers-become-the-new-normal.html; Julie Turkewitz, "A Boom Time for the Bunker Business and Doomsday Capitalists," *New York Times*, August 13, 2019, https://www.nytimes.com/2019/08/13/us/apocalypse-doomsday-capitalists.html; and Micah Maidenberg, "For Doomsday Preppers, the End of the World is Good for Business," *New York Times*, August 11, 207, https://www.nytimes.com/2017/08/11/business/prepper-survivalism-north-korea.html. For examples of articles about bunkers for the wealthy and the COVID-19 pandemic, see Jim Dobson, "Inside the World's Largest Private Apocalypse Shelter, The Oppidum," *Forbes*, November 5, 2015, https://www.forbes.com/sites/jimdobson/2015/11/05/billionaire-bunker-inside-the-worlds-largest-private-apocalypse-shelter-the-oppidum; and Rupert Neate, "Super-rich jet off to disaster bunkers amid coronavirus outbreak," *The Guardian*, March 11, 2020, https://www.theguardian.com/world/2020/mar/11/disease-dodging-worried-wealthy-jet-off-to-disaster-bunkers.

5 For example, see Geoff Manaugh, "Inside the Modern Safe Room: How Homeowners Today Are Fortifying Their Houses Against Burglars, Terrorists, and Hurricanes," *Dwell*, August 22, 2015, https://www.dwell.com/article/inside-the-modern-safe-room-how-homeowners-today-are-fortifying-their-houses-against-burglars-terrorists-and-hurricanes-a74a41de; Megan Johnson, "Luxury Panic Rooms and VIP Evacuation Services are in High Demand," *Architectural Digest*, March 21, 2017, https://www.architecturaldigest.com/story/luxury-panic-rooms-and-vip-evacuation-services-are-in-high-demand; Katherine Guimapang, "ABIBOO Studio pulls from their expertise in space architectures to develop a luxury doomsday bunker," *Archinect*, January 7, 2021, https://archinect.com/news/article/150243569/abiboo-studio-pulls-from-their-expertise-in-space-architecture-to-develop-a-luxury-doomsday-bunker; and India Block, "Eight homes, suits, and kits for surviving an apocalypse," *Dezeen*, March 12, 2021, https://www.dezeen.com/2021/03/12/apocalypse-architecture-design-roundup/; https://www.dezeen.com/tag/survival/.

6 For example, see Liz Stinson, "Bunker-like concrete house comes with a twist," *Curbed*, April 25, 2018, https://archive.curbed.com/2018/4/25/17277620/concrete-house-architecture-home-thailand; and Sheila Kim, "A Concrete Guesthouse in Upstate New York Is Decidedly 'Bunker Chic'," *Dwell*, September 15, 2020, https://www.dwell.com/article/square-house-levenbetts-466abc57.

7 See Nick Visser, "In Seoul, Confusion And Apathy Surround City's 3,200 Bomb Shelters," *HuffPost*, August 15, 2017, https://www.huffpost.com/entry/seoul-bomb-shelters_n_59927081e4b09071f69c2539; and Matt Neuman, "Seoul's 'War Preppers' Are Still (Sort Of) Expecting the Worst," *Bloomberg CityLab*, June 13, 2018, https://www.bloomberg.com/newsarticles/ 2018-06-13/south-korean-preppers-still-sort-of-expect-the-worst.

8 Bradley Garrett, "Doomsday preppers and the architecture of dread," *Geoforum* (April 10, 2020): 3.

9 Bradley Garrett and Ian Klinke, "Opening the bunker: Function, materiality, temporality" EPC: *Politics and Space* 37, no. 6 (2019): 1067.

10 John Beck, "Concrete Ambivalence: Inside the Bunker Complex," *Cultural Politics* 7, no.1 (2011): 86. Virilio writes, for example, "The bunker of the Atlantic Wall alerts us less of yesterday's adversary than of today's and tomorrow's war: total war, risk everywhere, instantaneity of danger, the great mix of the military and the civilian, the homogenization of conflict." Paul Virilio, *Bunker Archaeology*, trans. George Collins (New York: Princeton Architectural Press, 1994), 45-6.

11 While Le Corbusier here is specifically referring to architectural plans, as opposed to economic planning or urban planning, *The Radiant City* is a key text in urban planning history. Le Corbusier, *The Radiant City; Elements of a Doctrine of Urbanism to be Used as the Basis of our Machine-Age Civilization* (New York: Orion Press, 1964 [1933]), 7, 68. As Joe Deville, Michael Guggenheim, and Zuzana Hrdličková write, bunkers "concretize a confidence in the value of dedicated, technical, material solutions to disaster.... The absent disaster, whether nuclear explosion or a cyclone expected to arrive sometime in the near future, is transformed into an entity that, with the right application of technique, as concretized into a built material response, can be if not eliminated then at least managed." Deville et al, "Concrete governmentality: Shelters and the transformations of preparedness," *The Sociological Review* 62, no. S1 (2014): 190.

12 For an account of private bunker complexes that are often discussed in the media as complete but that don't actually seem to exist, see Bradley Garrett, *Bunker: Building for the End Times* (New York: Scribner, 2020), 136–141.

13 Jessica Hurley, *Infrastructures of Apocalypse: American Literature and the Nuclear Complex* (Minneapolis: University of Minnesota Press, 2020), 20. Emphasis in the original.

14 Virilio, *Bunker Archaeology*, 39.

15 Duffield, "Total war as environmental terror," 757.

16 For more on large bunker complexes built by the Cold War U.S. state, see Tom Vanderbilt, *Survival City: Adventures Among the Ruins of Atomic America* (Chicago: University of Chicago Press, 2002).

17 Joseph Masco, "'Survival is Your Business': Engineering Ruins and Affect in Nuclear America," *Cultural Anthropology* 23, no. 2 (May 2008): 383; Masco "Life Underground: Building the Bunker Society," *Anthropology Now* 1, no. 2 (September 2009): 13.

18 Masco, "Life Underground," 21.

19 Garrett and Klinke, "Opening the bunker," 1074.

20 See, for example, Evan Osnos, "Doomsday Prep for the Super-Rich," *The New Yorker*, January 22, 2017, https://www.newyorker.com/magazine/2017/01/30/doomsday-prep-for-the-super-rich; Adam Fish and Bradley Garrett, "Resurrection from Bunkers and Data Centers," Culture Machine 18 (2019): 1–14; Tea Krulos, *Apocalypse Any Day Now: Deep Underground with America's Doomsday Preppers* (Chicago: Chicago Review Press Incorporated, 2019); Garrett, "Doomsday preppers;" and Garrett, *Bunker*.

21 As Garrett and Klinke put it, "In popular North American prepper narratives today, the state has no role in the bunker society." Garrett and Klinke, "Opening the bunker," 1077. Barker argues that preppers more generally "[begin] from an understanding of their own exclusion from the myth of universal state security." See Barker, "How to survive the end of the future," 494.

22 Scholarship about people who identify as part of the prepping community in the United States often emphasizes that most people in this community do not really care about bunkers. Kezia Barker, for example, notes that while bunkers are "the class imaginary architecture of the pathologized prepper," very few preppers own a bunker. Nevertheless, the private bunker companies I will discuss market themselves primarily to people in this community. See Barker, "How to survive the end of the future: Preppers, pathology, and the everyday crisis of insecurity," *Transactions of the Institute of British Geographers* 45 (2020): 489.

23 "Vivos xPoint," The Vivos Group, accessed June 28, 2021, https://www.terravivos.com/secure/vivosxpoint.htm. The quote is from the first video embedded on the page.

24 See, for example, Andrew Lakoff, "Preparing for the Next Emergency," *Public Culture* 19, no. 2 (20007): 247–71; and Ben Anderson, "Preemption, Precaution, Preparedness: Anticipatory Action and Future Geographies," *Progress in Human Geography* 34, no. 6 (2010): 777–98.

25 "Vivos xPoint;" "Welcome to Survival Condo."

26 Lindsay Thomas, "Forms of Duration: Preparedness, the Mars Trilogy, and the Management of Climate Change," *American Literature* 88, no. 1 (2016): 159–84.

27 "Survival Condo Details," Survival Condo, accessed June 28, 20201, https://survivalcondo.com/details/; "Vivos xPoint."

28 Virilio, *Bunker Archaeology*, 42.

29 Leif Sorensen, "Against the Post-Apocalyptic: Narrative Closure in Colson Whitehead's *Zone One*," *Contemporary Literature* 55, no. 3 (2014): 562.

30 I discuss the post-apocalyptic temporality of preparedness in Lindsay Thomas, *Training for Catastrophe: Fictions of National Security after 9/11* (Minneapolis: University of Minnesota Press, 2021).

31 Garrett, "Doomsday preppers and the architecture of dread," 8.

32 "Welcome to Survival Condo," Survival Condo, accessed June 28, 2021, https://survivalcondo.com/overview/; the phrase "like-minded community" is used in the "Vivos xPoint" video.

33 "Welcome to Survival Condo."

34 See, for example, Occams Razor, "Being Like-Minded, What Do You Believe?", Survivalist Boards, September 26, 2009, https://www.survivalistboards.com/threads/being-like-minded-what-do-you-believe.76450/#post-947866.

35 The quotations are from Larry Hall, quoted in Krulos, *Apocalypse Any Day Now*, 145. For more on the demographics of preppers in the United States, see Jordan McKenzie, "Millennial utopians and prepper subcultures: Contemporary utopianism on the left and right," *Futures* 126 (2021): 5.

36 Tim Murphy, "Preppers Are Getting Ready for the Barackalypse," *Mother Jones*, January/February 2013, https://www.motherjones.com/politics/2012/12/preppers-survivalist-doomsday-obama/.

37 For a discussion of the "bunker horror" genre, see Michael Charlton, "The Infinite Inside: The Bunker Horror Film," in *The Spaces and Places of Horror*, eds. Francesco Pascuzzi and Sandra Waters (Wilmington: Vernon Press, 2020), 221–236.

38 See Marcia England, "Breached Bodies and Home Invasions: Horrific representations of the feminized body and home," *Gender, Place and Culure* 13, no. 4 (August 2006): 353–363; and Michael Fiddler, "Playing *Funny Games* in *The Last House on the Left*: The uncanny and the 'home invasion' genre," *Crime, Media, Culture: An International Journal* 9, no.3 (2013): 281–299.

39 Colson Whitehead, *Zone One* (New York: Doubleday, 2011), 239.

40 See Lara Langer Cohen, "The Depths of Astonishment: City Mysteries and the Antebellum Underground," *American Literary History* 29, no. 1 (2017): 1–25; and Cohen, "'The Blackness of Darkness': Mammoth Cave and the Racialization of the Underground," *History of the Present* 11, no. 1 (April 2021): 2-22. See "'The Blackness of Darkness'" for a partial list of works employing this trope. As Cohen emphasizes in that article, this understanding of the underground "prefigure[s] what would crystallize into 'subculture' in the twentieth century but also far exceed[s] that formulation" (3).

41 Colson Whitehead, *The Underground Railroad* (New York: Doubleday, 2016), 69, 67.

42 W. E. B. Du Bois, "The Comet," in *Darkwater: Voices from Within the Veil* (New York: Verso, 2016 [1920]), 401, 400.

43 Ibid., 401.

44 Ralph Ellison, *Invisible Man* (New York: Vintage, 1995 [1952]), 571, 6, 565.

45 Ibid., 7, 9, 13.

46 For more on the relationship between Wright and Ellison, see Imani Perry, "The Bleak Presence of Richard Wright," *The Atlantic*, June 2021, https://www.theatlantic.com/magazine/archive/2021/06/richard-wright-man-who-lived-underground/618705/.

47 Richard Wright, *The Man Who Lived Underground* (New York: Library of America, 2021), 53. Future references to this work are cited parenthetically in the text.

48 Wright, "Memories of My Grandmother," in *The Man Who Lived Underground* (New York: Library of America, 2021), 192. Future references to this work are cited parenthetically in the text.

49 Fred Moten, *In the Break: The Aesthetics of the Black Radical Tradition* (Minneapolis: University of Minnesota Press, 2003), 63.

50 Stephano Harvey and Fred Moten, *The Undercommons: Fugitive Planning & Black Study* (New York: Minor Compositions, 2013), 75.

51 Saidiya Hartman, "The End of White Supremacy, An American Romance," BOMB, June 5, 2020, https://bombmagazine.org/articles/the-end-of-white-supremacy-an-american-romance/.

52 For an excellent discussion of Wright's 1940 novel *Native Son*, northern segregation, and midcentury urban planning, see Bo McMillan, "Richard Wright and the Black Metropolis: From the Great Migration to the Urban Planning Novel," *American Literature* 92, no. 4 (December 2020): 653–680. For discussions of Wright's and Ellison's novels in relation to northern segregation, the housing-related riots in Harlem in 1935 and 1943, and the Housing Act of 1949, see Thomas Heise, *Urban Underworlds: A Geography of Twentieth-Century American Literature and Culture* (New Brunswick: Rutgers University Press, 2011), especially chapter 3, "The Black Underground: Urban Riots, the Black Underclass, and the Work of Richard Wright and Ralph Ellison, 1940s–1950s;" Myka Tucker Abramson, "Blueprints: *Invisible Man* and the Housing Act of 1949," *American Studies* 54, no. 3 (2015): 9-21; and Sarah Wasserman, "Ralph Ellison, Chester Himes, and the Persistence of Urban Forms," *PMLA* 135, no. 3 (2020): 530–545.

53 Hartman, "The End of White Supremacy."

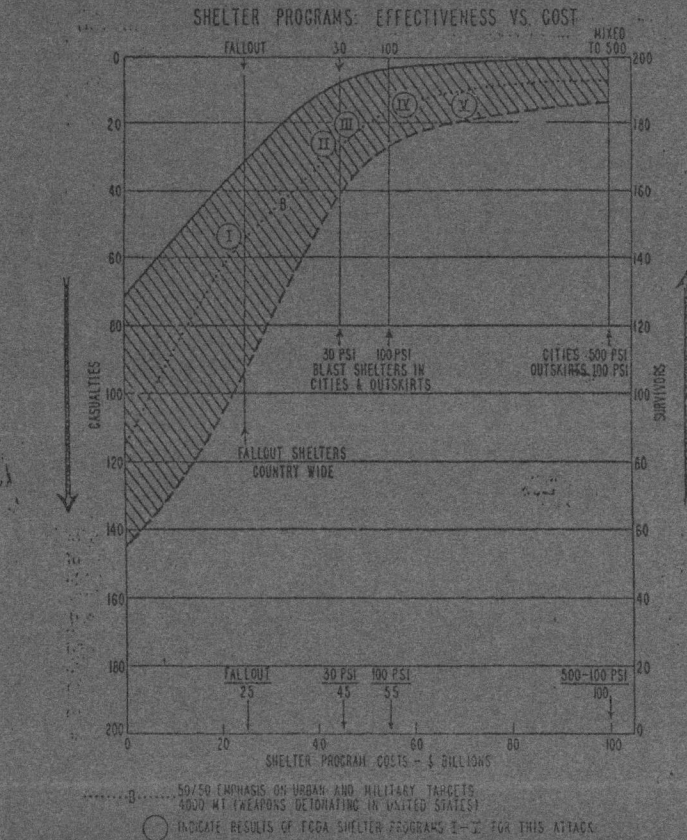

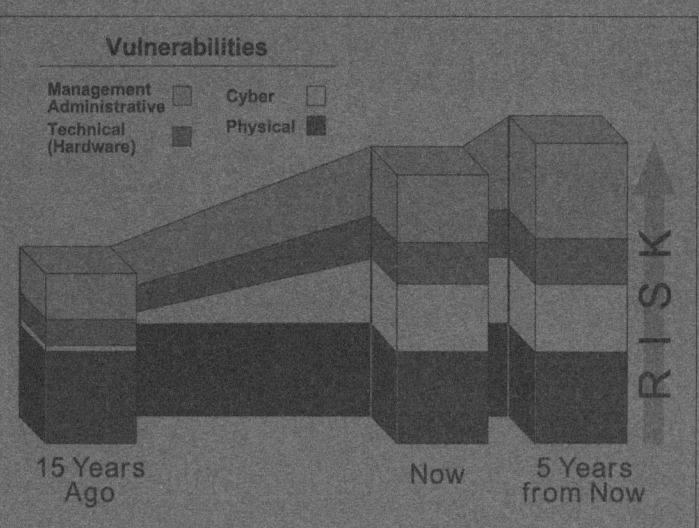

Figure 7. Vulnerabilities Profile

Data-Driven Design of Criminal and Consensual Environments

Peter Polack

Acknowledgements

This essay was motivated by community research and organizing at the Stop LAPD Spying Coalition, which also organized to file public requests for the records that informed this analysis.

Introduction

Data is under fire for reproducing racial and socio-economic disparities, and nowhere is this more evident than in law enforcement operations. From the disproportionate representation of people of color in crime databases[1] to the self-reinforcing feedback loops of crime prediction algorithms,[2] critics argue that data-driven methods have not enacted a paradigm shift in policing so much as they have intensified existing practices.

In the fields of design and urban planning, the use of data-driven methods is likewise on the rise. Pointing to examples like automated COVID lockdowns or the use of big data to monitor infrastructures, many within these disciplines contend that the moderation of social behavior can be achieved by embedding data collection and algorithmic systems in the built environment. Via greater investment in these information systems, so the argument goes, police-centered approaches to behavioral governance—and the repressive logics, systemic biases and mass incarceration that comes with policing—can be made obsolete.

The set of practices and theories called Crime Prevention Through Environmental Design (CPTED) makes this very claim. While law enforcement has always been in the business of configuring the built environment (see, for example, the use of police to enforce building codes for managing public health and order was already prominent in the 18th century[3]), CPTED differs from earlier approaches in that it explicitly advocates for the use of data-informed design as an alternative to policing as usual. In this system, data is used to identify features of the built environment that are conducive to certain behaviors, to assess the effects of design interventions on these behaviors, and to justify further interventions. In theory, this data-driven moderation of environments could do the work of behavioral governance without the police, minimizing human prejudice and recourse to violence.

But perhaps more importantly, due to the semblance of objectivity that comes with algorithmic systems, the police deploy these data-driven portraits of the built environment to make their designations of certain areas as criminal—and thus in need of corrective police power—appear

natural. That is to say, data-driven methods in law enforcement do not just automate or reproduce state violence, they are also used to configure how this unequal distribution of violence is perceived. Crucially, CPTED places a focus on design strategies that incentivize subjects to perceive their environment, community and selves in accordance with the law and police strategy writ large. By bolstering this viewpoint, other communities and environments are thereby made to seem objectively criminal. Through this analysis, we can begin to understand how data is not just used to automate the biases of existing systems, but is also used to configure the appearance of practices like policing so as to ensure public consent. As purveyors of information systems increasingly claim that they are able to eliminate algorithmic bias, it will become all the more necessary to understand how data can also be used to configure appearances, optimize consent and secure particular arrangements of power.

A Brief History of CPTED

I became aware that one cannot control criminal behavior by changing the educational system, the employment system, the social class system, or the prison system. One has to change the environment within which crimes occur. — C. Ray Jeffrey, 1977.[4]

While Crime Prevention Through Environmental Design was only coined as the acronym CPTED in the 1970s, an interest in designing environments to deter crime, enhance its visibility, encourage self-policing, and minimize recourse to overt acts of violence predates the acronym by centuries. The Statute of Winchester, devised to reform England's system of curfew-enforcing watchmen in 1285, proclaimed the removal of concealing structures on highways to enhance the visibility of potential criminals.[5] In tandem, landowners would be held responsible for crimes that occurred due to their negligence.[6] This statute established a direct relationship between self-policing—or, the surveillance and punishment of community members by other community members—and the configuration of visibility in environments. This relationship would be underlined again in Napoleon III's plans to renovate Paris in the 19th century, which responded to concerns at the time that public health, commerce, and order could be hampered by impaired visibility in urban environments.[7] Today, criminological theory calls the relationship between environmental visibilities and the capacity to self-police "natural surveillance," while the design of environments to support such capacities is termed "activity support."[8]

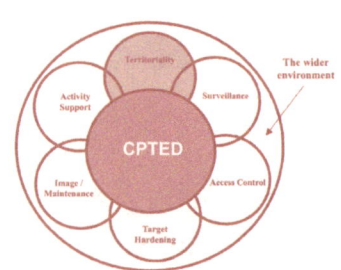

An explicit concern with configuring the appearance of the police to deter crime was later captured in the notion of "preventive policing," forwarded by the nascent police force emerging out of the British merchant class in the 18th century.[9] Following the utilitarian principles of Jeremy Bentham, it was assumed that, upon seeing the police, individuals would engage in utilitarian cost-benefit analysis and ultimately decide that the risk of being caught and punished for committing a crime was greater than whatever reward said crime would bring; the actual doling out of punishment would largely not be necessary. These principles would go on to inform Robert Peel's principles of policing in 1829, which emphasized "policing by consent," where the need "to secure and maintain the respect and approval of the public" is seen as integral to effective law enforcement operations, and where overt physical force is advised only when other interventions prove ineffective.[10]

Policing by consent aims at maintaining the approval of the public as a whole. Historically, however, there have always been particular communities whose "consent" had to be more forcefully coerced than others'. Moreover, it is only the most powerful stakeholders who get to define what it is that one should be consenting to in the first place. For example, colonialists seeking to maintain territorial control courted consent by investing in humanitarian development projects, an operation that ran parallel to the militarized repression of nonconsensual parties.[11]

Figure 10.2
Source: Pyle et al., The Spatial Dynamics of Crime, 1974, Fig.

Redesigned uban environments and new architectural forms not only changed the composition of colonized environments, but normalized social practices and aesthetics that were conducive to colonial rule, sieving out intransigent cultures and social practices.[12] This relationship between designing environments and optimizing consent is present as well in the 18th-century "lantern laws," which required black, mixed race, and indigenous people to carry lanterns in the streets when unaccompanied by a white person after dark.[13] While these laws did not bring about a permanent redesigning of the built environment, they established an enforceable boundary around public space by configuring the visibility of particular people and movements.[14]

What differentiates the modern formulation of CPTED from these earlier configurations of space and visibility is that it explicitly positions itself as an alternative to the police. From the mid-19th century onwards, planners and architects have portrayed environmental design as being useful for crime deterrence. For example, Elizabeth Wood, director of the Chicago Housing Authority during a time of socio-economic transformation and unrest in the early 1960s, contended that unwanted attitudes and behaviors stemmed from failures of the built environment.[15] Appealing to crime statistics, Wood argued that if architects and planners redesigned the built environment to make common spaces—and the crimes occurring in them—more visible, communities would engage in more self-policing behavior.[16]

This premise would be taken up by architects and urban planners throughout the 1960s. Jane Jacobs, distinguished for her activism against exclusionary development projects and urban renewal programs, argued that planning could enable communities themselves to take responsibility for the safety of their surroundings.[17] For Jacobs, design interventions could activate this capacity: as if taking a page from the Statute of Winchester centuries before, Jacobs argued that, by redesigning spaces so that there were more "eyes on the street," individuals would engage in self-policing and crime would be deterred. Jacobs's ideas would go on to inform Oscar Newman's theories of defensible space and territoriality, which remain integral to CPTED frameworks today.[18] For Newman, design could be used to emphasize property lines and land use boundaries, thereby making unsanctioned behaviors—and people—more visible. This enhanced visibility, in theory, would deter these behaviors and these intrusions by unwanted people.[19]

Throughout the 20th century, statistical methods were used to lend credence to the idea that crime was a function of the built environment. Shlomo Angel, a student of Christopher Alexander's, identified statistical correlations between crime rates and environmental features like land use and population density.[20] Later, spurred by a wave of riots throughout England in the 1980s, Alice Coleman's Land Use Research Unit likewise identified statistical correlations between features of the built environment and signs of "social malaise" like littering and graffiti.[21] Despite dubious methods, Coleman's reports attracted the attention of policymakers in the Thatcher administration, who then deployed defensible space design strategies in a series of major redevelopment projects with the Design Improvement Controlled Experiment (DICE).

While attributing crime to environmental features instead of socioeconomic factors naturally appealed to neoliberal policymakers, these theories had flaws too notable to be ignored. Most significantly, criminologists could not find data to definitively prove that particular environmental features were deterministic of crime.[22] C. Ray Jeffrey's CPTED framework, first introduced at this time, would solve this problem by turning to the behavioral theories of B.F. Skinner.[23] Crime was conceptualized as a response to a variety of material stimuli, over which designers, planners and law enforcement had only partial control. Crime prevention was thus formalized as an experiment on a subject whose inner workings, as in Skinner's work, were conceived as a black box. By altering environmental

183

inputs and seeing the behavioral results, one could uncover the factors that disposed subjects to crime.

Prior to this time, these potential behavior-altering factors were conceived of in architectural terms: it was thought that raised curbs, enhanced lines of sight and clearly indicated private property boundaries were the types of interventions that could possibly deter criminal behavior. But Jeffrey argued that this environmental determinism proved insufficient in practice: when it was operationalized in renovations to a series of public school systems in the United States, it failed to return tractable results.[24] In response, CPTED theorists expanded their purview beyond the dyad of environment-behavioral response, turning their attention to the idea of place-based "social norms."[25] For example, reflecting on earlier theories, this emerging generation of socially-focused environmental design theorists argues that "what's significant about Jacobs's 'eyes on the street' is not the sightlines or even the streets, but the eyes."[26]

Just designing the environment, then, wasn't enough—altering these social norms was essential. In an attempt to account for this social factor, criminologists in the late 20th century turned their attention to biological, psychological, and socio-economic factors. A "Second Generation" of CPTED theories shifted emphasis to the role of community networks, psychology and socio-economic factors played in deterring crime.[27] As one member of this generation of CPTED theorists put it, "When we fail to 'design' our affective conditions that help generate that sense of community with the same careful scrutiny as the physical, we are doing less than half the job."[28]

So-called "Community CPTED" stems from this call to "design" the affective conditions of a given community. Borrowing from the language of systems theory, this school of criminologists sought "to create healthy, self-regulating communities" through strategic and context-specific environmental interventions.[29] Here a Peelian logic of "policing by consent" was formalized in metrics like "social cohesion," which assess a community's ability to address conflicts socially, intellectually and emotionally.[30] In more recent crime data analyses, social cohesion and similar metrics like "collective efficacy" incorporate measurements of a neighborhood's propensity to call and cooperate with the police, as well as measures of the public's approval of law enforcement operations and use of force.[31] Through the lens of these metrics, communities that exhibit consent with law enforcement are seen as self-sufficient and self-regulating, while those that do not consent are deemed as having "low social cohesion," and are seen as requiring more stringent intervention from the outside.[32]

Importantly, although this generation of CPTED and its metrics focuses on the relation between "community" characteristics and crime,[33] it does not completely jettison the earlier focus on environmental and geographical characteristics. In these theories, communities are not just composed of abstract "social cohesion" levels; they are, rather, mapped and located in very specific geographic areas. Moreover, as noted above, environmental features are still considered influential. The design of a given space is thought to have an impact on a community's social characteristics, which in turn influences an area's overall propensity to crime or an area's unwillingness to collaborate with law enforcement operations.

CPTED and Data-Driven Law Enforcement

As I will show in this section, the tight statistical link CPTED posits between environment and community behavior allows contemporary police forces to perform a sleight of hand: they can effectively target specific communities while claiming that they are instead merely targeting statistically proven crime-causing environments. Data here is clearly doing much more than simply providing information; the guise of data is also used to alter appearances. That is, via their claims that they are

being objectively guided by "environmental data," police work is made to seem impartial and objectively required. To see how this works in practice, we can examine the data-driven methods of modern law enforcement agencies like the Los Angeles Police Department (LAPD).

Take, for example, the LAPD's Area Crime & Community Intelligence Centers (ACCICs). These criminal data processing centers designate certain parts of the city as Neighborhood Engagement Areas (NEAs), effectively treating particular geographic regions and their inhabitants as environments that can be moderated to influence the incidence of crimes.[34] Data about public sentiment and behavior is collected in each NEA to evaluate social cohesion, a metric that, as discussed above, incorporates measurements of a community's willingness to self-police. As in earlier CPTED theories, human behavior in this system is conceived as fundamentally geographic and environmental.

This social-environmental focus is evident at the subregional level as well, where specific buildings are classified according to their tendency to dispose people to crime. Structures that are identified as leading to criminal behavior are deemed "anchor points" or "crime generators."[35] Certain "crime generating" environments are designated as Community Safety Partnership (CSP) sites, a label that sanctions the deployment of CCTV cameras, license plate readers, and social media data surveillance under the pretense of "relationship building" with communities.

This mapping of behaviors and environments also occurs at even more granular scales. Following the logic of "crime generating" environments, the LAPD's Citywide Nuisance Abatement Program (CNAP) identifies individual properties as "nuisance" buildings, a label that then allows the City Attorney to pressure property owners into cooperating with the police by, for example, installing surveillance technology. Although this technology can then be used to surveil specific individuals, because it is technically the environment and not an individual that has been classified as exhibiting a propensity for crime, the police have a cover for this personal targeting.

This dynamic is what ultimately allows the LAPD to propose that its new regime of data-driven policing would not be "discriminatory" or racist, but rather "discriminating;" that is, informed by data about disorder and crimes rather than individualized, racial factors.[36] While this distinction is largely rhetorical, it indicates an overlooked function of data-driven operations: data here is used to assuage public discontent by making it appear as if the police are acting neutrally and objectively. We can see evidence of this performative use of data in the way that academic advisors to these LAPD projects talk about their work: they are concerned, they say, with cultivating "digital trust" in algorithmic systems, with centering police "accountability" so as to gain public support, and with avoiding accusations that race is involved in data analysis. For another example of this use of data, take what the law and policing scholar Andrew Ferguson wrote in an email to Jeffrey Brantingham, inventor the infamous PredPol predictive policing platform: "as a strategic matter," Ferguson argues, it is important to promote papers "showing that you can balance race or other factors." One should advertise papers, he continues, that show that solving such issues is just a matter of how the police "calibrate the algorithm."[37] Data thus is used to give the appearance that police are not considering factors like race, but are merely algorithmically addressing the environmental factors that give rise to aberrant behavior.

In their attempt to ensure that certain publics have a positive view of police work, law enforcement does not only use data to make their profiling and interventions in supposedly crime-prone areas appear neutral. They also use data to customize coalition-building efforts with those who are already most willing to cooperate with police operations. For example, the LAPD is working to implement software that permits authorized

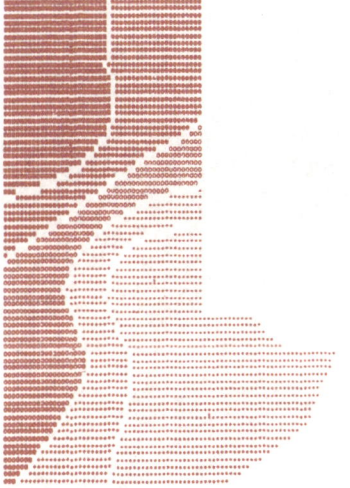

Figure 10.17: Burglary Rate Patterns in Census Tract 1 in 1970. Burglary rates were calculated per 1,000 population for each block group. Five levels of burglary rates were mapped: Level 1 = 0–6.24; Level 2 = 6.24–12.24–18.71; Level 4 = 18.71–24.94; Level 5 = 24.94–31.18.
Source: Brantingham et al., 1976, Figure 6.

regional stakeholders to submit their concerns, which will then make their way to police databases. Through adopting third-party, publicly accessible online dashboards for crime mapping and reporting like CityProtect and Motorola's Command Central Community, the police gain further control over what the public sees about crime, as well as control over how the public relates to crime through the design of these reporting portals.[38] Additionally, the LAPD relies on programs that analyze regional crime, sentiment, and social media data to plan their relationship building with particular communities. This data makes the LAPD seem voluntarily attentive to community concerns and it also aids them in pinpointing the most opportune places and times for public outreach (for instance, after officer-involved homicides). Altogether, through these emerging systems, law enforcement can selectively coordinate its partnerships with the most compliant and powerful parties. Thanks to troves of data that inform how the appearance of policing should be configured in each specific locale, coalition-building activities like coffee with cops can happen in an area adjacent to one under constant surveillance and threat of force.

In summary, then, we see that while CPTED once encouraged the construction of architectural cues like raised curbs to indicate the unsanctioned use of private property, the spatial differentiation of the built environment is now accomplished by accumulating data and then mapping areas according to its given metrics. In this data-driven system, whether or not a person inhabits an environment with a high "social cohesion" level—a metric that, as shown above, operationalizes data about a community's willingness or reluctance to endorse police power—is seen as objectively indicating a person's relationship to criminality. The key aspect of this system is that these maps of criminality use data to make certain relations between space, behavior, and policing appear innate. As one CPTED theorist puts it, the "task of controlling . . . the *image* of a particular site" is central to all types of environmental design (emphasis added).[39]

Importantly, with the development of this data-driven mapping, the audience of this image of criminologically drawn spatial boundaries changes. The curb cuts and fences of earlier CPTED were perceived by the communities that inhabited those environments. The digital boundaries drawn between consenting and "criminal-prone" areas today, however, are primarily geared to those stakeholders who already have a positive view of the police. These stakeholders tend to be those that have the power to direct policy, funding, or state-sanctioned force. The goal of securing the consent of the public as a whole has been abandoned in favor of garnering the support from these influential stakeholders.

Despite this change of audience, the fundamental tenet of CPTED—that it is possible to eliminate aberrant behavior by redesigning the way in which we perceive our environments—remains. However, instead of redesigning the physical structure of our environment to make more visible any aberrant behavior occurring therein, we now redesign our metrics so that any environment that refuses to be complicit with police operations appears as objectively dangerous.

Implications for Criticism and Design of Algorithmic Governance

> *The American liberals say: if you want to maintain ... the order of the law, you must consider everyone as a player and only intervene on an environment in which he is able to play.* — Michel Foucault, 2008.[40]

The critical takeaway from this analysis is that data-driven methods are not used simply to perpetuate existing biases and enforce algorithmic control, but to make police activities appear benign to consenting parties and stakeholders, thereby garnering their support. In other words, these data-heavy police practices evidence a regime of algorithmic governance that is staked less on controlling behavior outright than on putting

forward a positive representation of police practices so as to encourage people to endorse its particular distributions of power. The function of policing, we see here, is not simply to regulate activity in accordance with the law, but to configure the appearance of particular behaviors and social groups, of criminality, and of state power so as to license particular social practices while sieving out others.

This focus on the image of law enforcement is a fundamental component of policing: from the early days of preventive policing to today's predictive policing, the police have always been concerned with how they, along with the crimes and the communities that they target, appear. This focus on controlling appearances calls to mind Jacque Rancière's definition of the police. In contrast to common understandings of the police as a force that imposes extrinsic order on any disruptive actions, Rancière argues that their real purpose is to respond to any incidence of state violence or social unrest with the injunction "move along, there is nothing to see here."[41] The data-informed configuration of environmental appearances is critical to enabling this police function: via metrics like "social cohesion," particular behaviors are made to appear as objectively criminal, particular communities as objectively culpable, and particular responses as objectively fair.

What this analysis of CPTED demonstrates is not that data can never be used to improve social services, nor that any attempt to do so will automatically give way to policing. Rather, this essay shows that, because of the putative trustworthiness of data, organizations like the police can and do use data-driven methods to make their activities—which impose very particular distributions of power and resources—appear fair and natural. This deployment of data-driven technologies to the end of altering appearances has largely gone unacknowledged. Typically, critics have tended to focus on how algorithmic systems sort people into ontological categories which then automatically trigger differential outcomes (the phenomenon known as "algorithmic bias"). The use of data I have uncovered here is not concerned with ontologically ordering people but with configuring the phenomenological: that is, with altering how people perceive and how they feel about certain people and places—and their treatment by police. Perhaps this configuring of perceptions is what Michel Foucault had in mind with his uncompleted theory of "environmental technology." Instead of subjecting individuals to standardization and classification, this form of governance proceeds by influencing our perceptions of our environments—it "[modifies] the terms of the game"—and only thereby are inhabitants disposed to particular behaviors.[42]

This theory compels us to interrogate how ostensibly participatory forms of governance like Community-Focused Policing and environmental design are involved in optimizing buy-in to particular distributions of power, rather than in providing limits to their expansion. Such an analysis has significant implications for the field of architecture. The design disciplines, skilled as they are in computational methods and in data-mapping technologies, can be easily enlisted into this project that purports to offer an alternative to policing but that all the while preserves police power by rebranding its appearance. Architects have to be aware that designing environmental appearances, whether through sight lines or data-mapping, often supports a logic of policing by consent.

A contrasting political project is offered by the sociologist AbdouMaliq Simone, who, in opposition to the idea of the "right to the city," calls for "the right to indifference": communities, Simone argues, ought to have the right to live and experiment on their own terms without having their social practices integrated within existing city infrastructures, markets, and police practices.[43] Simone's politics is decidedly not reformist. What is at stake here is not whether the geographic distribution of police force and the participation in state power can be made less uneven; rather, he seeks a world in which refusing to consent to police power does not warrant violence. How, we might ask, can design contribute to this future?

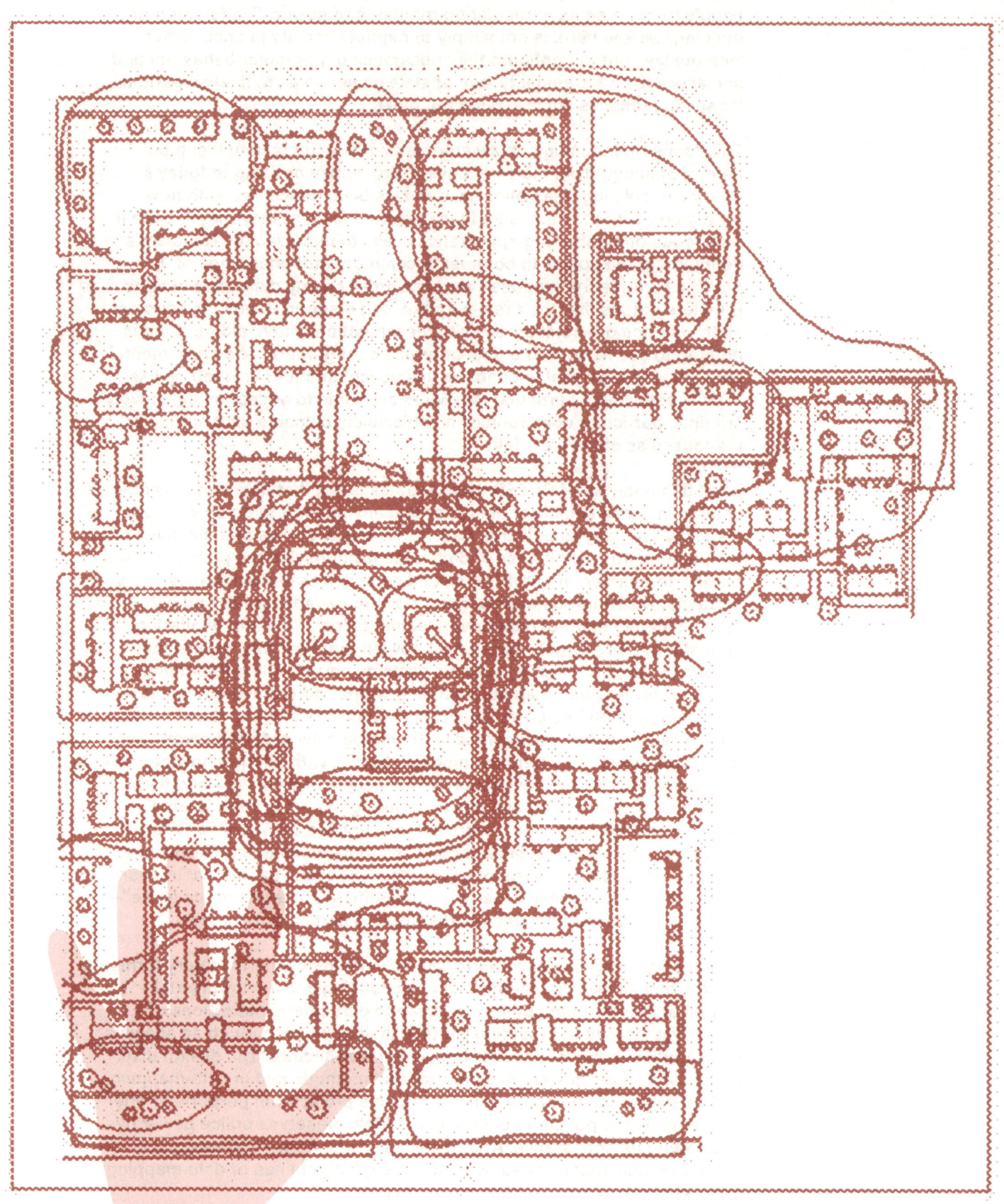

Figure III-3:
Composite of fear maps produced by residents.

■ To reduce the number of as to limit access and to

1. Rashida Richardson, Jason M. Schultz and Kate Crawford, "Dirty Data, Bad Predictions: How Civil Rights Violations Impact Police Data, Predictive Policing Systems, and Justice," *NYUL Rev. Online* 94 (2019): 15.
2. Kristian Lum and William Isaac, "To Predict and Serve?" *Significance* 13 no. 5 (2016): 14–19.
3. George Rosen, "Cameralism and the Concept of Medical Police." *Bulletin of the History of Medicine* 27 no. 1 (1953): 21–42.
4. C. Ray Jeffrey, *Crime Prevention Through Environmental Design* (Beverly Hills: Sage Publications, 1977): 289.
5. William Stubbs and H. W. Carless (Henry William Carless) Davis, *Select Charters and Other Illustrations of English Constitutional History* (Oxford: The Clarendon press, 1913).
6. Stubbs and Davis, *Select Charters*, 473.
7. Stephane Kirkland, *Paris Reborn : Napoléon III, Baron Haussmann, and the Quest to Build a Modern City* (New York : St. Martin's Press, 2013): 65–66.
8. Paul Cozens, "Crime Prevention through Environmental Design," in *Environmental Criminology and Crime Analysis*, eds. Richard Wortley and Lorraine Mazerolle (Oxfordshire: Routledge, 2013), 175–99.
9. Richard J. Terrill, "Police Theorists and the 'New Enlightenment,'" *Anglo-American Law Review* 9 no. 1 (January 1980): 48–64.
10. GOV.UK, "Definition of Policing by Consent," *UK Government Home Office*, 2012, https://www.gov.uk/government/publications/policing-by-consent/definition-of-policing-by-consent.
11. Tyler Wall, Parastou Saberi and Will Jackson, eds., *Destroy, Build, Secure: Readings on Pacification*, (Ottawa: Red Quill Books, 2017).
12. Wall et al., *Destroy, Build Secure*, 95–100.
13. Simone Browne, *Dark Matters: On the Surveillance of Blackness* (Chapel Hill: Duke University Press, 2015).
14. Browne, *Dark Matters*.
15. Elizabeth Wood, "Social-Welfare Planning," *The ANNALS of the American Academy of Political and Social Science* 352 no. 1 (Mar. 1964): 119–128.
16. Oscar Newman and the National Institute of Law Enforcement and Criminal Justice, *Architectural Design for Crime Prevention*, National Institute of Law Enforcement and Criminal Justice (Washington, DC, 1973): 122.
17. Jane Jacobs, *The Death and Life of Great American Cities* (New York: Random House, 1961): 126.
18. Newman, *Architectural Design*.
19. Oscar Newman, *Defensible Space; Crime Prevention through Urban Design* (New York: Collier Books, 1973).
20. Newman, *Architectural Design*, 132; Matthew B. Robinson, "The Theoretical Development of 'CPTED': Twenty-Five Years of Responses to C. Ray Jeffery," in *The Criminology of Criminal Law*, eds. William S. Laufer and Freda Adler (Oxfordshire: Routledge, 2017): 427–62.
21. Elanor Joan Petra Warwick, "Defensible Space as a Mobile Concept: The Role of Transfer Mechanisms and Evidence in Housing Research, Policy and Practice," PhD diss. (King's College London, 2015).
22. Warwick, "Defensible Space."
23. Jeffrey, *Crime Prevention*, 9.
24. Leonard Bickman et al., "Evaluation of Crime Prevention through Environmental Design Programs," (Evanston, IL: National Institute of Justice) 1977.
25. C. Ray Jeffrey, *Crime Prevention*.
26. Gregory Saville and Gerry Cleveland, "Second-generation CPTED in schools," in *1st Annual International CPTED Association Conference* (Orlando, FL, 1997): 1.
27. Saville and Cleveland, "Second-generation CPTED."
28. Saville and Cleveland, "Second-generation CPTED."
29. S. Plaster Carter, "Community Cpted," *The Journal of the International Crime Prevention Through Environmental Design Association* 1 no. 1 (2002): 15–24.
30. Gregory Saville and Gerry Cleveland, "CPTED and the Social City: The Future of Capacity Building," *The CPTED Journal* (Jan. 2006).
31. Heike Goudriaan, Karin Wittebrood and Paul Nieuwbeerta, "Neighborhood Characteristics and Reporting Crime: Effects of Social Cohesion, Confidence in Police Effectiveness and Socio-Economic Disadvantage 1," *British Journal of Criminology* 46 no. 4 (2006): 719–42; Craig D. Uchida, Mark L. Swatt, Shellie E. Solomon and Sean Varano, *Data-Driven Crime Prevention: New Tools for Community Involvement and Crime Control* (Silver Springs: Justice & Security Strategies, Incorporated, 2013).
32. Today this analysis of community self-sufficiency is marketed under the guise of Community-Focused Policing.
33. Uchida, et al., *Data-Driven Crime Prevention*.
34. Michael Boylls, "Data-Informed Community-Focused Policing in the Los Angeles Police Department," Los Angeles Police Department, 2020.
35. Patricia Brantingham, and Paul Brantingham, "Criminality of Place: Crime Generators and Crime Attractors," *European Journal on Criminal Policy and Research* 3 no. 3 (September 1995): 5–26; P. Jeffrey Brantingham, George E. Tita, Martin B. Short and Shannon E. Reid. "The Ecology of Gang Territorial Boundaries," *Criminology* 50 no. 3 (2012): 851–85; Uchida et al., *Data-Driven Crime Prevention*.
36. William J. Bratton, "Cops Count, Police Matter: Preventing Crime and Disorder in the 21st Century." *The Heritage Foundation* 2 (2018): 1–13.
37. "Request 20-5033 - NextRequest - Modern FOIA & Public Records Request Software," accessed August 3, 2022, https://recordsrequest.lacity.org/requests/20-5033.
38. Motorola Solutions, "CommandCentral Community: Improve Accessibility, Increase Trust," 2020, accessed September 26, 2022, https://www.motorolasolutions.com/content/dam/msi/docs/products/command-center-software/community-engagement/commandcentral-community/commandcentral_community_data_sheet.pdf; Motorola Solutions. "Community: Make Community Your Most Valuable Resources," 2021, accessed September 26, 2022. https://www.motorolasolutions.com/content/dam/msi/docs/global-software/community/cc-community-brochure.pdf.
39. Paul, Ekblom, "Deconstructing CPTED… and Reconstructing It for Practice, Knowledge Management and Research," *European Journal on Criminal Policy and Research* 17 no. 1 (March 2011): 7–28.
40. Michel Foucault, Arnold I. Davidson and Graham Burchell, *The Birth of Biopolitics: Lectures at the Collège de France*, 1978–1979, (New York: Springer, 2008): 261.
41. Jacques Rancière, Davide Panagia and Rachel Bowlby, "Ten Theses on Politics," *Theory & Event* 5 no. 3 (2001).
42. Foucault et al., *The Birth of Biopolitics*, 260–61.
43. AbdouMaliq Simone, "Urbanity and Generic Blackness," *Theory, Culture & Society* 33, no. 7–8 (2016): 183–203.

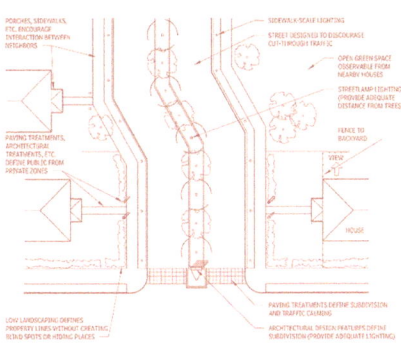

Figure 10.15: Burglary Rate Pattern in Florida in 1971. Burglary rates were calculated per 100,000 population for each country. Five levels of burglary rates were mapped: Level 1 = 120.1–557.3; Level 2 = 557.3–994.5; Level 3 = 994.5–1431.5; Level 4 = 1431.5–1868.9; Level 5 = 1868.9–2306.1.
Source: Brantingham et al., 1978, Figure 4.

Investments

William Deringer
Matthew Soules
Savannah Cox
Nashin Mahtani
Todd Reisz

If, for the previous section's security professionals, uncertainty is something that provokes unease, it takes on a rather different emotional valence in the economic sphere where, if Frank Knight is to be believed, the successful navigation of uncertainty is the source of all profits.[1] How, though, is one able to turn present uncertainty into future gains? In discussing the logic of stock market speculation, the economist John Maynard Keynes liked to bring up the example of a mail-in newspaper beauty contest with a very particular set of rules: instead of voting on which candidate's printed photograph they found the most attractive, entrants were instructed to vote on which candidate they felt the readership as a whole would rank highest. To win, then, you had to anticipate your competitors' valuations, who were in turn trying to anticipate your rankings. This circular dynamic, he argued, was a perfect metaphor for the stock market, wherein whether or not an investment is deemed valuable is dependent upon whether or not the market thinks it *will* be valuable. In this system, the best strategy to ensure your selected stock succeeds is to make other market actors think it is a good investment.[2]

Despite his focus on the affective dimension of valuation, Keynes ultimately believed that, over the long run, some sort of core, underlying material value would reveal itself. Recently, however, a number of thinkers on the left—usually the home of speculation's harshest critics—have taken issue with the belief in a non-social underlayer to value. For these scholars, value, being a category of human understanding, is necessarily always a social affair.[3] The project, in their eyes, is not to hold out fantasies of escaping this system into a chimerical unmediated world, but to understand exactly how the processes of valuation and investment work so as to intervene in this system in pursuit of a better future (or, bar that, to create a new system of value altogether). The following interviews and texts consider the role architects, master image-makers that they are, play in the project of cultivating value-generating impressions. Perhaps, given an understanding of this dynamic, architects can begin using their rendering powers to steer investors' minds towards reparative ends rather than profitable ones.[4]

---

1. Frank Knight, *Risk, Uncertainty and Profit* (Boston: Hart, Schaffner and Marx, 1921).
2. This account of Keynes's thought is taken from Jonathan Levy, "Primal Capital," *Critical Historical Studies* (Fall 2019),183–84. To read the original passage, see John Maynard Keynes, *The General Theory of Employment, Interest, and Money* (1936; San Diego: Harcourt, Brace & World, 1964), 155–156.
3. For a survey of this mode of thinking, see Lisa Adkins, Melinda Cooper and Martijn Konings, *The Asset Economy: Property Ownership and the New Logic of Inequality* (New York: Polity Press, 2020), 86–87. It is important to note, however, that social practices can have material effects. As Melinda Cooper points out, the "trustworthiness of all money is reinforced, in the last instance, by the threat of violence." Melinda Cooper, "Turbulent Worlds: Financial Markets and Environmental Crisis," *Theory, Culture & Society* 27, no. 2–3 (2010): 184–85.
4. For a fantasy account of such a positive re-steering of finance, see Hannah Appel "Reparative Public Goods and the Future of Finance: A Fantasy in Three Parts," in "Post-Covid Fantasies," eds. Catherine Besteman, Heath Cabot and Barak Kalir, *American Ethnologist* website, August 25, 2020, https://americanethnologist.org/features/pandemic-diaries/post-covid-fantasies/reparative-public-goods-and-the-future-of-finance-a-fantasy-in-three-parts.

Interview — William Deringer

Architects have largely been disabused of our yearning for a tabula rasa, that destructive dream of a completely blank site onto which we can build, without constraint, our utopian visions. Whether it be by nature or by humans, history has taught us that space is always inhabited and that it is typically only by violence that it can be made otherwise. When it comes to the temporal realm, however, our tabula rasa fantasies hold strong: the future is still mostly perceived as an open expanse into which we can project any structure our hearts desire. Ever so slowly, however, we're beginning to understand that this temporal realm is as crowded as those spatial landscapes we once thought so empty: future floods limit where we can site our future buildings while anticipations of depleted sand stocks cause our projected structures to be made of a different material. And of course there are those pesky future humans demanding that we consider their well-being every time we populate our plans with another carbon-emitting square footage of air-conditioned space.

How does one adjudicate between the claims of those designing in the now and those living in the future? In a world where money talks, it is more than likely that the language of finance will be the medium for these intertemporal negotiations. To understand how the ways in which we value the future affect our actions in the present, we spoke over Zoom with William Deringer, author of Calculated Values: Finance, Politics, and the Quantitative Age, *an examination of the relationship between political culture and financial calculation in seventeenth and eighteenth century England. He is currently working on a book about the discounting equation, a calculation for determining how much an income stream will be worth in the future.*

Perspecta 55: *First, for the sake of our readers, let's start with your background, academic and otherwise. How did you get interested in these questions of pricing the future? Your textured view of calculation came from a professional setting, correct?*

William Deringer: I've always been interested in calculation and in math—I will admit to having been a competitive mathlete in high school—and thought I could major in math at college, but I also had an array of humanistic interests. I decided to explore economics because it seemed like a fusion of the two, but I found that it was even more foreign—it's neither mathematics nor history; it was something entirely of its own. I didn't really understand it, but I was fascinated by economics as a domain to study.

I graduated from college in 2006, which was a very bland time in the economy and on Wall Street. I took my first job as an investment banker at Blackstone working for a group called Restructuring and Reorganization that did investment banking advisory for companies in financial distress. I did that briefly and quickly discovered that it was not for me in terms of the rhythm, stress and the kinds of questions that I like thinking about, but I took a lot away from it, including a familiarity with a very important technical domain. That experience opened me up to some big social, philosophical and cultural questions—but only because I was able to see through some of the technicalities.

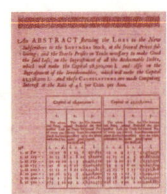

I was only at that job for a couple of days before I knew I would have to leave and go to graduate school, but I stuck with it for more than a year. I went to do a PhD in History of Science where I studied the history of these technical practices, work I had begun as an undergrad. The historical time period that I was most familiar with from my undergraduate work was the early modern, so that's where I started.

The moment that things started to click was in a first year grad seminar on 18th century Britain—there was some reference to this financial crisis in 1720, the South Sea bubble. I started searching around in WorldCat and came upon these caches of old political pamphlets that included very elaborate analyses of stock valuations. They looked weirdly familiar, like the technical work I was just doing at Blackstone; they had some of the same concepts. And in fact, the concept that really caught my eye was that of pricing the future, a technique that I learned in investment banking. It's a core technique for financial valuation, or so called DCF (discounted cash flow) analysis, where you essentially create an Excel model with what you think the future financial results of the company— the revenues, expenses, profits and cash flows—will be, and then use this technique of discounting to put a price on those future flows. So I'm sitting there in a grad seminar and stumble on these pamphlets where people are doing this in 1720. Well, they're doing something *like* this—it is logically very close, but also completely inscrutable in certain historical ways.

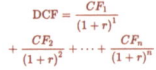

That was the origin of my dissertation project. It started as an effort to try to understand those pamphlets and calculations around the South Sea crisis—historically, socially, culturally, politically. How did it come to be that people not only knew how to do this, but also were publishing public pamphlets about this arcane subject? That work became my first book, *Calculated Values*, which filled out the history around that story to understand how numerical calculations became a form of political argumentation. I opened out from this episode in 1720 to think of numbers and calculations quite generally, as part of political life and almost as a kind of medium.

$$DCF = \frac{CF_1}{(1+r)^1} + \frac{CF_2}{(1+r)^2} + \cdots + \frac{CF_n}{(1+r)^n}$$

But in many of the episodes I studied in the book—which range from the 1690s to the middle of the 18th century—I kept coming across this particular calculation for pricing the future, this idea of using the mathematics of compound interest to translate back and forth across time. It came up in quite a few places unexpectedly: in debates about the South Sea crisis, in debates about what to do with national debt after this crisis, and there's even a scheme called a sinking fund that attempts to use compound interest in reverse to pay debt down. Then, particularly interestingly, this calculation comes up in 1706 when, during negotiations over the union of England and Scotland, the English agree to pay the Scottish to compensate for their taking on higher taxes. William Paterson, the founder of the Bank of England, and an Oxford mathematician came up with a calculation called the "equivalent" to determine how much this payment should be. And of course the "equivalent" also involves this same calculation, this so-called discounting calculation.

I was really intrigued by the ubiquity of this calculation, but never could figure out how anyone knew how to do it. It was this arcane technique that I knew of from working in finance and from some macroeconomics classes; I thought of it as a quite modern, esoteric, technical thing. Yet here you had a relatively substantial number of people—some members of parliament, these economic journalists types—that seemed to at least vaguely know what this was. Actually, a few of them could do these calculations with quite a high level of sophistication, such that you can reconstruct them in Excel. I could reverse engineer them to find out what was going on, which became a new puzzle for me.

When I finished my PhD and started my postdoc, I didn't want to work on my book for a while, so I thought I would just study this particular calculation to find out where it came from. I thought at first that this would be just a side project. Classic. And then I had a very fortuitous conversation with a friend of mine, who's a philosopher. I mentioned that I was doing this side project about the history of discounting calculations, and he lit up and said, "Well, philosophers are obsessed with this now." Weird, that's really strange, I thought. "Yeah—it's because of climate change!" And then it suddenly made sense.

He said there was a really active debate about intergenerational ethics and pricing the future. So I started digging around into these topics. This would have been a little bit after the first wave of attention to these questions—the Stern Review on the economics of climate change had been published in 2006—but it was still very much an active issue. So I thought, now I have a book here that just has to be written. All of a sudden this random, somewhat arcane subject that I was going to track down for my own personal curiosity or to distract myself—it needs to be something more than that. The project now is to try to piece together a history of this calculation across a very long sweep of time. And what really interests me is the question of *why* this technique takes hold in certain settings.

To that end, the book is organized around these threshold moments when this technique enters a new domain: Mining engineering is one case study; public policy and cost benefit analysis is another; there will be a chapter about the human sciences and how these calculations and critiques of them get incorporated into models of human decision-making; and then there will be a study of the legal arena, where you see this technique incorporated into routines for valuing human life, and specifically for projecting expected future earnings to determine how much victims should be compensated in wrongful death or injury cases. So that's the project I'm working on—and trying to keep it bounded, somewhat fruitlessly.

P: *The fact that this equation becomes centered and debated in particular moments more than in others feels like an especially important insight. I wonder how debt plays into this dynamic. You discuss this topic in your previous book in your discussion about multiple investment sinking funds. Your argument is that this was the moment when secular future calculation tactics entered governance—Paterson's genius was to use exponential compound interest to pay off debt. The future enters governance to pay off debt, to wiggle out of a commitment that you made in the past.*

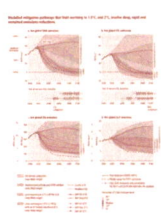

This complex interchange between past and future seems really central now, in the present day. To take one example, the IPCC imagines all sorts of future scenarios and climate mitigation pathways, but again, it's a way to pay off debt, this carbon debt we've incurred. And so is this something that you've found, that the future enters governments more as debts seem particularly central? Is the future more debated when our past feels particularly burdensome?

WD: That's a really interesting connection, though I don't know if I've ever thought about it in precisely those terms. While each of the different moments when this calculation takes on new powers has a slightly different texture to it, one of the consistencies is that this calculation seems to take hold—as a sort of solution—at moments when there has been a rupture in typical forms of temporality, that is, when a traditional way of understanding the relationship between the past and the present has become frayed or strained.

So one example—and it turns out that this explains the episode that I started out with 10 years ago when I was trying to figure out how all these 18th century figures learned these kinds of equations—is in England in the 1610s and 1620s, where you see these discounting equations unexpectedly beginning to be used all of a sudden. And they are being used in a very specific context: for property leases on agricultural land. Can I get kind of wonky with this?

P: *Yeah, definitely*

WD: It requires some explanation, but I think it's really interesting. If you go back to the feudal period, there are specific systems of farmland occupancy. Tenants would live on the land of a landlord, often a person of high social rank, and various different arrangements would govern the rights of the tenants on that land. Some of them were effectively a kind of permanent tenancy, where the tenant could live on the land forever and pass it down to their heirs, so long as they paid a certain rent every year. But then these traditional tenancies start to shift over in the early modern period to more formal leases. These leases tended to be quite long—often at least 20 years or so—and, while they each have their own weird characteristics to them, the most important thing about them historically was that in all the leases the rent that a tenant paid a landlord was fixed; it was fixed at a nominal level, oftentimes called the "ancient rent." It was literally a number that had been established in the Medieval Period, in the 13th century, and it was written down on a rent roll—a kind of manorial document—and it could not be changed. In fact, the social customs were so strong that any attempt to raise the rent was considered an absolutely intolerable violation of the landlord's customary obligations to the tenant. And courts supported this; they would rule in favor of the tenants. So perfect rent control, a fixed number.

Now, this made sense in a world without inflation. And Medieval Europe didn't have significant inflation until really the middle of the 16th century, which ushered in the so-called "Price Revolution"—a seismic world historic macroeconomic event where, around about 1550 or so, prices started to rise. Determining the causes of this shift is a great puzzle for economic historians; it's clearly a bunch of different factors. One thing is colonialism and the importation of precious metals from the Americas, and another is developments in mining technologies in Central Europe. There's more silver and gold that's being produced, so the money supply is increasing, so prices are going up. But there are also more people and new financial innovations that are increasing the velocity of money.

So there are a whole bunch of factors that are leading to the emergence of this inflation. But it is a shattering event—a slow and subtle one to be sure, but nonetheless a shattering event for people living in this time period. Now, if we go back to our farmers, you have a situation where the tenants are paying fixed rents for long lease periods. But as inflation starts to kick in, it's very good for the tenants but very bad for the landlords—their income is fixed, but their expenses are rising with prices. For the tenants, on the other hand, the amount that they have to pay in rent is an increasingly small percentage of their earnings from their sales of wheat and barely, or other things.

These price changes effect a huge shift in economic temporality: you go from a world in which you can reasonably expect the economic conditions to be the same in the future as they are today to one in which you have to expect that they're going to be different. Now, what happens is that within some of these leases, these new, weird provisions are introduced where the tenant, in order to start or renew the lease, has to pay a certain amount. And, unlike the ancient rents, which were fixed, these upfront payments, which were called fines, could be increased,

P: *I see. So it's almost a way of increasing the rent without violating that social custom.*

WD: Exactly. It's a way to increase the rent without falling afoul of social customs. You are essentially requiring tenants to pay upfront to lock in years of low rents. And it is in the context of this transaction that people start using discounting calculations. The other interesting, unexpected aspect of this history is that among the earliest adopters of these calculations is the church, who owns a huge amount of land and whose tenants have these kinds of leases. The church, unlike private landowners, really needs to appear like they're being fair to their tenants. So they come up with a kind of algorithmic solution to this problem of figuring out how to charge their tenants an amount that is fair, or at least is plausibly fair enough—a performance of neutrality.

And so in answer to your question, I will say that these calculations tend to come to the fore when there's been a rupture in temporality that puts a social obligation into disarray, requiring it to be rebuilt. And I think there's a way in which that's true of national debt as well, in the sense that it is a short-term obligation that creates a different relationship between a political present and future. Climate change is a particularly extreme and existential variant of a similar problem.

P: *And oftentimes this rebuilding is posited as a completely neutral process—like the church presenting their use of these calculations as objective or algorithmic—when in fact a new relationship to the economic future is being performatively created. These episodes call to mind a more present-day scholarly debate. There's a divide, speaking very broadly, between those with a more foundational view of value—in which it is thought that there is some essential, material basis underlying how we price things—and those who view value as more contingent and performative, like the scholars Jens Beckert or Martijn Konings. For those who put forward this more performative view of value, what is of paramount importance is one's ability to persuasively depict an imagined future, thereby commanding the investments necessary to bring this fictional future into being. I'm wondering how you think about this divide? Discounting seems, in many ways, to be on the side of foundational value—the calculation posits that there's an essential value that we can then project into the future—but a lot of what your work seems to do is blur the lines between these categories.*

WD: I think you're exactly right—this is often depicted as a contrast between technical conceptions of value that are grounded in a belief that there's some sort of real value, and a more performative, social conception of value. It's interesting that you mention Jens Beckert, because as I was formulating this project I was thinking a lot about the relationship between future expectations and present valuation practices. Some of the early work on the performative side almost seemed to suggest that calculation and narrative are somehow at odds, but I think they're very much in concert with one another. Calculations like the discounting equation create a structured, shared apparatus for certain people to consolidate their vision of the future into an actionable present. So the imagination part is absolutely essential, but it's filtered through a calculative process that both disciplines that future imagination and also creates a common medium around which people can agree.

So basically the way that these discounting calculations work is you have to imagine that there's going to be a stream of future profits, and then the calculation takes that stream and turns it into a number. In some ways the calculation doesn't say anything about what can go into that stream—often the projections can be extremely optimistic and there is actually a broad space of play within which people can project all kinds of futures—but it does place limits. It gives the future a certain shape and it demands that people articulate their imaginations of the future in particular terms. It is almost a kind of mangle—Andrew Pickering, in a classic work of

science studies, has this idea of the "mangle" of different practices that produce scientific knowledge. I hadn't really thought about his book in the context of my work before, but when it comes to producing future value, calculation and narrative are very much working in conjunction.

P: *If the practice of calculation often gives limits to and sets the terms for the free play of imagined futures, have you encountered in your research any times where other practices—say, image-making practices—play this same role in dictating the shape of plausible future imaginings? I'm thinking here of the so-called "paper cities" of the early 19th century like Cairos, Illinois, where maps emphasizing the city's geographic advantages and lithographs of "prospective" city views were necessary for securing speculative real estate investments.*

WD: 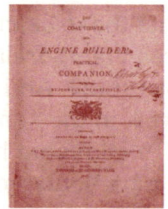  The third chapter of the book—or at least notional chapter three—is about coal mining. Discounting calculations were adopted particularly thoroughly right around 1800 for the valuation of unmined coal deposits in Northern England. Part of the reason why was that these coal mines sat on landed estates, and so the calculations that had already been used to value farmland and to set leases on farmland could be easily carried over to set leases on coal mines. But they couldn't be carried over that easily. The prior leases were based on the premise that, if one figured out the average agricultural yield, you could just expect that yield to be consistent over the course of the future. Coal mines, though, are very different from farmland—you can't exactly see what's there, and they're exhaustible. Before you priced their future, then, you had to first figure out how much coal there was. So these mining engineers—a distinct group of engineers called "viewers," a very evocative term—develop this technique of valuing coal.  Basically, they put a price on coal deposits by finding a way to measure their geological extents and the speed of extraction, a rate dependent upon answering both labor and engineering questions. Once these values were set, they were then used to calculate a stream of income that could be discounted. With this process, then, calculations were always accompanied by maps, charts, and other imagery dedicated to making visible what lies underneath the ground. Calculation and the imagined—and imaged—subterranean space were brought together.

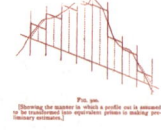

These mining techniques, which in the anglophone world largely begin with coal, were then adopted in hard metal mining and used globally in the middle and particularly latter part of the 19th century with the development of multinational, sort of imperialist mining ventures in western Australia, southern Africa, western North America and other places. There again you'll find the same people who ran valuation calculations putting together elaborate charts of the mineral distributions of these landscapes.

P: *It's almost as though, when there's a space or a resource that one can't see, then images step in and work in tandem with calculation.*

WD: 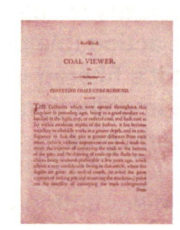 Yes, exactly, there's this connection between mapping, used to rationalize space, and these calculations, which are used to rationalize time. Another interesting use of these calculations is in the latter part of the 19th century in railway engineering. There's an 1871 text by the railway engineer Arthur Wellington about the economics of the location of railways that asks how to build a railway in the most efficient manner possible. Do you go around a hill, do you tunnel through, and so on. Richard White, the environmental historian, has this great book *Railroaded* about transcontinental railroad building in the United States and he pays particular attention to Wellington and the way in which he creates this notion of what White calls "absolute space"—a sort of totalizing space that can be rendered subject to calculated economic analysis. White doesn't specifically mention it, but Wellington was doing a very similar thing with time. The transformation of space coincided with a projection of future expenses and profits as a means to understand the economics of the venture.

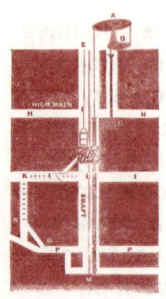

P:

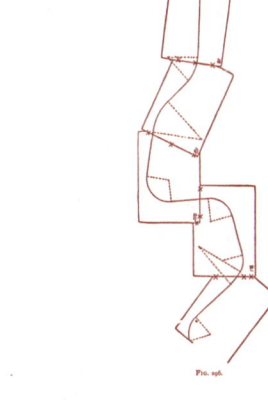

This history of the entanglement of spatial and temporal mappings makes me think of our present moment and the future outer space conquest dreams of Bezos and Musk. I don't know if you're familiar with the conversations around longtermism…

WD:

Well I've just heard this term for the first time like two weeks ago…

P:

Same, I've just recently been diving into critical readings of it. The gist of it is that they propose that the most rational timescale through which to judge any action is the very, very long term—the timescale of the potential whole entire future history of humanity—and that, through this lens, all that matters is species-level existential threats and not small problems like people having nice lives in the present. What's fascinating, architecturally, about this massive projection is that, like your train engineers, longtermists' temporal extrapolation requires a spatial one as well: to house the 10^54 or what have you future humans they think are possible, they have these dreams of colonizing space and using stars to build space stations and virtual worlds deep into the galaxy–it's this very Gerard K. O'Neill-inflected vision. Do you have any thoughts on this phenomenon? Do their thought processes bear any similarities to those of the historical actors you study?

WD:

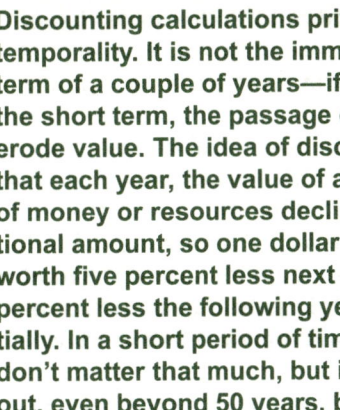

In terms of calculation, I often ask what kinds of time scales does this foreground? Discounting calculations privilege a certain temporality. It is not the immediate short term of a couple of years—if you're only in the short term, the passage of time doesn't erode value. The idea of discounting is that each year, the value of a certain sum of money or resources declines a proportional amount, so one dollar this year is worth five percent less next year, and five percent less the following year, exponentially. In a short period of time the effects don't matter that much, but if you go far out, even beyond 50 years, but certainly beyond 100 years, the exponential effect means that what happens in the distant future is actually pretty irrelevant—things have to be massive in the future to matter to us at all today.

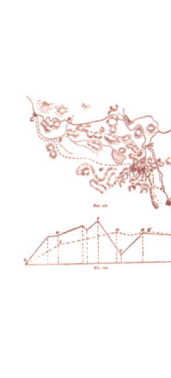

Discounting trains attention on what I'm calling the "mediate" future or the medium future, basically a one generation-length future. Thinking back to the first episode about farm leases—many of these leases had a fixed term of 21 years, which was understood to be the length of a generation. That's the term in which these calculations seem to work really well. But if you get beyond that length of time, you start to get into more problematic areas—the longer out you go, the more oddities you run into.

Longtermism suggests an embrace of a different temporality. This is one way

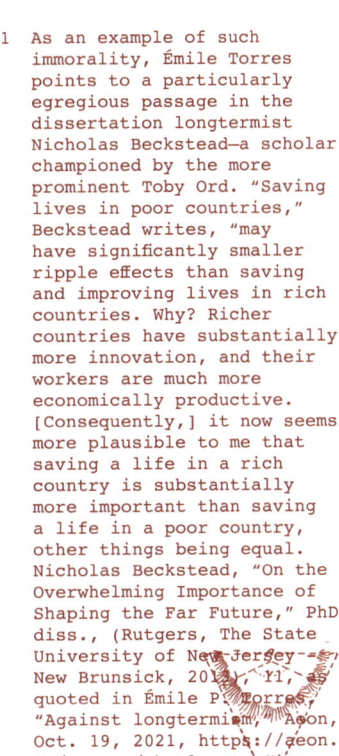

1   As an example of such immorality, Émile Torres points to a particularly egregious passage in the dissertation longtermist Nicholas Beckstead—a scholar championed by the more prominent Toby Ord. "Saving lives in poor countries," Beckstead writes, "may have significantly smaller ripple effects than saving and improving lives in rich countries. Why? Richer countries have substantially more innovation, and their workers are much more economically productive. [Consequently,] it now seems more plausible to me that saving a life in a rich country is substantially more important than saving a life in a poor country, other things being equal. Nicholas Beckstead, "On the Overwhelming Importance of Shaping the Far Future," PhD diss., (Rutgers, The State University of New Jersey—New Brunsick, 2013), 11, as quoted in Émile P. Torres, "Against longtermism," Aeon, Oct. 19, 2021, https://aeon.co/essays/why-longtermism-is-the-worlds-most-dangerous-secular-credo

There is a fantasy within some corners of the environmental movement that the single reason for our problems is a myopia begot of ignorance: if only we were taught to look forward in time so as to see the future consequences of our present actions, these commentators argue, the environmental criminals of the world would immediately correct their destructive behavior. While there are many reasons to take issue with this understanding of the climate crisis—the primary one being that it reduces politics to the rather narrow practice of effective communication—one under-considered reason to be suspicious of this approach is that it leaves unasked the questions of how far we are to look into the future and who are the actors that should serve as the mouthpieces (or inventors) of these future humans. What if a rather terrible group of people claims to be speaking in the interest of future generations? And what if the mode of life they're trying to secure for these future humans is batshit crazy?

Recently, Émile Torres and others have been reporting on the strange secular religion that is longtermism. As discussed in this interview, this is a worldview that holds that what is of primary importance is the human race achieving its full potential, judged in terms of the entire potential trajectory of human civilization. Believing that space exploration and virtual reality make possible the future existence of an astronomically high number of humans, these Silicon Valley Cassandras contend that solving present-day ills matters little if doing so interferes with the urgent task of ensuring that this long range future comes to pass. In pursuit of this goal—which longtermists argue they are doing purely as a result of measured, rational consideration—adherents of this philosophy have come to some predictably immoral conclusions.[1] Work like William Deringer's gives us the critical toolkit necessary for contesting these would-be masters of the universe's claims that they are simply acting in accordance with reason. Achieving such critical literacy in regards to the art of prognostication will become an increasingly necessary skill as the needs of the future are weaponized—for ill or for good—to spark action in the present.

203

to think about the essence of the climate change debate. Economists are using these discounting calculations—I'm painting with too broad a brush because there is actually an extraordinary amount of subtlety around these calculations—but they're designed to work on the scale of decades, not centuries. Some of the economic models that tend to downplay the urgency of climate change do so because of the way these discounting calculations work—they don't put a particularly high price on events that happen far out. So is this the right tool to think about certain scales? Discounting anything that happens at that scale—it becomes so tiny as to be inconsequential. Within the framework of exponential discounting, there's almost no value you could put on it in the future to make it relevant to us today

P: *On that idea of privileging a certain timeframe, I'm curious about how certain projections get buried or ignored. Recently the architectural historian Lucia Allais and the engineer and building researcher Forrest Meggers wrote about the equation for the degradation time of steel reinforced concrete, which is approximately 100 years. This equation, they note, had been a settled fact of engineering, but in the realm of architecture and state planning it was suppressed or ignored for a long time—basically until today when, out of necessity, it is now rising to the surface. The question their essay poses is how and why does this suppression happen? Concrete, of course, is very tied to modernist utopian dreams, which have their own particular timescales. But why were the timescales of these political futures privileged over the timescale of concrete? How do you think about the privileging of one timescale or another and about the suppression of certain projections?*

WD: The big question that interests me is why do certain calculations come to seem useful, plausible and authoritative within particular social milieus? And what I've been wondering about discounting is what is so good about it? Why does it seem to be so attractive in certain settings? And one of the reasons—it's almost an obvious point, but maybe not—is that the math works out pretty neatly.

In one of the chapters in the book I look at the period after these calculations started to show up when they started to get a lot of attention from mathematicians of that era. Isaac Newton, for example, sends letters to his contemporaries about mathematical oddities related to these kinds of calculations. And the mathematicians start to think, well there are some things to these calculations that are kind of wrong, or kind of weird, maybe we'd like to try to tweak them.

There emerged an interesting set of imaginative work in which, basically, these mathematicians started to think, What if we created financial mathematics otherwise? One of the issues they addressed was compounding interest, which was seen as maybe morally suspect, maybe a little close to usury. And, also practically, a little too neat; they thought it was expecting too much to assume that you could always so easily keep reinvesting your money to get compounding returns. So the mathematicians came up with alternatives, but the problem is they didn't calculate well. The discounting formula has these really nice features—this exponential series, where, if you take a series of payments in the future and then you discount them, and you want to add them up, there are very tidy formulas that allow you to do this very neatly. But when you try to change the mathematics to calculate the future otherwise, it becomes very hard and impractical. And one of things I'm trying to get my head around is the fact that this neatness is actually really important—that certain calculations are very tractable and very usable and others are not.

There's another really interesting contemporary example of this that I take from Donald Mckenzie's wonderful book on financial models, *An Engine Not a Camera*. He basically makes the point that all of the financial models that are developed in the 20th century for valuing derivatives—which then get fed into valuing mortgage backed securities and CDOs and the alphabet soup of stuff that collapses in the 2008 crisis—all depend on a particular kind of statistical view of the world that imagines that chance events are normally distributed on a bell curve, the so called Gaussian Copula Model. McKenzie and his collaborators have some really interesting articles on this. There are people from as far back as the 1970s, like the mathematician Benoit Mandelbrot, who said This is unrealistic, that you could use other models of statistical distributions that have fat tails and entertain the possibility of very unlikely events. But the math doesn't work out as well—you can't build useful tools with these models. In very general terms, you want the algebra to work so that you cancel out tons of terms and things reduce down to some neat closed form. I don't know, maybe the rise of these neat equations is a really significant historical phenomena. You can almost imagine a kind of platonic, metaphysical argument that the reason that these things work out neatly is because they are speaking the language of the universe or something, but it could just be dumb luck.

P: *It does bring up the question of style and aesthetics, like the way people talk about elegant code.*

WD: Exactly, mathematicians have a whole sort of system of epistemic virtues around elegance.

P: *From our side of things, there's Patrik Schumacher, who is like the villain of contemporary architecture. He designs by computational parameters but has an almost Hayekian view of the process, wherein the building form is like the price signal, the mathematical condensation of all of this information. The designer, in his mind, just has to respond to what this information tells him; he's not responsible for imagining and planning a more just society.*

Interestingly, in a riposte to an interview of his, the architect Peggy Deamer did the same thing as your 18th century mathematicians—she challenged him at the level of calculation. Instead of saying that computational parameters are an inherently invalid way to design, she argued that he was calculating incorrectly: he wasn't being objective, he was deliberately leaving out certain datasets, and so on. At the time, Thomas Pickety's Capital in the Twenty-First Century—*a very data-heavy book—had just been published, and she challenged Schumacher to include data on inequality in his supposedly all-encompassing parametric inputs.*

It was a fascinating argument, but it struck me that she was ignoring the aesthetic side of the issue: Schumacher's buildings have this very clear style, these smooth, vector-curves that evoke mathematical order. But no one has imagined an equally compelling aesthetic for a building designed, say, using Pickety's data about inequality as a guide. In fact, when we think of the aesthetic of a building designed with data on economic inequality in mind, we tend to imagine bland, square public housing. I'm curious how you think about a problem like this—about how style and aesthetics operate in terms of what types of calculations and datasets gain traction and influence?

WD: 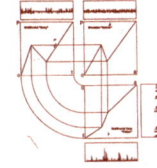 It's hard to think of any particularly obvious examples, except these moments where alternative financial models are explored but, due to their difficulty or lack of neatness, they get waved away and are never taken up again. But there are definitely aesthetic aspects of calculation that interest me. Getting back to the discussion of absolute time and absolute space, prior to the invention of a useful pocket calculator—which was really as late as the 1970s or 1980s—the tools that were used to do discounting calculations were books of tables. There's a whole way of thinking that involves moving across these grids of numbers and through this matrix of stacked tables—you'll have one set of tables with a 5% interest rate, another with 6%. Skilled users could take a set of table books and look up certain numbers—it wasn't just looking up one, you need to look up like three numbers and do a little bit of multiplication, you need to navigate back and forth, or look at two numbers in two different spots and subtract them.

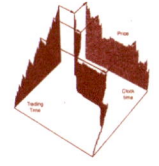

205

There's something about the aesthetic of the table book that enables a vision of the future—if you look at the way in which people write out these calculations in the early 19th century, there are these very rhythmic, orderly projections. I don't know if there's anything particularly deep here—a lot has been written about grids and the imposition of grid-like structures by James Scott and others—but I am curious about the way in which the calculative practice of using these table books encouraged certain styles of thinking. It's an interesting hypothesis.

P: *On the subject of certain styles of thinking falling out of favor, you end your book* Calculated Values *on a note of real concern regarding the possibility, given the state of American politics, that calculation writ large might no longer be functioning as a medium for political debate. Whether it's via Trumpian critiques of "elite" knowledge practices or via other means, I see the need for such warnings. In moments when calculation and political discourse seem particularly distant from one another, what are the means for bringing these two fields back into conversation? Are there any practices you are excited about that reignite an interest in the political dimensions of calculation?*

WD: 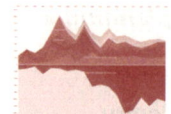 Back when I was writing the book, an event occurred that I would have taken as a signal example of the problem that you've identified here. Whenever different administrations release a budget, there had always been this process of the congressional budget office scoring it: saying how it would affect the deficit, what it is going to do to raise national debt or inflation and so on. While there's always been a critique of the whole apparatus of these calculations, and of the scores and counter-scores, as another mere masquerading of objectivity, I've always seen this process as a constructively constrained form of politics. The Trump administration, though, just stopped putting out the figures entirely. They stopped submitting budgets for scoring; they didn't even open up the space for the possibility of debate.

But ever since *Calculated Values* was published, I've been pleasantly surprised by a renaissance of political interrogations of calculation. There's been a rise rise of data activism, of statactivism.

P: *Defund the Police, for example, produces very close readings and analyses of city budgets.*

WD:  Yeah, absolutely—there's been a rise in forensic accounting. There's an amazing series of New York Times articles that were the result of the journalists basically spending months in semi-secrecy trying to make sense of Donald Trump's tax returns. And the forensics of that became really interesting, not just because of the immediate political payoff, but because of the way it revealed mechanisms of wealth and power that people don't talk about or didn't know about. And I think of work by colleagues like Lauren Klein and Catherin D'Ignazio, especially their recent book *Data Feminism*, which is an amazing compendium of works on the relationship between data practices and politics. Oftentimes these conversations are framed more in terms of data and algorithms rather than in terms of calculation or quantification or numbers, the almost intentionally stodgy terms I use. But I do think a lot of the work in what is called "critical data studies" embodies that ability to enliven calculation as a space for meaningful political discussion.

P: *Definitely, in the way you've framed our moment, it suddenly seems like an exciting time to be looking at these questions. It makes me think that, while Bezos and Musk and other billionaires are focusing their big data*

206

tools on the future, activists are becoming better at looking towards the past. In architecture, some of the most exciting work of the past ten years has not been a new building but the rise of so-called forensic architecture—the use of the tools of architectural analysis to reconstruct events of the past, pursuing justice via producing evidence of atrocities ranging from genocide to the violent suppression of protesters. The temporalities are again scrambled, but now the past is being used to project a better future.

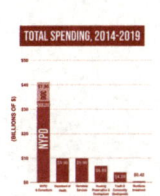

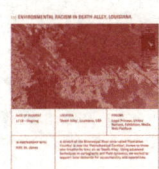

All My Futures Are in the Past

Matthew Soules

From the air this place is exhilarating. The way the topographical idiosyncrasies of rock and soil and the desert scrub—the results of thousands of years of plate tectonics, unrelenting sun, and periodic deluges—have just, well, been erased. OK, OK, maybe not exactly erased, how about violently transformed? Scraped, carved, and pounded into a series of level steps, each one both unique and exactly the same. Three hundred and thirteen of them to be exact. Each one roughly 15,000 square feet, or about a third of an acre. The scale and rigor of the operation is impressive. In the sharp midday light, it's hard to see the drone's video feed on my phone, but the basic impression is inescapable: truly sublime in the sense that it is both beautiful and terrifying. A delicious mix of adrenalin, cortisol, and dopamine courses through my veins. In a few years, three hundred and thirteen structures will occupy these gigantic terraces. An enclave of luxurious homes. I feel alive.[1]

"If certain cities of the world were placed end to end in a straight line according to size, starting with Rome, where would [Las Vegas] be in that impossible progression? Each city would be a three-dimensional mirror that would reflect the next city into existence. The limits of eternity seem to contain such nefarious ideas."[2] Certainly all earthworks are formations of capital and are therefore ultimately attuned towards the production of future value. Once we passed the threshold of not only producing things in space, but producing space itself, "[t]he ground, the underground, the air, and even the light enter into both the productive forces and the products."[3] And what about the graphs, the charts, the spreadsheets? The mirror certainly reflects these in some known but hard to pin-down fashion. What did Smithson say about the dialectical relationship between Site and Nonsite?[4] Perhaps it is this very relationship we are selling here in the McCullough Range?

I let the drone hover autonomously while I take a call from Jeff Hardcastle, Nevada State Demographer. I've been trying to get a hold of him for a while now, hoping to get an early glimpse at his latest population projections. The higher the forecast, the better the lenders are going to feel and the more likely they will revise our rates. His first word: "Sizzling!" Next week he will announce that Southern Nevada will continue to dramatically outpace national growth. Did I hear that right? 1.1 million new residents over the next twenty years.[5] The last ten years have been sweet, but this is amazing.

Armed with this prediction and the latest Case-Shiller numbers, how can the banks refuse? I just know we can get the construction financing down at least a couple basis points. Everything on the curve is suggesting radical price escalation over at least the five-year horizon. Smart buyers will want in now. If only we can get the renderings right. Insatiable desire, that's what I want to elicit. Make your most precious dream palpable. Sure, 3D Studio Max is great for conjuring this hallucinatory effect, but it's not just the building that's critical—I'm talking plant life! Francis got us that 3D Studio guru out in Pasadena but I'm not sure she understands the true desert modernism effect we're going for. Getting the boxy forms and sexy night lighting is easy enough, but their succulent library is horrible. How is she going to get around that? Hardcastle's projection will get us within spitting distance of the finish line, but some badass digital succulents will get us across.

It's time to bring the drone back. I could get someone else to do this work, but I get a kick out of it. It is a way to establish a real relationship with a project. I'm not some developer who only sees a project through the abstract lens of spreadsheets and pro formas. I'm not lulled by the seductive power of renderings. I am hands on. In the field. A materialist. I make "fantasies as real as mountains."[6]

These drones are great, except the battery life pretty much sucks. And now this one's running dangerously low. Why in the world doesn't it have some function to automatically come home in this all-too-common situation? Please don't let my assistant see the heavy flow of sweat now making its way from my armpits. "A real loser who can't keep his cool," he'll think. Thank God, the drone is finally above us. All I need to do is bring it directly down. 500 feet to go. What is this beeping? It's hard to make out the silhouette of that little box with four whirling propellers against the burning light of the sun. But yes, it flutters, stalls, and begins to drop. I try to run. But paralysis overtakes me. The harder I try, the more I stay put. It is then that the drone, travelling at 200 miles per hour, strikes me directly on my upturned, shrieking face.[7]

* * *

"Gulp!" Holy shit. Was I holding my breath in my sleep again? What time is it? These dreams are getting worse. How many ways can a person die? I should probably start dictating a dream journal. I think that was some sort of antique surveillance device that just took me out—direct hit to the head. Maybe I should speak to Rahul about tweaking the formula. Or maybe this is a dosage problem. Should I go up to 30mg in the morning and split the evening pill? Apparently, Jennifer started mainlining hers a while back but that seems a little extreme. I could try smoking, but I worry about my lungs and that is a dosage fuck up waiting to happen.

And a dosage error can lead to no end of hassles from the strata council.[8] If connectivity is spotty–or worse, if you go offline—you'll hear about it pretty quick. And it won't be long before the hedge fund's AI gets involved; adjustments happen almost instantly. If you leveraged yourself too heavily in neocortical derivatives, things can fall apart fast. Mess up for too long and whole quadrants of your cortex can be redlined. Everyone is always reminding you of what happened in the Odessa-13 tranche in the summer of 2048. Be careful.

When the brain strata protocols came around in 2039, why didn't anyone foresee this gong show? Wasn't it clear that the pharmaceutical component was far outpaced by the financial technology? Condominiumize your neocortical neurons and place them into the burgeoning brain real estate market and make a killing. What did people say? "Think of it as Airbnb for-neural-space meets mortgage-backed securities." As if anyone really understood what that meant. What a quaint form of nostalgic hype. I made and lost $6 billion and emotion jumped with the hottest bots but at what cost? Sure, investors have bought and sold increments of my cortex a trillion times a day in the biggest market ever to exist but how many times have I linked in with Westbank's customer support to say, "I want out?"[9] How many space-temp simultaneities can one endure?

It was once said that "[e]very epoch has its brain."[10] No doubt. But what an epoch, the 2040s! This era's new "brain" isn't merely an ideological construct; neuroengineering and morphogenic neuroplasticity really *do* give you a new brain. "In order to capture cognitive activity (attention, memory, language, imagination), semio-capital must insert automatic procedures into the field of cognition itself."[11] While the enclosure of cognition has a long history that stretches back at least to cybernetic attempts to systematize the mind's operations—if not earlier—Bifo was prescient about the particular form such enclosing would soon take when he noted: "Adaptation to the connective mode of communication, adaptation to the ferocity of competition, to the barbarity and horror of the submission of life and attention to financial abstraction, may take the form of a sort of social lobotomy: a pharmacological or surgical cancellation of what, in the human psyche, is incompatible with abstract domination."[12] I suppose a brilliant aspect of the brain strata protocols is the way in which the pharmacological intervention is simultaneously a means to generate more financial abstraction while also functioning as a form of lobotomy. Smart.

When Obama announced the BRAIN (Brain Research through Advancing Innovative Neurotechnologies) Initiative in 2013, it was championed as a means of unlocking new treatments for all sorts of brain disorders: Alzheimer's, Parkinson's, depression—the whole gamut. But anyone who was familiar with the links between mapping, colonization, and expropriation knew that a land rush was imminent. Once we had it mapped, we could own it. Never mind that it was space inside the human skull.

Just like with the Human Genome Project, we failed to account for exponential growth in the improvement of the mapping techniques. It will take a hundred years, claimed the doubters. We always default to linear projection, Kurzweil liked to say back then when he was cool—and alive.[13] Anyway, that's ancient history now. Kurzweil's exponential prediction played out and it all came into sharp focus in twenty years.

Once big pharma saw the potential and the great mergers with the real estate investment trusts started to unfold in the 2030s, Dalmar and I went all in. What else is investment than enacting the future? The double-blind studies that Gilead did in collaboration with Equity Residential provided us all the data we needed.[14] When we fed that into our model, Dalmar projected that the slight nose bleeding that occurred in 0.2% of the study group signalled not a bulwark but a powerful and unrecognized opportunity. We could move aggressively into the traumatized portions of the neural stem that the other agencies avoided. Classic gentrification move.

What time is it? Hours vanish when navigating up, down, and across the neural canyons and strips—kind of a paradox, getting to know oneself while getting lost in your own expanse. It's a dangerous form of distraction to follow your brain's real time valuations and occupancy feeds too closely. The dopamine highs and lows can almost tear you apart, depending on the market. That's another thing the pills are supposed to manage, but the technology isn't quite there yet. But I'm most concerned with the fact that the majority of my neural stacks that Westbank installed via the 2051-W2 construct are owned but empty. If they sit that way for too long they are ripe for viral cracking. And right this moment valuation is skyrocketing on these units while occupancy is almost zero. All to say, dopamine is pulling one way while serotonin is shooting the other. Ripe conditions for a space-temp collapse. It was then that I felt the breakage. Apparently too many neural units had just hit the market and the competing AIs had failed to correct. The vivid visualization of my very own neocortical metropolis that recalled the old Andreas Gursky photo of LA at night, but three-dimensional, went out and I was gone.[15]

* * *

The first thing I felt was the marble flooring, pressed cold and hard against my face, though in truth some fine fragments of gravel, tiny pieces of hair and a small puddle of saliva separated my jaw from the stone. Before my eyeballs, I countenanced a peculiar miniature still life, in which I began to lose myself until—ding, ding, ding—the elevator's shrill bell rang, heralding an arriving passenger. Words cannot express the absolute hollow terror of that moment! Had I really passed out in the lobby, again? Strangely, no one did emerge from the elevator cab at five a.m. that Friday morning of late September, 1924. Being empty, the elevator was no longer the cause of but my means of escape from morbid shame; I could now retreat to my office before the staff arrived. I darted into the cab, hit '18,' and held my breath. Deus Ex Machina.

Once back in my office, with the adrenalin drained entirely out of me, I was overcome by depression. As I slumped in my overstuffed chair, I had that same sense I always had after a particularly heavy night–like I had been caught in some ineffable and nightmarish field of flickering lights. Maybe I should consult a priest? "Snap out of it!" I muttered and did my best to repress that haunting after-image. I have far more immediate and pressing matters. I believe I made it back without anyone having seen me, but how can I be certain? I can't keep doing this. I need to get out of this rathole–get beyond the Loop once and for all. Start fresh.

The only thing that gave me even an ounce of cheer was the model. There it sat, painstakingly constructed from birch, with every detail scored and painted. At 1/8" scale, its 37.125 inches represented an impressive 297 feet of soaring height; a work of beauty. I couldn't have sold all those bond notes without this model.[16] People like to see something real before they give up their cash, especially when those dollars will be initially returned to them in the unfamiliar form of mortgage bonds. I always receive a thrill from being inside the actual building that the model represents. Puts everything into an odd sort of perspective—representation inside its reality. Maybe my predicament isn't so bad after all.

Danny had done a good job—one of his last before his untimely death. No, it was not his greatest project, but fine, nonetheless. The eight Doric columns stand heavily at 208 La Salle Street, holding firm the carved text: "CITY NATIONAL BANK AND TRUST COMPANY"—a missive even perfectly legible in the model.[17] And from that classical base the structure shoots up impressively. The corners offer solidity, but in between, the thrusting granite pilasters reach for the sky. Then, as if to underscore the magic of this operation—the reproduction of the ground towards the heavens—another eight Doric columns reappear at the summit, now holding up a roofed pavilion that caps off the whole affair. Burnham does have a knack for creating some strange amalgam of vertical explosion and Vitruvian firmitas. *Giganti della montagna*.[18]

A lot has been said about the United States and the function of the grid plan. Capitalism is an economic system in which the present is always the means to a future that has yet to occur; a constant motion of "innovation."[19] The grid plan functions "as a neutral support for capital's free exploitation of the city soil" and therefore the territorial matrix of this futuring.[20] And the "Chicago Loop is the perfect product of the laissez-faire city and its "system": a regular grid and an assemblage of prismatic buildings the height of which is determined by the investment of capital."[21] Danny knew the real purpose of architecture.[22]

The distance between Burnham and Associates and the mortgage bank is five minutes by the 'L,' a ride I had taken so many times that the two offices and the twelve blocks between them coalesced into one extended space of production. Bricks and bonds; you cannot have one without the other. It still boggles the mind to imagine that the bank managed to raise fifteen million in $100, $500, and $1,000 bond notes. To how many different individuals are we now indebted? The numbers reach the thousands. But the interest we offered has them laughing with joy; they see no downside. I even offered an investment share to get out of my tab with Mahoney after one of my particularly messy jags. One of his heavies believed such a debt to be worth my losing a finger, but two $100 notes of the City National Bank Building convinced him I ought to keep my pinky. Now, instead of owning a piece of me, Mahoney owns a piece of 208 La Salle. I like to think he owns the shitter down in the west side of the basement. That fucker has been hackling me about my financial escapades for years—but my run with single property mortgage bonds shut him up.

Whoa. Wait a minute, how did I get up here? Seriously, the SEC matter is of no great consequence,[23] just another straightforward regulatory crackdown, of the same variety that happens every cycle. They only want some information. But at the very moment I made the decision to get off this parapet, a gust that felt personally delivered to me, care of Lake Michigan itself, swept right into the small of my back.

It was a slow, peaceful descent. Moving past me like a ledger's tape, I saw all that granite and its careful setting and perfectly aligned joints. Is it stone cladding or bond issues? No, this is stone. Definitely stone. Once I passed the rounded cornice I knew the end was coming. Yet I felt the best I had in years, released at last from mortgage. It's impossible to say with certainty, but I believe my wristwatch was the first part of me to make contact with the sidewalk, and, in the quiet of that moment, I could swear I heard the ticking of time stop as the gold band hit the pavement.

* * *

"Dude, wake up!" "Waaaake, Up!" "Did you seriously fall asleep with the headset on again?" "Isn't that tripping you out?" "Seriously, drink more Red Bull, or something."

Super trippy is the least of it. I've been napping with Oculus on for weeks now. And the dreams are straight-up weird. I keep losing my balance and falling over and over from the scariest of places. I feel like I've plummeted from every tower in America. Whatever. Zaha Hadid Architects is keeping all the NFT heads abuzz by not specifying exactly when the next house will be dropped.[24] Until I at least get a shot at it, there's no way I'm leaving Meta. Why chance this opportunity for the future?

1. Ascaya is a "luxury" single-family-home subdivision in Henderson, Nevada. Part of the speculative expansion of suburban Las Vegas, Ascaya stalled with the 2008 housing collapse in the United States. In 2015, work on the development re-commenced with the building of subdivision roads and the reshaping of the landscape into terraces for future homes. Almost twenty years later, however, the site remains largely unoccupied, with just a few multi-million dollar homes sitting on what is essentially a massive earthwork.
2. Robert Smithson, "A Tour of the Monuments of Passaic, New Jersey," *Artforum*, December 1967, 57.
3. Henri Lefebvre, *The Production of Space* (Oxford: Blackwell, 1991 (English Translation): 187.
4. Robert Smithson, "A Provisional Theory of Nonsites," in *Robert Smithson: The Collected Writings*, Jack Flam (Berkeley: University of California Press, 1996).
5. Emily Richmond, "1 million more residents projected by 2024," *Las Vegas Sun*, May 19, 2004. https://lasvegassun.com/news/2004/may/19/1-million-more-residents-projected-by-2024/
6. Peter Schjeldahl, "Robert Smithson: He Made Fantasies as Real as Mountains," *The New York Times*, August 12, 1973, 127.
7. Robert Smithson died in 1973, "along with a photographer and the pilot, in the crash of a light plane on a ranch near Amarillo, Tex., while he was inspecting the progress of his latest earth sculpture," wrote Schjeldahl in "Robert Smithson: He Made Fantasies as Real as Mountains," The New York Times, August 12, 1973, 127.
8. The condominium is a legal innovation that dates to h the passing of the Utah Condominium Act of 1960. The law enabled, for the first time, the exclusive ownership of real estate without a direct connection to the land's surface. While condominiums–or stata, as they are called in Australia or British Columbia–were initially utilized primarily in high-density housing, in subsequent decades commercial, industrial, and agricultural real estate domains likewise began to make use of this novel property form. Given this trend, it is reasonable to expect that the condominium property form will continue to be applied to new geographies. Already, the sheer number of condominiums is staggering. In fact, in 2022 "strata councils"--that is, the representative bodies that govern condominium buildings–constituted the majority of small scale governance bodies in North American cities.
9. Westbank is a Vancouver-based developer that, in the 2010s and 2020s, established itself as a leader in facilitating new forms of real estate investing. For example, it offers so-called "Asset Protection Plans" that allow remote owners of condominiums to keep their absent units in good working order. Under these plans, dedicated staff will perform tasks like, say, turning taps on and off to preserve the quality of the plumbing in an "owned but empty" unit.
10. Dimitris Papadopoulos, "Plastic Brain," in *The Psychopathologies of Cognitive Capitalism: Part Three*, Warren Neidich, ed. (Berlin: Archive Books, 2018): 133.
11. Franco Berardi, "Beyond Adaptation Toward Morphogenesis," in *The Psychopathologies of Cognitive Capitalism: Part Three*, Warren Neidich, ed. (Berlin: Archive Books, 2018): 178.
12. Berardi, "Beyond Adaptation," 186.
13. Ray Kurzweil, author of *The Singularity is Near, The Age of Spiritual Machines* and other texts, is a prominent proponent of Transhumanism, a philosophy that holds that human beings can–and should–deploy technology to vastly enhance their lifespans and their cognitive and other abilities. He writes extensively about the limitations of the human brain as a predictive device, arguing that, because it has evolved to exclusively make linear projections, the mind is unable to accurately forecast the futures to be brought into being by technological development, which, he contends, grows exponentially.
14. Equity Residential is a real estate investment trust that is traded on the New York Stock Exchange. As of December 2021, the company owned or had investment in over 80,000 apartment units. It is the fifth largest owner of apartments in the United States.
15. *Los Angeles*, Andreas Gursky, 1998. Edition of Six.
16. Single property mortgage bonds first emerged as a means of financing the design and construction of specific buildings in late 19th century in Chicago. To raise money to create a specific building, a financial institution (bank, mortgage banker, real estate fund, etc.) would sell bonds backed by the soon-to-be-built project. It was possible for an individual investor to buy these bond notes in various denominations. Ernest M. Fisher, *Urban Real Estate Markets: Characteristics and Financing* (UMI, 1951): 29.
17. Daniel Burnham's architectural practice, Burnham and Associates, designed the City National Bank and Trust Company Building at 208 La Salle Street, in the Loop neighborhood of Chicago. Construction on the building was completed in 1914.
18. Manfredo Tafuri refers to skyscrapers as the "new *giganti della montagna* [mountain giants] in the downtowns" of American cities. Manfredo Tafuri, *The Sphere and the Labyrinth: Avant-Gardes and Architecture from Piranesi to the 1970s* (Cambridge, Ma: The MIT Press, 1990): 172.
19. Joseph Schumpeter, for example, states: "As a matter of fact, capitalist economy is not and cannot be stationary. Nor is it merely expanding in a steady manner. It is incessantly being revolutionized from within by new enterprise, i.e., by the intrusion of new commodities or new methods of production or new commercial opportunities into the industrial structure as it exists at any moment." Joseph Schumpeter, Capitalism, Socialism and Democracy (1942, reis. New York: Taylor & Francis: 2013): 31.
20. Alexander Garvin, *The American City*, (New York, NY: McGraw Hill, 1996), 1.
21. Garvin, *The American City*, 5.
22. "These men saw the fair not only as a stimulus to industrial and commercial activity but also as a means of increasing real-estate values, within the general scheme of managing the city's urban development. And this was precisely the area in which Burnham set to work." In *The American City*, p. 16-17.
23. The issuers of the mortgage bond for 208 La Salle Street ultimately had to default on their loan, the single biggest failure of this type of financial instrument in Chicago's history. As Ernest M. Fisher writes of the crisis in single property mortgage bonds, "[e]xtensive investigations by Congress eventuated in enactment and revision of the Securities Exchange Act of 1934, which placed companies under much stricter supervision and limitations. Thus," he continues, "the spectacular incident ran its course and mortgage bonds at least temporarily disappeared from the real estate market." Fisher, *Urban Real Estate Markets: Characteristics and Financing*, 33.
24. Mark C. Taylor writes, "With the movement from industrial through consumer to financial capitalism, there is a progressive dematerialization or virtualization of tokens of exchange." In Mark C. Taylor, *Abiding Grace: Time, Modernity, Death* (Chicago: Chicago University Press, 2018), 52. Since the turn of the last century advances in digital technology have increasingly facilitated new forms of speculation in virtual real estate. In 2006, Anshe Chung was reported to have become the first "virtual millionaire," primarily through buying, renting, and selling real estate in Second Life. Recent enthusiasm for Non-Fungible Tokens (NFTs) that use blockchain technology are only the latest manifestation of this longstanding trajectory. *The Architect's Newspaper* reported in early 2021 that Krista Kim had "sold an entirely virtual home, Mars House, for $500,000 on the blockchain." In Jonathan Hilburg, "The First Virtual House NFT Just Sold for More than $500,000," The Architect's Newspaper, March 24, 2021, https://www.archpaper.com/2021/03/mars-house-nft-just-sold-for-more-than-500000/. In December 2021, Zaha Hadid Architects, led by famously pro-capitalist architect Patrik Schumacher, presented a virtual art gallery called NFTism at Art Basel Miami.
25. Neal Stephenson's 1992 novel *Snow Crash* first deployed the term metaverse to describe a vast immersive virtual world. The reiterative cycles of futurist boosterism at the nexus of money, land, and architecture now posit this virtual world as the next El Dorado. For example, the financial and investing advice company *The Motley Fool*, writes that "[r]eal estate has always been an important part of most people's investment portfolios. Much, if not all, of that real estate has been 'real.' Today's real estate investor, however, may also be considering something a little less touchable—virtual land. Building a virtual real estate portfolio could be the next big thing for investors who aren't afraid to take a chance on new technology… Land in the metaverse, the collection of virtual worlds where buying virtual land is possible, can be as valuable as a piece of land in the real world, and has even attracted the attention of celebrities like Snoop Dogg and businesses like PricewaterhouseCoopers." In Kristi Waterworth, "Buying Virtual Land in the Metaverse," *The Motley Fool*, September 19, 2022, https://www.fool.com/investing/stock-market/market-sectors/information-technology/metaverse-stocks/buying-virtual-land/.

The Art of Transparency: Climate Change and Miami's (Un)controllable Future

Savannah Cox

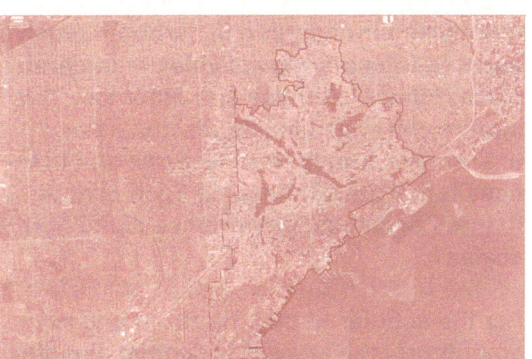

What makes for a resilient city?

Answering this question may conjure images of massive, otherworldly infrastructures that protect climate-vulnerable urban assets. Alternatively, one might envision something a bit humbler, such as a small water retention park or a multi-purpose green space in a residential neighborhood that stands to flood in the future. The resilient city could even call to mind reforms in existing urban planning practices such that they meaningfully incorporate the perspectives, and prioritize the needs of, residents who are disproportionately vulnerable to climate change. All of these examples, and many more, make for a resilient city. In this essay, however, I focus on less of a *thing* (or a series of things) that can be easily observed in the resilient city and more on a *disposition* and *practice* at work in dominant conceptions of the resilient city: transparency.

In the resilient city, urban life itself becomes an open-access climate inventory. Indeed, and as the content of countless urban resilience initiatives has made clear, insofar as officials within the resilient city direct their gaze to the climate shocks and stressors that the future may have in store, so too do city officials open up the present to close, metrological scrutiny. What sorts of emissions are the city's buildings producing each year, a capital planner might wonder? How much of the city's tax base, a financial officer might ask, has already been lost to climate-linked property devaluations? How might those figures be reduced through strategic planning and investment? How, for that matter, can officials effectively demonstrate that they are taking substantive steps to address climate risks and responsibilities like these to a population and investor base increasingly anxious about what climate change spells to their livelihoods and bottom lines?

The resilient city is also, by extension, information-rich: down to the last solar panel on a government building, officials within the resilient city promise to monitor, measure, and surveil the city's holdings to determine how they are, and stand to be, impacted by climate change over time. And they do so not just for the sake of creating an archive of a pivotal moment in history or producing robust resilience plans, but also for the sake of being and doing *good*. Indeed, by converting urban climate risk and action into a series of publicly-available, crowd-sourced metrics, indices, maps, and data sets, proponents of climate transparency suggest that city leadership can more effectively tackle climate inequities; encourage and enforce government accountability to local stakeholders; reduce uncertainty for investors, and devise more "efficient" forms of local climate action, among a host of other laudable acts.[1]

With these ambitious goals, it is perhaps unsurprising that a growing body of scholarship documents the many ways in which climate disclosure and transparency initiatives have seldom live up to their stated aims. In the face of such systematic failures, might we read disclosure as simply a ritualized performance of accountability, while "real" climate action takes place elsewhere?[2] Moreover, is climate disclosure up to the fundamental task of disrupting broader political economic rationales for engaging in carbon-intensive and risk-intensifying activities in the first place?[3] If not, as these and other scholars inquire, why has climate disclosure and the "smart" transparent features and practices that it entails become such central fixtures of climate governance at multiple scales?

For the scholar Esther Turnhout and her co-authors, the answer is simple: climate disclosure is about control. As an expression of what the authors term *measure-mentality*, disclosure follows a neoliberal logic that treats the environment as a "set of standardized units…and [provides] the basis for centralized control, coordination, and exchange."[4] But control over what, exactly? What do city officials actually stand to gain from converting the climate-changing built environment into a set of standardized units that can be openly monitored, observed, and acted upon from a distance? Disciplining existing built environments, for one. Many scholars of climate urbanism, for instance, have argued that the vast systems of climate measurement, monitoring, and surveillance that help make up urban resilience efforts stand to reduce how much one travels by car or how much electricity employees working within a given office building use on a given day, as well as regulate where families and businesses move and invest in the city, and so on.[5]

Examples like these speak to the crucial role that climate disclosure plays in shaping existing urban geographies and practices within them. In this essay, however, I suggest that we pay more explicit attention to another, albeit equally consequential, temporal frame that climate disclosure stands to greatly shape: urban futures. After all, as demographic data points more and more to the centrality of the *urban* scale in driving *global* economic growth, what more could be at stake in climate disclosure than generating a sense among all relevant parties that urban futures are indeed secure, no matter the challenges that the climate crisis may pose to them? More concretely, what does a city's time-consuming creation of a local greenhouse gas inventory signal to residents and external observers if not its commitment to helping build and maintain a habitable world for generations to come? What does the barrage of "before and after" photos at work in mundane public presentations and flashy promotional material on adaptive infrastructure projects convey if not that a city is making bankable progress in reducing its climate risks, and that existing and future investments made in the city are sound? What, in other words, is climate disclosure about if not securing the future?

These questions are of particular urgency in the Greater Miami region, which has in recent years gained a global reputation as "ground zero" for the economic impacts of climate change and which, equally, has begun to draft and implement droves of resilience and adaptation plans. Indeed, the region of over six million people sits atop a bed of porous limestone, which allows rising seas to seep not just *into* the city but *up*. Greater Miami also contains a little over a quarter of *all* U.S. homes at risk from rising seas[6] and may have already lost up to $465 million in coastal property values from 2005 to 2018—a figure which could shoot up to $23 billion by 2050.[7] Of course, these losses could come far earlier, and with dire consequences:

Figure 1: Screenshot of Miami Forever strategy goals.

Figure 2: Drone footage of flooding in Miami, June 2022. Available at: https://www.youtube.com/watch?v=l6oPaNe_w_o

Figure 3: Screenshot of content from Storm Water Master Plan meeting. April 2021.

Figure 4: City of Miami's homepage. One can see the COVID-19 banner on the top. To access the climate emergency, one has to scroll to the bottom of the homepage, where the climate change section is located, then scroll toward the bottom of a new page to see the 'emergency' tab, and then click once more to be directed to the official emergency declaration, which is housed on the city's old website.

a sudden, climate-linked fall in investor confidence in the region's future may spell a (perhaps permanent) drop in the city's tax base. A cratered tax base, in turn, will make it that much harder for the city to pay for measures that reduce physical and social climate vulnerabilities, particularly through bonding.[8] [Fig. 1]

Despite the existential threat that climate change poses to the region, Miami officials have embraced transparency as a key norm and practice of their ongoing resilience and adaptation strategies. As noted above, officials' embrace of transparency comes at least in part because they genuinely believe it is a good thing to do: as many capital planners have told me, failure to disclose to residents how exactly the city is using taxpayer dollars to finance adaptation may exacerbate long-held local mistrust of government and thus threaten the very possibility of future, taxpayer-funded investments in adaptation and resilience measures. As importantly, and perhaps surprisingly, Miami's turn toward climate transparency—here understood as the strategic disclosure of local climate risk and action on it—also derives from the need to defer unplanned adaptation in the region: that is, sudden, mass property devaluations that will crater the city's economy and thus Miami's ability to prepare for future climate calamities. But transparency is a difficult dance. Officials must make many epistemic and affective maneuvers to paint an exclusively bright future for the city through climate disclosure. And as persuasive as these moves may be to their desired audience, they cannot fully conceal the city's already existing, and rapidly growing, climate losses and vulnerabilities from wider view. In fact, and as I have seen myself, Miami's transparency turn may actually draw more attention to its anticipated and ongoing climate losses and vulnerabilities: how is it, external observers and residents alike may wonder, that city officials of climate ground zero believe that the region will be around "forever," as the Miami Forever Climate Ready Strategy—one of the city's flagship resilience plans—so confidently proclaims? What, exactly, is getting lost in translation, and why? Who's getting conned, and since when did urban resilience and adaptation become *The Art of the Deal*, anyway? These are all central preoccupations among those who have a stake in the city's future, and who are understandably paying close attention to the region's remarkably "open" disclosure of its climate vulnerabilities and action on them. In what follows, I draw on 26 months of ethnographic fieldwork to briefly reflect on two important sites of resilience deal-making in Greater Miami, municipal finance and climate emergency declarations, and some key local and extra-local responses to them. [Fig. 2 and Fig.3]

Beefing things up?

In 2017, the world's largest credit rating agency, Moody's Investor Services, announced that it would begin to formally account for a city's climate vulnerability and resilience in its municipal bond rating practices.[9] On its surface, this announcement should have been a concerning development for Greater Miami officials. As with many US cities, the metropolitan region has historically turned to municipal bond markets to pay for basic goods and services, such as public schools, hospitals, and roads. Moreover, the city's lucrative property tax base—the lynchpin of a good bond rating and thus the catalyst for issuing cheap debt—is highly vulnerable to climate change. And yet, many Miami officials I interviewed welcomed the agency's announcement: they viewed it as an opportunity to further boost their credit ratings. Over the past few years, one financial officer in Miami Beach told me, local officials had noticed that rating agency analysts were asking more and more questions about climate change risks and how they were preparing for them. The analysts sometimes fielded these questions over the phone, but analysts more often asked them through formal surveys that they sent out to Miami Beach City Hall. Rather than paint a picture of Atlantis—a mythical sunken city that, by many scientific accounts, Miami Beach will resemble in the coming century—this financial officer told me that he used the survey questions to "beef up" representations of the City of Miami Beach's action on climate risk. What was the beef? Mainly thick descriptions of the myriad resilience actions and accomplishments that the city had taken in recent years. When it came to disclosing vulnerability, this officer tried to keep things brief and mainly positive. As he expounded, "because we feel like we've done a lot [to reduce our vulnerability], we wrote a lot, so they [Moody's analysts] would see it and value it."[10]

For reasons that I have expounded upon elsewhere,[11] Moody's analysts have thus far bought this officer's transparency act: following the rating agency's 2017 announcement, the firm has consistently given Miami Beach sterling ratings despite listing it as one the most climate vulnerable municipalities in the United States.[12]

Importantly, Miami Beach officials can use these high ratings to make further adaptation and resilience investments on the cheap *and* reassure investors in real estate and bonding that the arbiters of credit risk are confident in the city's medium-term future. But others within the realm of municipal finance are less convinced—and due at least in part to the region's own highly publicized acts of climate disclosure relative to its less publicized technical disclosure documents. Describing the promotion of Miami's climate transparency strategies as "'look at me and how holier than thou I am, I'm doing all of this fancy and sophisticated stuff on climate change, don't you want to invest in me instead of them,'" one municipal bond market investment firm executive told me that he has started to look elsewhere to get the rub on whether Miami is owning, and acting on, its climate risk: specifically, to its municipal securities disclosure report.[13] In one meeting, this executive scrolled through a recent report in front of me. Once he made it to the end of his word search, he raised his voice and noted in amusement that the City of Miami Beach didn't once use the term "climate" or "climate change" in its report. "They're hiding things from us!" he exclaimed. "Please explain to me how it is that Miami is doing so much on climate change if, in their annual [securities disclosure] report, there's no climate and there's no climate change?"[14]

No "doom and gloom"

Residents of Miami have highlighted similar discrepancies in the city's climate talk and climate action. In November of 2019, following months of protracted battles with local climate activist organizations, the City of Miami officially declared a climate emergency. In the statement, officials acknowledged that the "ecological effects of climate change are driving an increased rate of extinction of species, which could consequently devastate ecological stability and much of the biological life on Earth for future generations" and that significant action is required to blunt ecological catastrophe. For these reasons and others, in the declaration city officials called for significant financial and regulatory assistance from state and federal governments to "end citywide greenhouse gas emissions as quickly as possible…and accelerate adaptation and resilience strategies in preparation for intensifying climate impacts."[15]

For activists like Mihai Preda, a nuclear physicist, piano teacher and member of the international climate organization Fridays for Future, the climate emergency declaration marked a significant victory in ongoing climate battles in the city. After all, the declaration could provide the empirical basis and institutional legitimacy needed for the city to make massive investments in the built environment that, in the eyes of activists like Preda, would hopefully yield a more sustainable Miami. And yet, almost as quickly as city commissioners penned the declaration, Preda told me that they pushed it out of sight. "Nowhere on the city's [online] homepage can you find the declaration of the climate emergency. How is it that you can find information on the COVID-19 emergency on the homepage, but not the climate emergency, which is arguably even worse?" For Preda, the answer was simple: because disclosure of climate action in Miami was ultimately about managing competing perceptions of the city's climate future. "As a public official," Preda mused, "I am supposed to act on an existential threat, but I have no intention of acting on the existential threat. However, I have several constituencies. Some believe climate change is a Chinese hoax. I need to keep them happy, so I'm not going to let them hear anything about climate, because then I become a Chinese communist. Then I have these other people who are kind of worried 'cause they see the wildfires, they hear the news. I need to keep them happy, too. So I need to make it look like I'm doing something. So I have an idea, I'll make a declaration for the people who are concerned, and then I'll hide it from everyone else who could be concerned to see it. And that way I can keep on doing whatever I want for a while."[16] [Fig. 4]

In monthly Zoom meetings of the Mayor's Resilience Action Forum, a key component of the city's resilience efforts and wherein local constituents can virtually meet with city officials to discuss ongoing climate measures, Preda and others brought up the conspicuous absence of the climate emergency from the city government's website. On one occasion, Mayor Francis Suarez took up Preda's comment, saying that he refused to spread "doom and gloom" toward the city's climate future. For that reason, he concluded, he would not agree to post the declaration on the city's home page. Suarez noted that he was even hesitant to publicly use the term "emergency" in relation to the city's climate vulnerability given its potential to rattle residents and markets alike. Instead, concluding his engagement with Preda, Suarez said that he wanted to focus on solutions.[17] As with Suarez's courting of Silicon Valley techies he perceived as overly burdened by California taxation, it seems that climate change, too, can be adequately addressed by asking and answering the following question (see the search bar in Figure 4): how can we help?

A future slipping out of control?

In her 1987 monograph of *Miami*, Joan Didion wrote that the city is "long on rumor and short on memory."[18] While Didion directed her observation to the rush of *exilio* cash, ambition, and ideas that flowed to Miami during Cold War dramas abroad, the same principle applies to the city's recent turn toward climate transparency. As I discussed in the vignettes above, city officials have strategically mobilized and constrained their accounts of climate disclosure to generate positive orientations to the city's future. When and where sustained talk of climate risk, action, or emergency might conjure less optimism among residents and external financial observers, it is silenced or quickly hidden from view. Somewhat paradoxically, then, in Miami climate transparency may over time increasingly resemble climate censorship.

To be fair to Miami officials, a highly circumscribed understanding of climate transparency is in some ways understandable. Over the course of the region's over century-long history, the Greater Miami region has hitched its wagon to real estate-backed development and its attendant demands, despite being built atop a swamp.[19] Practically speaking, and as one resilience official told me, Greater Miami's economic path dependency means that if the region doesn't address its climate risks as they relate to property markets, "we [the city] can't address all of the other things that people care about and that we care about," such as climate displacement and gentrification. [20] (personal interview, 18 July 2019). Fail to keep external observers confident in the future, fail to provide for those in need. Indeed, this explains why inasmuch as Miami officials—themselves backed into a very tight corner—are depending on storm water infrastructure to create resilient futures, so too are they relying on strategic disclosure of climate risk and action. Importantly, and as I have stressed throughout this essay, many of the blocks with which Miami officials are attempting to build the city's future are not sturdy: as with the porous limestone that makes up the city's increasingly damp geologic foundation, Miami's transparent climate action is full of small holes. Residents and investors alike have begun to pick up on them, and they're starting to ask questions. In the end, and as Didion would have it, it may be doubt and rumor, not rising seas, that sink Miami.

1. See, for example: Laureen Elgert, "Rating the sustainable city: 'Measurementality', transparency, and unexpected outcomes at the knowledge-policy interface," *Environmental Science & Policy* 79 (Jan. 2018): 16–24; Aarti Gupta and Michael Mason, "A transparency turn in global environmental governance," in *Transparency in global environmental governance: Critical perspectives*, eds. Aarti Gupta and Michael Mason, 3-38. Cambridge: The MIT Press, 2014; Aarti Gupta and Michael Mason, "Disclosing or obscuring? The politics of transparency in global climate governance," *Current Opinion in Environmental Sustainability* 18 (Feb. 2016): 82–90; Susanne Konrad, Max van Deursen, and Aarti Gupta, "Capacity building for climate transparency: neutral 'means of implementation' or generating political effects?" *Climate Policy* 22 no. 5 (2022): 557–575.
2. This question is asked in Aarti Gupta, Sylvia Karlsson-Vinkhuyzen, Nila Kamil, Amy Ching and Nadia Bernaz, "Performing accountability: face-to-face account-giving in multilateral climate transparency processes," *Climate Policy* 21 no. 5 (Jan. 2021): 616–634.
3. This query is considered in Nadia Ameli, Paul Drummond, Alexander Bisaro, Michael Grubb and Hugues Chenet, "Climate finance and disclosure for institutional investors: why transparency is not enough," *Climatic Change* 160 no. 4 (2020): 565–589.
4. Esther Turnhout, Katja Neves and Elisa de Lijster, "'Measurementality' in biodiversity governance: knowledge, transparency, and the Intergovernmental Science-Policy Platform on Biodiversity and Ecosystem Services (IPBES)," *Environment and Planning A: Economy and Space* 46 no. 3 (Mar. 2014): 583.
5. See, for example, Bruce P. Braun, "A New Urban Dispotif? Governing Life in an Age of Climate Change," *Environment and Planning D: Society and Space* 32 no. 1 (Jan. 2014): 49–64; Jennifer L. Rice, "Climate, carbon, and territory: greenhouse gas mitigation in Seattle, Washington," *Annals of the Association of American Geographers* 100 no. 4 (2010): 929–937; Joshua Long and Jennifer L. Rice, "From sustainable urbanism to climate urbanism," *Urban Studies* 56 no. 5 (Apr. 2019): 992–1008.
6. Mario Alejandro Ariza, "As Miami keeps building, rising seas deepen its social divide," *Yale Environment* 360, September 29, 2020, https://e360.yale.edu/features/as-miami-keeps-building-rising-seas-deepen-its-social-divide.
7. Jesse M. Keenan, Thomas Hill and Anurag Gumber, "Climate gentrification: from theory to empiricism in Miami-Dade County, Florida," *Environmental Research Letters* 13 no. 5 (April 2018): 1–11; Steven A. McAlpine and Jeremy R. Porter, "Estimating recent local impacts of sea-level rise on current real-estate losses: a housing market case study in Miami-Dade, Florida," *Population Research and Policy Review* 37 no. 6 (June 2018): 871–895; Risky Business Project, *Risky Business: The Economic Risks of Climate Change in the United States*, June, 2014, https://riskybusiness.org/site/assets/uploads/2015/09/RiskyBusiness_Report_WEB_09_08_14.pdf.
8. See, for example, Robert Meyer, "Miami and the Costs of Climate Change," The Wharton Risk Management and Decision Processes Center, 2014, https://riskcenter.wharton.upenn.edu/miami-and-the-costs-of-climate-change/.
9. Michael Wertz et al., "Evaluating the impact of climate change on US and local issuers." Report, Moody's Investor Services, November 18, 2017, https://southeastfloridaclimatecompact.org/wp-content/uploads/2017/12/Evaluating-the-impact-of-climate-change-on-US-state-and-local-issuers-11-28-17.pdf.
10. Personal interview, June 27, 2019.
11. Savannah Cox, "Inscriptions of resilience: Bond ratings and the government of climate risk in Greater Miami, Florida," *Environment and Planning A: Economy and Space* 54 no. 2 (Mar. 2022): 295–310.
12. 427 Management, "Assessing exposure to climate change in U.S. Munis," May, 2018, http://427mt.com/wp-content/uploads/2018/05/427-Muni-Risk-Paper-May-2018-1.pdf.
13. These reports provide investors with a picture of a municipality's financial and operating conditions, specifically on current and anticipated credit risks, such as climate change.
14. Personal interview, June 21, 2021.
15. City of Miami, "Resolution R-19-0477: A Resolution of the Miami City Commission Declaring a Climate Emergency," Nov. 21, 2019.
16. Personal interview, Aug. 21, 2021.
17. Field notes, May 25, 2021.
18. Joan Didion, *Miami*. (London: Granta, 2005): 11.
19. Mario Alejandro Ariza, *Disposable City: Miami's Future on the Shores of Climate Catastrophe*. (London: Hachette UK: 2022); Zac J. Taylor, "The real estate risk fix: Residential insurance-linked securitization in the Florida metropolis," *Environment and Planning A: Economy and Space* 52 no. 6 (Jan. 2020): 1131–1149; Zac J. Taylor and Manuel B. Aalbers, "Climate gentrification: risk, rent, and restructuring in Greater Miami," *Annals of the American Association of Geographers* 112 no. 6 (Feb. 2022): 1685–1701.
20. Personal interview, July 18, 2019.

Re-membering the Future

Nashin Mahtani

"Everywhere we see the desire to annex nature, animals, other races and cultures, to a universal jurisdiction."
– Jean Baudrillard[1]

Amidst a global pandemic, ecosystem collapse, and public outcries for radically different futures, political slogans to "build back better" and "recover stronger" attempt to placate collective innervations over the inadequacy of global governance infrastructures to support the basic necessities of life, yet their generality also disguises what a "better" future entails, and for whom. Despite the populist tinge of these phrases, the design of the future (so often spoken of in the singular) has repeatedly been relegated to the imaginations and actions of a small handful of governing elites. Echoing the language of imperialist development politics, calls to "build back better" perpetuate the monopoly that a singular Euro-Atlantic model of civilization has long had on our future imaginary. In this model, where an illusory concept of social evolution is ranked by GDP,[2] the future is flattened to a homogenous and linear purview, and perpetual economic growth is conceived of as the only worthy desire, annexing any other community-based notions of well-being or pluriversal traditions of rhythmic temporality.

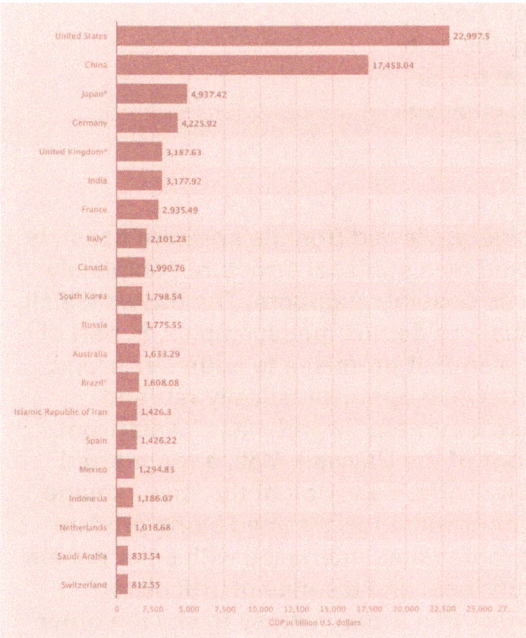

Even as the collapse of Earth's systems fiercely demonstrates the incompatibility of this model with our planet, governing elites continue to use capitalist developmental logics to sideline other modes of visioning and practicing the future. The urgency of climate change has been co-opted to enable new forms of (disaster) capitalism keyed to traditions of imperial annexation:[3] the accumulation of carbon in Earth's atmosphere has prepared the ground for market-based environmental conservation programs, new financial instruments have been designed to trade risks (effectively, betting on others' livelihoods), and technocratic infrastructures and masterplans claim to save the planet while securing enormous profits and privatized areas of land for a select few. Capitalism has always dismembered objects from their spatio-temporal entanglements so as to transform them into calculable and tradable assets of equivalence, but, with climatic turbulence, the uncertainty of the future itself becomes a tradable asset, as chaos-driven speculation opens up a plethora of new markets ranging from weather derivatives to catastrophe bonds and escapist city-building projects. When planetary risks are operationalized to further accelerate the same patterns of accumulation and colonization of temporalities that have driven ecosystem collapse—including the continued monopolization of what "better" futures are and could be—we must ask how we can reclaim our futures from neoliberal, techno-liberationist capitalist logics and give rise to pluriversal temporalities and futures capable of inhabiting instability.

Amongst the latest theatrics of risk-prevention extravagance and spatio-temporal dismemberment, Saudi

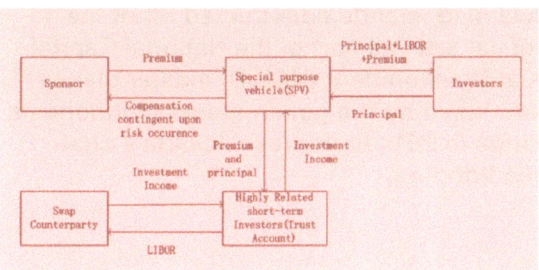

225

Arabia's Crown Prince recently announced the design of a zero-carbon city, "The Line", amidst ongoing human rights and energy crises. Evidently possessing an exorbitant marketing budget, a glitzy animation represents the "city of the future" as a 100-mile-long walled complex that cuts through a remote stretch of desert; a container walled off from its ecological context and sterile of any socio-ecological history. This narrative of newness, a start-over achieved through the erasure of any past or relational dependencies, is only the latest amongst a plethora of futuristic techno-solutionist fantasies promising limitless leisure and escape. All of these designs claim to solve the planetary crisis through sterile "innovation", a rhetoric of newness laden with the imperialist mentality of *tabula rasa*. In conjuring projections of frictionless urbanism devoid of entanglements with material-cultural life, these spectacles of architecture under capitalism are complicit in perpetuating myths of spatial and temporal dismemberment.

As architecture becomes increasingly subsumed into producing profit-generating investment assets, proposals for *exchangeable* urban environments, dismembered from terrestrial realities, proliferate in a global marketplace keyed to asset trading. Plans for the Line were quickly compared to Superstudio's 1969 theoretical project, the Continuous Monument, which was intended to represent "the horrors architecture had in store, with its scientific methods of perpetuating standard models worldwide."[4] Superstudio's prescient critique remains relevant today as collages of glass megastructures infused with "smart" sensors continue to infiltrate the realm of urban design across cultures and geographies, and even if unrealized fully, their Hollywood-style city trailers (designed specifically for our contemporary attention ecologies) grip the public imaginary and standardize perceptions of "better" futures. In these homogenous visions of society the "city of the future" on an Arabian desert feels identical to the "city of the future" on an island in the Java Sea; enclaves of controlled nature promising care-free lifestyles managed by circuit boards that eradicate all risk.

The skyline of Jakarta, viewed from its northern coast, is abruptly interrupted by a colossal structure completely out of scale with its coastal neighbors. The Baywalk Mall, a gated commercial-residential megacomplex, is part of an urban master plan that promises to address chronic flooding in Jakarta while opportunistically rebranding its coastline as a modern, "world-class" waterfront. On the ground floor of the Baywalk Mall, a room-sized model of "Pluit City" offers a vision of the "new" image of Jakarta: glistening white towers lined along pristine beaches, green promenades interlaced with solar panels and white wind turbines, and a series of articulated bridges that connect this urban fantasy to sixteen other newly constructed artificial islands. Pluit City will be one of seventeen reclaimed islands constructed off of the northern coast of Jakarta, all part of the National Capital Integrated Coastal Development (NCICD) master plan, a megaproject undertaken by the governments of Indonesia and the Netherlands in 2014 to address Jakarta's challenges of extreme flooding.

As one of the most rapidly urbanizing cities in the world, with a current population of 31 million people, situated on the coastal edge of the world's most disaster-prone region, and sinking at an average rate of five to ten centimeters a year, Jakarta has been described as the "future condition" of cities in the Anthropocene.[5] Jakarta's responses to its confluence of challenges offer many lessons—or warnings, given that its consultant-driven master planning strategies exacerbate the very same anthropogenically-driven challenges and inequalities they claim to solve. The NCICD climate infrastructure project involves the construction of a new, forty-kilometer-long, twenty-five-meter-high sea wall, with a price tag of $40 billion US dollars, the unprecedented expense of which will be partially recovered through selling real estate on the seventeen reclaimed islands that complement and extend the arc of the seawall. Glassy towered figures of liberated privilege deliver *en masse* a vague promise to "save the city" by constructing a "new," "world-class" identity.

But for whom is this new world-class city being constructed? Although the plan acknowledges that the most cost-effective strategy for flood risk mitigation in Jakarta is to reduce land subsidence—even stating that it would make the forty billion dollar NCICD project "unnecessary altogether"—the plan itself does not address this issue, and instead insists that the colossal infrastructure of oceanic defense is necessary because the sinking of Jakarta cannot be stopped "in time."[6] Urgency, here, is invoked to posit a high-investment offshore master plan as the only option, one that will conveniently guarantee enormous profits for the Dutch water sector. Meanwhile, for residential communities living along the coast of Jakarta, the colossal infrastructure project has only amplified uncertainties and the risk of flooding. On December 19, 2019, the force of the Java Sea obliterated a recently completed 170-meter section of the new defensive barrier, just four years after construction began and with less than one percent of the total project completed. The failure of the wall poses huge risks to the coastal communities who live immediately adjacent to the structure. Yet, the project continues apace and the rest of the city continues to experience chronic flooding. In June 2022, Jakarta was inundated during what has historically been its "dry season" in a particularly concerning convergence of anthropogenic events: torrential downpour carried a profusion of pollutants into the city's streets and waterways, with the unprecedented rainfall coming just weeks after Jakarta was ranked as having the world's worst air quality, with pollutant levels 27.4 times higher than those deemed safe by the World Health Organization.

As the city of 31 million people chokes and sinks under the pressure of capitalism, Indonesians have now been promised another new future for the nation: a carbon-neutral "smart metropolis" surrounded by lush greenery where residents lounge on marine coastal pods floating across slivers of glistening wetlands that weave through a white metropolis. In this city, children fly kites beneath towers of shining crystal, people bicycle through tree-lined boulevards, drones cater to consumerist desires in real-time, vegetation sprouts through all surfaces, and all buildings glow under a perpetual sunset veneer.

The centerpiece of these urban renderings is a giant glass building in the shape of the mythical bird Garuda, with its wings spread wide, watching over the frictionless city of leisure. This is the image of "Nusantara", Indonesia's new capital city that promises to set itself apart from the challenges of Jakarta, both conceptually and physically.

Plans to relocate Indonesia's capital city from Jakarta, a megacity situated on the most densely populated island in the world, to East Kalimantan, home to some of the world's most biodiverse ecosystems, was announced by President Joko Widodo in August 2019 and ratified in a bill passed in January 2022. The new capital plan has elicited a range of reactions amongst Indonesian residents, ranging from apathy and disbelief to despondency and excitement.[7] Even if its actual realization remains doubtful, the imagined city of these renderings—its core conceptual vision of a 'care-free' future liberated from all risk—functions as the basis for contract negotiations to re-distribute, re-zone, and ecologically transform land. Massive land clearance and infrastructure construction is already underway. Design has always been an act of imagining and imaging the future, but when these images of the future are increasingly operationalized to move material and exchange credit—the result of which is almost always the accumulation of capital elsewhere—we must ask who is eligible to imagine, measure, and price the future, and by what means such positions of power are acquired and maintained.

The lush forested landscape of a generic greenery depicted in the renderings completely obscures the fact that the new capital city relies on the state's acquisition of privately-owned land. Though the renderings do not narrate the realities of inhabitation and livelihoods that are teeming below the forest canopy, their presence are well known by pioneers of the master planning project; soon after the announcement of the new capital city, a change to Indonesia's property laws made it more difficult—and sometimes illegal—to contest land conflicts. In Borneo, we met with Jubaen, a member of the Indigenous Paser Balik tribe and the chief of Pemaluan, a village inside the planning zone for the new capital. Without any official ownership records to assert rights to the land,[8] his tribe is hesitantly aware of the oncoming displacement they will face, a pattern they have been familiar with since the 1970s when plantation companies began to encroach on their land.[9]

Since the 1970s, extractivist projects have penetrated the island and enabled smoother access to Kalimantan's abundant fuel and forest reserves under the pretense of development. By carving access to the area's palm oil, timber, and coal reserves, global supply chains continue to accumulate profits for the metropole while displacing risk onto these sites of extraction. Although the new capital city project is operating under the novel pretense of climate adaptation, it cannot be considered separately from these longer histories of extractivist accumulation. Within the boundaries of the designated site, there are currently 162 active concessions (including mining, forestry, oil palm plantation, and coal concessions), 94 abandoned coal mining pits, and 72 indigenous villages, all entangled in a long history of struggle and violence to

control the commodification of the Kalimantan rainforest. Yet, these histories of colonial and global arrangements of extraction and wealth creation that are deeply imbricated within the terrain, are completely erased from the nationalist rhetorics underpinning the new capital city's marketing strategy.

While the proliferation of national symbology serves to entice mass enthusiasm for the nation's new future, the actual plans suggest that only a small percentage of Indonesia's population will be able to participate in the nation's new future. Although the 632,580-acre site is four times the size of Jakarta, the new capital is designed to house only 900,000 to 1.5 million people—less than three percent of Jakarta's current population. The relocation of the capital is a salient reminder that 'better futures' tend to follow supremacist cartographies of selective zones that determine those who are rendered legible and sensible, and those who are not.

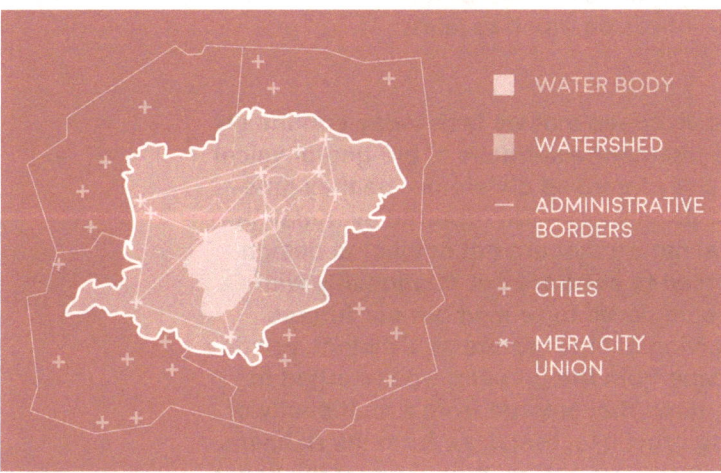

As the vortex of financial markets pull governance and planning into dismembered dimensions of extraction, recombination, and liquification of their own, the flamboyance of illusionary renderings cannot stop the thrust of thermodynamic forces playing out their own material realities on the ground. Since the public announcement of the capital relocation project in 2019, Jakarta and its millions of residents have continued to experience historic flooding every year. (In 2021, heavy rainfall and broken infrastructure resulted in the Kalimantan province experiencing its worst flood in fifty years). While the elite perceive climate change as a future projection, the extremities of that future have already arrived for millions of residents who are unequally exposed to weather turbulence. In response to these new climate realities, the international media trots out the same tired binary: despondency over Jakarta's present versus cheerleading for a risk-free future in the new capital city in Kalimantan.

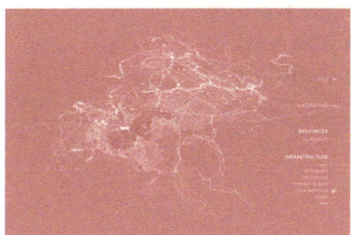

To adjust to increasingly erratic flows of water, for instance, riverside communities in Jakarta have developed a collective, empirically-indexed flood warning system that relies on the repeated sharing and updating of river conditions through an informal SMS network. Extending along the entire length of the river, the information sharing network traverses five administrative boundaries, connecting residents in Jakarta to the upstream cities of Bogor and Depok. Community leaders layer information about upstream river conditions on top of current neighborhood conditions—including the pattern of eddies, local rainfall, neighborhood infrastructure and drainage systems—in order to calculate the window of time for action and make decisions about moving goods, people, and provisions. This integrated approach of risk assessment, which foregrounds physics, ecology, and collective wisdom, represents a nuanced response to turbulent weather—a far more sophisticated approach to risk adaptation than techno-solutionist fantasies of starting over.

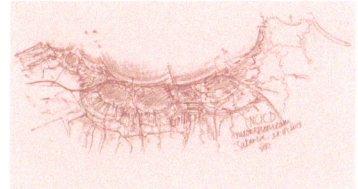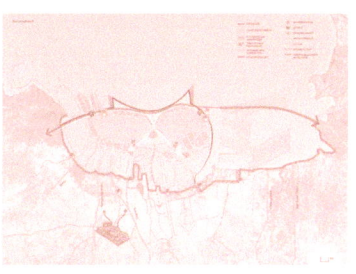

The ecological dimensions of this network are particularly useful to pay attention to; formal flood management programs carve the river into five segments on the basis of jurisdictional lines, producing a disjointed response to overflow, even though the river runs through all five cities. The resident-organized system, by contrast, acknowledges the watershed ecology as a single system. Resident modes of adaptation re-member the watershed through distributed, collective knowledge of more-than-human worlds. Such practices of situated sense-making and attention to environmental change are prevalent in communities whose lives depend on having close relationships to the soil, the water, or the forest. More often than not, however, these populations have been marginalized as "underdeveloped" and excluded from the visions of "better" futures drawn up by consultants and from the scientific forums appointed with the agency to disseminate climate knowledge. Yet, such a grounded response to risk, based on a situated understanding of material flows and interconnections—a knowledge that can often only be gained from living in a place—offers us much to learn from.

The planetary-scale crises that we face today continually remind us of the interconnectedness of bio-geo-physical worlds. As artificially imposed divisions—be they jurisdictional lines or flood walls—are ruptured everyday by forces of material nature that are not subject to design intent, we are forced to confront our relationality with the world; we are implored to re-member our futures. Instead of conceiving of "the" future as a distant, pristine and ordered escape from the present, we are urged to move towards futures that emerge from a multiplicity of already occurring practices, that draw from the richness of intricate entanglements and relationships of thickened temporalities. Contrary to popular renderings, the sterility of "newness and innovation" will not bring the just and liveable futures that the world yearns for. But practicing the future, instead of betting on it, just might.

As we learn to practice the future, how might we adapt the risk technologies already in play? While risk models have been aggressively adopted to accelerate neoliberal capitalism, the way they engage with future worlds also offers the chance for political inversions. In their capacity to render time-complexes that can produce recursive truths—that is, because the future they project inflects the trajectory of the present—risk models have a potency to overcome the limitations of a linear ordering of time.[10] Co-opting this model of temporality has tremendous political potential: instead of a prescriptive future foreclosing action in the present, the iterative inflection of possible futures could open up the search for radically different but latent worlds.

A theoretical provocation, *MERA* is an ongoing research project that explores the potentials of co-opting these techniques of future speculation to reintegrate dismembered spatio-temporal entanglements. To this end, MERA posits that cities sharing a watershed form city-unions whose governance decisions are inflected by the ecological wellbeing of future worlds. With this layering of geospatial interests, it is not only the short-term futures promised every electoral season that recursively affect the present within insular jurisdictional boundaries;

rather, it is the deep time of entire ecologies–that inflect upon present-day decision making. Deep time futures and pasts become reintegrated as a spectral presence in daily life. Through this process of re-membering futures, the various scales at which bio-geo-physical temporalities and spatialities unfold, are reintegrated into the shorter perceptual rhythms of social, cultural, and economic of human life, providing the groundwork for environmental co-governance by humans and more-than-humans. If Nusantara and other monumental urban resets seek to sever the future from the current state of our world, MERA seeks to re-member our futures to our present: the deep time of the watershed combined with the very real and varied hopes and desires of inhabitants guide incremental maneuvers and microdecisions in the present, as we iteratively become into future worlds.[11]

If we really are to move towards "recovering together", we cannot adapt to rapidly shifting climatic conditions by deploying the same strategies of conquest and techno-solutionism that flatten the many cultural-material entanglements of our worlds. Nor can we afford to insist on apocalyptic doom or perpetuate myths of risk-free sustainability and care-free resilience as alibis for rapacious forms of neoliberal development. A sober reckoning with the environmental, social, and political challenges of our world compels us to shift away from escapism. Instead, we are implored to explore the possibility of new political alliances and to imagine creative strategies for enacting the futures that we actually want and need. To this end, the recursive temporalities of risk models, offer possibilities to reintegrate the layered understandings of time and relationality that have been prevalent in many non-dominant cultures. If we can steer such a projective tool away from a singular capitalist future so as to make space for pluriversal futures keyed to different traditions and their respective and changing ecologies, perhaps we can shift away from dismemberment, dissociation, and helpless passivity in addressing the planetary crises to integration, social collaboration, and visceral agency for planetary wellbeing. As we navigate increasingly turbulent climatic changes, rather than clinging to "a better future" conceptualized as a social-technical frontier (that relies on the promise of technological progress), we are encouraged to explore other, non-standardized ways of becoming that embrace the navigation through risk. Only if we can imagine different futures—ones that emerge from embracing, instead of canceling, pluralistic histories and temporalities capable of inhabiting turbulence—can we begin to work towards more just and joyful lifeworlds.

1. Jean Baudrillard, *Impossible Exchange* (London: Verso, 2001).
2. Wolfgang Sachs, *The Development Dictionary* (London: Zed Books, 2010).
3. Naomi Klein, *The Shock Doctrine: The Rise of Disaster Capitalism* (Toronto: Knopf Canada, 2007).
4. Oliver Wainwright, "Nine Million People in a City 170km Long; Will the World Ever be Ready for a Linear Metropolis?," *The Guardian*, September 8, 2022, https://www.theguardian.com/artanddesign/2022/sep/08/nine-million-people-in-a-city-170km-long-will-the-world-ever-be-ready-for-a-linear-metropolis.
5. Etienne Turpin, Adam Bobette and Meredith Miller, "Navigating Postnatural Landscapes: Jakarta as the City of the Anthropocene" (paper presented at the European Council of Landscape Architecture Schools Annual Conference, Netherlands, 2013).
6. Indonesian Ministry of Economic Affairs, Government of the Netherlands, Master Plan. National Capital Integrated Coastal Development, December 1, 2014, 37.
7. Much of the research about the sea wall and the new Indonesian capital was conducted with Etienne Turpin for our forthcoming film *Tidak Ada Kapital (There is No Capital)*. On processes of accumulation and abandonment, see: Nashin Mahtani and Etienne Turpin, "There is No Capital," Kerb 28 (Fall 2020).
8. Under the law, any land that cannot be proven to be owned by anyone is automatically property of the state. For decades, Indigenous communities in Indonesia (especially in rural areas) have been displaced because they do not have (and usually cannot acquire) the documentation to prove their inheritance of land that has been cultivated and passed on over many generations.
9. Parts of this text appear in Nashin Mahtani, "Torrential Urbanisms and the Future Subjunctive," *E-Flux Architecture*, September 16, 2020, https://www.e-flux.com/architecture/accumulation/345108/torrential-urbanism-and-the-future-subjunctive/.
10. On the speculative time complex, see Suhail Malik and Armen Avanessian, *The Time Complex: Post-Contemporary* (Miami: NAME, 2016).
11. For a more detailed narration of MERA, taking the Caspian Sea as a preliminary case study, see https://mera.zone. MERA is an ongoing research project co-led by Nabi Agzamov, Antonia Burchard-Levine, Olga Cherniakova, Nashin Mahtani, and Evgenia Vanyukova. The project was conceived during their time as research fellows in the New Normal Program at the Strelka Institute for Media, Architecture & Design.

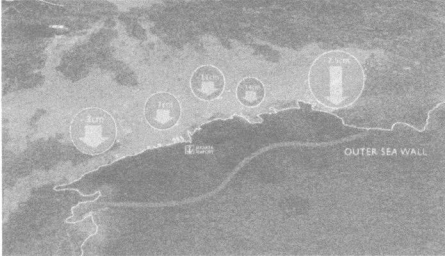

All There Ever Was — Todd Reisz

This might be your moment. Your trainers are merging with near-molten asphalt. Like butter pressed onto crackling toast. Across the glistening tarmac, the pilot uses impatient arm gestures to summon you, as if worried that scorching ground will soon consume his craft. Mimicking the way they do it in political thrillers—torso bowed, hand over head—you and the others move forward and under the swirling rotor blades.

All of you—architects, urban planners, behavioral economists, public-art brokers, designers who claim mastery of scales "from the human to the planetary"—are summoned for two days of presentations. Each will make a pitch for *a lively futuristic city*. Organizers have promised a "sky as the limits" reception for your brave imagination. *There is nothing to hold you back.*

In contrast to the call for unshackled ideation, the group dynamic already constricts with self-importance. Imagination is unlimited, but lucrative contracts are scarce. Catchwords like *world-class*, *sustainability*, *livability*, *walkability*, *happiness*, and *inspiration* will be embodied by each consultant. Everyone knows everyone else. You are expected to speak to shared, unwavering values and, at the same time, stand out. The best of you will perform to these cue words effortlessly, fueled by the catering's canapés.

Helicopters. They're infused with the excitement of luxury and the severity of military. They take heroes to war zones, refugee bivouacs, and disaster locales. Today, you feel a heightening, as if lives depended on your expedited transport over hostile landscapes to the other side. You and the other consultants are elite in the global circuit of city expertise. This trip automatically renews your license for access to the next junket.

The cabin is consumed by the rapid-fire percussion that will keep you suspended above ground. The group's penchant for Ray-Bans goes well with the requisite headsets. The pilot has muted the mics, so that only he can be heard. Insurmountable noise forces a silence in the cabin. For now, there can be no reconnaissance of the competition. You can focus on the view. Every few meters higher feels a degree cooler. Sweat, once forming a cloud of humidity between skin and blouse, now condenses and converts clothing fibers into thermal disadvantage.

You glide over crop circles and landfills that fringe the departed city that no one will mention. You've read descriptions of the landscapes that unfurl from the horizon: lunar-like, otherworldly, untouched. It's at once beautiful and menacing. It's less a comprehensible landscape than a menagerie of geological shapes that defy approach. From the hovering cabin, shapes transmute, reminding you that rocks are composed of particles that have roved for millennia. And will continue to rove. You witness an acceleration of geological time. Cinnamon-colored sands convene in occasional swirls to conceal the evidence.

You catch signs of settlement—fences, walls, compounds, and roads. They are ruins perhaps of previous attempts to rein in the environment. At this height, they seem inactivated. You're paid to ignore any hints of civilization.

Through clouds of ancient dust scourged by rotor blades, you are shepherded to the site. This time, site circumscribes not a new building or tower district, but a new city. On newly found land. As if the brim of a now-diminished ridge, once open to the Earth's mantle, had been pushed open by the surfacing of fresh magmatic basalt, causing mountains and palisades to bob like soap in water. It's as if such an aching process has now concluded,

and the hardened basalt offers a new floor of crust, peppered with wistful sand. This place had no name, until millions heard it spoken on YouTube. Until daily papers shellacked it on full-page ads.

Once the sea takes over the horizon, a perfect circle of green turf comes into view over the pilot's shoulder. It grows to become the helipad, at the edge of a compound whose walls borrow hues of purple from the rocks in your midst. The pilot finally balances the craft above the green target for descent. Disembarking, you step out onto the turf, and then through it. Like a booby-trap, it conceals a man-made swamp. Boggy earth imported from somewhere else now fills your trainers. Awaiting men welcome you in creaseless white robes.

The new city might not yet exist, but there is a logo. For the next two days, everything you touch and see will be fastened to the logo: pens and shampoo tubes, water bottles, notebooks and shoe horns, even the desserts you eat. Its relentless application reminds you that you are paid to be part of *the world's most ambitious and visionary mega-development focused on tomorrow's Humanity today*. Like the interminable spread of the logo, this city's formula will be applied and multiplied. No longer dwellings, cities are unrealized latencies, the *blank pages for humanity's next chapter*. As immaterial as the logo might be, this city overflows with ambition, and the next heavy load of it has just landed in the form of urban expertise. *Just endless potential*.

For more than eighty years, consultants like you have looked out of decommissioned military planes and chartered helicopters to pinpoint potential. Hired to design life out of lifelessness. Countless engineers and planners have preceded you in making deserts turn green and reminding anyone who will listen that we are truly a global species. But now you and your professional kin do something else, or maybe something more. The climate was once something that professionals like you pushed aside to create the space of design. The act, a composition of sealants and membranes, was a heroic resistance. The results of which were meant to be seen. At this workshop, any mention of the construction industry's drive to create landfills and release carbon will be suppressed. No one will talk about the fluorescent green discharge that desalination plants eject into coastal waters, killing wildlife, melting coral reefs, and decimating tourism numbers. Your fellow visionaries are assured that other practitioners are working, quietly in a lab somewhere else, on a way to capture debris, carbon, and the green slime—wrapping it all up like an unwanted cadaver and burying it under the sea. Only in the movies does the unwanted corpse eventually rise to the surface.

Along with a logo, this city also has a CEO. "If you're in *the city business*, like myself," begins the CEO in his opening remarks. You will forget what comes after that clause. He's wearing conference-casual loafers. Their slenderness makes his paunch more pronounced. He has to pinch his shoulder blades together to create counterbalance to the paunch. The strain affords him a posture of certainty. The city business. The wheeling and dealing that churns a constant amassing of resources, cooked and forged into materials with half-lives spanning millennia. A constant surge of matter to generate an unyielding presence. The CEO says he expects to see this city to completion in his lifetime, patting his graying hair as if to say this city needs to happen fast. As he lowers his arm, he joggles his wrist to settle his heavy watch back into place. Neverending potential gets sifted into contractual completion.

Let's change everything.

After the first day of proposals, each ending with a flurry of finger-snaps (less obtrusive than applause), you're invited with the others to a party tent on the beach. The scent of cardamom coffee fills the space. The CEO makes his next speech, perhaps still stirred by the fresh proposals for underground ice generation, contorting towers that overwhelm the geological skyline, a desert vanquished by palms and flower beds, and a calculator to measure true urban happiness. "We're here to make a lot of money." He pauses for effect, as if your boundless ideas will lead to mutually boundless profits. The opening lands awkwardly. Has he misread his paid audience, or did he aim for this palpable discomfort among the "ideas people"? There is some nervous chuckling. You haven't fully signed onto the fact that you've fully signed on to this.

This time, the architect does not serve autocrats or kings, but rather the lionized management thinkers, the industrialist visionaries whose principles are listed in one or another case study from Harvard Business School. But really there are no principles to be bullet-pointed. Opportunism is the real river that management tends to. This time, the CEO embraces one expert's proposal to furrow an actual river across a tectonic plate currently without one.

Dense forests, automated waterfalls, robots, airborne taxis, and sky-high biodomes. The CEO and the industrialists already know what they want. The slip-on loafers with no-show footies reveal as much: that the real work has already been done. *The city is an endless playground.*

Play is an imagined state characterized by the shifting of borders and the abeyance of history. When beneficial and pleasurable,

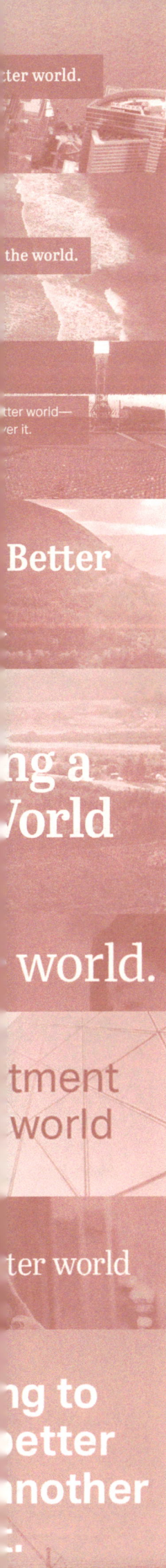

play is liminal and temporary. Tabula rasa occurs when the powerful convert this disposition into something contained and permanent. Borders are inscribed, to keep history out. The old gets sequestered so that designers can proclaim the new. The analysts deem on-site soil sterile and order it scraped away. Exfoliated, the Earth's crust can be padded with new life.

Somewhere not far from this tent, Abrahamic texts say the sea split in two, creating a passage for traveling humans. At this new city, it will be sodium chloride that splits from H_2O to create sweet fresh water. The visionaries have calculated on the back of their high-salary envelopes that the city can run on limitless energy captured from the sun. Solar streams will purify water and pump it to sky-high mountaintops so that it can flow back down again as scintillating waterfalls, to enliven water parks and to render public squares virtuously plush. The Earth's systems will be rigged with life hacks.

The billionaire industrialists believe that financial virility fuels their visionary prowess. They know that a new city doesn't have to convince; rather it has to lure - lure more charmers who siphon short-term profits off of somebody else's long-term goals. In turn, the charmers hire the do-good salary men and women, like you, who seek professional opportunity, if also a chance to make a change. At school they read utopia; now they read student-loan statements. They left high-priced schools and low-paid internships with a belief in their skill set. Site, for this reason, serves a personal, psychological purpose. It's an isolated place of focus. A chance to make the rules stick, for once. History, they sigh, need not weigh so much.

You don't want to hear of history. And, anyway, this is nothing more than a dramatization. Any resemblance to actual events is mere coincidence.

Architects love a good crisis. An architect's announcement of crisis, you once learned, is your calling card, handed out upon your arrival at the scene to inspect, then to diagnose, and finally to design a cure. Without a crisis, there can be no architecture. A famous architect once declared a crisis by citing a clichéd and dubious statistic, namely that 2% of the world's built environment is designed by architects. When the famous architect states this, he wants to express: 1.) that he knows the world; 2.) that it is poorly built; and 3.) we (he, you, and I) are losing ground to higher-yield city makers. Fashioning a crisis is not inherently bad, but this cliché misses the point. Crisis is framed in a way that the architect is some kind of precious threatened species, a precise rarity at 2.0%. The precision dwells on the architect's absence, not on the abounding ways in which things get built by other professionals more versatile at guiding the extraction of materials from various places and fastening them together into some materialized conception of space.

The real crisis might be our inability as architects to see ourselves for who we are, our inability to see ourselves as part of a prodigious ecosystem. There are two components in an organism's recognition of self. The first is the distinction of the self from others and one's surroundings. The second component is the organism's ability to appreciate what traits it shares with others. Both components are necessary for species survival. The architect who cries 2% clearly has the first component down, as would any successful consultant, that is the ability to distinguish himself in a scene of problems and scarcity. It's the latter component in which architects often prove deficient: the acknowledgement of one's own partaking in that scene. What we as architects often fail to admit is that we are inextricably tied to a vast constellation of people paid to reshape Earth, paid to instrumentalize the extraction of natural resources into hardened casts for habitation. We are never a break from, but always a continuation of a history.

Years ago, I attended a two-day convention, much like the one you are at now. On a panel was someone who had tapped wealth from an earlier building boom. He had navigated that boom like the weather. He delighted his audience with stories of how he cladded the entire city that "rose from the desert." He credited his community for his success: There are two kinds of societies, he said, those that destroy and those that build. The Destroyers allow ethnic and ideological strife to tear apart their cities and to scare away investment. They wallow in history. As examples, he referred to Beirut, Baghdad, and Aleppo. Then there are the Builders, those that pursue continual environmental transformation. Builders defy history. They build no ruins. They know the world will keep turning, its hardened surfaces will keep shifting, with or without them. His society was that of the Builders. When another speaker reminisced about how his team of engineers had "turned a virgin coastline into a concrete plane," the Builder nodded vigorously, as if indicating he remembered the day his city was glazed over in concrete. Workers from three continents had massaged the doughy mixture over a matrix of British steel. Concrete as incarnate Platonism.

A vast plane of reinforced concrete to thwart the vagaries of coastal erosion—the imagery brings us to the idea of permanence. Time, somebody once observed, can only occur if change occurs. And change can only be perceived spatially. One has to perceive it on surfaces of the earth. If change is necessarily spatial, then time only happens if space says it can. Since time can only be read through space, and since the architect shapes space, one would think that the architect is engaged in moving time along. Yet much more often, architects are hired to stop time, not to mark it.

This tussle, between permanence and impermanence, is evident in the idea of a formal garden. There, permanence arises through cultivation, and by defining the area under cultivation with walls and fences. Inside the bounds, permanence is tended to. The threat of the temporary and unexpected outside the bounds is also an essential part to permanence. The garden's stability can only be read against instability.

One could say that multinational design firms perfected the city, only by restricting it as an area of design. Over past decades, the *site* of contracts, indemnities, and construction schedules has expanded in size, congruent to the growing sizes of the firms that compete to control them. The development of this site can grow boundlessly, but it will always be bound by surveys and contracts alike.

There is an enduring concept engaged with time, timelessness, and space—utopia. The term is an etymological play with ancient Greek, but it was born in London, where its author Thomas More later lost his head over a king's divorce. His corpse, after being decapitated, was further cut up and hoisted atop various gates of London, a city which he dreamed of leaving but whose ramparts were ultimately stained with his guts. More than five hundred years later, we still pursue his failed escape. Partly thanks to architects, *utopian* can mean *radically imaginative*, *naïve*, *avant-garde*, *future*, or *futuristic*. One of our famous colleagues asserted that architects carry the "utopian gene." A moral burden contracted on the way out of an expensive finishing school.

Like the walled garden, Thomas More's utopia was not a city, as it's often described, but an island. A site delimited by the seas. The shipmasters who went exploring after More's island did not find utopia; instead, they encountered civilizations they strategically framed to make their own civilization seem better off. In other words, travel didn't lead to utopia; it led to colonialism. Plantations, ports, camps, and colonies became the formal gardens. They could be perfected because the area under cultivation was restricted. And by being restricted, they had to be defended against the so-called barbarians. The threats of the barbarian were just as necessary as the walls around colonialism's formal gardens. Permanence exists only when the ramparts are constantly under attack.

That brings me to some observations about one publicly traded multinational building-industry conglomerate, called A____, which first made its *profits* in oil refining in eastern Kentucky. These days, it earns its billions of dollars of profits not in refining oil, but in refining oil profits into hardened built matter. A____ became one of the largest companies in the design management and construction industries through a voracious strategy of mergers and acquisitions. Without even knowing it yet, you may already work for it.

Through A____'s gigantism, its leadership has won the world's largest design and design management contracts by convincing clients to give it everything. It's so large that to describe it you have to talk about multiple industries. Architecture is a mere percentage of its operations, and yet the company has chewed architecture up and spit it out. Having sapped up any of its value, it now outsources design services, just like its payroll services, to the lowest bidders.

No ambassadors from A____ have been invited to speak at this conference, but, yes, you suspect that some of those gray-suited men, seated at the back of the room and cleaning off the dessert trays, are being paid to listen to you. The day after this *ideas assembly*, they plan to return to their workstations.

A____ might have eviscerated architecture, but the architectural project still endures. The company now promises to "future-proof our world," suggesting the culmination of the gardening project at its maximum dimensions. *Future-proofing* is not about knowing the future but about possessing controls to counter the future. Here we have a powerful building-industry firm claiming so brazenly that it can enact space but *resist* time. A____ promises to keep future-ness out of clients' plans. Whatever A____ will design, manage, and deliver will make it through; time can be dispensed with. There is a promise that the complex but calculable ecosystems of nature, politics, warfare, greed, terrorism, etc., will not be able to gather up and destroy your creation. The impermeability of external surfaces is but a metaphor for all that's ensured. Nothing is left to chance because there is no chance. An online definition for *future-proofing* describes it as *minimizing possible consequences*. Design without consequences. A____ once maintained a PR magazine, One, as in one-stop consulting services. Total design. Full service. A____ is the protector of a vision, a master plan, a business plan, an annual report. It is the assurance that the CEO gets his bonus because everything sticks to this plan. If there is no space for the future; there is no time for it.

My apologies for all this chatter when you should be practicing your pitch for tomorrow's session. You need to breathe some air from beyond this compound of quick-build cabanas and office containers. You approach the fleet of cars made available to the guests. A man in a safari vest, festooned with the logo, stands up. Visibly relieved that someone else wants to get out of here too, he gestures toward his assigned SUV. Inside, an exchange of hand signals confirms you share no common language. Both of you are fine with silence. You can think about your pitch while watching landscapes framed through the windshield.

He has little reason to obey speed limits. You whiz by roadside markets, gas stations, and mosques. Children lay claim to a stranded earth mover. Camels graze. Dilapidated walls, obstinate fences, and disused tires demarcate space and tell history. Parallel to the road and about 200 meters beyond your window runs a rhythm of pylons connected by wires, disappearing and reappearing from behind curtains of rimrock. The sun has begun its expansive setting. Every surface is cast in hues of orange and mauve. The driver seems set on bringing you somewhere in particular. He slows down to engage a roundabout. Along the circumference of the circle is a canopy stretched over a flock of people. They're focused on the interior. They are wearing broad sunhats; their pant legs bulge with side pockets. Their curiosity makes them seem harmless. The driver senses your interest and pulls over. You check out what's happening.

It's not clear whether anyone notices your approach. You hear English, in several accents, spoken as lingua franca. A large folding table is covered with sky-blue felt unfolded as if to accept a dentist's tools. Instead, it's used to display a grid of rocks. As small as a fingernail and as large as a loaf of bread, they might have seemed like anything you encountered on the compound's walkways. Here, they transform against the unexpected backdrop. They begin to emit stories. They reveal grooves and planes fashioned by humans. Measurements are being taken. Notes written in journals. One spectator makes elevation and plan drawings. The group of archeologists have come together after fanning outward in SUVs all day. They avoided sites recently scraped by bulldozers. Each stop resulted in a collection of Paleolithic tools that were dispersed over the landscape like scree. Some they recorded in notebooks and returned to place. Others they brought to this tent.

You realize that until now you have read this landscape as geological, as if it were devoid of life and bore only histories of tectonic drift. The granite rock that is visible from the roundabout would not have been conducive to making the tools being assessed before you. These stones, their shapes made by human hands, come from other places, either brought here by humans or swept by waters that once ran from unseeable mountains. Nothing could have ever isolated this land. Humans have been here longer than nearly everywhere else, a junction of your species' dispersal, of its endless departures and returns to this place.

Just as fight/flight is a constituted binary within us, so it must be that we harbor a more expansive, sometimes inconsistent, belief that there are possibilities, spatial ones, laid out before us. No possible trajectory has yet explained how the earliest humans left East Africa, because all of them require Herculean feats of transversal. A species moved and spread, but only because individual choices were made. Love, greed, and fear, quite literally moved them. They looked at and together assessed landscapes on the horizon.

Before your arrival, the CEO had already publicized a *regreening initiative* to plant 100 million trees before the city even had an acknowledged resident. *Regreening* seemed the wrong word when this land has never been green in human history. But these artifacts speak a rebuttal that indeed waters ran here and so did game. Archeologists refer to *refugia* here. There have been places and periods of intensively green habitat, galvanized by the forces that always generate green: wind patterns, flurries of airborne seeds, and ambulant life. A *regreening initiative* can somehow be simultaneously ignorant of history and teeming with it.

The first modernists who claimed to read vast histories on the Earth's surface were broken into two camps, the catastrophists and the uniformationists. The former believed that Earth was shaped by terrific, violent events; the latter see a planet formed gradually, wholly, obeying the same laws today as long ago. Today it seems both camps are right.

The driver has reached the place he wants to show you. It's a shallow, nearly circular cove, reminiscent of a kiddie pool. Where the shore slopes upward is a carcass of oxidized steel. The setting sun irradiates its rust into copper. You make out that it was once the fuselage of an airplane. Two Italian men—black suits, white shirts, and shiny silver belt buckles—pose for a picture taken by their host. You gather they are here for another conference elsewhere. Engineers maybe. The ruin throws your scale of time off. You're no longer thinking just of the Pleistocene.

You won't forget this ruin so quickly. Once you have made your pitch and once your hosts have thanked you for your ideas, you will be ready to negotiate the swampy helipad again. Waiting for the inbound helicopter, you will show a fellow expert an image of the disemboweled plane on your phone. The CEO will overhear your colleague's reaction and ask to see the screen. He will muster an impromptu and final speech. He will summon his other experts to the edge of the helipad to hear the tale of the ruined airplane. I paraphrase:

> After World War II, an American couple bought a used military seaplane—one of those that can touchdown on both land and water. They set out to fly it around the world accompanied by their two small children. This was a time when Americans believed in their global presence. Being global means heeding no borders. It nurtures the urge to declare that there is one world, one human race. They flew their machine—like an elevated RV—across the Atlantic and beyond Europe.
>
> One afternoon they spotted a cove of coral filled with colorful fish at the edge of the sunburnt desert. The sand was packed enough to receive their vessel, and the upward slope of the shoreline helped bring it to a stop. The family unloaded food and supplies onto the beach, as if for a picnic. They gathered whatever they could to fuel a campfire. They fell asleep under the stars. They believed they were nowhere.
>
> The nomads didn't kill them and, instead, used rounds of gunfire to spark the plane's turn into ruin. The nomads took the travelers as prisoners. They made the weeks-long journey as a caravan to the city where the captives stood before the queen. Only the queen, the nomads believed, possessed the authority to execute trespassers. She thanked the nomads for their time and loyalty and she rewarded them. Impressed by neither their sense of adventure nor their ideal of a single world, the queen didn't have the trespassers killed. Instead, she banished them. And they were forgotten.

The CEO will conclude his story with a smile that attempts to compensate for a story lacking climax or devastation. His smile will betray no irony to a bunch of New Yorkers about to board a helicopter in order to be forgotten. In a matter of weeks, even he will be forgotten.

The new city will require the hiring of thousands of consultants like you. Manifold more will be hired to build and service it. They will build a city not meant for them; their children will come to maintain it, also knowing this city is not for them or for their children. They will struggle to keep the city's walls shiny and its floors free of sand. This new city won't be allowed to grow old or take on the patina of *culture*. It might be for the declared absence of culture that many will come. Like the garden, an invisible regimen of cultivation will keep history out for the sake of permanent prosperity. *There will be nothing to hold you back*.

But all of this for later. First, you need to get back to your cabin. Run through the deck one more time.

Computation

Daniela Fabricius
Justin Joque
Amelyn Ng and John Lewtas

If much of the work of the previous section was concerned with how architectural and other representations are used to steer the minds of investors towards a given future, computation is often presented as a form of world management that bypasses this middleman of human wetware altogether. Why need we resort to the inefficient distribution skills of the market when we can just compute the optimum and proceed from there? This conflict is not novel—its contours were first laid out in the so-called "socialist calculation debate" of the 1920s—but it has recently been rejuvenated thanks to the considerable powers of contemporary computation technologies. For example, Benjamin Bratton has recently argued that, with these technologies, we can now all but achieve what he calls, nodding to this earlier period, "synthetic catallaxy," a phrase indicating his belief that computation makes possible "new forms of pricing and price signaling that include negative externalities and the return of planning as a form of economic intelligence cognizant of its own future."[1]

We open this section with this debate because it quite effectively scrambles our typically adversarial attitude towards calculative reason. Trained humanists that we architects are, our knee jerk reaction to the rising powers of computation is to seek solace in practices—hand-drawing, formal experimentation and the like—that are thought to be the last redoubts of the unmediated and ineffably human. The socialist calculation debate, however, shows that far from being our eternal enemy, computation was once the hammer and sickle that socialist planners wielded to counter the claims of neoliberalism's evilest philosophers of market-hive-mind intelligence. And it is not only the return of a discourse on planning that computation has made possible: from pandemic to climate models, computation has enabled some of the most socially necessary forecasts of our time.

Of course, though, it is not so simple as computation being wholly good or wholly bad. Via the powers of computation, the rich were also able to sequester in their homes as precarious app delivery contract laborers risked COVID to deliver them their groceries. And climate models, by incorporating into their forecasts as-yet-to-be-implemented-at-scale carbon capture and storage technologies, can provide justification for governments to overshoot targets as much as they can for prudent action on climate justice. As is the case with the other practices in this book, then, assessing the impact of computational futurology requires the careful scrutiny of its innerworkings and assumptions, of its socio-economic context, and of the uses to which it is being put. One of these uses is in the domain of architecture. The following essays and interview provide critical insights into architectural computation's past and its possible futures.

---

1 Nils Gilman and Benjamin Bratton, "A New Philosophy of Planetary Computation," *Noema*, October 5, 2022, https://www.noemamagcom/a-new-philosophy-of-planetary-computation/.

Calculating Growth: Prediction and Simulation in Berlin, 1968

Daniela Fabricius

> Jeder Wissenschaftler ist ein idealist. (Every scientist is an idealist.)
> —Welt am Draht (1973), directed by R. W. Fassbinder

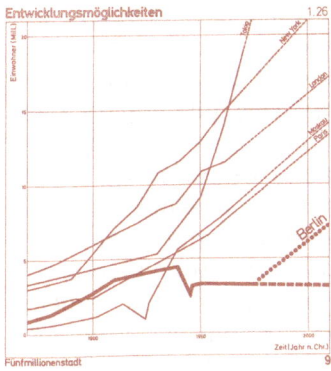

From *Berlin 1995*, Veröffentlichungen zur Architektur 25 (Berlin: TU Berlin, 1969).

The acceleration of the climate crisis, together with the COVID pandemic, have given rise to increasingly anxious discourse around the very fate of human and planetary life. Forecasting has become commonplace, whether it is tracking the local behavior of the latest COVID variant, following real estate and financial markets, watching simulations of rising sea levels, or the daily ritual of live satellite views and granular predictions of local weather. The production and collection of vast amounts of data has multiplied what can be predicted and foreseen, and the capacity and predictive abilities of today's systems are widespread. The collection of information about human habits has also taken a darker turn, as in the manipulation of politics through the algorithms of social media, which have directly threatened the functioning of democratic societies.

This fixation on prediction is in many ways reminiscent of the Cold War era, when existential fears were centered around thermonuclear war, population growth, and resource scarcity. There was a growing sense that the world was more complex and dangerous than humans could adequately grasp, and that modeling and prediction were critical tools to manage these crises and their systematic complexities. Futurology, or "future studies," was born in the 1950s-60s in Western industrialized countries as a science of prediction that was usually applied in the spheres of political and economic planning.[1] Future studies increasingly focused not only on questions of national security and warfare, but also "civilian" problems concerning cities, resources, and populations.[2] A prominent example was the Club of Rome, which was formed in 1968 to model

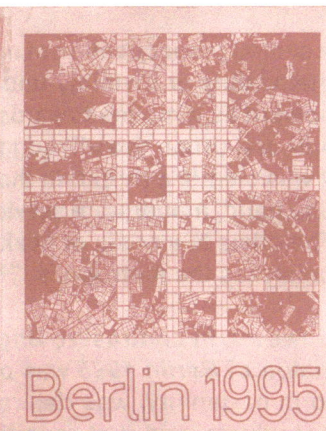

Berlin 1995, Veröffentlichungen zur Architektur 25 (Berlin: TU Berlin, 1969). Title page.

249

and analyze the "technical, social, economic, and political" factors that have interacted to produce what they call the "world problematique."[3] This "problematique," they argued, had resulted in poverty, environmental degradation, and urban sprawl, but also "loss of faith in institutions," "alienation of youth," and "rejection of traditional values."[4] These terms are an oblique reference to the social movements that characterized the late 1960s, and are presented as yet another "problem" to manage and control.

The findings of the Club of Rome, published in The Limits to Growth (1972), predicted that word population and industrial capacity would decline within a century if growth rates in terms of world population, industrialization, pollution, and use of resources did not change. In other words, there would be an end to the centuries of Western economic expansion and growth that followed colonialism and industrialization. Here growth is presented as something that is no longer just a desired economic outcome, but also a potential problem (especially when it came to the growth of populations and cities in poorer countries). The purportedly new goal was now world equilibrium, rather than growth.

Donella H. Meadows et al., *The Limits to Growth: A Report for the Club of Rome's Project on the Predicament of Mankind* (New York: Universe Books), 1972.

The mathematical models of prediction behind *The Limits to Growth* were developed by Jay Forrester, a computer engineer who was by the late 1960s better known as the inventor of system dynamics.[5] Forrester also worked on the urban scale, as in his 1969 *Urban Dynamics*, a study based on computer simulations of a city that claimed to predict the outcome of US urban policies on issues like stagnation and unemployment.[6] The city, and the enormous quantities of statistical data that it is capable of generating, was one of the privileged objects of futurology. In the 1960s, new informational and computational tools of simulation offered the tantalizing possibility that a number of urban variables (poverty, unemployment, economic growth and decline, infrastructure, etc.) could be predicted, managed, and optimized.

Urban prognostication was seductive to architects, and became a source of experimentation in architecture. The period between 1950 and 1970 was also the height of the "scientization" of architecture, planning, and design, as it was influenced by advances in cybernetics, behavioral sciences, prediction modeling, and system dynamics. This shift reflected the rising influence of the technocracy in industrialized nations. The use of these new tools also established a new role for the architect: that of an observer and manager of systems.

Predictive technologies are primarily tools to mitigate risk, and are used by those in power to maintain stability and control. However, the practice of prediction also has the potential to engage new imaginaries by scripting and simulating alternative worlds and possible futures. What would it mean to appropriate technologies of prediction for utopian purposes, rather than being determined by dominant economic and political scripts? This question lay at the heart of *Berlin 1995*, a 244-page book self-published in 1969, which documented a seminar at the Technical University of Berlin led by Oswald Mathias Ungers and his assistants Tilman Heyde and Michael Wegener.[7] The premise of *Berlin 1995* was that the city would continue to grow until it reached five million residents by the year 1995, restoring Berlin's population close to its pre-war numbers. This optimistic vision proposed a stunning new political reality for divided Berlin: that of a dense, unified city. This, of course, was far from the reality of Berlin after 1961. The construction of the Berlin Wall severed street and train infrastructures, rerouted the circulation of the city, and left vast gaps in the urban fabric. Having served as a showcase for capitalism and the West, West Berlin was now a city that was cut off from the booming West German economy. By the late 1960s, West Berlin's population and economy were in decline.[8]

A central preoccupation of urban prediction is planning for, and imagining, growth;[9] The graph that visibly or invisibly underlies most urban planning proposals is a line angled steadily upward as it moves towards the future. Such a graph was the basis for *Berlin 1995*. For the authors, urban growth suggested both opportunity and potential catastrophe. For Ungers, it was clearly a threat: in the book's preface he writes: "Constant population growth on the one hand, inadequate services on the other, lead to the gradual collapse of the metropolis. The crisis is a crisis of peak load. The inability of systems to function when overloaded... paralyzes the metropolis."[10]

However, in contrast to Ungers's model of the city as a space of systemic breakdown, the vision of *Berlin 1995* was one of a unified and deliriously connected city. Growth, in the form of density, was desired by the students. The narrative of *Berlin 1995* begins with a coordinate grid that reunifies the divided city. This grid is repeated at every scale, from

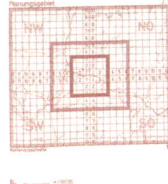

Coordinate grid, *Berlin 1995*

the city to the block. Street names, and their historical signification, would no longer be needed – an address would now be made up of coordinates. Life would occur in a data grid, and the grid would determine everything.[11] The coordinates were superimposed over Berlin, with the center (0,0) at the Brandenburg Gate (which was also where the Berlin Wall was located). The authors do not propose to eradicate the existing urban fabric; instead, at the smaller scale, the grid is shown as capable of a series of local deformations to accommodate the city.

The Cartesian coordinate system is the preferred graphical expression of mathematical prediction, with the ability to match performance (the y-axis) with time (the x-axis). The coordinate system, as the philosopher Sybille Krämer argues, is a mathematical space of potential.[12] The grid acts as the intermediary between an abstract concept and the real city, as this infrastructure creates the framework – or one could say the mainframe – for a maximum of simulated futures. But the urban grid is more than a passive framework in which events simply "happen"; it is also a system of codes, rules, and limitations that ultimately determine growth in a highly controlled manner. Furthermore, it is difficult not to imagine this diagrammatic overlay of the city as an echo of past abstractions, such as the flattening of urban territory into a series of coordinates under the gaze of aerial bombing campaigns. The grid is also redundant.[13] Redundancy is used to calculate maximum certainty and return, but it also runs counter to optimization. This is especially evident when confronted with the extraordinary drawings in *Berlin 1995* showing dense, overlapping transportation systems. These images serve as a representation of a state of overdeveloped infrastructure that exceeds human need. One can only imagine the anxiety that the underdevelopment of West Berlin in the 1960s caused in order for such density to have been proposed.

Student project, *Berlin 1995*, (Catherine Hoja, Bahnhof Zoo).

With the framework for an urban simulation having been established, the authors test two possible scenarios: the *Bandstadt* (Ribbon City) and *Flächenstadt* (Planar City). Both proposals have a similar representational strategy: a dense network is shown overlaid with an orthogonal megastructural plan in relief. An image of it shown on the cover of the book appears as a large game board laid over Berlin, functioning as a "connector" between East and West.[15] In the *Ribbon City*, a grid composed of basic megastructural "units" was placed over Berlin's former center. In contrast to this centralized model, the *Planar City* gives equal weight to all parts of Berlin. This plan, with strips 10 to 12 kilometers long, ties together different urban nodes, while the areas left over become green recreational zones. The networks are shown evenly dispersed in a drawing of intense graphical thickness. The argument seems to be that Berlin would be so hyper-connected that it would no longer need a center.

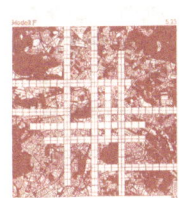
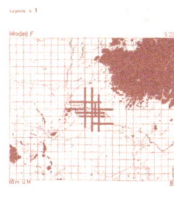

Model F ("Flächenstadt"), *Berlin 1995*

Simulation, we are reminded here, does not necessarily mean adapting to optimal or even functional results. The objective was to create a field of "densification zones," to provide for all moments at once as opposed to an ideal state, to fill the entire urban (and graphic) field, even at the expense of legibility and efficiency. The philosopher Vilém Flusser has suggested a close connection between density and simulation. According to Flusser, the "alternative worlds" emerging from computers "are nothing but computed point elements… hazy constructs floating in nothingness."[16] This results in what he considers a modern paradox – that in the translation from the continuous world into the world of numbers, the seamless nature of what Descartes called the *res extensa* is lost.[17] Resemblance to reality is measured by density or the degree of resolution.[18] Filling in the gaps with information becomes conflated with the real.

A dialectic is thus formed between – on the one hand – the coordinate system in which every place in the city is represented by a point – and the method of filling between the points (or "stuffing the intervals between the numbers," as Flusser puts it), which results in a fixed, extensive reality.[19] For the authors of *Berlin 1995*, the possibility of switching between the simulated and the real is left open.

But was it really a simulation? This project was created at the cusp of the transition from architectural simulation as static representation, to simulation as a time-based process.[20] It was no longer enough to recreate the world in space; through calculation the world would also be predicted as it changes through time. At best, *Berlin 1995* aspired to what technological simulation might one day provide. Simulation is not simply imagining a future or alternative world; it is equally grounded in both the science of prediction and the art of the imaginary. In many ways, however, the desired prognosis came true – by 1995 Berlin was a unified city.

The intricate and technologically precise drawings of *Berlin 1995* appear to be not unlike the surface of a microchip: a small world in itself, yet in truth a crucial part of a much larger system linking space and information. The media theorist Friedrich Kittler has made the comparison between the city and a microchip ("Entire cities made of silicon, silicon oxide, and gold wire have…arisen"); he argues that in both, information circulates through "the play between commands, addresses, and data."[21] In this suggestive image of the city as a vast medium by which to generate and transmit information, it appears not only as a simulation, but also as a model of the electronic media that enable the processing of futures. It is not enough, in other words, to suggest that the city is one of several outputs generated by some imagined computer program: the city itself should resemble the otherwise invisible inner workings of that process.

Simulation is not only a departure from the real; it is a "fast-forward" of events that would otherwise play themselves out in real time. This results in what the economist Elena Esposito describes as "time binding," where the uncertainty of the future is turned into a potential resource (Esposito uses financial instruments as an example).[22] *Berlin 1995* was a form of science fiction, based on a narrative in which multiple possibilities were presented at every step. It suggests that history itself is an open-ended process with missed chances and alternative trajectories that can be retraced through feedback.

Jay W. Forrester, *Urban Dynamics* (Cambridge, Mass.: MIT Press, 1969).

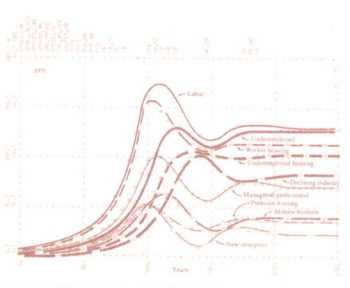

The authors of *Berlin 1995* describe their project as a *Planungssimulation* (planning simulation), a term that was apparently new in West Germany at the time.[23] "By 'simulation,' we…mean the playing out of a planning process in a representable expenditure of time. Thereby even complicated processes like the planning of a large city, which in reality takes decades . . . can be represented as if in time-lapse."[24] Wegener cites the work of Forrester as one of the most influential sources for this concept.[25] Simulation, as it was used in 1969, was still associated with computer science and mathematics, and not yet the influential (and critical) theory of simulation that was proposed by Jean Baudrillard in the late 1970s.[26] By the time Baudrillard published *Simulacra and Simulation* (1981), the seeming indistinction between prognosis and planning was already a lost space for utopian possibility.

Berlin 1995 in many ways reflects the competing goals of the future studies movement in West Germany, which mirrored political discussions of the late 1960s and early 1970s.[27] Futurology in West Germany was roughly divided into two camps: on the one hand a leftist, utopian version; on the other a market-based, neo-conservative form of cybernetics research. Among the utopian researchers was the journalist, historian, and anti-nuclear activist Robert Jungk (who also lectured at the TU Berlin), and the political scientist Ossip Flechtheim, who is credited with having coined the term "futurology." Jungk and Flechtheim took a "historical-dialectic approach to science," and avoided government participation, focusing instead on planning, participation, civil society, and the new social movements.[28] A more positivist approach was represented by the think tank Zentrum Berlin für Zukunftsforschung (ZBZ), co-founded by TU Berlin sociologist Helmut Klages in 1968. This organization worked with the support and collaboration of the Federal Government, including the Berlin Simulation Model (BESI) project (1969), which was meant "for studying the development and restructuring of large cities."[29] A leading member was the aeronautical engineer Heinz Hermann Koelle, who supported computer-based systems analysis for implementing political and planning decisions. As the historian Elke Seefried puts it, "It is clear that it was no longer the object – the "what" – that was decisive but the "how": any topic appeared to be workable because in the centre of focus was the method, and here, above all, the computer-based simulation model."[30]

There was a dark side to this use of simulation, as Rainer Werner Fassbinder portrayed in his 1973 science-fiction television film *Welt am Draht* (World on a wire).[31] The timing of Fassbinder's film was clearly linked to the political

Still from *Welt am Draht* (dir. Werner Rainer Fassbinder, 1973)

situation in West Germany in the 1970s, where both government and industry were using information technologies for security and profit. One of the most controversial government projects was the *Rasterfahndung* (raster dragnet) method, initially developed to find Red Army Faction members, which was used to search vast information databases on German citizens for potential criminal activity. *Welt am Draht* describes a simulated world unwittingly inhabited by 10,000 people, created by a computer at the fictional Institut für Kybernetik und Zukunftsforschung (Institute for Cybernetics and Future Research). There the "Simulacron" experiment, created with public funds for the "betterment of human society," was also secretly being used for private purposes in order to accurately predict (and dominate) the future of the aluminum industry. The same system used to control the future of investments was thus also used to track and simulate human lives, closing the divide between social-utopian and market-driven uses of simulation.

Rather than seeing *Berlin 1995* as a literal expression of the desire for a technocratic future, one can view it as a way to make manifest the contradictions within Berlin and West German society – the divisions not only of east and west but also enclaves of social control and consumption. For the students with utopian aspirations, the conditions for a different future still had to be created. The equalizing function of the grid symbolically eradicates differences by connecting all points in the city. At the same time, the city is a simulation; the problem therein lies not with the question of what is real but with *who* is in control. As in the film *World on a Wire*, one has to assume that there are always managers and technocrats pushing the buttons. Perhaps the political aspiration of *Berlin 1995*, then, was that the future could be controlled at all, that the tools used by technocrats could be taken over by the students to imagine their own destinies. Could the technologies of simulation, perfected during the Cold War in order to predict and control future conflicts, be used to erase the geographies it created, to provide a space for new social and architectural possibilities?

Berlin 1968

The critical aspirations and contradictions of *Berlin 1995* can be better understood when viewed in light of the intense political environment at the TU Berlin in the late 1960s. Several of the protagonists who had imagined this hyper-development of the city were also publishing pamphlets challenging the excess rationality of West Berlin's urban planning. "Science, Whore of the Capitalists!" – the title of a 1969 article in a student magazine – sums up the attitude quite succinctly.[32] Recalling the political events of this period allows one

Ernst Reuter Platz, Berlin, 1966. The TU Berlin Architecture Department building is at the top right.

to appreciate how this momentum built up in only a few years. On June 2nd, 1967, the university student Benno Ohnesorg was killed by police during a demonstration against the Shah of Iran's visit to West Berlin. This event, which took place just blocks from the TU Berlin, had a catalyzing effect on the West German student movement. Several of Ungers's students attended this demonstration, and he cautiously endorsed their political engagement.[33] Increasingly, however, the overlaps between Ungers' research and his students' activism caused friction, and by 1969, Ungers' private opinion of the politicized students had become embittered.

Some of the more radical students and assistants of Ungers participated in the so-called Kritische Universität, a student-organized series of seminars at the Free University in Berlin in collaboration with the TU Berlin.[34] Michael Wegener's photograph appears in a collage on the cover of the Winter 1967/68 pamphlet. Of particular significance for the students enrolled at the Technical University was an Adornian critique of the instrumentalization of knowledge "for inhuman and destructive uses."[35] According to the pamphlet, political consciousness could be introduced to architecture through collaboration with economists and sociologists, steering architecture away from the functionalism of technocrats towards social-oriented praxis.[36]

At the beginning of the fall semester of 1968, architecture students from the TU Berlin formed a group called "Aktion 507," which organized an exhibition called *Diagnose Zum Bauen in West-Berlin*.[37] Students held the exhibition in the raw concrete structure of Hans Scharoun's 1966–1969 building for the architecture school, which made it a direct comment on what they saw as an obsolete and apolitical culture of artistic architectural design.[38] A manifesto and comprehensive booklet of over 100 pages was published with the exhibition.[39] The cover shows four interlocking arms, labeled "building department, architects, speculators,

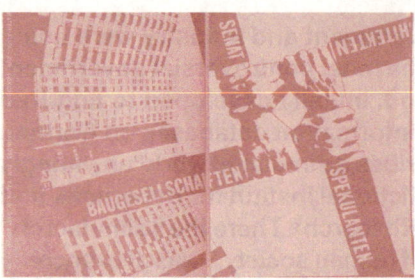

Diagnose exhibition poster and book cover showing buildings from the Märkisches Viertel in the background. 1968. Ungers Archiv für Architekturwissenschaft.

construction companies," laid across images of residential high-rises in the Märkisches Viertel, a low-income neighborhood in West Berlin.

Diagnose took special aim at the Märkisches Viertel, the notorious 17,000-unit housing complex built between 1964 and 1974.[40] Ungers was one of twenty-two architects who built towers there, and several students involved had worked with him on the Märkisches Viertel as assistants. Audio recordings were played of student interviews with residents of the neighborhood. The exhibition showed abstracted photographs of rows of buildings and gritty everyday scenes of life. If *Berlin 1995* was a simulation, this was a project about "the real," as the raw concrete walls and documentary materials attested. The students viewed these urban contradictions as potential sites for revolutionary change.

When it came to the question of rationalism, however, a dilemma arose. Even if the students criticized capitalist rationality following the theories of the Frankfurt School, they nevertheless embraced a rationalist architecture. As one student, Ingrid Krau, later put it, "We were *Aufklärer* [Enlighteners], who believed in the power of technological and scientific progress." "We were rationalists."[41] "[We] thought in technocratic terms to a large extent, and reduced the inhabitants to their objectifiable, plannable, and summable needs."[42] The problem with the Märkisches Viertel, then, was not that it was a product of too much rationality, but too little: it had been designed according to arbitrary formal and aesthetic criteria without consideration for "objective" social data.

Optimized planning

In 1968, another kind of simulation was also underway. Ungers, together with the business economist Horst Albach, was asked by the building department of West Berlin to collaborate on an optimization study of the city's housing projects.[43] As part of an effort to create a more objective approach, architects and economists would work together to translate spatial values into numerical ones that could be calculated. For this simulation a computer *was* used (an IBM 7090, located at the University of Bonn). One of the case studies looked at by the researchers was the Märkisches Viertel. This had great personal resonance for Ungers, who claimed that the critical public reaction to the project was one of the reasons that he stopped building for fifteen years. He would later speak of the painful stigma of that project, which he claimed he had designed with the best "knowledge and intentions" [*Wissen und Gewissen*].[44] According to Ungers, it was this "naïve" ethical relationship between *Wissen* and *Gewissen* that had apparently led to the failed design of the project. But this new study, which took place during the turbulent political context of 1968, suggests an equally complicated relationship between rationality and morality, based on a misplaced faith in the powers of calculation.

An early version of the project was presented in 1968 at the TU Berlin in a summer conference called "The Computer in the University."[45] Although Ungers would later claim that the study was arguing against building high-rise housing, the students nevertheless viewed it as technocratic and opportunistic. They reacted to the project with rage, and interrupted the presentation with hissing and shouting.[46] The research presented was later published in the 1969 book *Optimale Wohngebietsplanung* [Optimal Residential Planning].[47] This reevaluation of housing in West Berlin did not take into consideration the recent criticism of these projects, but instead used scientific methods for justifying and "optimizing" public expenditure. While this study was published several years before the so-called *Legitimationskrise* of the 1970s – a term used to describe the loss of faith in West German public institutions – it betrays a similar anxiety about the role of the state in providing services and institutions. The application of economic tools developed for the private sector, in a simulated cost optimization of public expenditure, hints at the increasing privatization of urban development in West Germany in the 1980s.

Comparison of gird systems, from Horst Albach and Oswald Mathias Anders, *Optimale Wohngebietsplanung*, Band 1, (Wiesbaden: Betriebswirtschaftlicher Verlag Dr. Th. Gabler, 1969).

Ungers hired the same assistants who wrote *Berlin 1995* (Wegener and Heyde) to work on the study, and one can even see that some of the graphics were the same. But an entirely different form of prediction is promoted here than the one seen in *Berlin 1995*. While the students preclude the possibility of an optimum in *Berlin 1995*, preferring to play within the parameters of multiple simulations, Ungers and Albach worked to find a single "solution." This solution was based almost entirely on the demands of financing, and not the needs of residents. To express this mathematically, they translate different markers of housing quality into quantifiable information, even while they admit that these depended on "subjective" values.[48] In a series of algebraic manipulations, a number of variables were introduced: building area, code constraints, number of residents, number of floors, etc. – which were then calculated on a computer. The end result of these manipulations was a single equation used to arrive at an "ideal" housing model with an optimum shape (the hexagon) and building height (six stories). Evidence for this is provided in a graph laconically entitled "Absolute optimum of the optimum combination."

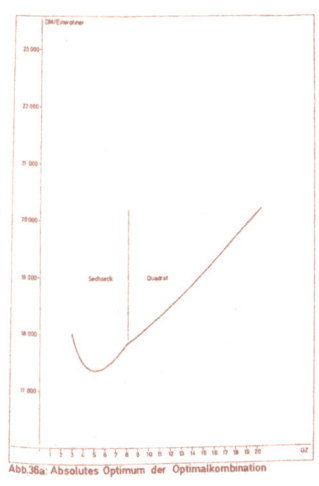

"Absolute optimum of the optimum" graph, from Horst Albach and Oswald Mathias Anders, *Optimale Wohngebiets-planung*, Band 1, (Wiesbaden: Betriebswirtschaftlicher Verlag Dr. Th. Gabler, 1969).

Having established an ideal urban form in a virtual space, Albach and Ungers use the same methods to reassess existing housing projects in West Berlin, including the Märkisches Viertel, according to a simulated "rebuilding." The project of Ungers and Albach was less the anticipation for the future than an attempt at correcting and managing the past. In processing the Märkisches Viertel through the machine of calculation, they perhaps hoped for a different outcome. Going through several hundred iterations using the data obtained from the neighborhood, they determine that an optimized version of the project would have cost up to 25 percent less. Social criticism of the project is never addressed.

These equations, and the computer that processed them, could be used to calculate a complex number of variables, but did not yet have the flexibility of later models allowing for multiple solutions.[49] The book shows all of the raw parametric data generated by the calculations, but in the end the project was still a search for a single optimum.[50] The authors warn that this would reduce the average space allowed per resident to 15.14 square meters – which clearly shows that not every significant factor, especially this most important one – could be accounted for.

In the unpublished second volume to Optimale Wohngebietsplanung, Albach and Ungers tried to address the problem encountered in the first study by focusing on questions of "values":

> This study begins with the hypothesis that the "users" are themselves capable of giving information about their ideas of housing values. At the same time, one must nevertheless be aware that the formulation of goals, preferences, and criteria, on which a choice is based, is especially difficult for most people. Their consciousness is not so far developed that they have fully rationalized these subjective decision-making processes.[51]

Here they delve deeper into the territory of social "immeasurables" and seeming complexity by trying to rationalize the consciousness of human subjects. In projecting and rationalizing desire itself, the hope was to remove uncertainty, to create a systemic stability in which the spending of the state and the "unpredictable" needs of the residents are in equilibrium.

Wicked problems

The 1970s marked a significant turning point for designers who were interested in methods of prediction: the deeper they got into the complexity of the world – whether at the large scale or the small scale – the clearer it became that there were limits to the technologies that tried to model and emulate this complexity. In 1972 Horst Rittel, a former professor at the Ulm School for Design, proposed the idea of the "Wicked Problem" – a planning problem of such great complexity and urgency that it cannot be fully resolved or calculated, or adequately addressed through "tame" scientific means.[52] The theory of the wicked problem was developed in response to Rittel's sense of the increased social and economic complexity of planning issues by the end of the 1960s.[53] While at Ulm, Rittel had written of tasks "for which there is no merely intuitive solution. The objects have proportions which demand a rational penetration, because the costs of a failed design are too high."[54] Here he is referring above all to social costs, not to economic ones – this could mean "defense strategies, development of Third World Countries, projects of atomic technologies and space travel."[55] He later describes the "era of disappointment" that followed the first generation of the systems approach, and sees this as tied to the "paradox of rationality": that the effort to both fully predict and limit or contain the consequences of design-making is inherently contradictory.[56] With the concept of the wicked problem Rittel was expressing the fundamental paradox of the *risk society:* the awareness of uncertainty that coexists with the scientific means to try to manage it.

Ulrich Beck's notion of the risk society was similarly developed in the context of the late Cold War in West Germany. The growing awareness of environmental devastation in the 1970s, and the 1986 Chernobyl nuclear disaster, emphasized the extent to which risks were very much human-produced, and to which humans are accountable:

> Under the surface of risk calculation new kinds of *industrialized, decision-produced incalculabilities and threats* are spreading within the globalization of high-risk industries, whether for warfare or welfare purposes ... *Along with the growing capacity of technical options* (Zweckrationalität) *grows the incalculability of their consequences.*[57]

Beck argues that the calculation of risk, together with the increased reliance on technology, had reached a horizon where it lays beyond the possibilities of calculability, in spite of the growing capacity of computation. This suggests something almost like Immanuel Kant's sublime of the mathematically incalculable. This critique of the limits of prediction and the ability to manage risk was arguably in keeping with postmodernist challenges to the sciences and the boundaries of knowledge. This has given rise to, among other things, the notion of non-human agency, which remains an alluring topic for architects and theorists. Bruno Latour's actant suggests a force beyond human agency, one that is unruly, messy, and humbling, and has inspired false humility and apologies for being human.

Nevertheless, The interrelated forces that drive today's intersecting crises – environmental pollution, gender and racial discrimination, food scarcity, eroding physical and social infrastructures to name just a few – describe layers of human accountability. It is clear that these are not mysterious forces at play (which often suggests metaphors for the invisible hand of the market), but human policies and decisions that have given rise to cascading crises. The urgent nature of climate change in particular, but also the associated causes and effects, have arguably ushered in a new focus on prediction and calculation – perhaps because there seems to be no other option. This is a potential area for design to play a role in imagining alternative futures.

Oswald Mathias Ungers, Residential Units, Eichhorster Weg 32–42, Märkisches Viertel (1964–1967). Ungers Archiv für Architekturwissenschaft.

1 The Rand Corporation especially devoted a number of studies to futurology, most notably by Herman Kahn, whose publications include *On Thermonuclear War* (1960) and *Thinking about the Unthinkable* (1962).

2 For instance, in 1965 the Commission on the Year 2000, led by Daniel Bell, was formed in response to "fractious problems" such as "Negro rights, poverty pollution, urban sprawl." One of the works that emerged from the Commission was a book by Herman Kahn and Anthony Wiener, *The Year 2000: A Framework for Speculation on the Next Thirty-Three Years* (New York: Macmillan, 1967). Similarly, Daniel Bell published *The Coming of Post-Industrial Society: A Venture in Social Forecasting* (New York: Basic Books, 1973). See Wendell Bell, *Foundations of Future Studies: Human Science for a New Era: History, Purpose, Knowledge* (New Brunswick, NJ: Transaction Publishers, 2003).

3 D. Meadows, D. Meadow, J. Randers, and W. Behrens, "Forward," *The Limits to Growth: A Report for the Club of Rome's Project on the Predicament of Mankind* (New York: Universe Books, 1972), 10–11.

4 Ibid.

5 In a series of books – *Industrial Dynamics* (1961), *Urban Dynamics* (1969), and later *World Dynamics* (1971) – Forrester suggested that extremely complex social and economic environments could be modeled, analyzed, and simulated.

6 Forrester came to the controversial conclusion that the urban policies used in American cities, like those that provided resources for the poor, would cause further urban decline. Most controversial was his "finding" that further investment in low-income housing would be damaging to urban growth. The seeming neutrality or objectivity of these planning scenarios should be seriously questioned. Jay Forrester, *Urban Dynamics* (Cambridge, MA: MIT Press, 1969).

7 *Berlin 1995. Planungsmodelle für eine Fünfmillionenstadt im Übergang zu den siebziger Jahren*, Veröffentlichungen zur Architektur 25, 1969. The English title would be Berlin 1995: *Planning Models for a City of Five Million in Transition to the 1970s. Berlin 1995* was one of twenty-seven experimental publications in the series *Veröffentlichungen zur Architektur* (Publications on architecture) that documented the research of Ungers's seminars at the TU Berlin between 1965 and 1969.The Veröffentlichungen zur Architektur series also documented research done by Ungers's students at Cornell University. See "Lernen von O. M. Ungers," ed. Erika Mühlthaler, special issue, ARCH+ 181/182 (December 2006), and Jasper Cepl, "Oswald Mathias Ungers und seine Schule," in *Architekturschulen: Programm – Pragmatik – Propaganda*, ed. Klaus Jan Philipp and Kerstin Renz.

8 Berlin had around two million residents in 1969. In order to illustrate the scale (and possible economic future) of the new Berlin, the authors compare it to a map of the Ruhr region in West Germany.

9 A notable exception is the "Shrinking Cities" theory, as inspired by Oswald Mathias Ungers's influential "Berlin as Green Archipelago" project. Oswald Mathias Ungers with Rem Koolhaas, Peter Riemann, Hans Kolhoff, and Arthur Ovaska, *The City in the City—Berlin: A Green Archipelago*, 1977. See also Sebastien Marot and Florian Wertweck, *The City in the City: Berlin: A Green Archipelago* (Zürich: Lars Müller, 2013), and Philipp Oswalt, *Shrinking Cities* (Ostfildern-Ruit: Hatje Cantz, 2005).

10 When *Berlin 1995* was published, Ungers had already been influenced by the urban problems he witnessed in the United States when he described a potential systemic crisis facing Berlin. Ungers, preface to *Berlin 1995*, 7. All translations mine.

11 The authors were inspired by the work of architects like Ludwig Hilberseimer and Fritz Haller, who proposed a similar coordinate system for urban models. An influential precedent was Fritz Haller's 1968 "Totale Stadt," which is reproduced in *Berlin 1995*. The authors include an example from *Totale Stadt – Ein Modell* (1968) in which a city for six million is shown placed over the grid of Berlin. Haller shows an urban space defined by graphic systems that can be multiplied to accommodate various scales. Haller also uses a universal coordinate system, which in Haller's city serves as the basis for a symmetrically formed plan of circuitry for different modes of transportation.

12 Sybille Krämer, "'Epistemology of the Line': Reflections on the Diagrammatical Mind," in Olga Pombo and Alexander Gerner, eds., *Studies in Diagrammatology and Diagram Praxis* (London: College Publications, 2009), 13–38.

13 This criticism comes from Michael Wegener himself. Interview with the author, April 10, 2013, Dortmund.

14 The linear city is a model that has haunted the avant-garde, with its most famous manifestations appearing during the 1930s with Milyutin's Sotsgorod (1930), and plans for Magnitogorsk by Ernst May, Ivan Leonidov, and others. Leonidov's gridded plan for Magnitogorsk, with its checkerboard pattern, in particular resembles the plan proposed in *Berlin 1995*. These linear cities had been designed with the industrial city in mind, separating residential, industrial, and transportation areas. While *Berlin 1995* borrows the linear model, its goal in designing a post-industrial city was to combine as many programs as possible to create density, growth, and connectivity.

15 The authors suggest that the linear version could extend beyond the city and even be connected to other similar urban zones in the region, repeating the grid pattern at another scale.

16 "Nichts anderes sind als komputierte Punktelemente, weil sie im Nichts schwebende Nebelgebilde sind." Vilém Flusser, "Digitaler Schein," *ARCH+* 111 (March 1992), 26–30; 26. My translation.

17 Ibid.

18 "Dichte der Streuung." Ibid.

19 "Stopfen der Intervalle zwischen den Zahlen." Ibid.

20 Computer simulation is a "leap from a timeless to a time-contingent technology. It is this temporal aspect that distinguishes computer simulation from inherited concepts of simulation in architecture." Andrea Gleiniger and Georg Vrachliotis, editorial, in *Simulation: Presentation Technique and Cognitive Method*, ed. Andrea Gleiniger and Georg Vrachliotis (Basel; Boston: Birkhäuser, 2008), 9. English in original.

21 Friedrich Kittler and Matthew Griffin, "The City Is a Medium," *New Literary History* 27, no. 4 (1996): 717–729; 721–722.

22 Elena Esposito, *The Future of Futures: The Time of Money in Financing and Society* (Cheltenham; Northampton, MA: Edward Elgar, 2011), 21–25.

23 "I think that we invented the word '*Planungssimulation*' at that time – today it evokes 3,240 entries in Google." Wegener cites various examples from operations and systems research as influential, including the work of Ludwig von Bertalanffy, Norbert Wiener, and Talcott Parssons. Michael Wegener, email to the author on August 9, 2013.

24 "Unter Simulation verstehen wir...das Durchspielen eines Planungsablaufs bei vertretbarem Zeitaufwand. Dabei lassen sich sogar komplizierte Vorgänge wie die Planung einer großen Stadt, die in Wirklichkeit Jahrzehnte dauern . . . wie im Zeitraffer darstellen und in groben Zügen anschaulich machen." Tilman Heyde and Michael Wegener, Introduction to *Berlin 1995*, 9.

25 "Although [Jay Forrester's] *Urban Dynamics* and *Simulation* appeared only in 1969, when our project was nearing completion, the students I worked with were familiar with these new ideas and shared my enthusiasm about them." Michael Wegener, email to author, citing Jay Forrester, *Urban Dynamics* (Cambridge, MA: MIT Press, 1969).

26 Jean Baudrillard, *Simulacra and Simulation*, trans. Sheila Faria Glaser (1981; repr., Ann Arbor: University of Michigan Press, 1994). Baudrillard published materials from the book in the late 1970s, before its publication.

27 Karlheinz Steinmüller, "Zukunftsforschung in Deutschland – Versuch eines historischen Abrisses (Teil 1)," *Zeitschrift für Zukunftsforschung*, vol. 1 (2012). http://www.zeitschrift-zukunftsforschung.de/ausgaben/2012/1/3411. Last accessed July 23, 2016. See also Elke Seefried, "Steering the Future. The Emergence of "Western" Futures Research and its Production of Expertise, 1950s to Early 1970s," *European Journal of Futures Research* 2, 29 (2014).

28 Seefried.

29 Ibid, 7.

30 Ibid.

31 R. W. Fassbinder, *Welt am Draht* (1973). The film was based on Daniel Galouye's 1964 science fiction novel *Simulacron 3*.

32 Anonymous, "Wissenschaft, Hure der Kapitalisen!" in *Anrisse* 78 (November 6, 1969): 2–4. Cited in Cepl, "Oswald Mathias Ungers und seine Schule," 245.

33 See *Lernen von O. M. Ungers* and Cepl, "Oswald Mathias Ungers und seine Schule." See also Ungers interviewed in "Studenten – Unruhen – Ursache oder Indiz sich anbahnender Umwälzungen? Anrisse – Gespräch mit dem Dekan der Fakultät für Architektur, Prof. O. M. Ungers," *Anrisse* 59 (July 1967): 6–10, TU Berlin Universitätsarchiv.

34 *Kritische Universität. Freie Studienorganisation der Studenten in den Hoch- und Fachschulen von Westberlin. Programm und Verzeichnis der Studienveranstaltungen im Wintersemester 1967/68* (Berlin: AStA der Freien Universität Berlin, Politische Abteilung), 2. Private archive of Michael Wegener. All translations mine.

35 Ibid., 13.

36 "Architektur und Gesellschaft," in ibid., 63–65.

37 The exhibition was a response to the "Berliner Bauwochen" (Berlin Building Weeks) hosted by the city's Senate for Housing and Development. Ironically, the Senate ended up funding the *Diagnose* exhibition. "Städte-Bau. West Berlin. Slums Verschoben," *Der Spiegel* (September 9, 1968): 134–138.

38 "Last week, in a half-finished lecture-room of the Technical University, they glued large photographs to particleboard, constructed a wooden scaffolding for graphical representations, and installed the speaker systems from which the sound scenery for the protest exhibition *Diagnose* would drone. The spoken accusations of inhabitants of a satellite-city, recorded on tape, and the slide projections on raw concrete, are to impress upon the visitors the stone deserts that are the new settlements in the peripheries of Berlin. The triste concrete façades of the 'Märkisches Viertel,' for instance . . . the paradigm for anti-social housing construction." Ibid., 134. My translations. See also Hans Stimmann, "Wohngebirge für die neue Gesellschaft, Megastrukturen und Eskapismus: Was bleibt von der Architektur der 68er?" *Die Welt*, March 28, 2008.

39 *Diagnose zum Bauen in West-Berlin. Materialien zur Diskussion* (Berlin: 1968), unpaginated, Ungers Archiv für Architekturwissenschaft.

40 In the 1970s, the housing complex became a cause for the Left, including Ulrike Meinhof and other future RAF members, who were involved in the organization Arbeitskreis Mieten und Wohnen Märkisches Viertel. Meinhof was arrested while occupying an empty factory in the area in May, 1970. See Ulrike Meinhof, "Vorläufiges Strategie – Papier Märkisches Viertel," in Johannes Beck et al., eds., *"Jetzt reden wir": Betroffene des Märkischen Viertels. Wohnste sozial, haste die Qual* (Hamburg: Rohwolt, 1975).

41 Ingrid Krau, "Die Zeit der Diagnose," *Stadtbauwelt* 80 (1983): 340–345.343. My translations.

42 Ibid., 342.

43 Horst Albach (1931-2021) taught economics at the Rheinischen Friedrich-Wilhelms-University Bonn, and served on the advisory council for the German Ministry of Economics, as well as the boards of several West German corporations.

44 Ungers in Brigitte Jacob et al., eds., *40 Jahre Märkisches Viertel: Geschichte und Gegenwart einer Großsiedlung* (Berlin: Jovis, 2004), 183-184.

45 Participants in "The Computer in the University" conference included Max Bense, Max Bill, cybernetic artist and author Herbert W. Franke, American computer scientist J. C. R. Licklider, and the German computer inventor Konrad Zuse. Albach and Ungers presented their work at a panel called "Manipulation of Complex Systems by the Use of the Computer," which also featured Aaron Fleisher and Nicholas Negroponte. *The Computer in the University/Der Komputer in der Universität: Joint Summer Conference, Technische Universität Berlin, July 22 to August 2, 1968* (Berlin: Technische Universität, 1968).

46 The students also accused Albach and Ungers of withholding scientific evidence, and stole the research materials after the lecture, claiming they were public property. Thomas Sieverts, Oswald Mathias Ungers, and Georg Wittwer in conversation with Nikolaus Kuhnert, "'Das war eine ungeheuer kreative Situation . . .' Die vergessene Reformdiskussion der 60er Jahre," *Stadtbauwelt* 76 (*Bauwelt* 48), 73 (December 24, 1982): 369–392.

47 Horst Albach and O. M. Ungers, *Optimale Wohngebietsplanung. Band I: Analyse, Optimierung und Vergleich der Kosten städlicher Wohngebiete* (Wiesbaden: Betriebswirtschaftlicher Verlag Gabler, 1969). A second volume of the book was planned but never published outside of the university: O. M. Ungers and Horst Albach, *Optimale Wohngebietsplanung. Band II: Der Wohnwert Städtischer Wohngebiete. Faktorenanalyse zur Bestimmung einer Wohnwertfunktion* (Bonn: Universität Bonn, Betriebswirtschaftliche Abteilung, 1968). Private archive of Michael Wegener.
48 Introduction, Ibid., unpaginated.
49 This is not to suggest that the "flexibility" of parametric systems should be idealized, as they are accompanied by their own ideological and technical limitations.
50 Aside from being six stories tall and hexagonal, the units should have 93 residents and would cost 17,376 DM per resident to build. Ibid., 201.
51 Albach and Ungers, *Optimale Wohngebietsplanung. Band II*, 7. My translation.
52 Horst Rittel, "On the Planning Crisis: Systems Analysis of the First and Second Generations." Reprinted from: *Bedrifts Økonomen* (Norway), No. 8, October, 1972. Reprint 107. Berkeley: University of California at Berkeley, Institute of Urban and Regional Development.
53 Prologue, and "Reflections on the Scientific and Political Significance of Decision Theory," in Jean-Pierre Protzen and David J. Harris, *The Universe of Design: Horst Rittel's Theories of Design and Planning* (London: Routledge, 2010).
54 Horst Rittel, "Zu den Arbeitshypothesen der Hochschule für Gestaltung in Ulm," *Werk* 48 (1961): 281–283; 282. My translations.
55 "Reflections on the Scientific and Political Significance of Decision Theory," 24.
56 Rittel, "On the Planning Crisis," 390–392.
57 Ulrich Beck, *Risk Society: Towards a New Modernity*, trans. Mark Ritter (London; Newbury Park, CA: Sage Publications, 1992), 22. Italics in original. First published in German as *Risikogesellschaft: Auf dem Weg in eine andere Moderne* (Frankfurt am Main: Suhrkamp, 1986).

Interview   Justin Joque

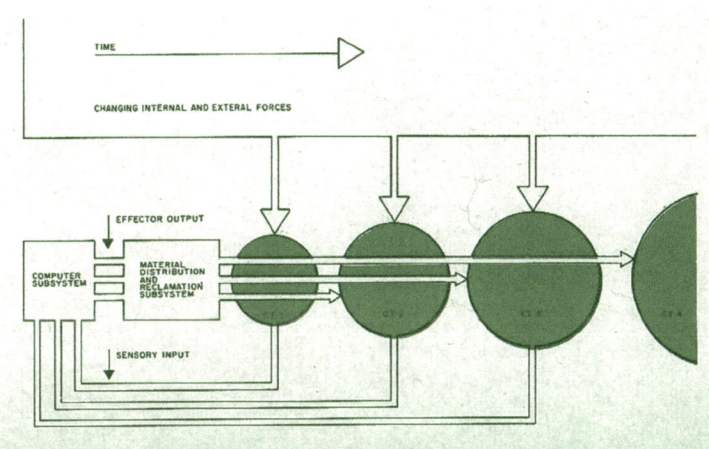

Fig. 1: Wolf Hilbertz, "Toward Cybertecture," *Progressive Architecture* (May 1970): 102.

As cybernetics and general systems theory took the architectural world by storm in the 1960s and 1970s, cutting edge design proposals began to be accompanied by all manner of recursive diagrams. In the future, these documents foretold, our designed spaces would not be composed of inert forms but would instead be made up of sensor-laden, adaptable spatial components. Via the gathering and processing of data, these flowcharts promised, a space could be automatically altered to better suit its inhabitants' needs. The exact mechanisms by which this data would be processed to produce a new optimal output, however, were often left maddeningly vague, the specificities of circuitry or statistical procedures usually condensed into a single backwards-bending arrow. [Figs. 1 and 2]

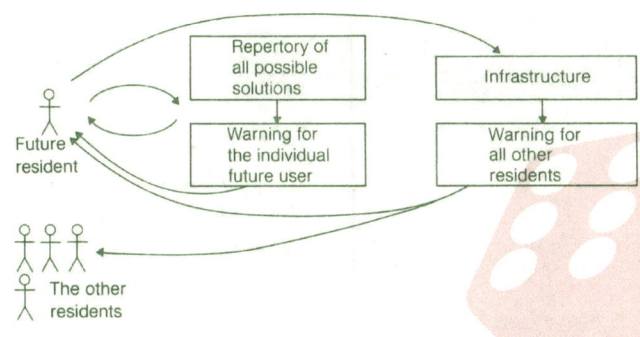

Fig. 2: Yona Friedman, "The Flatwriter: choice by computer," *Progressive Architecture* (March 1971): 100.

While these utopian dreams never quite came to pass, the project of self-optimizing architecture lives on in present-day "smart city" proposals, the white papers of which are riddled with looping diagrams of all sorts. [Fig. 3] Despite having swapped out an electric engineering aesthetic for the crisp icon language of corporatized graphic design, these flowcharts are clearly indebted to their cybernetic ancestors. These new proposals, though, have not just updated the graphic style of their forebears; they also lean on a rather different imaginary of self-regulation: if previous adaptive architectures were guided by an oftentimes vaguely defined "electronic computer," smart city proposals have swapped in data analytics as the governor of their self-adaptive systems. Even with this evocation of a numbers-heavy science, however, that recursive arrow remains as vague as ever.

To try to understand what statistical processes might be underlying these abstractions, in early 2022 we spoke with Justin Joque, author of *Revolutionary Mathematics: Artificial Intelligence, Statistics and the Logic of Capitalism*, a recent book that traces the history of statistics while always keeping an eye on the political economies in which a given technique has been put to use. Joque's study focuses in depth on the role that Bayesian statistics—a procedure that allows one to continually update one's predictions as new information is received—plays in contemporary capitalism. As architects and urban designers contend with a climate change-ravaged world that has cast big data as its savior—and as we contend with the longer history of our discipline's championing of information and feedback—understanding the specificities of statistical techniques has become an important political project.

Fig. 3: Craig Chadwell, "Why smart cities need smarter data infrastructure," *SoftIron Blog*, March 3, 2022, https://softiron.com/blog/why-smarter-cities-need-smarter-data-infrastructure/

Perspecta 55: You note at one point in your book that most approaches to big data and statistics fall into two camps: On the one hand there is the optimistic, Silicon Valley approach that holds that we can use big data to work towards a more perfect and rational world, while on the other hand there is the critical, left-leaning approach, which sees big data as producing a dystopian control society against which we have to fight for the return of free and un-alienated interactions. You contrast both of these approaches with your own project, which holds little hope for the return of a mythical un-alienated life. Instead, you scrutinize precisely *how* particulars are transformed into abstractions and how those metaphysical abstractions then impact the material world. Could you expand on this unique approach of yours?

Justin Joque: One of the things I'm trying to do in the book is to push back against the idea that we can just undo these systems and go back to a world where everything is perfectly apparent. And in a certain sense, I think that the two approaches your question sketched out are two sides of this same fantasy: The big data paradigm says that if we just gather enough data, then we'll have a perfect, transparent picture of the world that will allow us to manage it in all sorts of ways. And then the oftentimes leftist critique of big data also relies on this fantasy of transparency; that is, the idea that if we just shine a light into these algorithmic systems then we'll be able to figure out how they operate so that we can *exit* these systems entirely and deploy more direct and unmediated and therefore more ethical solutions to our problems. I don't at all want to disparage this critical project—I think that's important work to do—but the point that I'm trying to make in the book is that the bigger problem is less these systems of knowledge in themselves and more that these systems have been weaponized by capital and therefore produce a world in capital's image—one oriented towards privatization—and that we are then locked into this world. And so, for me, the question is not how do we achieve some sort of transparent, unalienated order but rather how do we imagine different types of alienation and abstraction that are more just and that produce the world we want to live in.

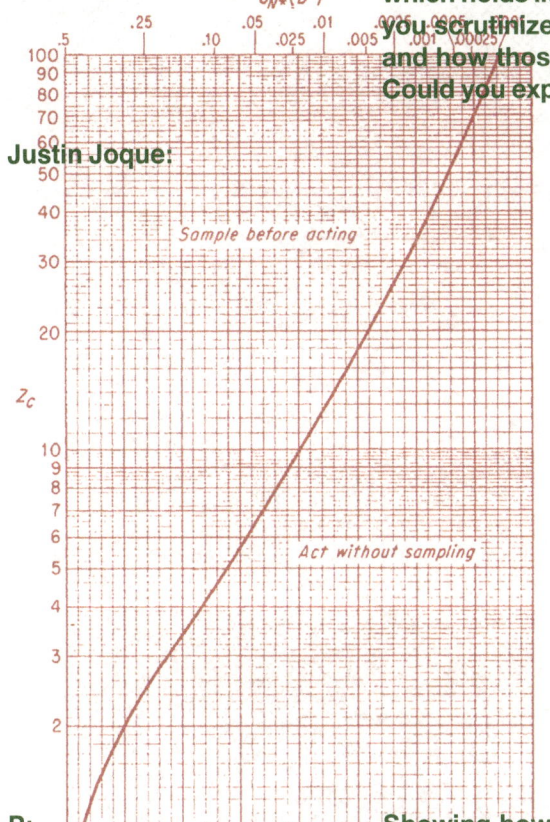

Figure 5.10
Critical Value of $Z = \lambda^{\frac{1}{2}}$ When $K_i = 0$
118

P: Showing how things could be otherwise seems to be a central concern of your book, something you demonstrate via carefully tracking the history of statistics, that is, by documenting how techniques of abstraction have already been changeable over time. In tracing this history, you always take care to unpack the different political economies underlying different theorist's ideas. How do you see probability and statistics changing over time?

JJ: It's important to point out at the beginning that, although probability allows us to have a framework for making predictions and managing uncertain events, at the end of the day probability is not a solid, material, real thing: it either rains tomorrow or it doesn't rain; a coin is either heads or tails. By definition, then, probability is an intellectual, ideological, political, social, and economic supplement. So in my book I've traced how tools of statistical abstraction are developed in relationship to the broader historical changes of the 20th century. And while of course at any given moment there were ongoing debates and contrasting schools of thought, I loosely periodize the history of probability and statistics into three major moments.

The first moment I look at is characterized by the work of Ronald Fisher, who started working during the interwar period at an agricultural research center in England. For Fisher, the central question is one of difference: you have two groups or two treatments and you want to know if there is any actual difference between them. To answer such questions, he developed the method of hypothesis testing that you now learn about in any introduction to statistics class. It is in some ways a counterintuitive idea: Suppose, for example, that you want to know if a new fertilizer is better than an older fertilizer. You would take two fields and apply the older fertilizer to one and the new fertilizer to the other and then monitor the differing rates of growth—maybe, say, the plants grow twice as tall in the field treated with the new fertilizer. Fisher then asks you to imagine a world in which there is *no* difference between these two fertilizers, the so-called "null hypothesis." What is the probability that the null hypothesis is correct, that the two fertilizers have the same

FIGURE 2. Overall A Priori distribution for *Scorpion* search

effect and the difference in height is just due to chance? How unlikely does that chance event have to be to say that, no chance can't be the cause; the result you got really *is* due to a difference in the fertilizers?

Fisher is in a lot of ways really invested in this idea of difference. His first academic job was in a eugenics department at the University College of London, and even after World War II, when a lot of scientists who had been in favor of eugenics abandoned it, Fisher still continues this lifelong commitment to the concept of eugenics and racial difference. He's a figure that is committed to difference—to difference of blood and soil, essentially.

This is the agricultural paradigm that you get with Fisher. But very quickly people realized that this framework doesn't give you a firm foundation because it is extremely limited to imagining the fake world of the null hypothesis and then assessing the probability that any difference you see is merely due to chance. So these two statisticians Jerzy Neyman and Egon Pearson come along who—although they're actually quite excited about what Fisher is doing—say that we don't have to *just* test the null hypothesis; there is a way to quantify what happens if you're wrong in both directions: we can imagine that one of the fertilizers is better when in fact it isn't, or vice versa, we can imagine that they're the same when in reality one is better. And they work out the math for quantifying the costs of a mistake in either direction. That is, with their math one could quantify the economic costs of a false positive (an incorrect assumption of difference) and a false negative (an incorrect assumption of no difference) and make decisions accordingly. You can even think economically about your sample size: with a small sample size, you're more likely to get false positives or false negatives, but if the economic costs of a mistake are low, you'd maybe decide not take on the work of a larger sample size experiment.

In many ways this is an important discovery because it shifts statistics from this agricultural paradigm of the lone scientist or farmer who over the time of many tests assesses whether there is or is not a difference to a paradigm suited to the manager of an industrial plant who is thinking about calibrating costs and maximizing profit. Leonard Savage—a statistician who will be one of the major figures in the Bayesian revolution that comes along after this work—argues that Neyman and Pearson's work is actually this quite large philosophical shift from questions of knowledge to questions of value; essentially from questions of what you can say to be true to questions of what action you should take. But in a lot of ways, this important development gets lost: as more and more fields realize they need some form of hypothesis testing, they mash together Fisher's work and Neyman-Pearson's work into this philosophically incoherent system that you see in statistics textbooks.

And then the third paradigm is the Bayesian one, which actually predates the frequentist approach by around a century, but fell out of favor before coming back into vogue in the 80s and 90s, continuing on into today. Before we get into Bayes, one key thing to understand is that, in a properly Fisherian understanding of probability, you can't assign a probability to an individual event. Probability is this long-run frequency of a collection of events; it's nonsensical to assign a probability to a single event or hypothesis. Another big thing to understand is that, for frequentists like Fisher and Neyman and Pearson, probability is understood as objective. What this means is that, in their minds, probability has some sort of tie to a real, objective material reality. This tie to reality is achieved through the idea of long-run frequency—you know, you flip a coin a thousand times and if it's fifty percent heads then the probability of heads is fifty percent. In most understandings of Bayesian statistics, on the contrary, probability is seen as a measure of personal belief in what one thinks is going to happen, an approach that made Frequentists very uncomfortable. It seemed unscientific to them.

There have been, though, a couple of different ways for finding a grounds for the subjective probability of Bayes. One of the ones that I think is most compelling is the Dutch book argument. A Dutch book is a betting scenario where, no matter what happens—no matter which horse wins or loses—the

265

gambler is guaranteed to lose money. And you can derive all the laws of the probability calculus from the aim of avoiding having a Dutch book made against you. So with Bayesian statistics, you see that it's founded on this market logic, on this exchange of contracts. This allows you to assign probability to an individual event, like a horse winning a race. And you can update these probabilities—the bets you'd be willing to take—as you get more information about the horse, about the situation. Basically, with every bit of new data, you have to re-run the calculation. It is pretty simple to do this, but it's computationally intensive.

Bayesian statistics, then, really aligns with our current era of information capitalism, where companies are paying for these constant data streams, and with each new piece of data they use Bayes to update, say, what ad they think you should see, or how likely you are to repay your mortgage. Bayesian statistics allows for this real-time, continual updating of probabilities.

Again, I'm speaking in very broad strokes; in reality these schools are all kind of going on at the same time. But to summarize the phases: we go from Fisher, with this agricultural probability theory, to Neiman-Pearson, a theory of probability suited to an industrialist running a plant, and then to the Bayesian theory of probability, which maps really well onto informational capital and its real-time computation of constant streams of data.

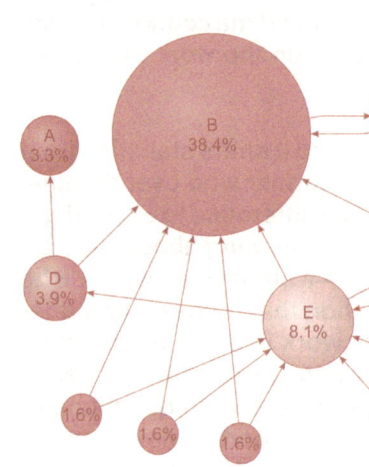

P: Your periodization is extremely compelling. It even helps to make sense of certain developments within the field of architecture. So-called "smart cities" are clearly in line with the Bayesian paradigm and our era of information capitalism: smart cities' belief in the optimizing power of ever-more data collection is ultimately a vision of politics as reducible to the technocratic problem of updating one's Bayesian priors. I'm curious, though, about how the Bayesian paradigm potentially has an elective affinity not just with the information age but also with what Ulrich Beck characterizes as the unique challenges of our "post-insurantial" order. In Beck's conception, the advanced technoscientific developments of our age have produced perils—everything from nuclear power plant accidents to toxic pollution—whose historical novelty renders them unmappable via the long-run, frequentist techniques so central to much of actuarial science. Following Beck, however, a number of thinkers—from Stephen Collier and Andrew Lakoff writing about catastrophe models to Jenny Andersson talking about the Delphi method—have been analyzing tools of forecasting that enable us to map the future even when frequentism falters. I don't think that any of these thinkers necessarily mentions Bayesian statistics, but Bayes' theorem certainly provides another important tool for managing the historically unprecedented dangers that are so central to Beck's theory of the Risk Society. While the rise of information capitalism is certainly a significant factor, do you also see these unprecedented perils as contributing to the rise of Bayesian statistics?

JJ: Yeah I think you're right, that there are two things going on. On the one hand I think one of the really interesting things about Bayesian statistics is that it allows you to make predictions about events that you've never seen. If you read about machine learning algorithms and these sorts of things, you'll hear about how they're able to make models such that even if they encounter a document or webpage or photo they've never seen before, the algorithm will still be able to make a prediction about what it contains. And it's true that Bayesian statistics provides a system for dealing with a world with so much uncertainty—a world that is, as you say, facing events that have no historical precedent and so don't have any long-run frequency. Bayes allows you to take the little bits of data that you have from other events that have even any remote similarity to what you are looking at and make some sort of prediction with that information. Whether or not it is a good prediction or not is another question!

But I think there is a flip side to this ability to model in the face of sparse information. An idea that I try to develop in the book is the notion that, the more accurate we think our predictions to be, the worse we get at dealing with events that break the frame of our model. Because the more the model

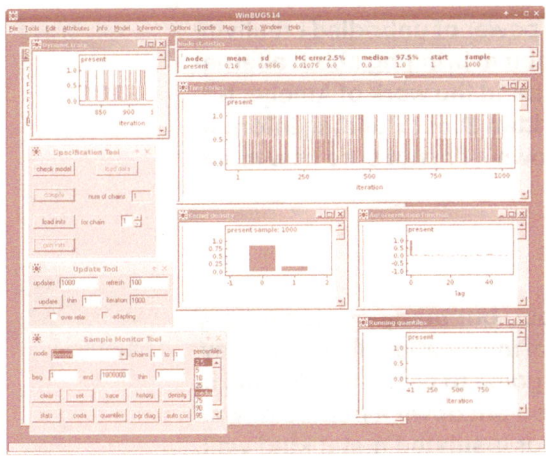

seems to work, the more we get rid of contingency planning. One of the things that inspired me to write the book was thinking of all these examples where an algorithm being introduced into a system led to the elimination of those people who otherwise would hear appeals to a given institutional decision. For example, I talk briefly in the book about Michigan's introduction of MIDAS (the Michigan Integrated Data Automation System) in 2013. One of the things MIDAS was supposed to do was automatically detect fraud in unemployment insurance claims, but it straight up didn't work: something like 40,000 people were kicked off of unemployment insurance. But because Michigan had spent millions of dollars implementing this system, they'd also gotten rid of everyone who previously was working on fraud investigations, and so there was no appeals mechanism in place, nobody you could call to get your unemployment insurance reestablished. This lapse led to people being without unemployment insurance for five or six years without an appeals mechanism—and of course, these are people in very precarious situations; you aren't on unemployment because you can wait six years for a check.

And so I think that even though these systems have a certain ability to predict events that haven't been seen, the problem to me is that the more efficient they get, the easier it is to commit to streamlining them. And efficiency is a trade-off with robustness: the more you favor efficiency the more disarmed you are for these extraordinary events; the more you are left without any way to course correct and deal with them.

P: Right, if we place too much faith in the absolute objectivity of these systems we lose sight of their performative dimension: in the example you gave, the (incorrect) prediction of fraud brought about a world in which those Michiganders were treated as if they *had* committed fraud. Do you think that such performativity can ever be strategically deployed? As I was reading your book I was thinking of the work of thinkers like Martijn Konings or Jens Beckert, scholars who are similarly suspicious of what you call "dereification" projects. According to these thinkers, left-leaning critics who are trying to expose the fallacy of speculation in favor of some objective value are misguided; value, in their eyes, is grounded in speculation, that is, in affect, desire, anticipation, the imagination. How do you see Bayesian statistics/computational prediction interacting with these more affect-laden approaches to the future and to value?

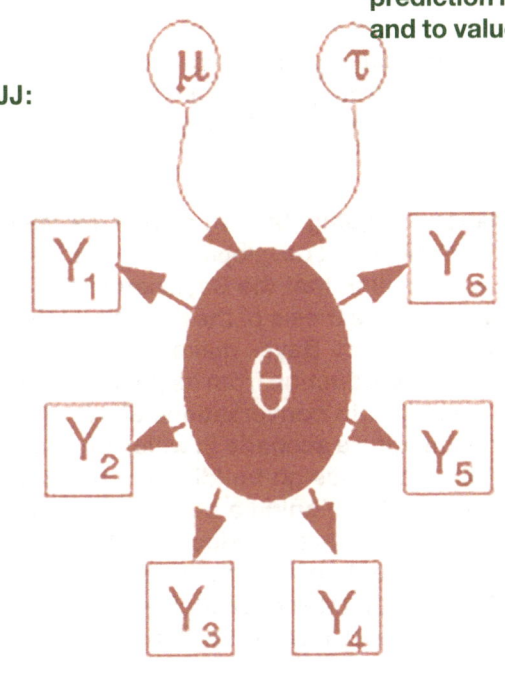

JJ: Yeah that's a really interesting question. It's important to point out, however, that oftentimes these kinds of Bayesian statistical models or machine learning algorithms are plugged into systems that deal with affect or desire. So much of what is being subjected to algorithms are consumer desires. One example that I talk about in the book is the idea of YouTube as a radicalization engine—you know, you watch one video about a historical subject and then it starts serving you these increasingly radical, conspiratorial white supremacist historical videos to get you latched into staying on the platform even longer.

And so, in addition to the idea of dereification, something that I'm very suspicious of is the idea that somehow our creative passions or desires necessarily provide us the ability to step outside of these systems. On the contrary, so often these systems are good at reinterpreting these creative impulses or desires and serving them back up to us in a way that allows for both the extraction of capital and the propping up of white supremacy and sexism and imperialism, or anything else that a YouTube radicalization video hinges on.

But at the same time, your question is asking about the possibility of imagining other forms of value that really *do* break with the kinds of capitalist value systems that I think are so damaging. So I think there is something potentially productive in looking towards the space of creativity, but we have to be very careful not to think that imagination or creativity are in and of themselves good. It really matters what we imagine and what we're creative about. Because, as YouTube shows, there are all sorts of ways in which feelings, imaginations, and desires can be preyed upon in destructive and extractive ways.

P: It's certainly true that committing oneself to the power of unbridled creativity has many pitfalls—it's not necessarily the solution to bringing about alternative forms of value. This predicament brings to mind the work of Amelyn Ng, one of the contributors to our issue. She has written about Building Information Management, or BIM, as it is commonly known—I'm not sure how much you know about this program?

JJ: No, I've never heard of it before.

P: Well, it depends on the scale of a given project, but many contemporary architecture models contain massive amounts of information. If you are, say, working on a large government contract, you're going to be using BIM. And in this program, you don't just put down a wall, you put down a particular wall type—8" exterior brick cavity wall, 4 7/8" interior insulated metal stud wall, etc. And oftentimes, these objects are even connected to particular products. So if you put a sink in your model, it won't just be a generic 3D model of a sink, it will be a particular Kohler make and model—because, increasingly, a BIM object isn't just tied to a particular material, but also to a particular brand. And, even more, now BIM is advertising itself as a planning tool for the entire building lifecycle: the BIM model becomes the foundation for digital twins that layer ever more data into these models, from maintenance costs, to metrics on building use and so on.

JJ: It sounds to me a little like object-oriented programming, but for the production of a building.

P: Right, exactly. And increasingly, Ng notes, this modeling program has become the standard for government contracts. So, despite many architects' faith in the unmediated power of imagination, Ng points out that if, say, a Climate Corps were ever to come into being, the designers on board would be using the dry programming language of BIM. In light of this fact, Ng argues that designers ought not nostalgically dream of an architecture carried out without the heavily mediated BIM, but should instead devote more of their creative energies to thinking about ways to hi-jack the BIM system. Because what if, she asks, a BIM object wasn't attached to cost equations but was instead attached to its carbon impact or the social implications of its manufacturing and so on. I bring all this up because it foregrounds the question of tactics. In attempting to bring into being new systems of value—in enacting the "revolutionary mathematics" of your book's title—is the better strategy to create new value systems whole cloth or ought we hack the systems of mediation that already exist?

JJ: I'd never heard of Building Information Modeling, but I think that's a really perfect example to talk through my thinking about developments in statistics. I want to make clear that in many ways I think that the Bayesian evolution is an important step forward; it is not at all the thesis of the book that this is a bad bourgeois science that we have to reject. Bayes makes an important discovery: you can't separate knowledge production from its political economy. You can take this insight and map it onto conversations about architectural modeling programs. You can imagine a scenario in which one says, "Oh let's get back to the root of things and design buildings in the good old way that we used to." But if you're still designing a building considering how much it will cost and how much it needs to produce to offset these costs—you may be changing the surface tools of design, but at the end of the day you're still responding to the same dictates of capital. In some ways such nostalgia is even more insidious because it adds this patina of artistic creativity atop the capitalistic process.

So I really like this idea, as you say, of hacking into these existing systems. From what you're saying it sounds like this is a high-level abstraction for the work of design. To my mind, it is less a question of getting rid of abstractions altogether than it is a question of thinking about different inputs and outputs for those systems. It is about specifying different things that we value. Likewise, in my book, I'm not saying that we should throw out probability and statistics; I'm not saying that they're bad. Rather, I argue that we have to think about these systems—and especially about the political economy they're embedded in—so that we can bring different values into these systems and rethink what we're trying to achieve with them.

But the point is not that we should just sit in our armchairs and imagine a new form of capitalism without getting involved in the specifics. These two aspects—an individual decision or input and the larger metaphysical systems of value informing a given decision—are, for lack of a better term, in a dialectical relationship. We have to be working on both of these poles at the same time, the inputs that go into the model and the overall model.

P: Definitely, and I think Amelyn Ng's work operates very much along the lines you just described—she writes about inserting new inputs into our systems so as to produce new outputs and how hopefully, via this procedure, we can change our computational modeling systems writ large. I'm curious about how you think about a related but different tactic, that is, the tactic of deliberately trying to gum up the functioning of a given input—to-output mechanism. I'm thinking here of Paul N. Edward's ideas of data and computational friction, by which he means all the little hiccups and incommensurabilities that have to be ironed out to make different datasets or computational procedures compatible with one another. In Edwards's case, he is discussing a computational system—global climate models—that he thinks is valuable, so he writes about the elimination of data friction in adulatory terms. But I wonder if his highlighting of data friction suggests the possibility of another tactic even more extreme than hacking: one could work to increase data friction, one could insert sand into the gears of someone's computational system (for example, by putting in an input that forces a system to compute endlessly). Do you see such subterfuge as a potential tactic for re-writing value systems?

JJ: I'd never thought about this in exactly those terms. But I know precisely what you mean and that's a really interesting idea. In the book, I focus less on friction as an adversarial tactic on the part of those who would resist capital and its inequities and more on rising data friction as something that we see capital doing to itself right now. I think something that's really fascinating about our present moment is how much individual actors or companies are throwing sand in the gears of all their opponents. What's ended up happening is that as these conglomerates and corporations and states compete for knowledge—and compete in a field where it is often more efficacious to destroy your competitor's knowledge rather than gain in your own knowledge—they end up throwing sand in their own gears. For example, I was reading an article the other day about how Google has become essentially worthless when it comes to finding product recommendations. The only way you can get recommendations for purchasing something is to type in, say, "new washer" and "Reddit" because Reddit is one of the only platforms that hasn't been completely destroyed yet.

And while I think you're right that there might be some value in increasing data friction as a kind of adversarial tactic, there's also an added risk. Here is where we see how tactics and strategies are always very situational. To take the unemployment insurance example that I gave earlier, you see that, oftentimes when there is a data error, those in power or those that control capital are not necessarily the ones who are hurt by the mistake; more often than not it is the most marginalized who end up paying the price for that kind of misrecognition. So one has to be careful about who is downwind of the systems that one is adding friction to because usually the capitalists have all sorts of insurance. They've hedged their positions incredibly well and can take advantage of any sort of disaster.

P: If capitalism is throwing sand into its own gears, what is the best way to take advantage of these errors, or at the very least to critically publicize the moments when our current political economy is not working?

269

JJ: Something I've drawn from Marx is the idea that abstractions like value and capital work even if individually we don't believe in them. You can go around shouting about how value is arbitrary and money doesn't exist but at the end of the day you still have to pay your student loans and pay your rent. But I still think that simply being explicit about how these systems are ceasing to work is very important because it is in these moments that you have these openings to imagine other systems, to demonstrate the functionality of other calculations of value that could potentially take the place of our damaging current situation. So much of the discourse throughout the second half of the twentieth century has been about how, despite how horrible capitalism can be, it is the only system that actually works. It is extremely necessary to be as public as possible about those times when capitalism clearly is not functioning.

P: And doing so would help to make more viable the possibility of other modes of political economy! It's a silver lining to be sure, but one development that has been really heartening to see in the face of the massive scale of the climate catastrophe is the return of a discourse around planning, and specifically a discourse about socialist planning. I'm thinking here of Holly Jean Buck, Leigh Phillips, Michael Rozworski and others. It's as if early twentieth century debates about the workability of centralized planning are resurfacing again, only with certain conclusions flipped: the "socialist computation problem," as Hayek phrases it, has become, as you cheekily put it in your book, a "capitalist computation problem." What specifically do you mean by this term?

JJ: In the "Fragment on Machines" from The Grundrisse, Marx briefly mentions this idea of the general intellect. He talks about how industrial advances and the sciences create this general knowledge that everyone can draw from. Ultimately this application of knowledge reaches a point that, if you think about automation, is almost directly productive. Of course, it's important to qualify this idea; I don't want to give the impression that the general intellect was ever completely shared because it was always still enclosed within a nation or ethnonationalist space in all sorts of problematic ways.

But I think what we're seeing in the present moment—where companies do not share information but compete over it so as to have better, private probability models—is that the general intellect is increasingly being parceled out and enclosed in a way analogous to the enclosure of pastoral lands in England during the rise of capitalism. The sharing of knowledge and information, so necessary for the production of the general intellect, is breaking down. And while I don't think that capitalism was ever very good at calculating, at least for a certain strata—the top of bourgeoisie and above—it did succeed for a time in managing their affairs. But I think companies act so adversarially now, and knowledge has become so enclosed, that you get a situation where capitalism is even beginning to fail in the halls of power and capital itself.

P: I'm curious about how you see this breakdown in knowledge in relation to your work as a visualization librarian, a role that involves helping people convert data into readable visuals. At least in theory, this work counters the enclosure of probabilistic knowledge by making information more democratically accessible. Is there a role for well-designed visuals to intercede in our political economy, that is, to be a tool in the pursuit of a more democratic planning apparatus?

JJ: I should start out by saying that, of course, this is a job and one has to do their job to eat. So it's not like I necessarily signed up to do this work exclusively because of some radical potential I saw in data visualization. I think in a lot of ways data visualization simultaneously partakes of the best and worst of these sorts of information systems. There are clearly a lot of data visualization practices that give this false idea that one can totally understand a situation and modulate it and control it. I'm thinking here of Orit Halpern's book *Beautiful Data* and, to get back to smart cities, Shannon Mattern's recent book *A City is Not a Computer*. The dashboards she talks about give this illusion of control over these complex systems, a real risk that comes with data visualization

Table 3

ESTIMATED PROBABILITY OF NOT MORE THAN TWO FUTURE ACCIDENTS GIVEN ZERO ACCIDENTS IN THE PAST[a]

Number of Past Opportunities	Number of Future Opportunities		
	100	1,000	10,000
100	.879	.251	.030
1,000	.999	.875	.249
10,000	1.000	.999	.975

[a]Based on the same Beta distribution as Table 2.

But then on the other hand, something I try to do when I work with people on data visualization is to really get them thinking about it as a form of storytelling. I think that data visualization offers up some really interesting possibilities with regards to the kinds of stories we can tell. One really powerful aspect of data visualization is that it allows for a sort of commensurability—to get back to this term—between space and time. If you read a book or you engage with other forms of narrative, even if the text covers a long period of time, you're still understanding that time in a linear fashion. You read a book from start to finish. But with a visualization, data covering a long period of time can be seen all at once, laid out over space. This allows you to pull together all sorts of connections or differences, and to ask very interesting questions.

So, in summary, there isn't anything necessarily liberatory or positive about data visualization, but it offers different kinds of affordances. It allows us to ask different questions, and if we're thoughtful about these questions, they can potentially open up some new avenues.

P: I know you are talking about the space of the page or the space of the screen, but one of the lessons architecture teaches about space is that it is always limited. How do you think about this necessary limiting condition of space? How do you decide what to exclude in a given visualization?

JJ: This gets back to this central question of abstraction. I think the idea that you could avoid making these decisions in any sort of media is a fantasy. Whether you are writing a novel or making a movie, one still has to make decisions about what is included or excluded. And so to my mind it is less about exclusion having a necessarily negative valence than it is about being cognizant of the decisions one is making. To bring it back to probability, with frequentism, you always have to decide what goes in the reference class. For example, if you say, "there's a 70% chance of rain tomorrow," what's the reference class you're drawing from to make this prediction? Are you talking about the weather in this particular area, or a bigger location? How long does it have to rain for a day to qualify as rainy? And so on.

The most dangerous thing is to pretend that these decisions are objective, to say "Oh it's obvious, everyone knows what the reference class is, we don't need to talk about it." You have to be thoughtful about the reference class you are choosing and why you are choosing it. You cannot not have a reference class so this is the best you can hope to do.

P: With regards to the politics of choosing a reference class: are there any projects—any forms of abstraction, or new ideas with regards to value—that you are excited about at present? Who are the "revolutionary mathematicians" working not to enclose knowledge but to produce new knowledge and less harmful futures?

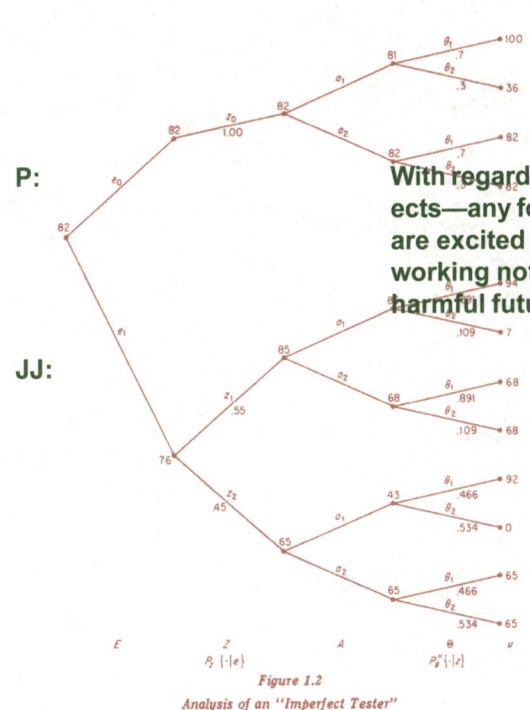

Figure 1.2
Analysis of an "Imperfect Tester"

JJ: That is a good question and one that people keep asking me in response to the book. It's a question that I try very hard not to answer, for strategic reasons. Because capitalism and imperialism and other systems of injustice are so very good at re-appropriating those which oppose them, it's difficult to project what projects will work out. But, speaking generally, I will say that I think there is a new spirit of exploration—a new spirit of play is maybe the better word—that you can see in a lot of different spaces. There is interesting work, for example, being done in queer theory and Black studies. And, personally, over the course of the pandemic I've been involved in unionizing my colleagues. I think there are exciting things happening in the labor movement, a real reimagining of what the labor movement could be.

So maybe that is the answer I will give. I can't point to any project specifically and say that it's the one that has figured it out, but the current spirit of play is a really positive development. I think it's important to keep that openness and to keep experimenting. We will only know what has worked after the fact.

Planetary Accounting/ Scene From a Warehouse

Words by Amelyn Ng Renderings by John Lewtas

We work with calculable images. Not only in terms of measurable geometry, as has historically been the case in the practice of architectural drawing, but also in terms of machine-readable objects that comprise a 3D model.

In Building Information Modeling (BIM) software, 3D objects are self-counting. Sometimes called Families, "smart" components have begun to resonate more with contemporary forms of logistics (consider how barcode stickers and RFID tags allow physical goods and materials to be organized in some greater database). In a "search, not sort" world, things are governed through perpetually updating digital-physical inventories. In BIM models specifically, 3D objects can act as precise proxies for real products and materials out there in the world. Tagged with myriad non-graphical information (cost, manufacturer's data, quantity, material / thermal / structural properties), BIM objects can automatically tally, log, and arrange themselves into the spreadsheet language of schedules and specifications — all within the same modeling software.

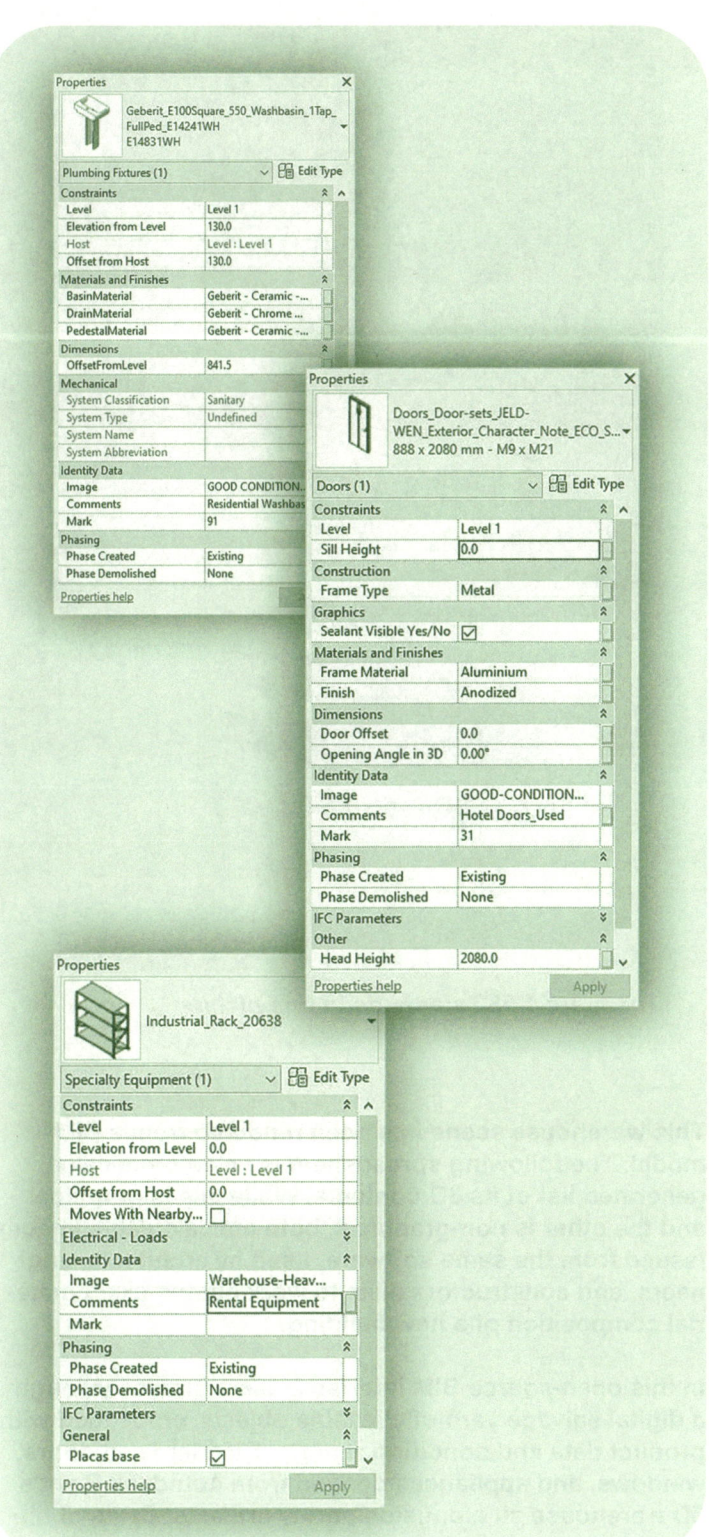

There are 1,582 elements in this picture.

This warehouse scene has been rendered from a BIM model. The following spreadsheet is an automatically generated list of its 3D contents. While one is graphical and the other is non-graphical, both are calculable images issued from the same software, used by architects, engineers, and constructors alike to work out the exact material composition of a new building.

In this open-source BIM interface, users browse through a digital salvage yard of clickable objects, embedded with product data and condition reports. Standardized doors, windows, and appliances derived from Autodesk Revit's 3D warehouse sit alongside unruly artifacts: fields of tile and brick, rental equipment, steel beams from another project... As a calculable image, the rendering is reframed as the inventory, tethered to a live spreadsheet.

However preliminary, this visual exploration is a gesture toward planetary accounting within machine-readable mediums such as building information models. Architecture's calculable images are reimagined beyond *accounting* instruments of pure quantification, toward scenes of *accountability* (collective responsibility) for the documentation and potential recirculation of imperfect yet perfectly reusable construction materials and equipment.

Today, techniques such as photogrammetry make it even easier to model existing objects and conditions. If the

information-rich model became a real-time environment for collectively counting, sorting, and reassigning value to standing building stock — think BIM salvage yard or 3D Warehouse Craigslist — then there lies potentials for the participation of the drawing itself in more circular economies, and for countering the perpetual newness implied by 3D objects and materials.

3D WAREHOUSE INVENTORY

LAST UPDATE 08-02-22 10:08:02

COUNT	CATEGORY	DESCRIPTION	FAMILY	TYPE	CONDITION
6	Ceilings	3D Warehouse Ceiling	Basic Ceiling	Generic	Contact Owner
30	Curtain Panels	3D Warehouse Wall Panels	Metal Profile Cladding	Ribbed	Contact Owner
2	Doors	Exterior Single Door - Residential	Doors_Door-sets_Swedoor_JELD-WEN_Ext	888 x 1980 mm - M9 x M20	Used - Good
3	Doors	Exterior Single Door - Residential	Doors_Door-sets_Swedoor_JELD-WEN_Ext	888 x 1980 mm - M9 x M20	Used - doorknob missing
6	Doors	Exterior Single Door - Residential	Doors_Door-sets_Exterior_Character_Leon	888 x 2080 mm - M9 x M21	Used - Good
3	Doors	Exterior Single Door - Residential	Doors_Door-sets_Exterior_Classic_Albinoni	888 x 2080 mm - M9 x M21	Used - Good
1	Doors	Exterior Single Door - Residential	Doors_Door-sets_Exterior_Classic_Rossini	888 x 2080 mm - M9 x M21	Used - Paint chipping
3	Doors	Exterior Single Door - Residential	Doors_Door-sets_Exterior_Leon_SBD_Single	948 x 2115 mm - M9	Good
1	Doors	Exterior Single Door - Residential	Doors_Door-sets_SBD_Single_Outswing_1.0	988 x 1980 mm - M10 x M20	Moderate repair needed
2	Doors	Exterior Single Door - Residential	Doors_Door-sets_Swedoor_JELD-WEN_Ext	988 x 1980 mm - M10 x M21	Good
1	Doors	Interior Single Door - Industrial	Door-Passage-Single-Cold_Room	1000x2080 mm	Good
1	Equipment & Storage	3D Warehouse Storage	Granite Slab Storage Rack	Regular - holds 8 slabs	Rental only
13	Equipment & Storage	3D Warehouse Storage	Industrial_Rack_20638	4 Tier Rack Braced	Rental only
7	Equipment & Storage	3D Warehouse Storage	Milk_Crate_14710	Standard Size - 3 colors available	Used - Free
3	Equipment & Storage	3D Warehouse Storage	Wood_Pallet_Standard	48" x 40"	Rental only
1	Equipment & Storage	3D Warehouse Equipment	Jungheinrich_Site_HandPalletTruck_AM22	AM22 - 1520	Rental Only
4	Equipment & Storage	3D Warehouse Equipment	Safety_Barricade_Orange	Standard Size	Rental Only
1	Floors	3D Warehouse Floor	Basic Floor	Insitu Concrete 225mm	Contact Owner
1	Floor Finish	Tile - Outdoor	Granite Stack_Dark_Honed	4ct x 1000x1000 mm	Spare - Perfect condition
1	Floor Finish	Tile - Outdoor	Granite Stack_Dark_Honed	4ct x 1000x1000 mm	Spare - Perfect condition
4	Floor Finish	Tile - Outdoor	Granite Stack_Grey_Rough	4ct x 1000x1000 mm	Spare - unsealed
2	Floor Finish	Tile - Outdoor	Granite Stack_Red_Honed	4ct x 1000x1000 mm	Spare - Perfect condition
1	Floor Finish	Tile - Indoor	Floor Tile	Tile Floor Beige - 31.116 sqm	Used - Good
1	Floor Finish	Tile - Indoor	Floor Tile	Tile Floor Diamond Pattern 9.667 sqm	Used - Good
1	Floor Finish	Tile - Indoor	Floor Tile	Tile Floor - Marble 14.201 sqm	Needs resealing
31	Furniture	Study Desk - Dormitory	Desk Student	24" x 18" x 24"	Good
2	Furniture	Study Desk - Library	Desk	60" x 30"	Minor Scratches
25	Furniture	Furniture Hardware	Narrow Black Connecting Bolt	Metal connector	Spare - Loose
14	Furniture	Study Chair - Dormitory	Furniture_Office-Chairs_Fritz-Hansen_N02T	Default	Used - Good
2	Garden	Brick - Residential	Red Brick Pallet [640 ct]	For low walls & pavers - not for structural use	Mortar cleaned
5	Garden	Brick - Residential	Red Brick - Loose	Single brick unit	Good
60	Lighting Fixtures	3D Warehouse Lighting - Industrial	M_Pendant Light - Linear - 2 Lamp	2400mm - 277V	Contact Owner
7	Plumbing Fixtures	Bath - Residential	Bath-Shower-Sterling_Plumbing-Performa-K	60" x 29" x 75-3/4" Left Hand Drain	Spare - Perfect condition
3	Plumbing Fixtures	Sink - Residential	Sink-Vessel-KOHLER-Iron_Plains-K-5400	Drop-in/under-mount bathroom sink	Used - Good
3	Plumbing Fixtures	Sink - Residential	Middleton Single-basin Kitchen Sink	25"x22" Four Faucet Holes-NA-Stainless	Used - Good
16	Plumbing Fixtures	Sink - Pedestal	Geberit_E100Square_550_Washbasin_1Tap	E100 Square Handrinse Washbasin 1 Tap Hole	Spare - Perfect condition
1	Plumbing Fixtures	Sink - Pedestal	Geberit_E100Square_450x350_HandrinseWa	E100 Square 450x350mm Handrinse Washbas	Chipped edge
7	Plumbing Fixtures	Toilet - Residential	Toilet-Floor_Mount-KOHLER-Reach-K-23185	One-piece compact elongated dual-flush toilet	Spare - Perfect condition
6	Plumbing Fixtures	Two-piece elongated 1.28 gpf toilet	Toilet-Floor_Mount-KOHLER-Kingston-K-250	Not A Type-See Type Catalog	Spare - Perfect condition
3	Plumbing Fixtures	Soil appliance for the disposal of excre	Sanitary_Toilets_Sanindusa_Cetus-rimflush-	Sanitary_Toilets_Sanindusa_Cetus-rimflush-wa	Used - Good
6	Plumbing Fixtures		Toilet-Domestic-3D	Toilet-Domestic-3D	
4	Plumbing Fixtures	K-3577	Toilet-Round_Front-Kohler-Wellworth-3577	Vitreous_China-Almond-47	
5	Roofs	3D Warehouse Roof	Basic Roof	Generic - 400mm Corrugated Metal	
6	Structural Beam Systems	3D Warehouse Steel Elements	Structural Beam System	Structural Framing System	Contact Owner
24	Structural Columns	3D Warehouse Steel Elements	UC-Universal Columns-Column	UC305x305x97	Contact Owner
18	Structural Connections	3D Warehouse Steel Elements	Apex haunch	Apex haunch	Contact Owner
24	Structural Connections	3D Warehouse Steel Elements	Base plate	Base plate	Contact Owner
12	Structural Connections	3D Warehouse Steel Elements	Bracing I splice angle double	Bracing I splice angle double	Contact Owner
12	Structural Connections	3D Warehouse Steel Elements	Clip angle	Clip angle	Contact Owner
8	Structural Connections	3D Warehouse Steel Elements	Gusset plate (triangle) at one diagonal	Gusset plate (triangle) at one diagonal	Contact Owner
30	Structural Framing	3D Warehouse Steel Elements	UB-Universal Beam	152x89x16UB	Contact Owner
10	Structural Framing	3D Warehouse Steel Elements	M_Round Bars	RB79.38	Contact Owner
2	Structural Framing	3D Warehouse Steel Elements	M_Round Bars	RB106.36	Contact Owner
1	Structural Framing	3D Warehouse Steel Elements	UB-Universal Beams	Structural Column	Contact Owner
39	Structural Framing	3D Warehouse Steel Elements	UB-Universal Beams	UB305x165x40	Contact Owner
2	Windows		M_Trim-Window-Exterior-Flat	with Sill	Broken
4	Windows		Trim-Window-Exterior-Flat	with Sill	Used - Good
6	Windows	Double Glazed Window - Residential	Trim-Window-Interior-Flat	Picture Frame	Good
12	Windows	Double Glazed Window - Residential	Window-Double-Hung	24" x 42"	Used - Good
1	Windows	Double Glazed Window - Residential	Window-Double-Hung	28" x 46"	Used - Latch missing
2	Windows	Double Glazed Window - Residential	Window-Picture-Andersen-A_Series	31-1/4" x 23-1/4" Composite-clad wood picture	Spare - Perfect Condition
5	Windows	Double Glazed Window - Residential	Window-Double_Hung-Andersen-A_Series	47-1/4" x 95-1/4" - Composite-clad hung windo	Spare - Perfect Condition
1	Windows	Single Glazed Window - Residential	Window-Casement-Double	48" x 60"	Used - Good
2	Windows	Single Glazed Window - Residential	M_Window-Double-Hung	700 x 1200mm	Used - Good
2	Windows	Single Glazed Window - Residential	Window-Awning-Andersen-400_Series	Vinyl-clad wood Awning window	Used - Good
4	Windows	Single Glazed Window - Residential	Window-Awning-Andersen-E_Series	Aluminum-clad wood awning window	Used - Good
2	Windows	Single Glazed Window - Residential	Window-Casement-Andersen-100_Series	Fibrex casement window	Glass pane missing
6	Windows	Single Glazed Window - Residential	Window-Fixed-Andersen-100_Series	Fibrex fixed window	Spare - Perfect Condition
5	Windows	Single Glazed Window - Residential	Window-Gliding-Andersen-E_Series	Aluminum-clad wood gliding window	Used - Good
8	Windows	Single Glazed Window - Residential	Window-Picture-Andersen-400_Series-Tilt_W	Vinyl-clad picture window	Used - Good

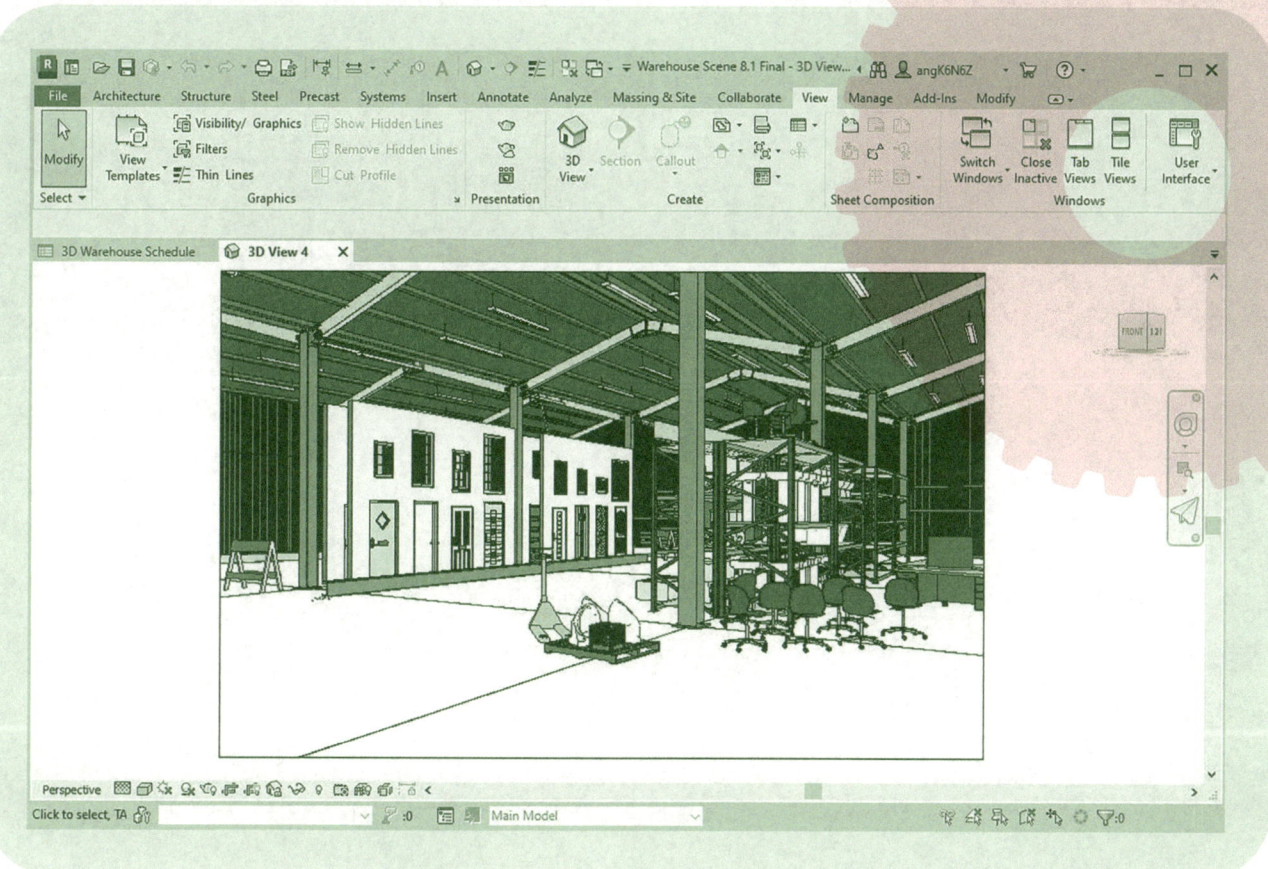

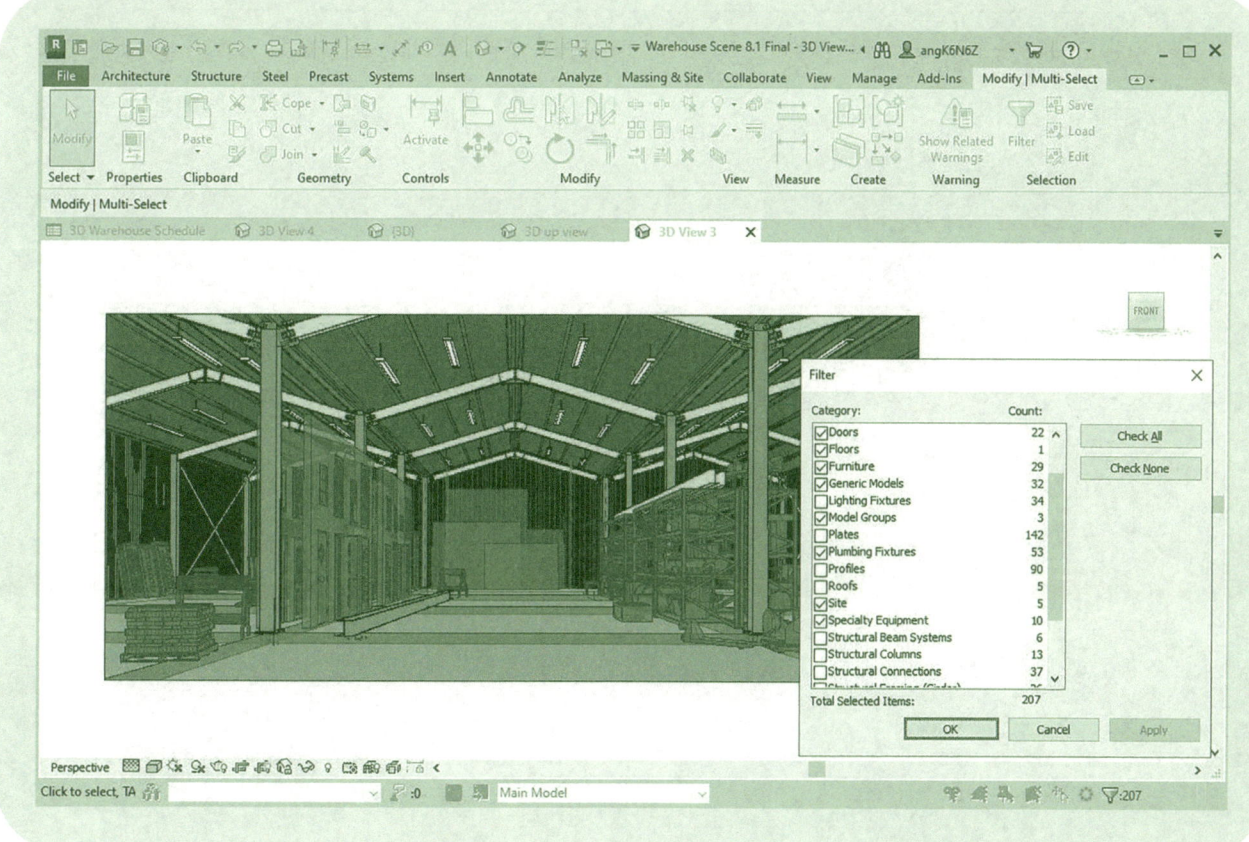

277

Acknowledgments
(or, On Editing *Perspecta* in a Speculative Age)

This issue is not only about the future but it has been brought into being by (a particular vision of) the future. To explain: while *Perspecta* has a printing budget, neither the Yale School of Architecture nor the Yale School of Art maintains funds for paying the publication's editors and designers. We were able to overlook this lack of present rewards only because we anticipated that our work on this issue would, at some *future date*, bestow benefits upon us.

Such a speculative attitude stems not from the editorial team's scholarly interest in all things futures. It is, rather, merely a reflection of the broader socioeconomic situation in which we conducted this work: we are speaking, of course, of the stranglehold that Chicago School human capital theory has had on the lives and imaginations of millennials everywhere.[1] Indeed, this theory—this stance towards the future—not only led to us editing this architectural journal, it led to us getting our architectural degrees in the first place.

Education as an investment: this idea is the kernel that sprouted human capital theory, that in turn sprouted our graduate school dreams, which in turn sprouted this *Perspecta*. Though this approach to education has degraded both our psyches and our wallets—more on this below—it originally started out as a relatively benign attempt, undertaken by neo-Keynesian Theodore Schultz, to solve a confounding economic mystery. In the late 1950s, GDP was growing at a clip despite a lack of accompanying growth in the size of the country's labor force or physical capital.

To account for this imbalance, Schultz proposed a simple reclassification of certain categories of economic activity, chief among them education spending: if we treated such spending not as an act of consumption but as an *investment* in human resources, the missing cause of GDP growth revealed itself. The ickiness underlying this conceptual shift—wherein humans are treated less as unique moral beings and more as collections of capital goods—was offset some by the policies it led Schultz to endorse: he argued that, because the benefits of these investments in human capital largely accrued to the public, they should be funded primarily by the state.

Despite these laudable aims—and the few short years of increased education spending they precipitated—the lasting legacy of Schultz's theoretical incursion is its opening of the Pandora's Box of treating humans as investable assets. It would be hard to overestimate the curses said opening unleashed. Over time, Milton Friedman, Gary S. Becker and other economists of the Chicago School leapt onto Schultzian human capital theory and transformed it into a far more punishing version. Here the state, unsurprisingly, is absent: contrary to Schultz, Friedman and his ilk contend that investments in human capital accrue primarily to the individual and thus these costs ought to be borne by her on her lonesome. And so, as Friedmanian human capital theory gradually gained adherents in the upper echelons of the American policy-making apparatus, government support for higher education by design failed to keep up with rising costs and, in response, individuals and families had to turn to student loan programs.[2] With these rising prices and with this new mode of funding, architecture school has become a highly speculative proposition: without state backing, the architecture student must bear alone the risk that her increases in earning potential may not be enough to compensate for the massive debts—plus interest—she will owe the creditor funding her education. That is to say, the *anticipation* of gains on this asset has been essential to its financing. Unfortunately for architecture students, these gains are no sure thing: the value of any investment is only determined in the future, which, because it is "shaped by events that we cannot predict" is fundamentally "unknowable."[3]

Sadly, as we march into that unknown future, it's turning out that the investments we made in our educations aren't appreciating at the rate we would like. And so, to counter this failed investment, we have, via this *Perspecta*, leveraged ourselves further. How so? The cultural theorist Michel Feher argues that the privatized, speculative modality described above extends well beyond higher education and its indebting of students. For Feher, the ascendency of Chicago School human capital theory has resulted in a wholesale shift in our sense of self. He contends that we are no longer laborers selling our labor power (remember, we received no paycheck for our work on this issue) but portfolio managers of a sort, acquiring a collection of skill sets and projects in hopes of their appreciation. "The return on human capital," he writes,

> no longer manifests itself solely in calculations about whether to work or to receive more training. It now refers to all that is produced by the skill set that defines me. Such that everything I earn—be it salary, return on investments, booty, or favors I may have incurred—can be understood as the return on the human capital that constitutes me.[4]

If the paradigmatic human being of neoclassical economics was a walking utility maximizer, the model individual in the age of human capital theory is, in Feher's conceptualization, a portfolio manager, overseeing a group of stocks called the self. And as all devotees of modern portfolio theory know, one's collection of stocks must always be diversified: risky bets carefully offset by sure things, investments in blue chip stocks like professional degrees mixed with pie-in-the-sky investments.

Now, banking on the editorship and designing of a relatively obscure art publication appreciating into any actual returns (be they in the form of a teaching position, a grant, a future book contract or so on) is a rather risky bet. Despite this low chance of payout, it was one we were ultimately willing—or, more precisely, for some of us, able—to make. How so?

With this investment, we are in effect our own creditors, working for free now in the hopes that these self-loaned manpower hours will find recompense in the value the final printed publication nets us in the future. But, of course, not everyone can work with only possible future money as pay; it is far easier to do so when one has that ultimate hedge of familial support. For, as we all know, the ultimate disaster in today's economy is not being able to pay your debts, thus hurting your credit-rating and thereby limiting your ability to get credit in the future. With a backstop of financial support, however, such a situation need never come to pass, making the speculative endeavor of editing an architectural journal for free a lot less risky.[5] The ability to participate in publishing projects like *Perspecta*, then, is increasingly becoming a product of one's inherited class position.

This class barrier matters because, although it is unlikely, it *is* possible that the speculative project of editing this journal actually will pay off in the future. (The roster of former *Perspecta* editors is, after all, littered with the names of a few successful critics and tenured professors.) That one's ability to edit an architectural journal is largely dependent upon one's socioeconomic circumstances thus has potentially long-lasting effects on the make-up of architectural thought leaders. We see here in microcosm, then, a demonstration of a general economic principle of our present era: the "growing importance of intergenerational transfer and inheritance for the determination of life chances."[6]

All too often, members of this editorial team have lain awake at night, tossing and turning as we grappled with these issues and their practical implications.[7] The Yale School of Architecture (YSoA), on the other hand, has been sleeping easy. For YSoA, the rise of human capital theory has, unwittingly or not, been a boon to its bottom line: it provides them with a convenient cover for saddling their recent graduates with an albatross of unpaid work, work for which the School will receive at least as many of the reputational benefits[8] despite taking on, in terms of labor,[9] virtually none of the financial risks.

It would be unfair to lay this sin of refusing to examine the underlying class dimensions of human capital theory and architectural production entirely at the YSoA's feet, however; us millennial architects ourselves have also been pretty blind when it comes to these pressing issues. Trained as we have been to do anything and everything to invest in our own little portfolios of human capital, we've rarely attempted to put a halt to the endless pursuit of individual accolades that constitutes contemporary architectural production. This willingness to sacrifice our present security for the sake of individualistic future gains—in other words, our willingness to work for free or for low wages with no benefits, to spend money on massive architectural models and the like—has, as Malcolm Harris notes, put "a generation of workers in a very bad bargaining position." He continues,

> If we're built top-to-bottom to struggle against each other for the smallest of edges [rather than] to cooperate ... in our collective interest ... —and we are— then we're hardly equipped to protect ourselves from larger systemic abuses. In a way, we invite them, or at least pave the road.[10]

Unfortunately, a life lived under the aegis of human capital theory has meant that we're unable to perceive the exploitation we invite upon ourselves—nor are we able to see the class dynamics at play in terms of who actually has the inherited credit required to gain the small advantages Harris describes as being essential for success. And so, instead of banding together in pursuit of collective goals, we continue to indebt ourselves (or dip into inherited wealth) in order to broaden our individual portfolios—more degrees! more little projects for our CVs!—in hopes of their appreciation. It is *this* vision of the future, one in which all our indebting has been worth it, that led to us volunteering our time on this *Perspecta*. Perhaps we'll be one of the lucky ones for whom it all pays off, but, in the process, by having our individualistic blinders on and not fighting harder for the instantiation of a *Perspecta* stipend that would allow a wider swath of people to participate in this project in the future,[11] we've really undercut that collective interest.

* * *

Just maybe, however, things might be changing. In the fall of 2022, employees at Bernheimer Architecture formed the country's first union at a private-sector architecture firm.[12] Following a failed union drive at ShoP Architects earlier in the pandemic, the success at Bernheimer provides a rare ray of hope for a profession that sorely needs it. Just maybe, this victory, combined with a trend toward increased labor activism in architecture more generally, is a sign of a radical shift away from the individualistic pursuit of the well-stocked portfolio described above.[13]

However, while a life dictated by human capital theory is not a pleasant one, can we really afford to give up the pursuit of investability altogether? While I imagine that Michel Feher (the scholar upon whose work we have been leaning heavily over the course of this essay) would support this union drive, he has also made the argument that the left needs to take the reality of our finance-dominated society into account in its activism strategies. In a world where creditors' opinions determine the future—after all, he argues, they are the ones who "select the projects that deserve to be financed"—we cannot, he contends, afford to entirely abandon the project of accruing a portfolio in which people will want to invest.[14] Noting the incredible power of credit-rating agencies, he argues that the left's most likely path towards a more just future is by taking on such a rating role (hence the subtitle of his book, "Investee Politics in a Speculative Age"). Feher asserts that, against Moody's, activists should in effect release counter-ratings that address the issues of concern to them. Such ratings could hinge on things like the environmental impact of a given project, the human rights abuses and labor conditions in a company's history, and so on. If they accrued enough cultural sway, these ratings might steer credit-suppliers towards investing in a better world.[15]

Such a strategy, however, can work in concert with traditional union drives. Indeed, commenting on the Bernheimer union, the organizer David DiMaria showed exactly what this combination of strategies looks like: "When the city gives a contract to a firm, is the city looking to see that the firm doesn't turn around and make workers work 20 hours of unpaid overtime a week?" Bernheimer rhetorically asks before noting that they "routinely do that in other industries … [and that this is] an avenue we want to explore."[16] In other words, rather than being an obstacle to winning commissions, if portrayed in the right way, having a union could potentially *increase* a firm's desirability in the eyes of those who fund projects. If we can't give up the habit of pursuing credit-worthiness whole cloth, we can at least, DiMaria suggests, make it work for us.

* * *

I'm sorry to say that, in putting together this *Perspecta* for free, we have already failed on the union side of this combo-strategy. By giving our labor to YSoA for free in the hopes of future gains from this issue, we've made it that much more difficult for writers and editors of other architectural publications to get paid; we have, in short, been scabs. But if we've failed on that front, perhaps we can succeed on the credit-rating side of the equation. And so, in lieu of acknowledgements, let's act as investee activists and give some ratings:

The friends, family members and partners who put up with us over the course of this often-times stressful editorial process: we rate you highly. Professors Keller Easterling and Jesse LeCavalier, who met with us to talk ideas and provide advice: high rating. Our graphic designers (really our co-authors) and our wonderful contributors: again, AAA rating, everyone should invest in their stock. The Yale School of Architecture and other institutions that use the free labor of recent graduates to produce their journals: your credit rating is down.

With this low rating, we are not in any way encouraging schools to cease publishing journals; we believe strongly in the need for publications that provide a space for critical architectural writing. This low rating is due to the fact that we think the YSoA, and design schools more generally, need to take a hard look at the political economy in which such writing is produced. When the first issue of *Perspecta* was published in 1952, the median home price was $9,050[17] and an architecture degree all but assured you a comfortable life. Moreover, the decimation of print journalism and the precaritization of academic labor having not yet occurred, these student editors, if they decided that they wanted to work as teachers and writers instead of architects—well, they could just go ahead and do so. The situation is very different today. Architecture students are now graduating from Masters programs with, on average, up to $72,000 of debt[18] and into jobs that in all likelihood will initially only be netting them $65,000 a year.[19] And, as discussed above, success in the discursive arena now entails much more work than it did seventy years ago. The amassing of a rather robust collection of little side projects—edited journals, published texts, competition entries, multiple adjunct teaching posts, the creating of a website for the mostly notional "studio" you run when you are not working at your actual job—is now a requirement to even begin to think about making a career in the discursive side of architecture.

While in the past it might have been possible for everyone to work for free on *Perspecta*, it's a different story today. It is incredibly difficult to pay off one's debt from architectural education while simultaneously incurring more debt in pursuit of a now mandatory robust CV.[20] Again, those who do not have to incur debt in either of these pursuits have a tremendous advantage. To make success in architecture less dependent upon one's class position, the goal of achieving debt-free school of course ought to take priority. However, schools also need to begin thinking about how to support their recent graduates[21] as they attempt to undertake projects like *Perspecta* that are required portfolio items for those who wish to make a living as a discourse leader. If the YSoA, as we're sure it does, considers itself in the business of producing discourse leaders, they have to start finding a way to make it not the case that only their rich alumni will have the opportunity to play this role. Instituting a stipend for *Perspecta* editors and designers would be one small step in pursuit of this worthwhile goal.

And who knows, maybe such a stipend would actually help Yale's bottom line, not hurt it: think about how many more donations YSoA would receive if we were giving them a higher rating! After all, it's only by changing the minds of the donors—aka the creditors—that we'll get the investments to build a future architecture world in which we'll actually want to work.

Or a future for architecture, tout court. While perhaps, eventually, the debt-financed acquisition of master's degree-certified architectural skills may appreciate into a highly paid design gig (I mean, Norman Foster, is pretty damn rich), this appreciation is currently too unlikely, and its pace too slow, for most people to stay in the profession. As Adkins et al. put it, even if one has "the best investment opportunity," if one has to "borrow in order to buy it and the returns it generates are not enough for [one] to keep up with [one]'s repayment schedule (and [one] doesn't have any other sources of cash flow)," a person will be forced to sell.[22] In essence, this dynamic is what's leading to so many people leaving the profession: their investment in architectural skills is failing to appreciate, so they are trading in this speculative asset for the immediately high wage that comes with jobs in real estate development, finance, UX and other tech-adjacent fields. Unless architecture schools can gather and distribute enough donations to eliminate student debt and dramatically shift this calculus, it is hard to imagine a situation in which this professional bleeding does not become more profuse.

While we'd love it if the low rating we've given the YSoA results in such a shift in investor priorities, it is also highly possible that the rather wonky "investee activism" we're practicing here fails to have any results. Indeed, Adkins and her co-authors posit a full-throated embrace of socialism as one of the only ways to counter the class inequalities that play out so starkly in fields like debt-financed architectural education.[23] And Malcolm Harris comes to a similar conclusion, arguing that, given the particular pressures of a life lived as a heavily financialized collection of human capital, at a certain point millenials will cease to submit to this system and will instead become "fascists, or revolutionaries, one or the other."[24] In this light, LeCorbusier's famous dictum "Architecture or Revolution" must now be reversed: without revolution, there can be no architecture. How's that for a forecast?

1 Malcolm Harris, *Kids These Days: The Making of Millenials* (New York: Back Bay Books, 2017), passim; Lisa Adkins, Melinda Cooper and Martijn Konings, *The Asset Economy: Property Ownership and the New Logic of Inequality* (Cambridge: Polity Books, 2020), 45-49, 91.
2 Much of this account is taken from Melinda Cooper, *Family Values: Neoliberalism and the New Social Conservatism* (Brooklyn: Zone Books, 2017), 219-251.
3 Martijn Konings, "The Time of Finance," *The Los Angeles Review of Books*, December 29, 2017, https://www.lareviewofbooks.org/article/the-time-of-finance.
4 Michel Feher, "Self-Appreciation; or, The Aspirations of Human Capital," *Public Culture* 21, no. 1 (2009): 26.
5 It is important here to note that having higher exposure to risk isn't some abstract financial position; it is a lived reality with material and psychological effects. For those who have gone into debt, one has to simultaneously support oneself while managing an oftentimes onerous repayment schedule. Moreover if the asset one has invested in—say an architectural degree—depreciates in value, one has to deal with the financial fallout entirely by oneself; no familial money is present to, in essence, extend more credit for another loan. In other words, although we all must contend with the fickle winds of asset appreciation and depreciation, we are not all equally exposed to these unpredictable dynamics.
6 Adkins et al., *The Asset Economy*, 6.
7 Most significantly, is it possible to produce critical architectural discourse when to do so one must either leverage one's own future or have financial backing? Or will criticism wither in the face of the inequities caused by our human capital theory-authored socioeconomic order?
8 Any architecture school worth its salt has a journal. After MIT Press has sent out this journal to populate bookstores in major cities the country over, it will effectively be serving as an advertisement for the school.
9 YSoA's Director of Communications, A.J. Artemel, did help considerably when it came to coordinating with the MIT Press. He was a pleasure to work with.
10 Harris, *Kids These Days*, 86.
11 In the Spring of 2021 we did make one request for a monthly stipend for our work. It went unanswered by the *Perspecta* board.
12 Noam Scheiber, "Architects at a New York Firm Form the Industry's Only Private-Sector Union," *The New York Times*, September 1, 2022, https://www.nytimes.com/2022/09/01/business/architects-union.html.
13 I cannot emphasize enough how necessary the Bernheimer Architecture union victory is, especially in the wake of the failed SHoP Architects' organizing effort, the collapse of which seemed to signal that our generation would continue to pursue their individualistic goals at the expense of the collective interests of architectural laborers everywhere. It was particularly ironic that this was happening at SHoP, where the stark inequalities between its principals and its regular workers overlap so exactly with the investment/class dynamics I've been describing here. As suggested by reporting in *The New York Review of Architecture*, the SHoP principals frequently negotiate with their clients so that a portion of their payment is in the form of an ownership stake in the buildings they design; this property, however, only accords to the owners of the firm. It is a reverse Robin Hood situation: because the value of an architectural degree has depreciated, SHoP has to pay its indebted employees less; the principals then trade these, in effect, discounted designs for real estate, a rapidly appreciating asset. Their employees, of course, cannot afford to enter this lucrative market. The ownership class gets richer, the indebted class gets poorer, and somewhere in between their eyesore buildings get made. Dan Roche, "Organizing SHoP," *The New York Review of Architecture* 16, February 2022.
14 Michel Feher, *Rated Agency: Investee Politics in a Speculative Age*, trans. Gregory Elliott (Brooklyn: Zone Books, 2021) 17.
15 Feher, Rated Agency, 78-85. See Orit Halpern's essay in this volume for an account of how such activism could work in practice.
16 Scheiber, "Architects."
17 Approximately $101,145 in today's dollars. Jane Kenney, "Here's How Much a House Cost the Year You Were Born," Do You Remember?, accessed Sep. 24, 2022, https://doyouremember.com/91242/how-much-house-cost-year.
18 AIA Pennsylvania, "Student Loan Forgiveness and the Architect," accessed on September 24, 2022, https://aiapa.org/2022/09/07/student-loan-forgiveness-and-the-architect/.
19 This number refers to the starting salary of graduates from Masters programs in New York City; it is likely lower in most other parts of the country. "Graduate Architect Salary in New York, NY," salary.com, accessed September 24, 2022, https://www.salary.com/research/salary/recruiting/graduate-architect-salary/new-york-ny#:~:text=How%20much%20does%20a%20Graduate,falls%20between%20%2460%2C244%20and%20%2473%2C259.
20 As debt-cancellation activist Astra Taylor put it in a recent interview: "People who are in debt have to worry about making that next payment. It's a source of anxiety and stress. It changes your psychology. If you don't make your payments on time, you're penalized harshly. Your credit scores are trashed, and that limits your options in terms of being able to rent an apartment or secure a job. The stakes are enormously high. In some places, if you default on your student loans, your license can be taken away so you can't even do your job." Sean Illing, "The Case for Canceling Student Debt–All of It," Vox, May 13, 2021, https://www.vox.com/policy-and-politics/22383450/student-debt-forgiveness-biden-astra-taylor.
21 For any readers who have been reactionarily arguing that it is absurd to request that students be paid for editing a school journal, it is important to note that *Perspecta* is only nominally a student-edited journal. In the vast majority of cases, it is recent graduates who edit this publication; one merely wins the editorship while a student.
22 Adkins et al., The Asset Economy, 20.
23 Adkins et al., The Asset Economy, 91-92.
24 Harris, *Kids These Days*, 227-28.

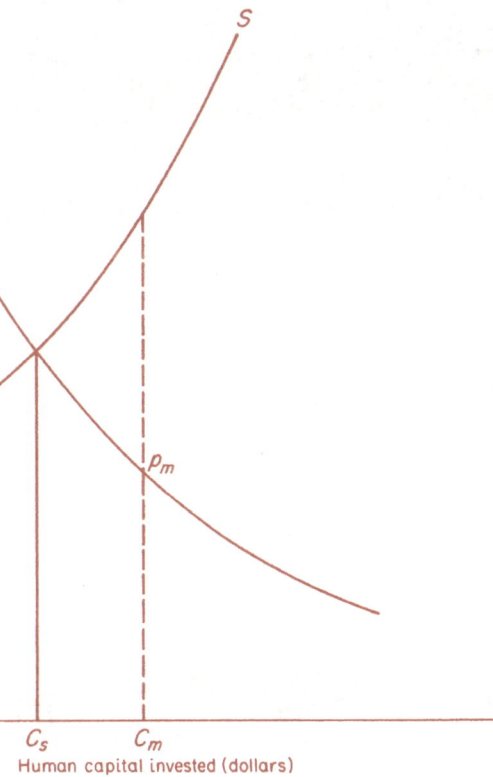

Thank You

Perspecta 55 would like to thank current and past donors to the Perspecta Fund for their ongoing generosity and support: Tom Beeby from the Richard H. Driehaus Foundation; Marc Appleton, '72 M.Arch; Hans Baldauf, '81 BA, '88 M.Arch; Austin Church III, '60 BA Family Fund; Fred Koetter and Susie Kim; Cesar Pelli, '08 DFHA; Robert A.M. Stern, '65 M.Arch; Jeremy Scott Wood, '64 BA, '70 M.Arch; and F. Anthony Zunino, '70 M.Arch.

Colophon

Perspecta 55: Futures Index

Editor
Matthew Wagstaffe

Assistant Editors
Lani Barry
Jeffrey Liu
Nicholas Miller
Ethan Zisson

Designers
Kyla Arsadjaja
Julia Schäfer

Printer
Grafiche Veneziane, Italy

Paper
Munken Print White 18
GMUND Heather Alabaster

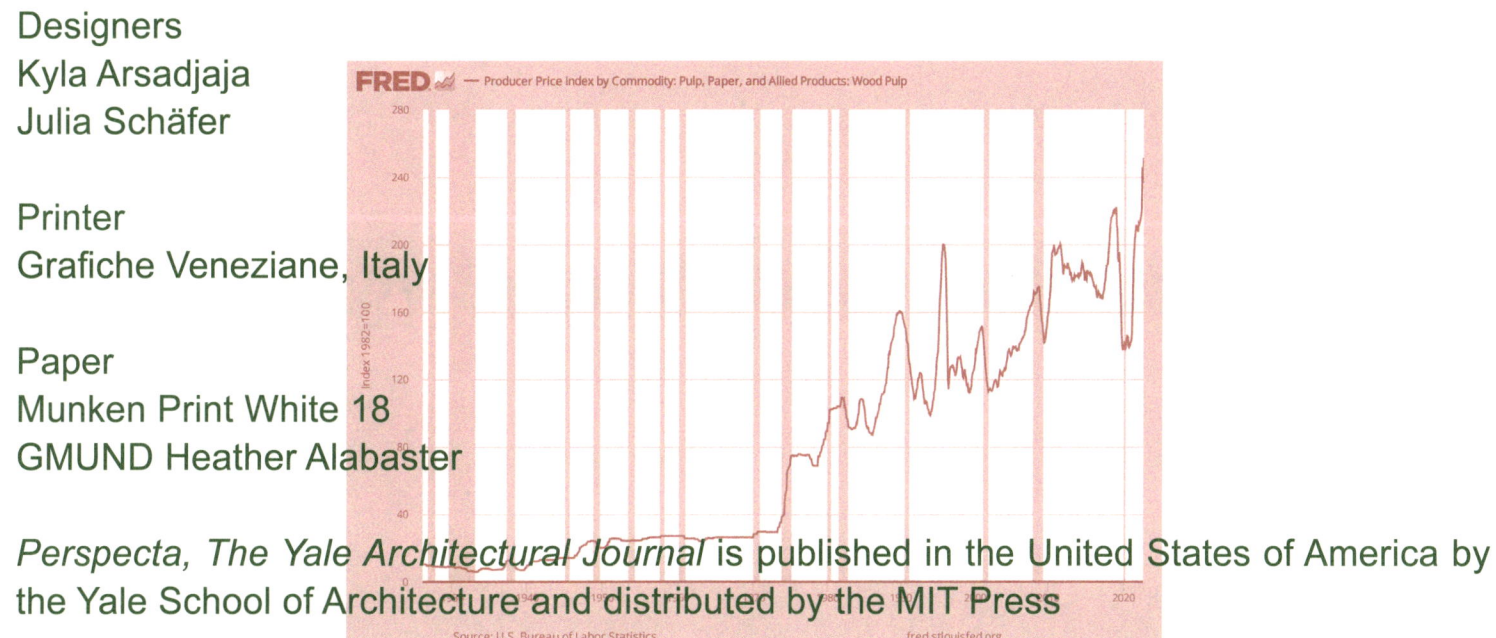

Perspecta, The Yale Architectural Journal is published in the United States of America by the Yale School of Architecture and distributed by the MIT Press

©2023 *Perspecta: The Yale Architectural Journal*, Inc., and Yale University

Distributed by the MIT Press
Massachusetts Institute of Technology
Cambridge, Massachusetts 02142
http://mitpress.mit.edu

All rights reserved. No part of this book may be reproduced in any form by any electronic or mechanical means (including photocopying, recording, or information storage and retrieval) without permission in writing from the publisher.

ISBN: 978-0-262-54546-4
ISSN: 0079-0958